Fushigi Yûgi: Genbu Kaiden™

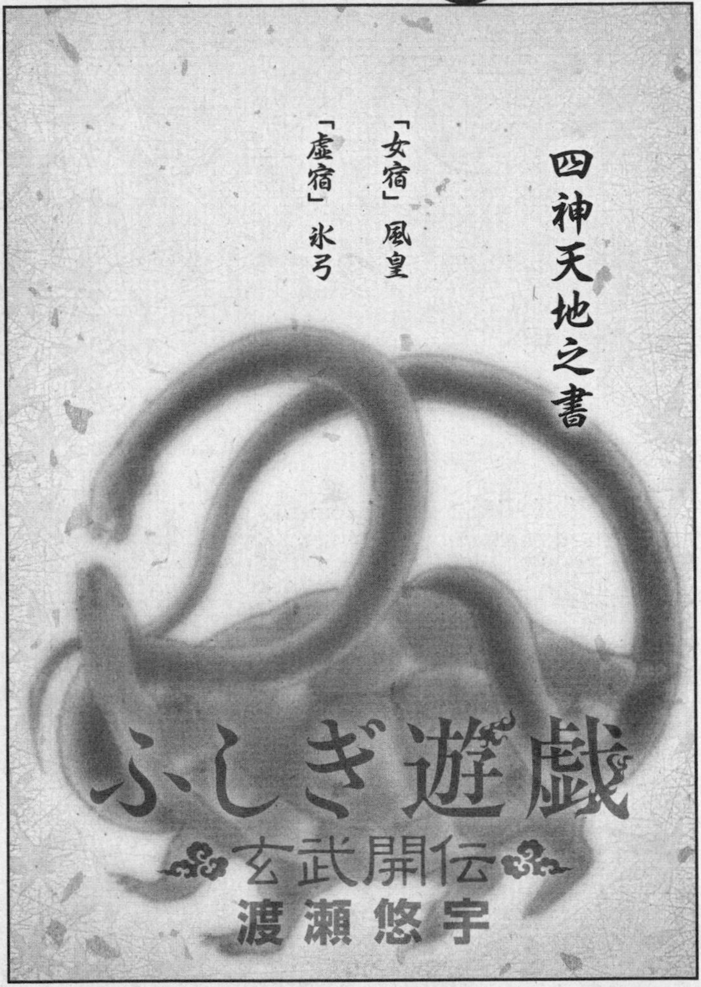
四神天地之書
「女宿」風皇
「虚宿」氷弓
ふしぎ遊戯
玄武開伝
渡瀬悠宇

story and art by **YUU WATASE**

Vol. 5

CONTENTS

TRANSLATION OF "THE UNIVERSE OF THE FOUR GODS"

Uruki: Wind Prince
Tomite: Ice Bow (Archer)

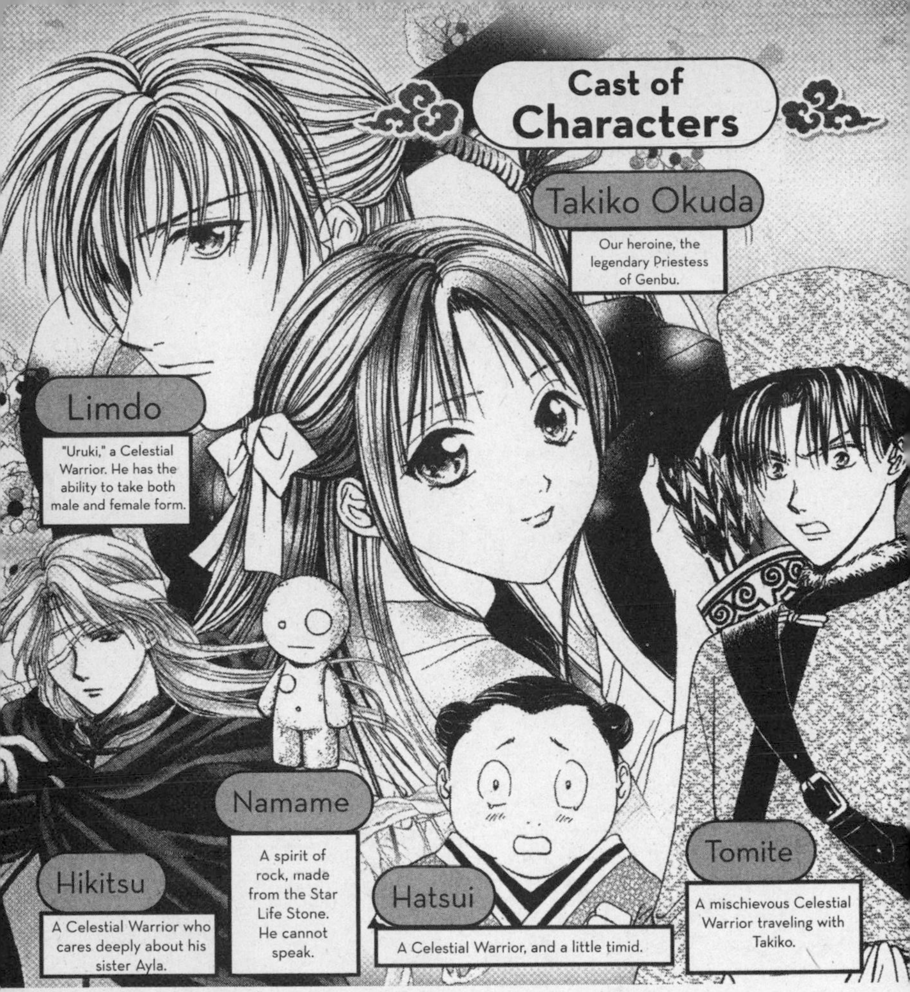
Cast of Characters
Takiko Okuda
Our heroine, the legendary Priestess of Genbu.
Limdo
"Uruki," a Celestial Warrior. He has the ability to take both male and female form.
Tomite
A mischievous Celestial Warrior traveling with Takiko.
Hatsui
A Celestial Warrior, and a little timid.
Namame
A spirit of rock, made from the Star Life Stone. He cannot speak.
Hikitsu
A Celestial Warrior who cares deeply about his sister Ayla.

The Story Thus Far

The year is 1923. Takiko is drawn into the pages of *The Universe of the Four Gods*, a book her father has translated from Chinese. There, she is told that she is the legendary Priestess of Genbu, destined to save the country of Bêi-jîa. She must find the seven Celestial Warriors who will help her on her quest. In Bêi-jîa, however, the Priestess and the Celestial Warriors are seen as ill omens.

Takiko has now been joined by five Celestial Warriors: Uruki, Tomite, Hatsui, Namame and Hikitsu. During a battle against monsters called the Maw, Takiko accidentally looks into Hikitsu's Mirror Eye and vanishes before her friends' eyes. She awakens to find that she has returned to her own world and time...

FUSHIGI YÛGI:
GENBU KAIDEN

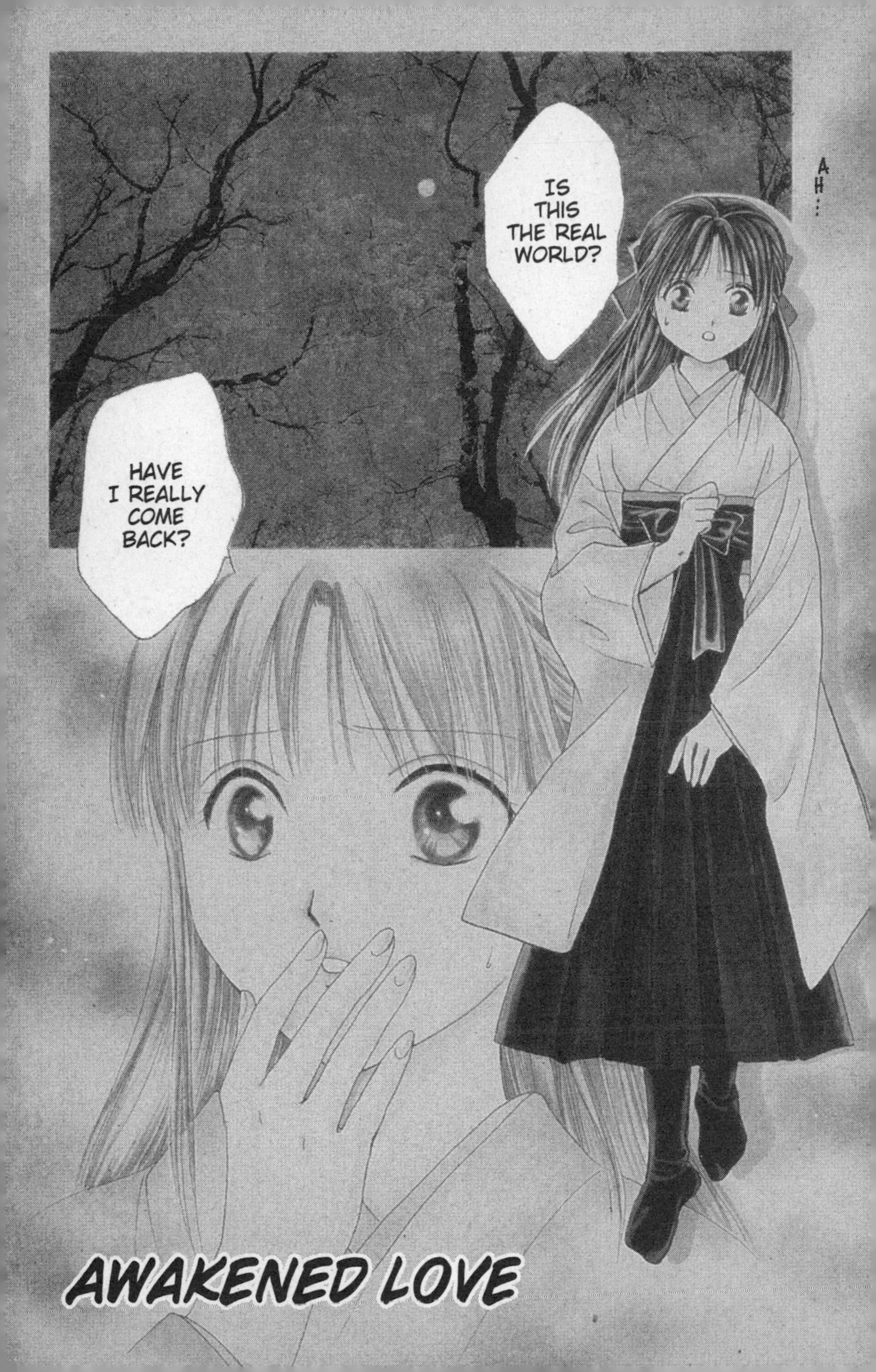
AH...
IS THIS THE REAL WORLD?
HAVE I REALLY COME BACK?
AWAKENED LOVE

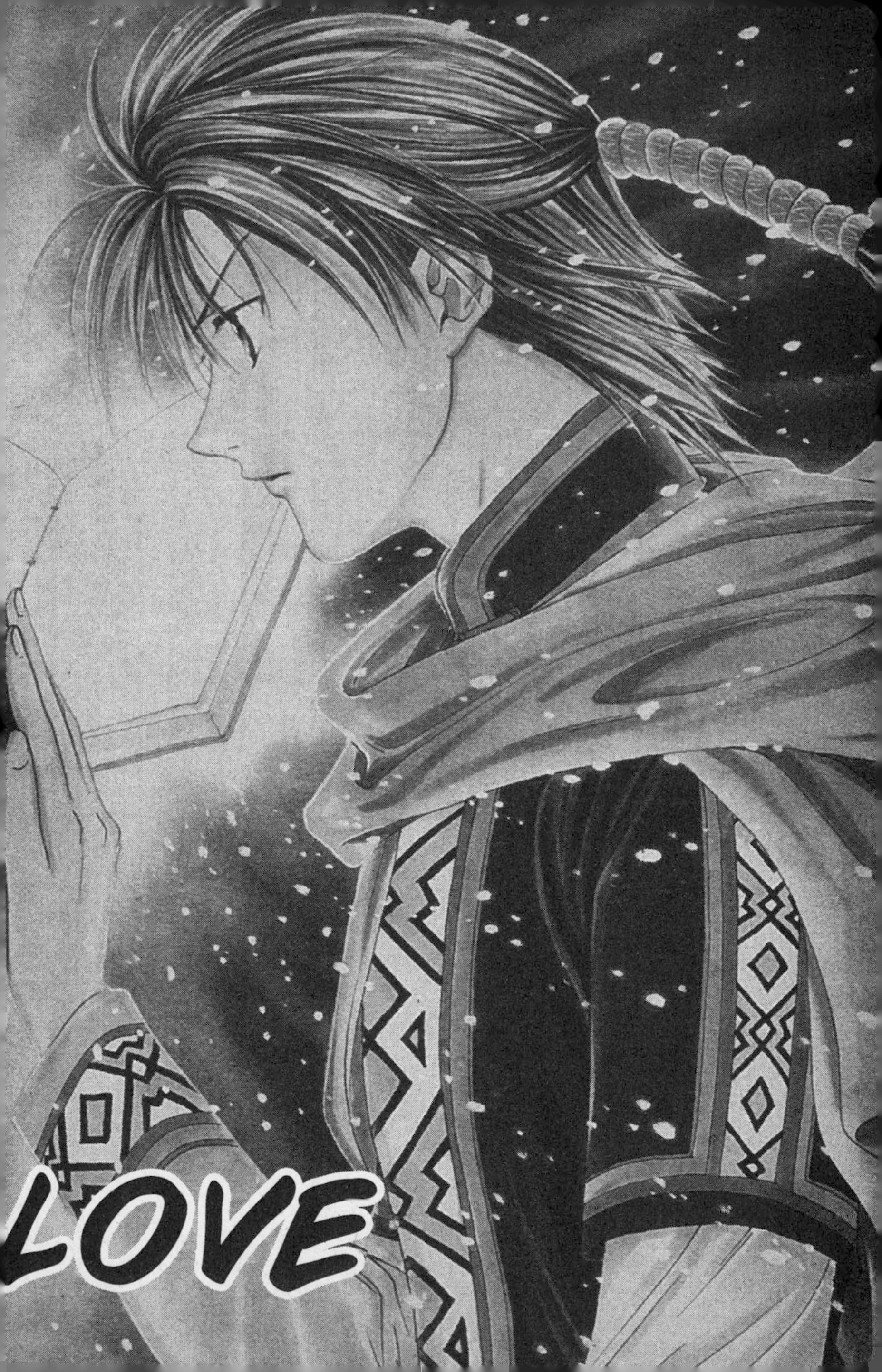
LOVE

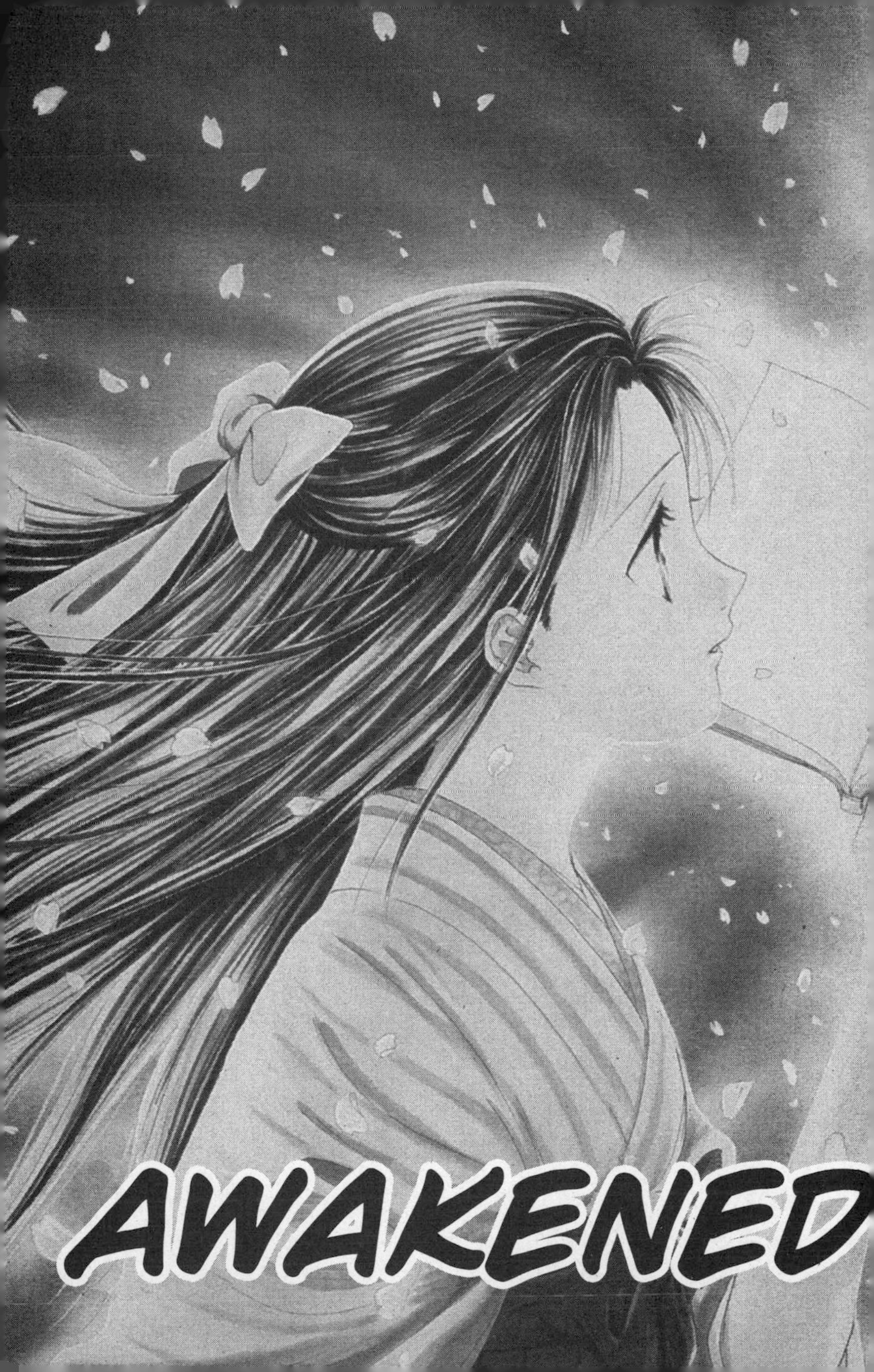
AWAKENED

②

Hi! Watase here!

Genbu is in its fifth volume! There's another special edition (with a bonus drama CD) in the works! Please enjoy!

Perfect World Volume 7 was supposed to go on sale around the same time, but it's been postponed until next spring...I'm sorry!! ^^ I asked for a vacation because I wanted to catch my breath and get in better health. The next issue will include a preview of my new manga (!), so please take a look when it comes out! (The *Shojo Comics* website should have updates on sale dates, etc.) Don't forget!

As for announcements, the game "Fushigi Yugi Genbu Kaiden Tales: the Priestess in the Mirror" and the drama CDs are on sale right now. The second CD came out in August, and the third is scheduled to come out in December. Also, the pocket edition of *Ceres: Celestial Legend* began its release in October! If you've never read it before, please take this opportunity to give it a try! (--)

The plot of the second drama CD centers around Hatsui. Ah, Hatsui...I was determined to have a chubby character this time. Sure, he may not be cool-looking, but I opted for variety. My inspirations were pandas and Tove Jansson's Moomins. ^^ But then, gasp! Ms. Megumi Ogata, the voice of so many beautiful characters, was chosen to play him! At the time, I thought, "What a waste!" (I'm sorry, Hatsui). But I also knew that he would be a difficult character to portray and required someone very good. And she did a great job, playing an adorable Hatsui. I guess I'll have to increase his page time!

The story arc about Anlu and Namame will be on the third CD. Ziyi will have a big part, too!

Yes...ever since the video game came out, Ziyi's popularity has skyrocketed!! I love his storyline in the game. ^^

②

But I hope people won't start expecting the Ziyi in the manga to be like the Ziyi in the game. ^^ He might be even more heartless. Well, I'm sure his past will eventually be revealed. What will happen? Feiyan couldn't be included in the game because of his severed arm. I finally got him a prosthetic in this volume. Oh, yeah... Xiu-luo, the character created for the game, was so cute. But he's not right for the manga. I'll have to increase the page time for Ziyi and Feiyan, too...

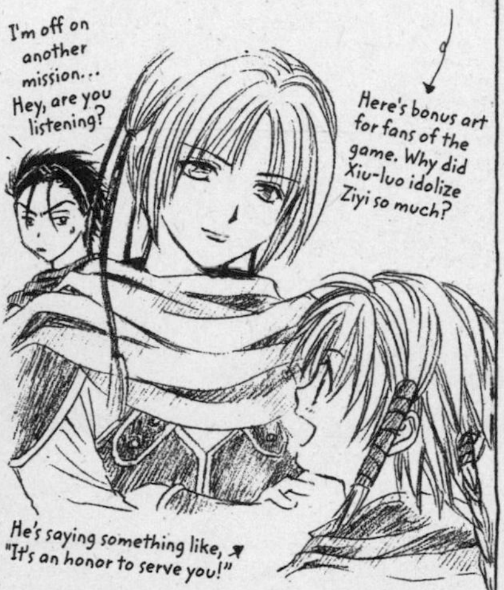
Here's bonus art for fans of the game. Why did Xiu-luo idolize Ziyi so much?
I'm off on another mission... Hey, are you listening?
He's saying something like, "It's an honor to serve you!"

I highly recommend the CD with the game's theme song, "Eternal Flower." It includes a sticker of the game cover art. (I put a lot of effort into that illustration...) Or was it only in the first edition? The third song, "Distance," is good enough to be an anime theme song... (Wishful thinking.) They're all such good songs!! Speaking of anime, Mr. Koyasu, the voice of Hotohori, is the voice actor for Hagus. Many people were surprised, but I wanted voice actors from the first FY anime. Ms. Yumi Toma is also in it.

Doesn't it seem more connected this way? If I do the Byakko storyline in the future, and it becomes a drama CD, etc., it should include voice actors from Genbu. I really like that kind of link. Or is it just me?

Vol. 6 will probably come out next year. I'm sorry it'll take time, but I'll see you in the next volume!

You can get CDs and books through Amazon. ← I use it often. ^^

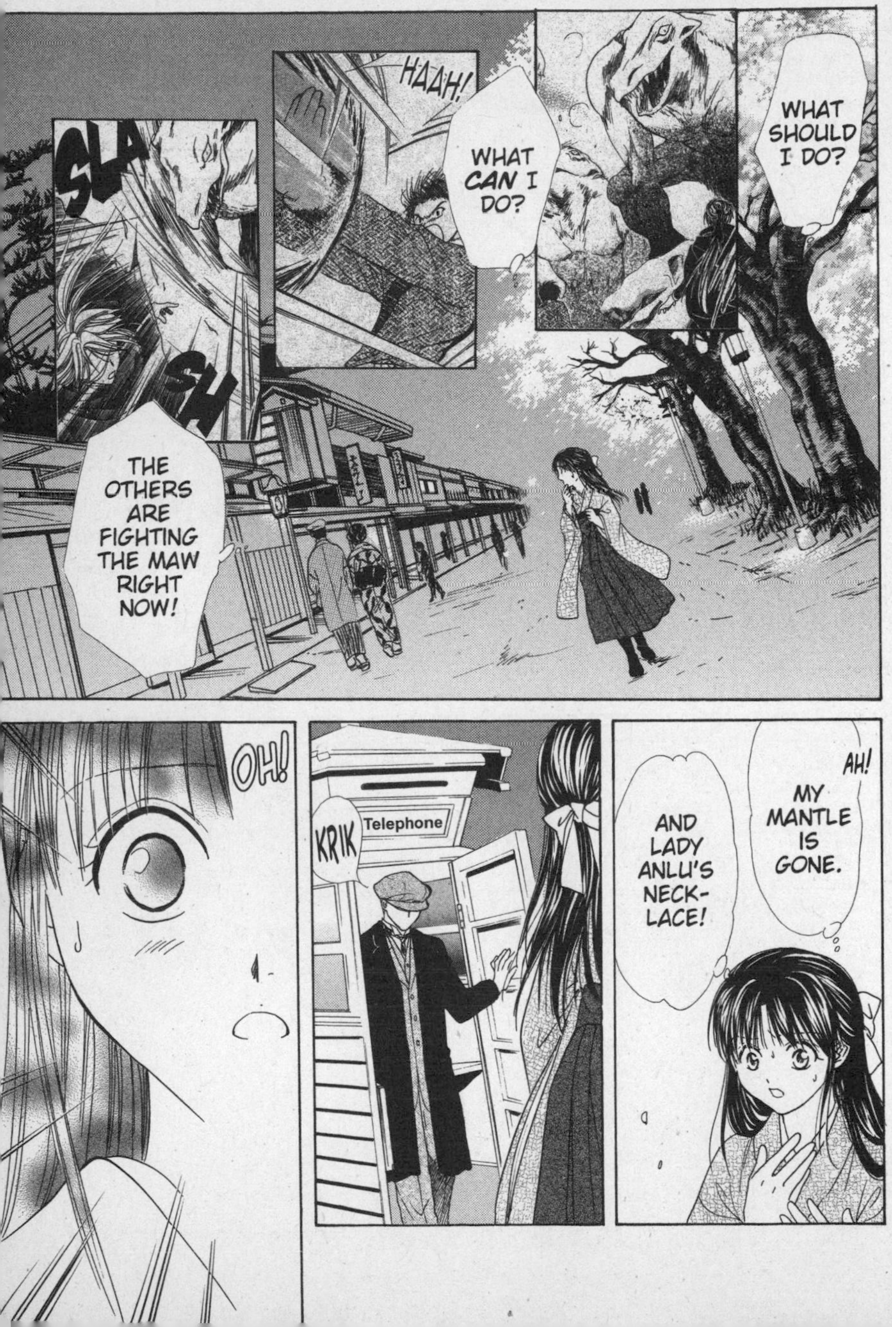
WHAT SHOULD I DO?
HAAH!
WHAT CAN I DO?
SLA
SH
THE OTHERS ARE FIGHTING THE MAW RIGHT NOW!
AH!
MY MANTLE IS GONE.
AND LADY ANLU'S NECK-LACE!
KRIK
Telephone
OH!

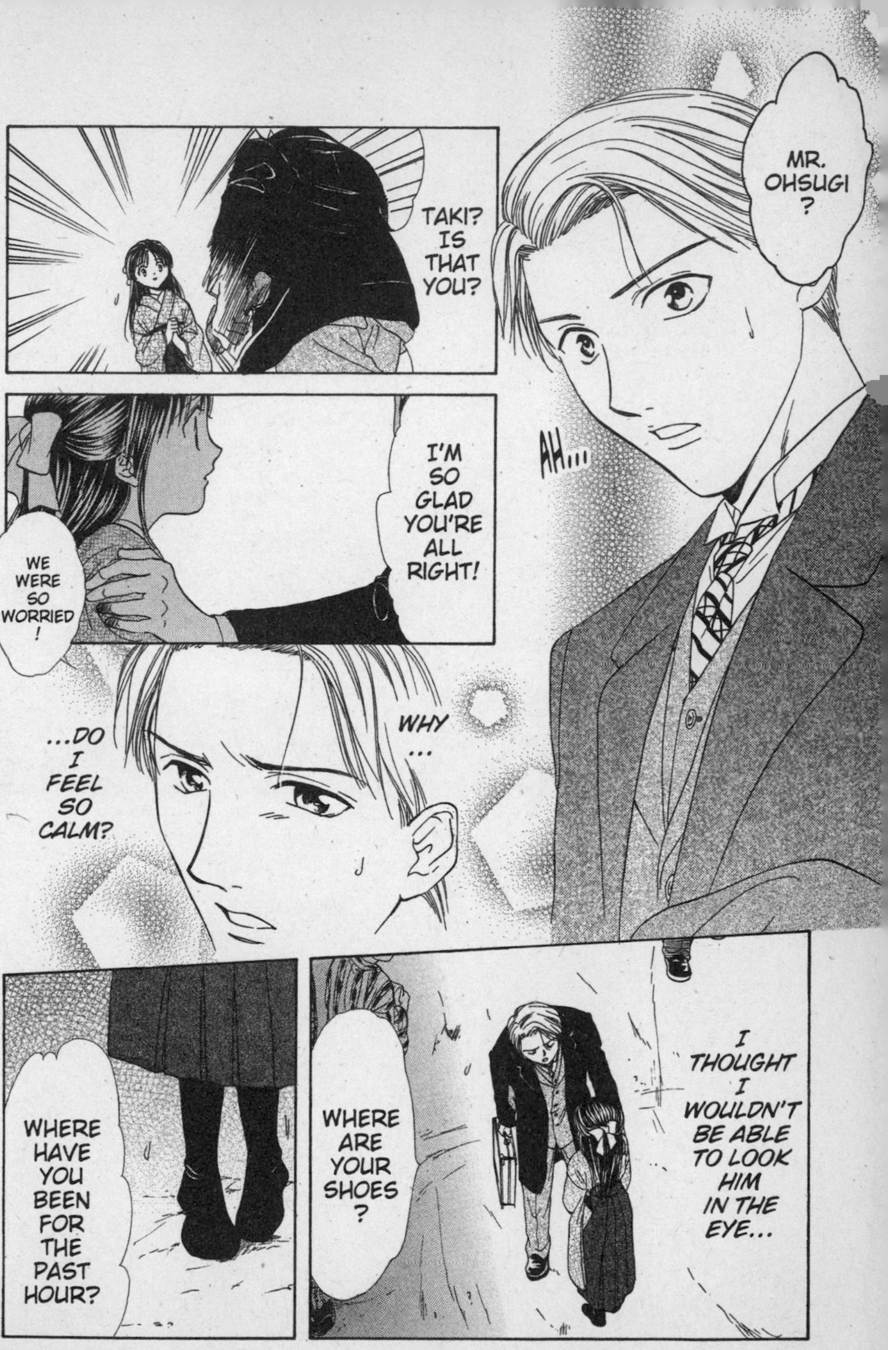
MR. OHSUGI?
AH...
TAKI? IS THAT YOU?
I'M SO GLAD YOU'RE ALL RIGHT!
WE WERE SO WORRIED!
WHY...
...DO I FEEL SO CALM?
I THOUGHT I WOULDN'T BE ABLE TO LOOK HIM IN THE EYE...
WHERE ARE YOUR SHOES?
WHERE HAVE YOU BEEN FOR THE PAST HOUR?

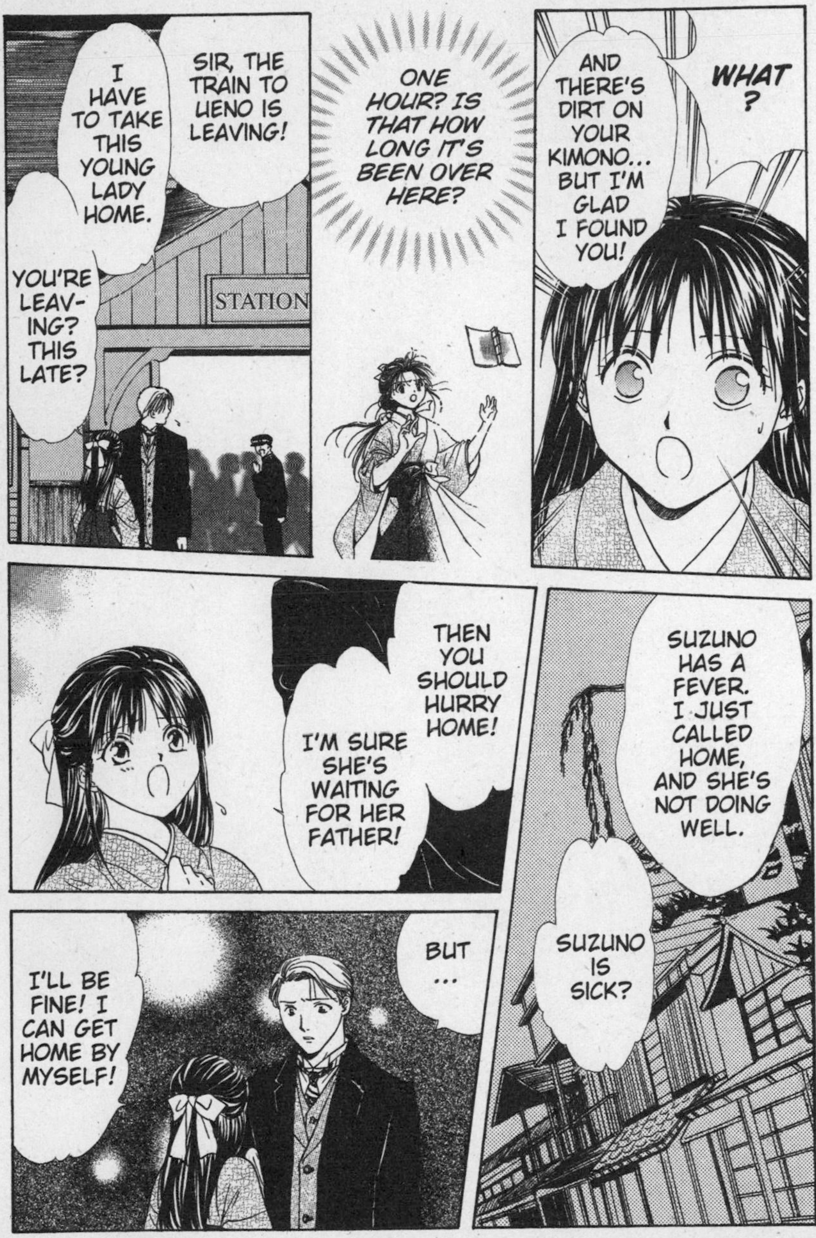
WHAT ?
AND THERE'S DIRT ON YOUR KIMONO... BUT I'M GLAD I FOUND YOU!
ONE HOUR? IS THAT HOW LONG IT'S BEEN OVER HERE?
SIR, THE TRAIN TO UENO IS LEAVING!
I HAVE TO TAKE THIS YOUNG LADY HOME.
STATION
YOU'RE LEAV-ING? THIS LATE?
SUZUNO HAS A FEVER. I JUST CALLED HOME, AND SHE'S NOT DOING WELL.
SUZUNO IS SICK?
THEN YOU SHOULD HURRY HOME!
I'M SURE SHE'S WAITING FOR HER FATHER!
BUT ...
I'LL BE FINE! I CAN GET HOME BY MYSELF!

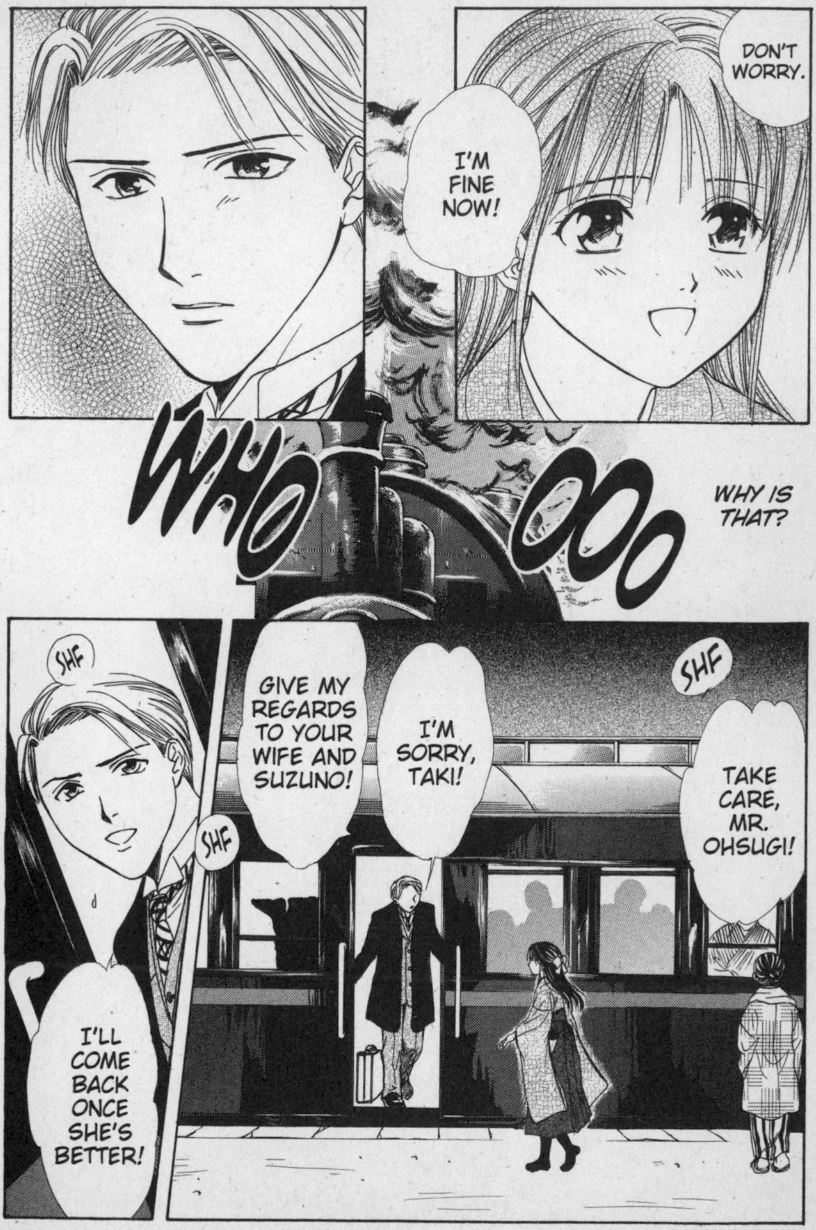
DON'T WORRY.
I'M FINE NOW!
WHOOOO
WHY IS THAT?
SHF
TAKE CARE, MR. OHSUGI!
I'M SORRY, TAKI!
GIVE MY REGARDS TO YOUR WIFE AND SUZUNO!
SHF
SHF
I'LL COME BACK ONCE SHE'S BETTER!

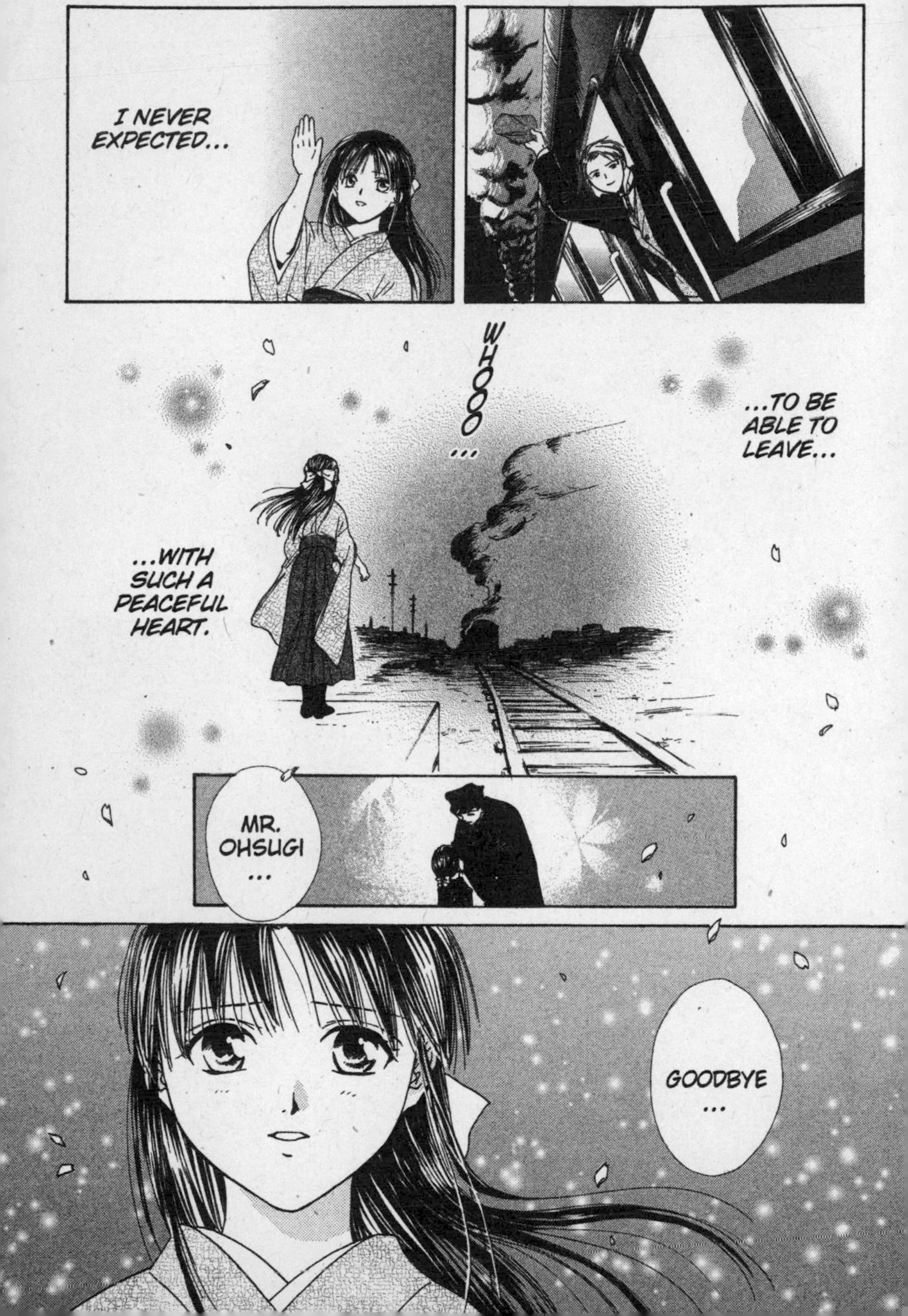
I NEVER EXPECTED...
...TO BE ABLE TO LEAVE...
WHOOOO...
...WITH SUCH A PEACEFUL HEART.
MR. OHSUGI...
GOODBYE...

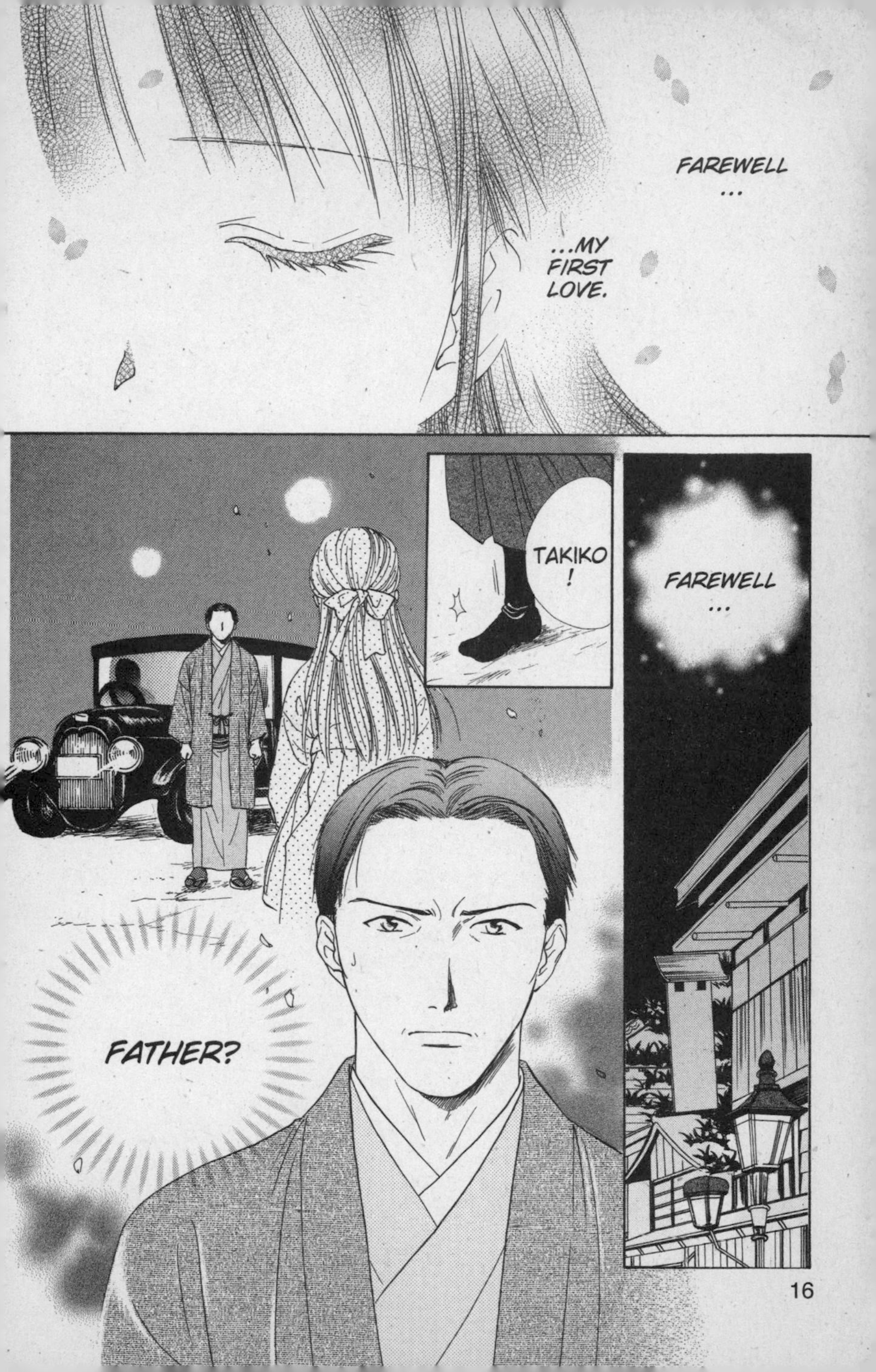
FAREWELL ...
...MY FIRST LOVE.
FAREWELL ...
TAKIKO!
FATHER?

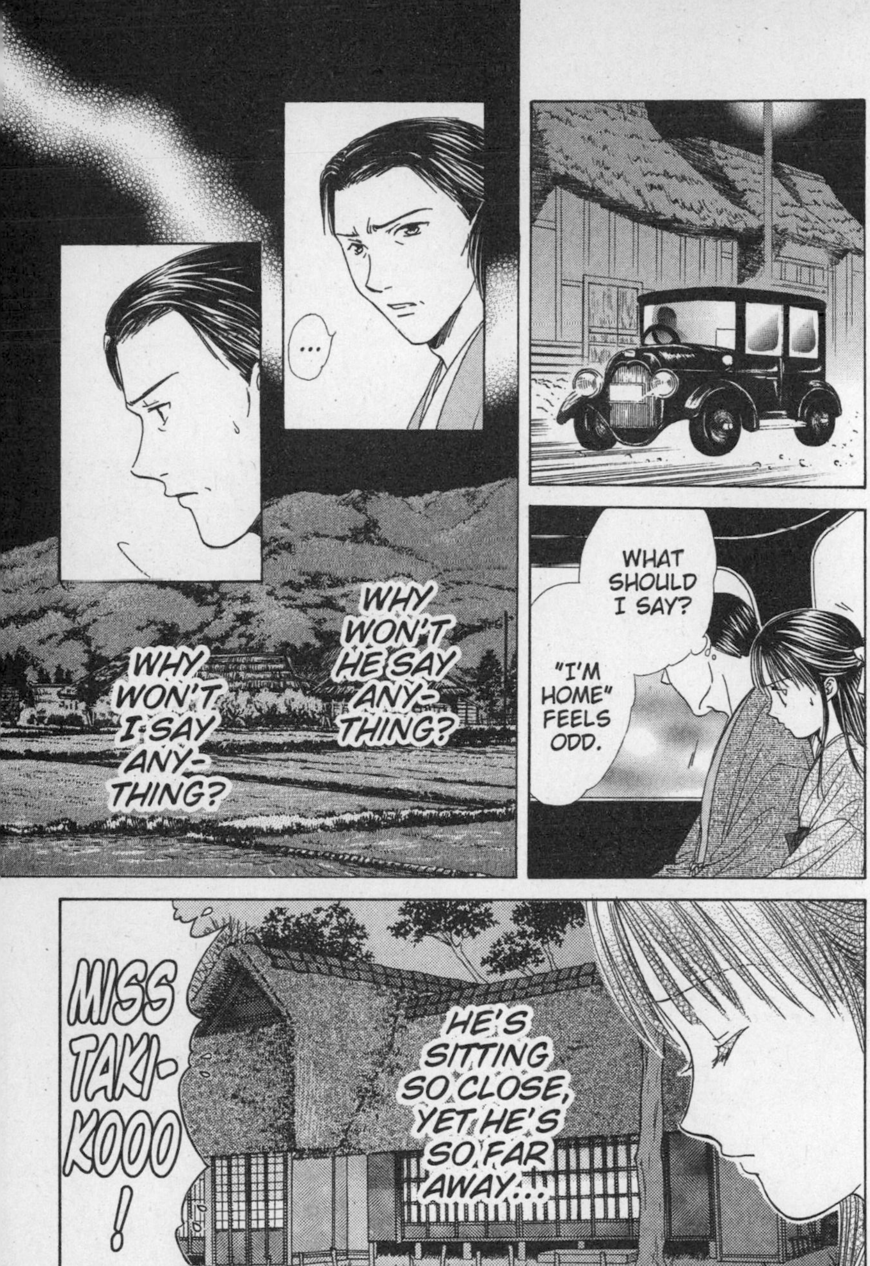
WHAT SHOULD I SAY?
"I'M HOME" FEELS ODD.
...
WHY WON'T HE SAY ANY-THING?
WHY WON'T I SAY ANY-THING?
HE'S SITTING SO CLOSE, YET HE'S SO FAR AWAY...
MISS TAKI-KOOO!

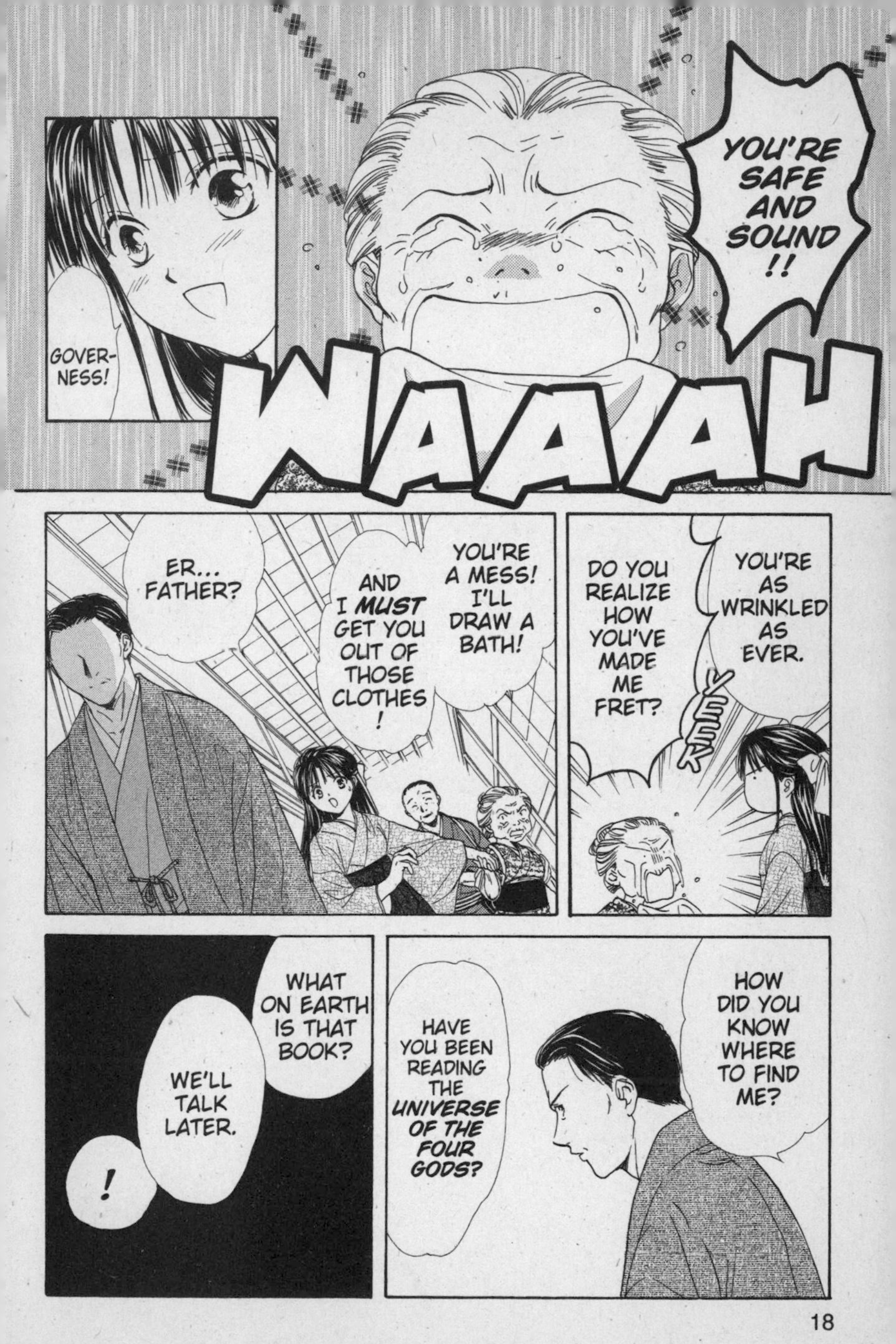
YOU'RE SAFE AND SOUND!!
WAAAH
GOVERNESS!
YOU'RE AS WRINKLED AS EVER.
DO YOU REALIZE HOW YOU'VE MADE ME FRET?
YOU'RE A MESS! I'LL DRAW A BATH!
AND I *MUST* GET YOU OUT OF THOSE CLOTHES!
ER... FATHER?
HOW DID YOU KNOW WHERE TO FIND ME?
HAVE YOU BEEN READING THE *UNIVERSE OF THE FOUR GODS?*
WHAT ON EARTH IS THAT BOOK?
WE'LL TALK LATER.
!

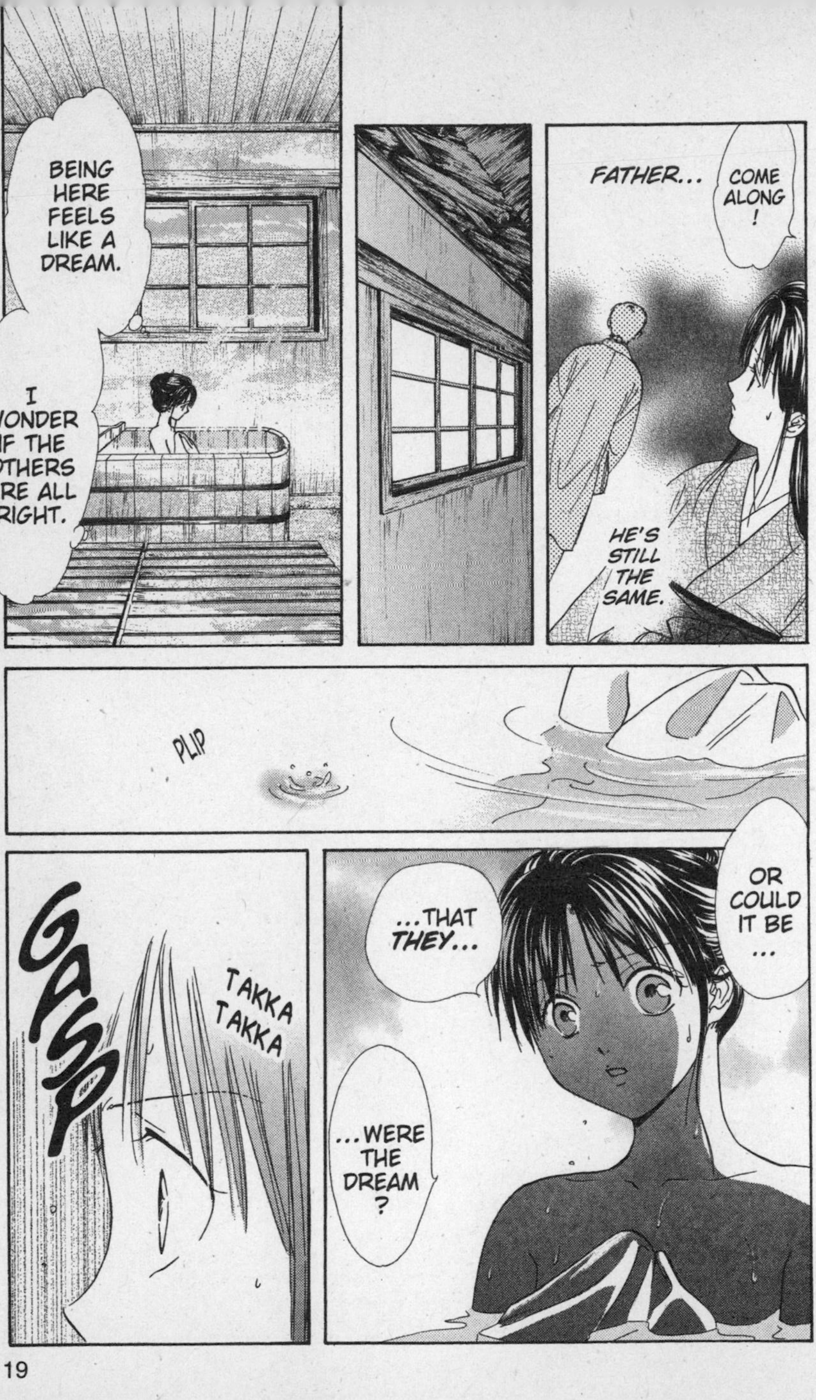
COME ALONG!
FATHER...
HE'S STILL THE SAME.
BEING HERE FEELS LIKE A DREAM.
I WONDER IF THE OTHERS ARE ALL RIGHT.
PLIP
OR COULD IT BE ...
...THAT *THEY*...
...WERE THE DREAM?
TAKKA TAKKA
GASP

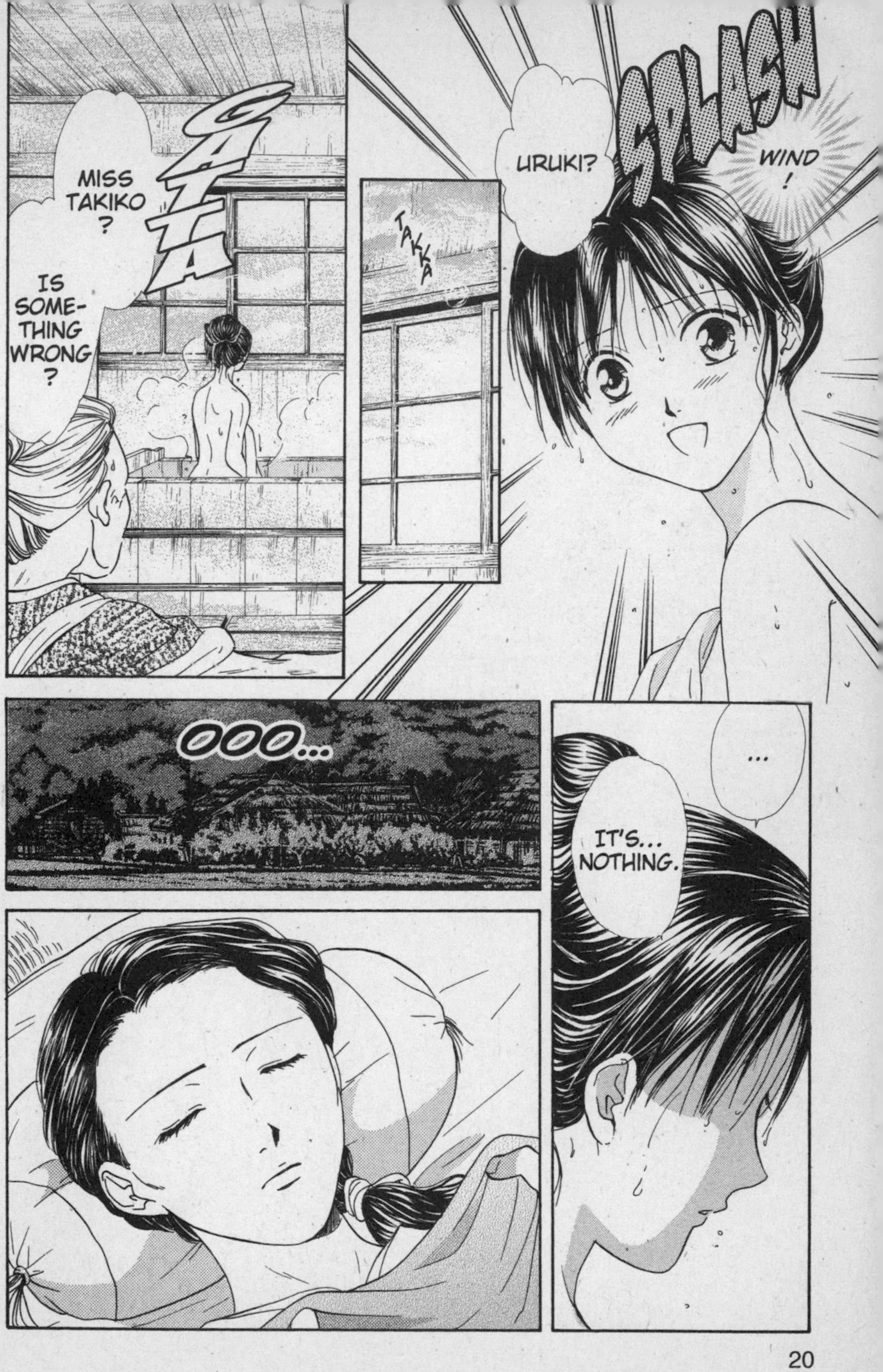
SPLASH
WIND!
URUKI?
TAKKA
GATA
MISS TAKIKO?
IS SOMETHING WRONG?
...
IT'S... NOTHING.
OOO...

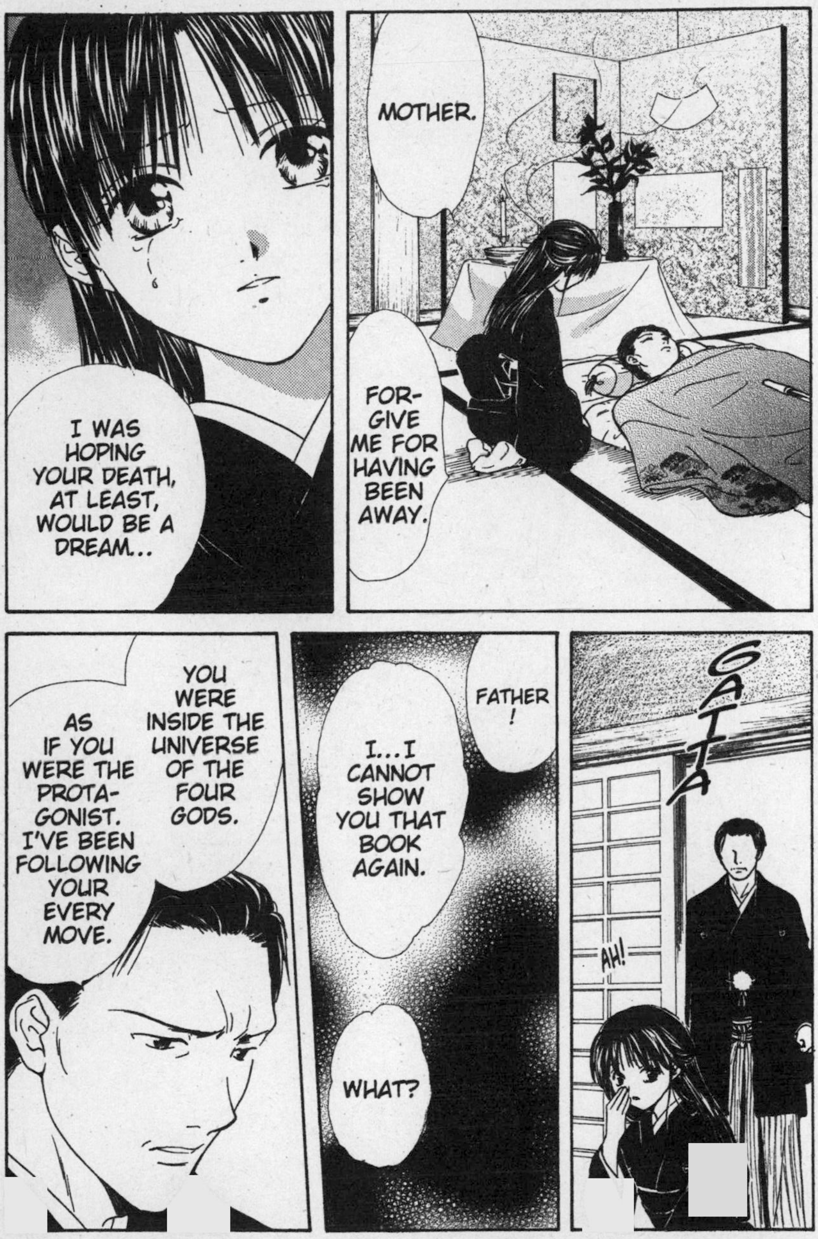
MOTHER.
FOR-GIVE ME FOR HAVING BEEN AWAY.
I WAS HOPING YOUR DEATH, AT LEAST, WOULD BE A DREAM...
GATTA
AH!
FATHER!
I...I CANNOT SHOW YOU THAT BOOK AGAIN.
WHAT?
YOU WERE INSIDE THE UNIVERSE OF THE FOUR GODS.
AS IF YOU WERE THE PROTA-GONIST. I'VE BEEN FOLLOWING YOUR EVERY MOVE.

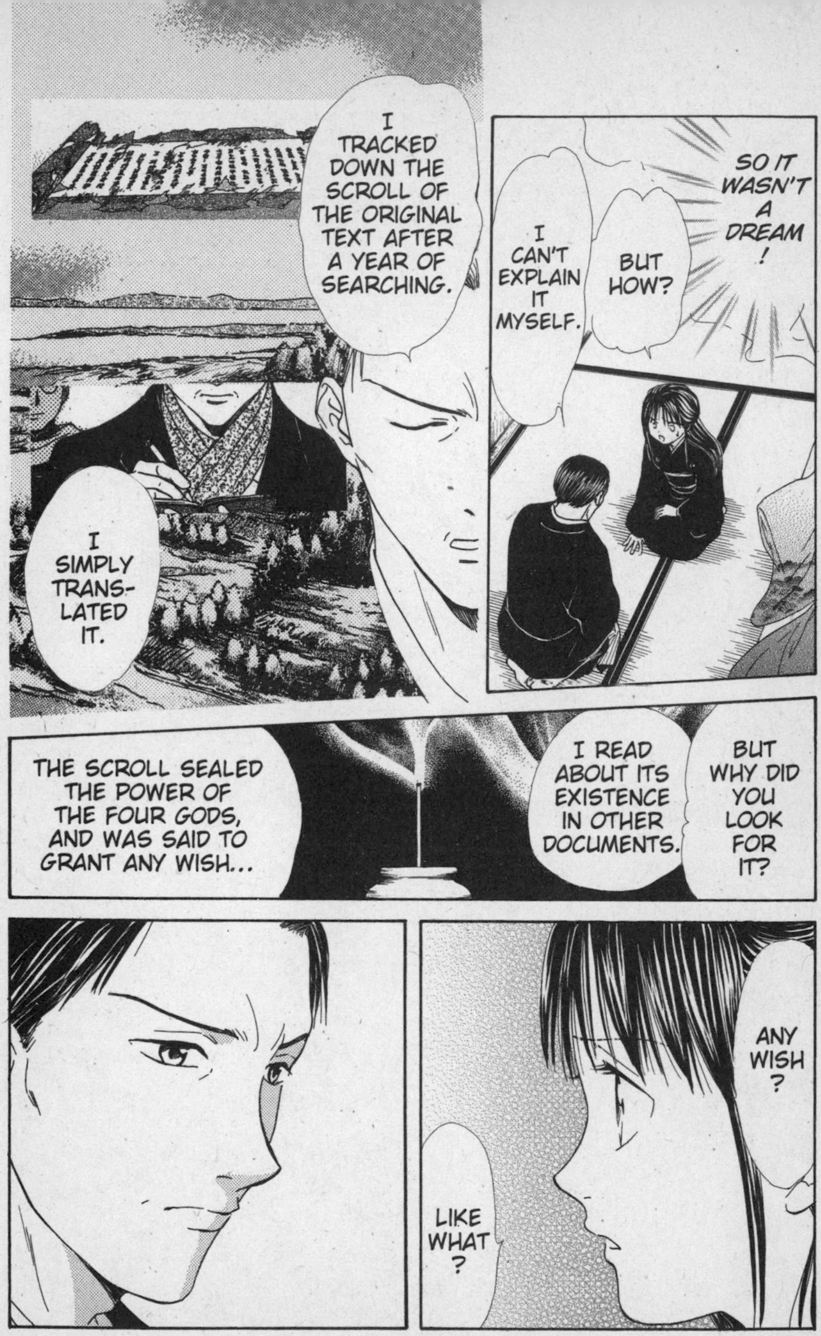
SO IT WASN'T A DREAM!
BUT HOW?
I CAN'T EXPLAIN IT MYSELF.
I TRACKED DOWN THE SCROLL OF THE ORIGINAL TEXT AFTER A YEAR OF SEARCHING.
I SIMPLY TRANS-LATED IT.
BUT WHY DID YOU LOOK FOR IT?
I READ ABOUT ITS EXISTENCE IN OTHER DOCUMENTS.
THE SCROLL SEALED THE POWER OF THE FOUR GODS, AND WAS SAID TO GRANT ANY WISH...
ANY WISH?
LIKE WHAT?

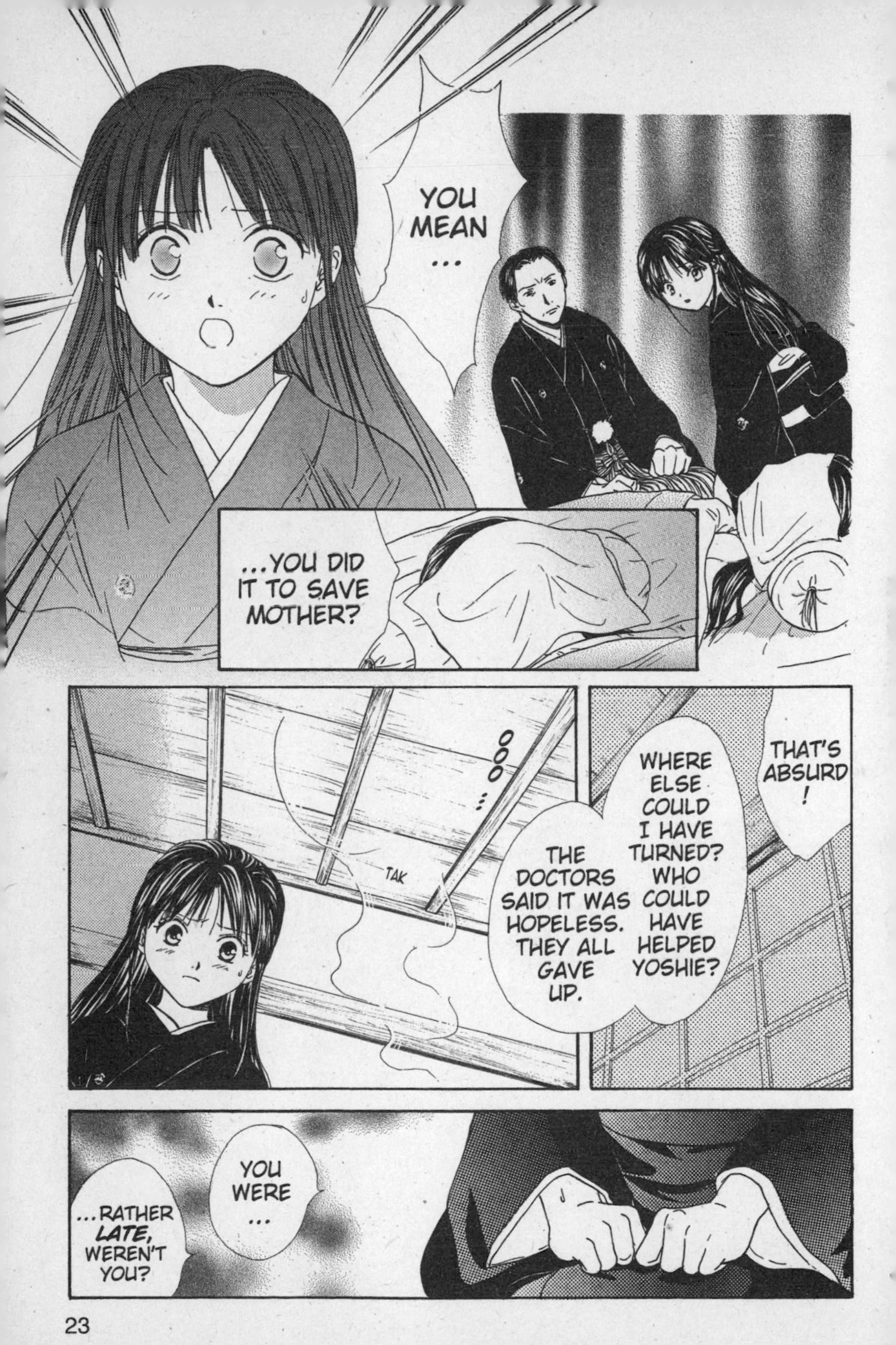
YOU MEAN ...
...YOU DID IT TO SAVE MOTHER?
THAT'S ABSURD!
WHERE ELSE COULD I HAVE TURNED? WHO COULD HAVE HELPED YOSHIE?
THE DOCTORS SAID IT WAS HOPELESS. THEY ALL GAVE UP.
OOO...
TAK
YOU WERE ...
...RATHER *LATE*, WEREN'T YOU?

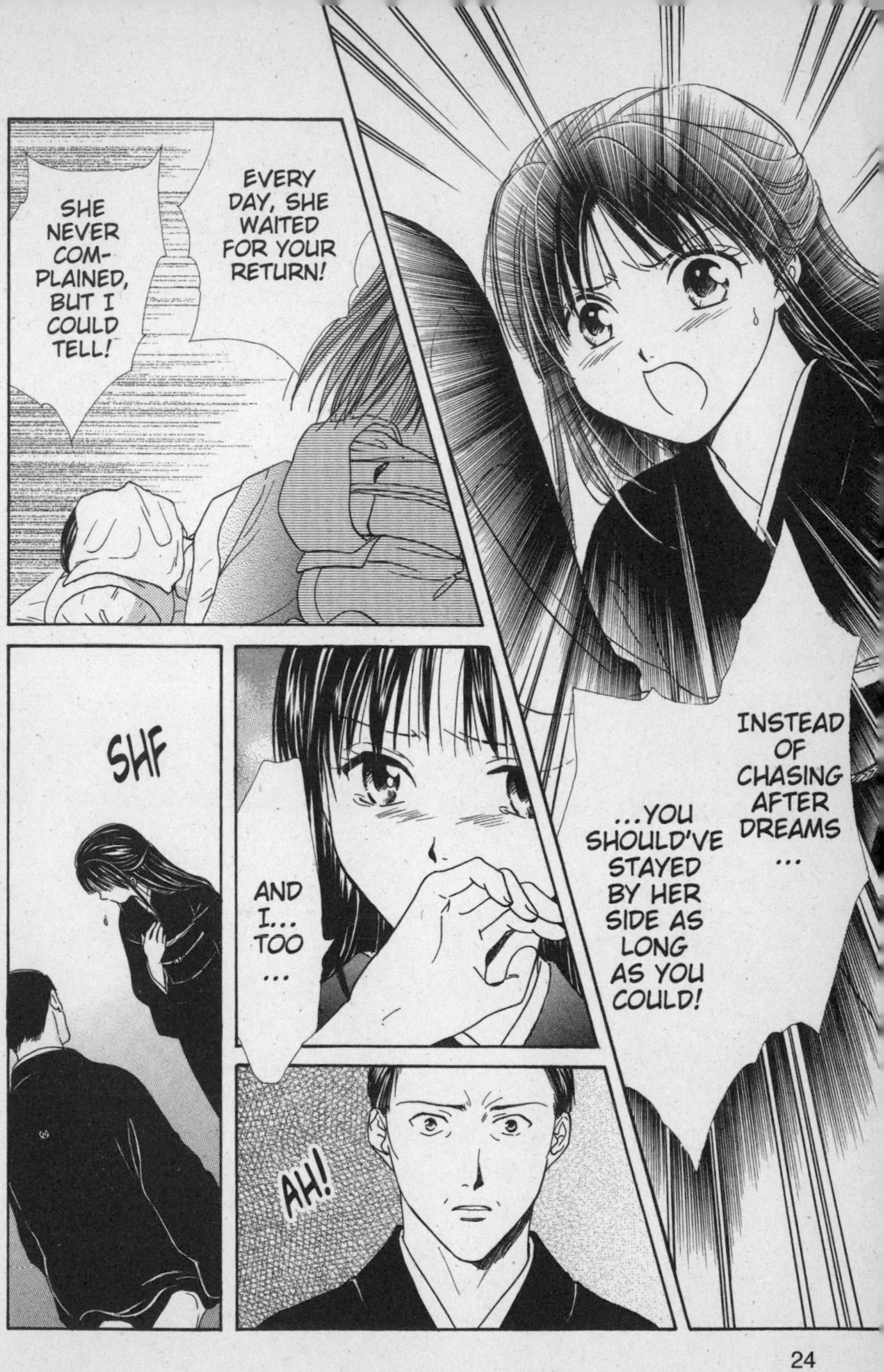
INSTEAD OF CHASING AFTER DREAMS ...
...YOU SHOULD'VE STAYED BY HER SIDE AS LONG AS YOU COULD!
EVERY DAY, SHE WAITED FOR YOUR RETURN!
SHE NEVER COM-PLAINED, BUT I COULD TELL!
AND I... TOO ...
AH!
SHF

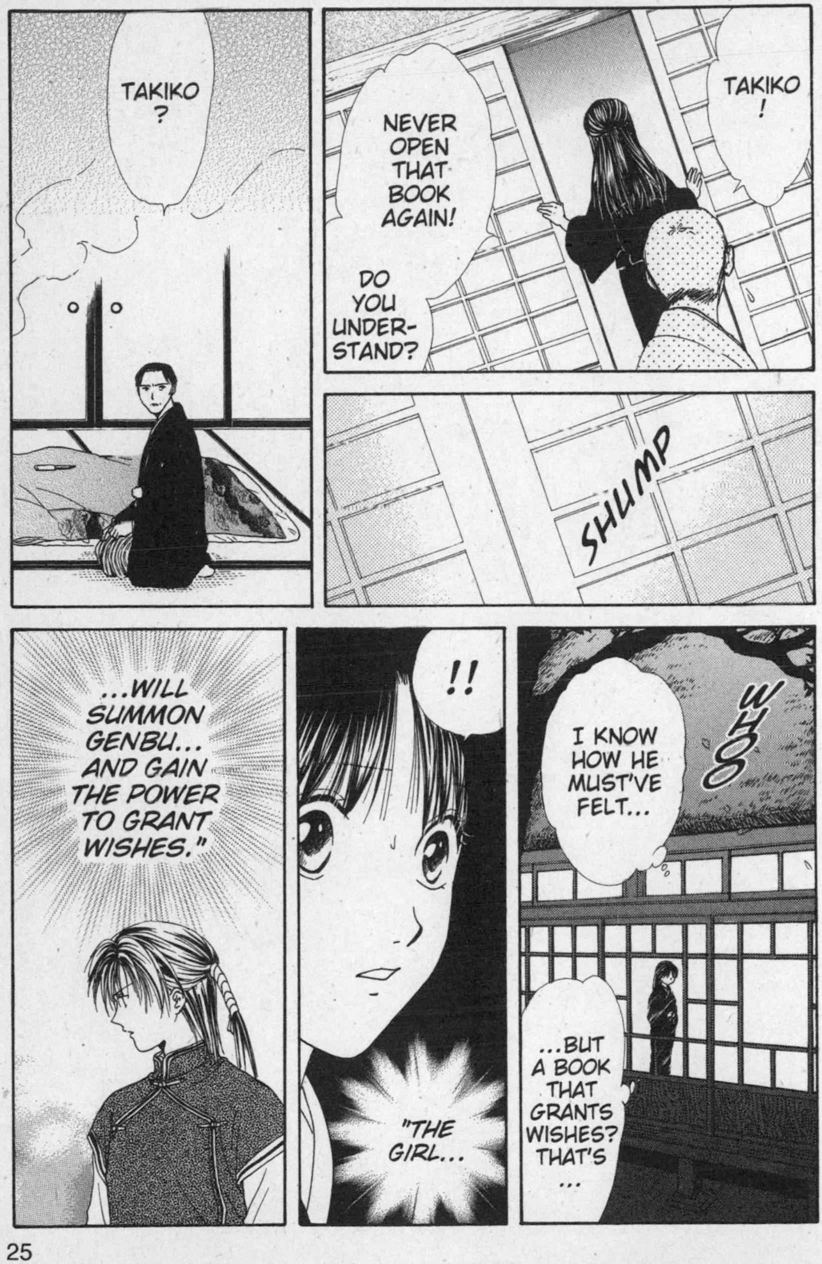
TAKIKO !
NEVER OPEN THAT BOOK AGAIN!
DO YOU UNDERSTAND?
SHUMP
TAKIKO ?
WHOO
I KNOW HOW HE MUST'VE FELT...
...BUT A BOOK THAT GRANTS WISHES? THAT'S ...
!!
"THE GIRL...
...WILL SUMMON GENBU... AND GAIN THE POWER TO GRANT WISHES."

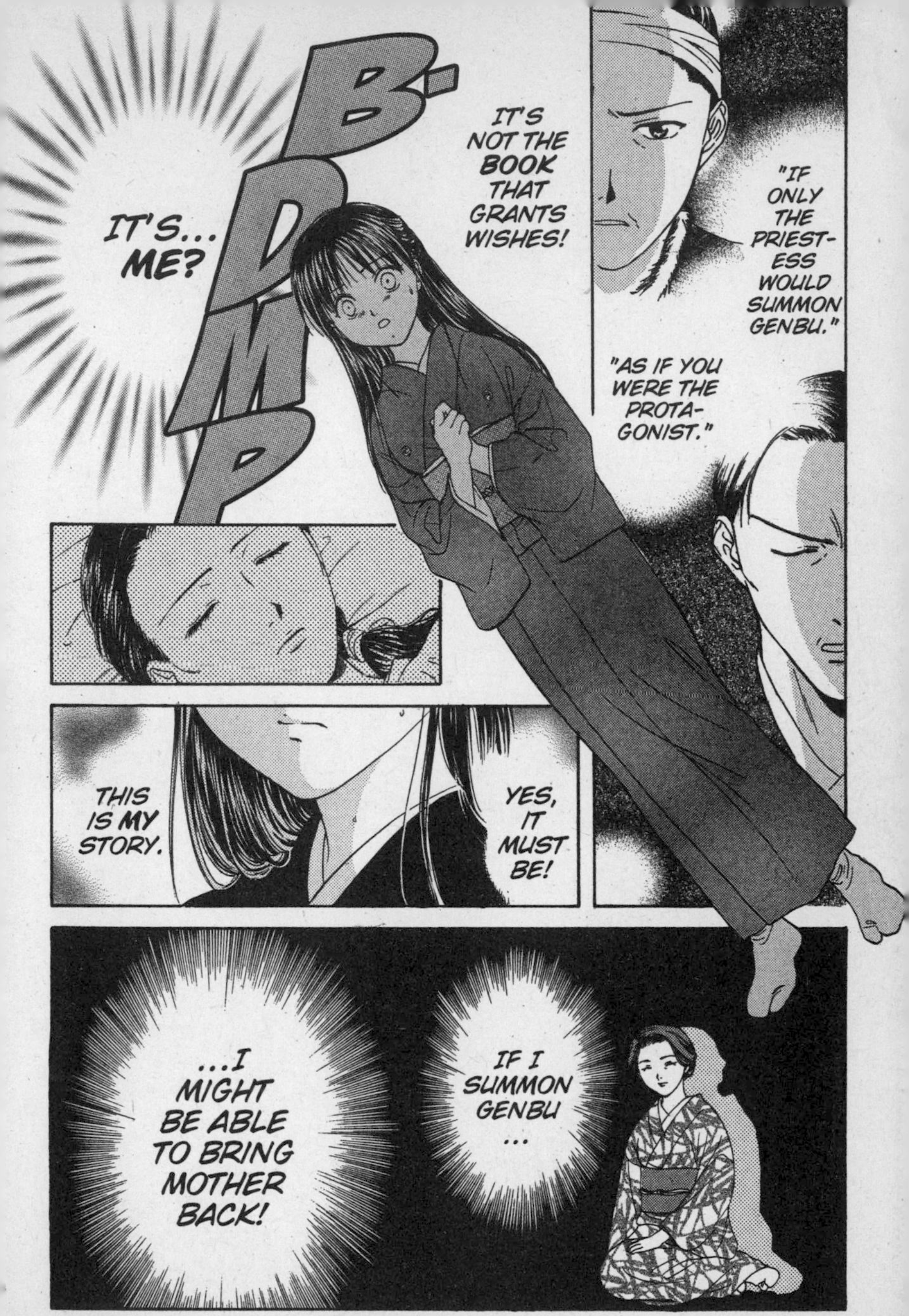
"IF ONLY THE PRIESTESS WOULD SUMMON GENBU."
"AS IF YOU WERE THE PROTAGONIST."
IT'S NOT THE BOOK THAT GRANTS WISHES!
B-DMP
IT'S... ME?
YES, IT MUST BE!
THIS IS MY STORY.
IF I SUMMON GENBU...
...I MIGHT BE ABLE TO BRING MOTHER BACK!

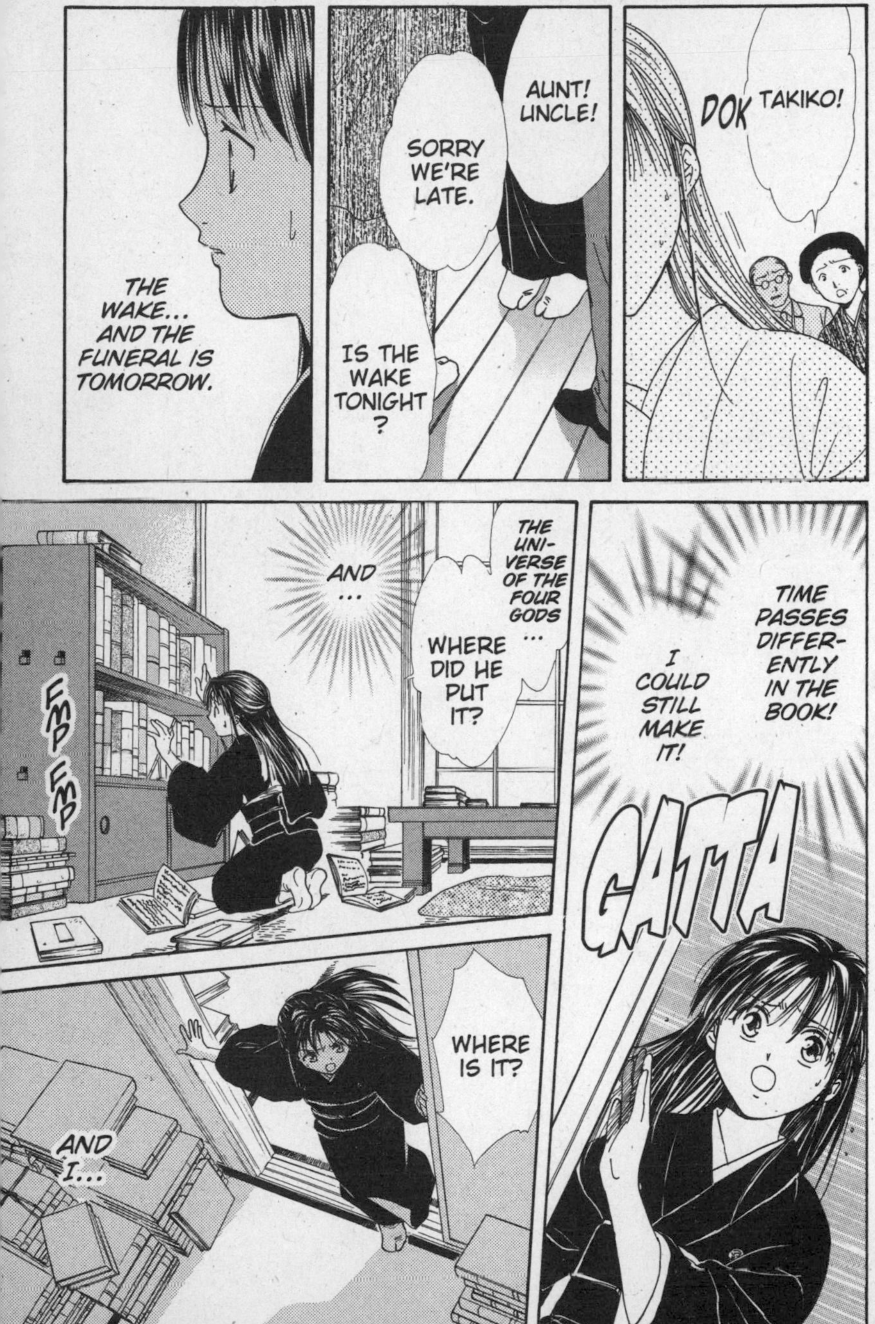
DOK
TAKIKO!
AUNT! UNCLE!
SORRY WE'RE LATE.
IS THE WAKE TONIGHT?
THE WAKE... AND THE FUNERAL IS TOMORROW.
TIME PASSES DIFFERENTLY IN THE BOOK!
I COULD STILL MAKE IT!
GATTA
THE UNIVERSE OF THE FOUR GODS...
WHERE DID HE PUT IT?
AND...
EMP EMP
WHERE IS IT?
AND I...

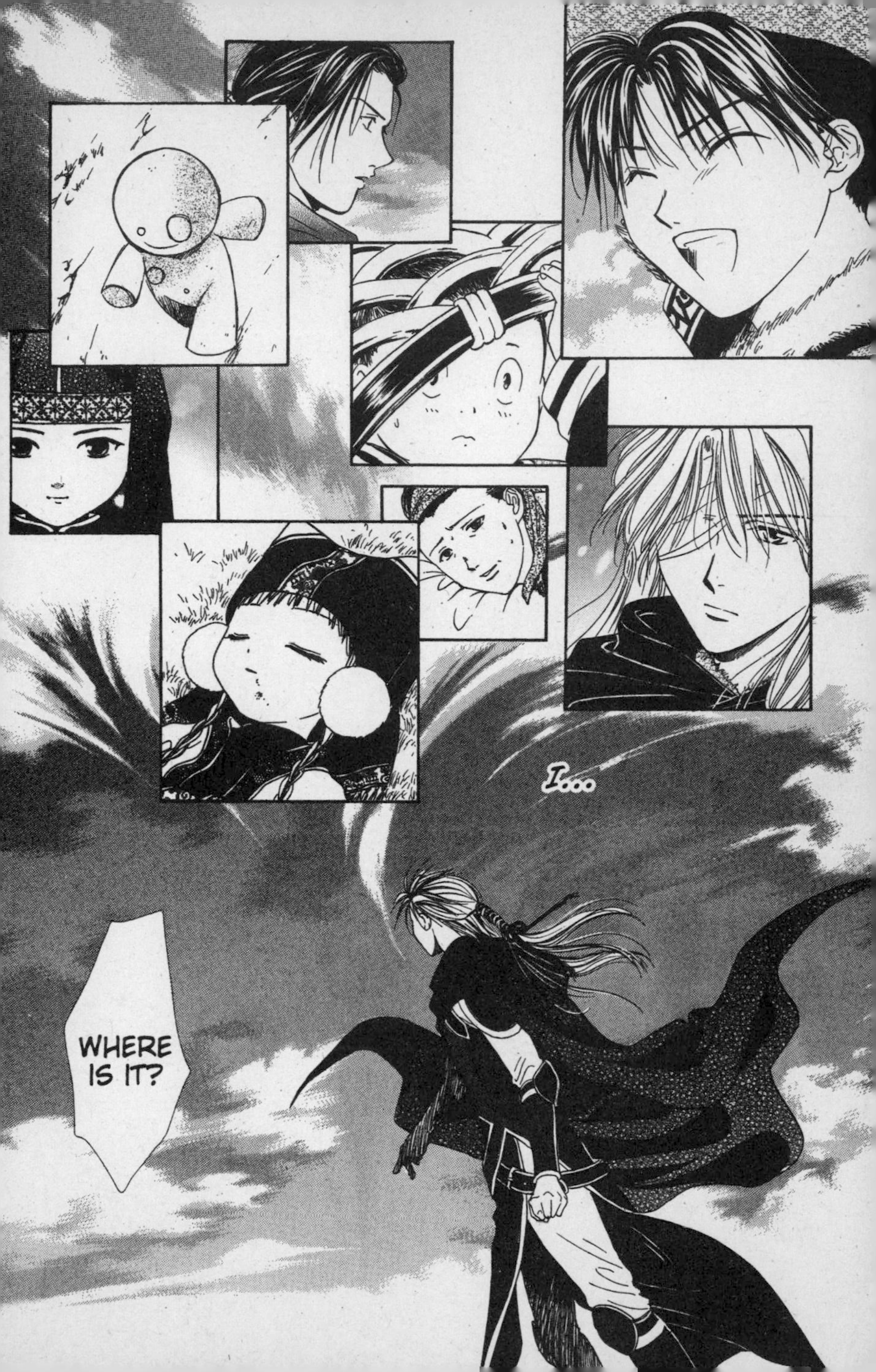
I...
WHERE IS IT?

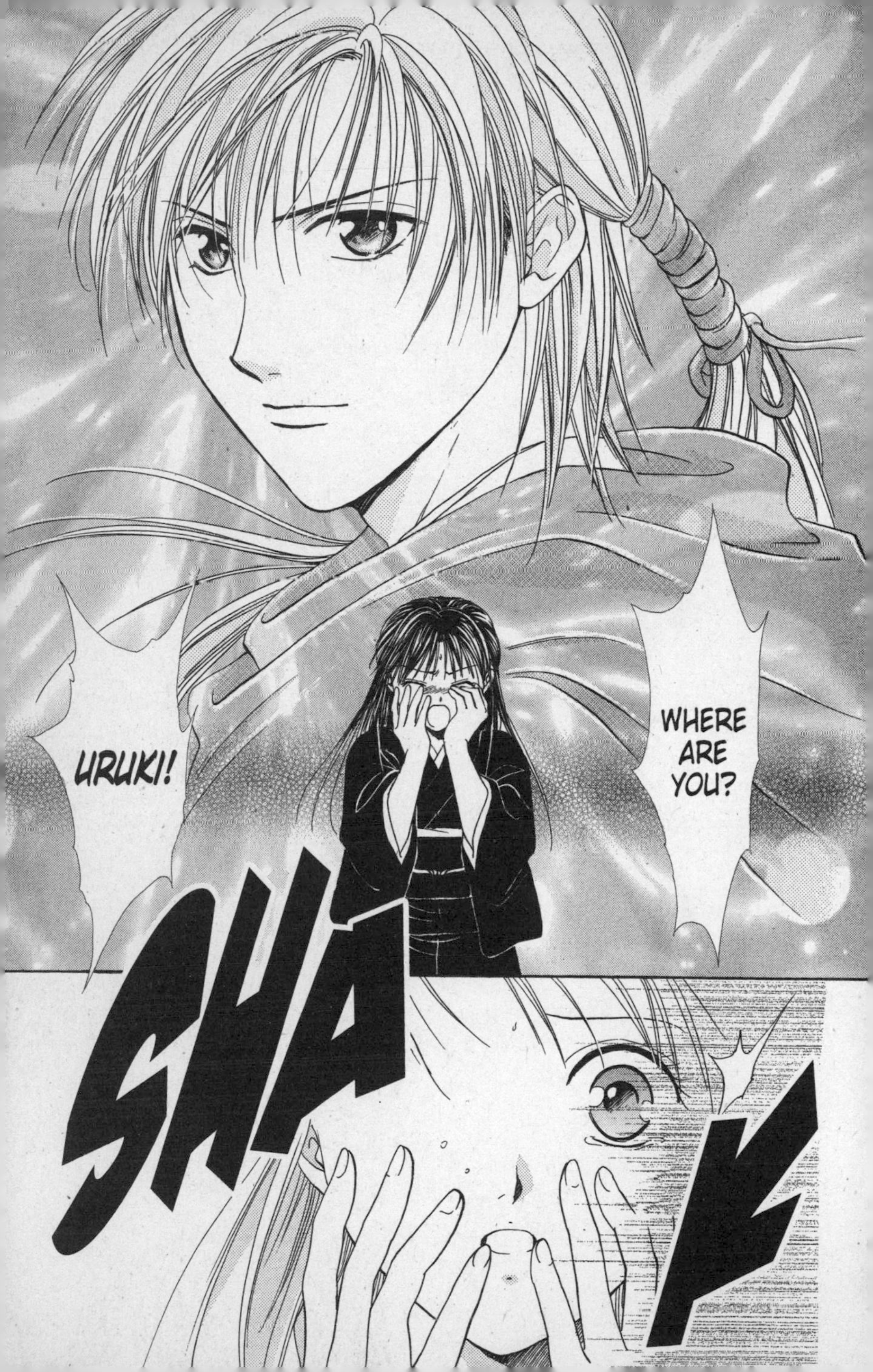
WHERE ARE YOU?
URUKI!
SHAK

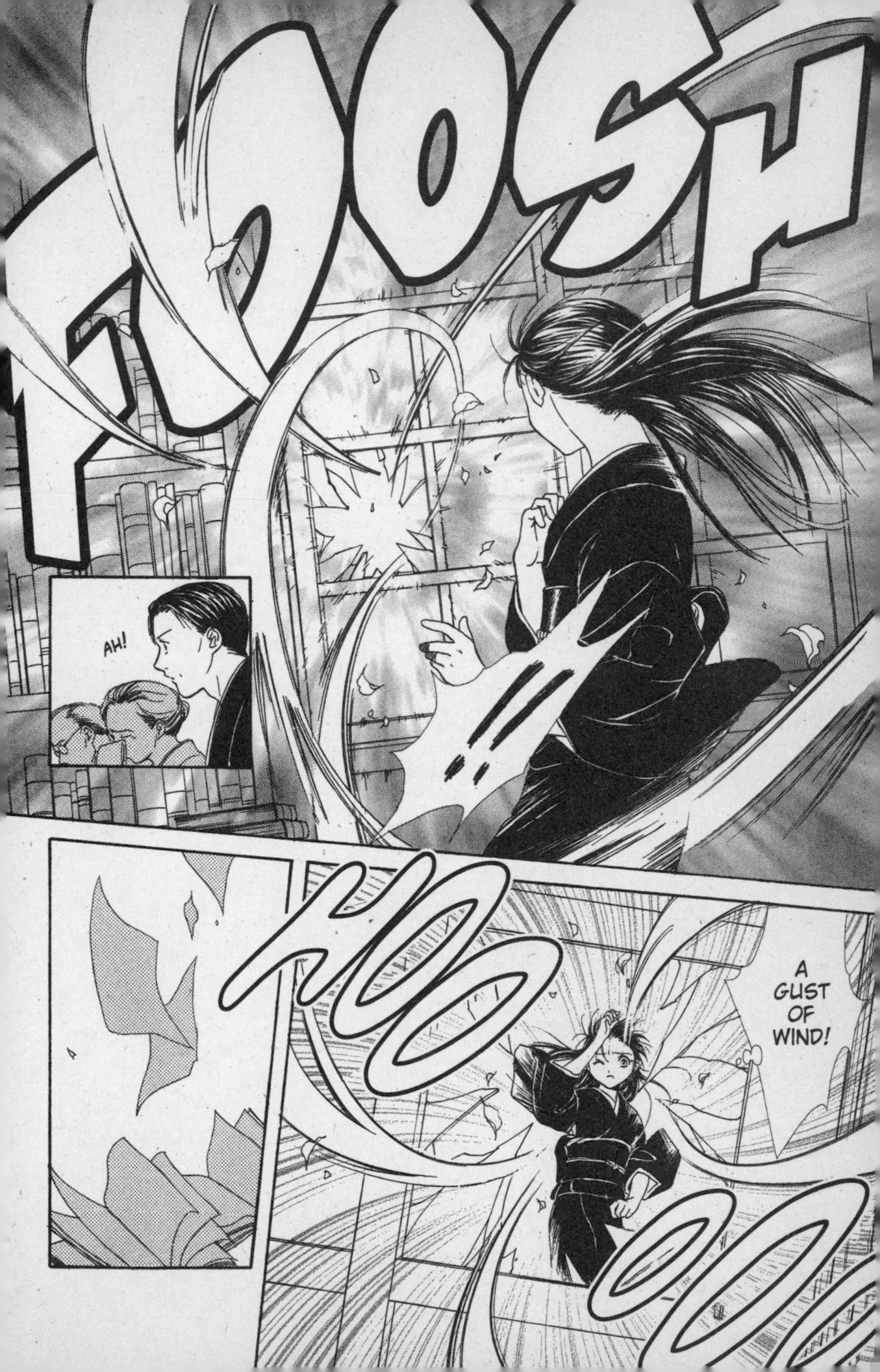
FOOSH
AH!
A GUST OF WIND!

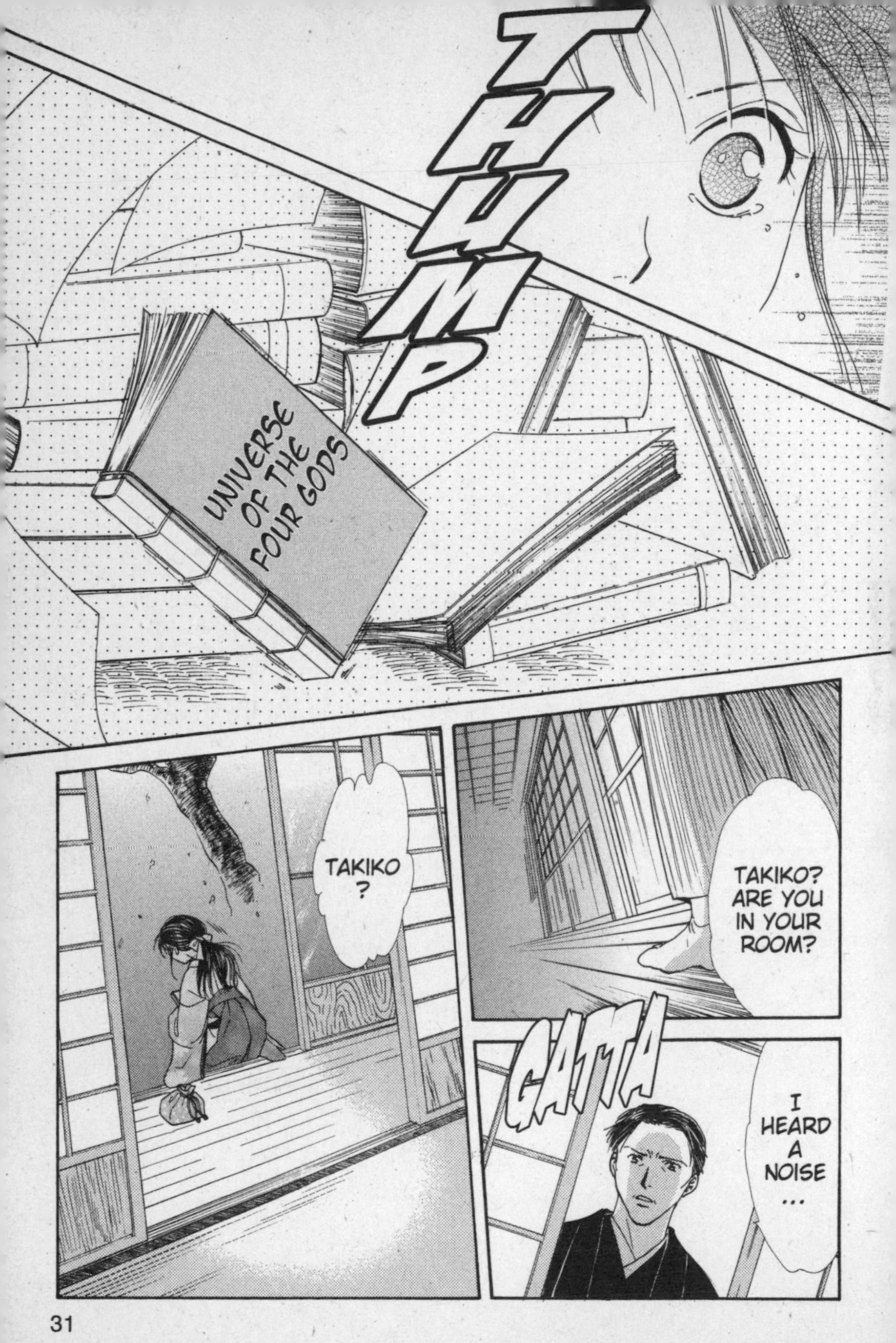
THUMP
UNIVERSE OF THE FOUR GODS
TAKIKO? ARE YOU IN YOUR ROOM?
GATTA
I HEARD A NOISE...
TAKIKO ?

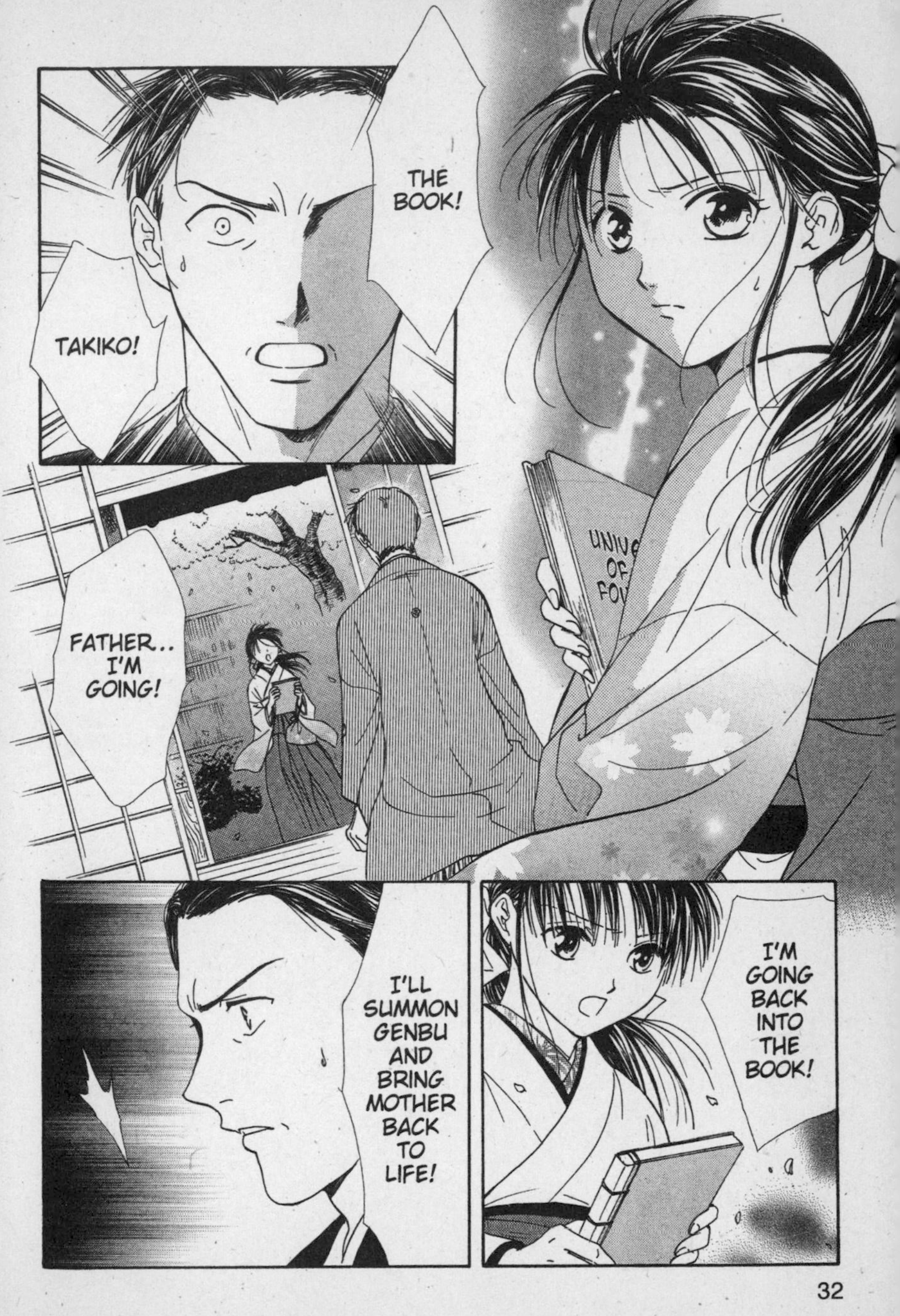
THE BOOK!
TAKIKO!
FATHER... I'M GOING!
I'M GOING BACK INTO THE BOOK!
I'LL SUMMON GENBU AND BRING MOTHER BACK TO LIFE!

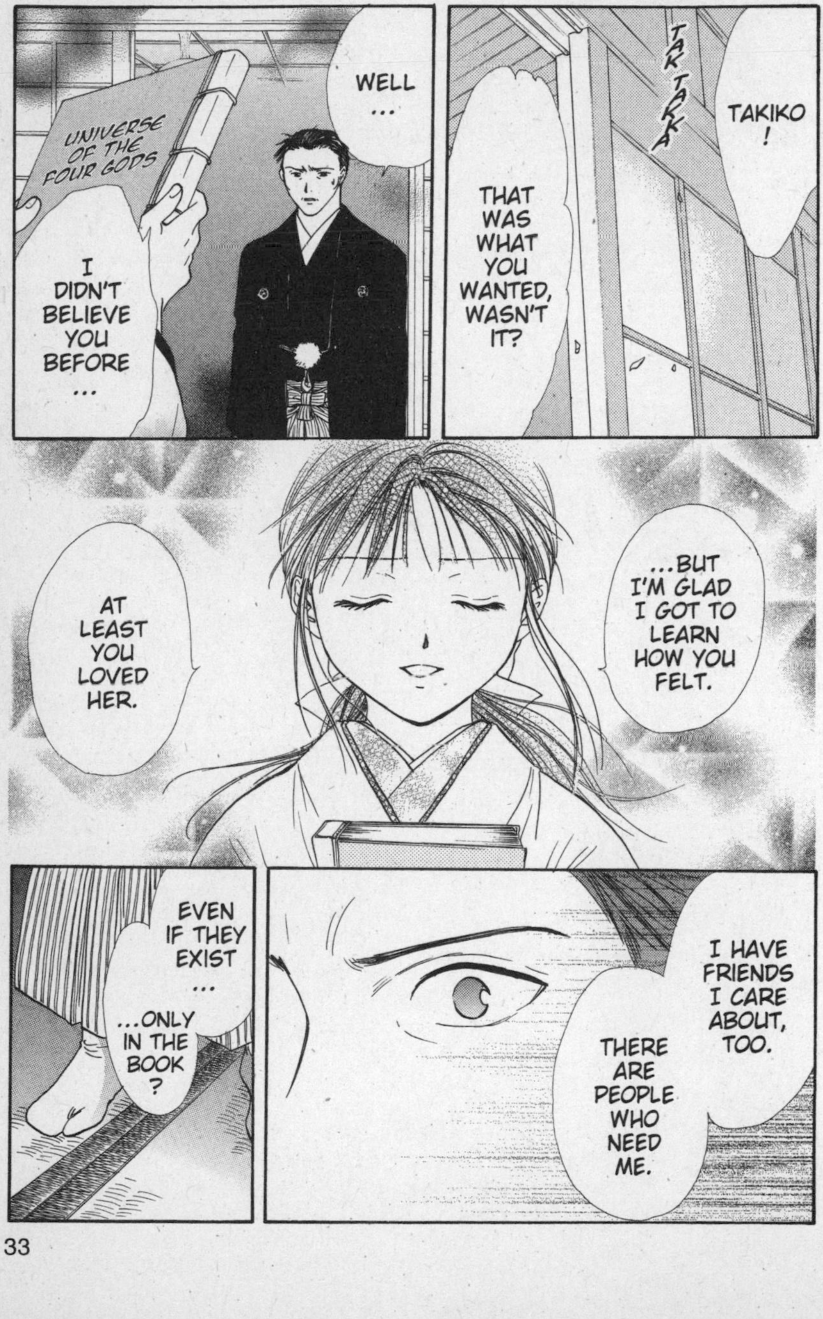
TAKIKO!
TAK TAKKA
THAT WAS WHAT YOU WANTED, WASN'T IT?
WELL...
UNIVERSE OF THE FOUR GODS
I DIDN'T BELIEVE YOU BEFORE...
...BUT I'M GLAD I GOT TO LEARN HOW YOU FELT.
AT LEAST YOU LOVED HER.
I HAVE FRIENDS I CARE ABOUT, TOO.
THERE ARE PEOPLE WHO NEED ME.
EVEN IF THEY EXIST...
...ONLY IN THE BOOK?

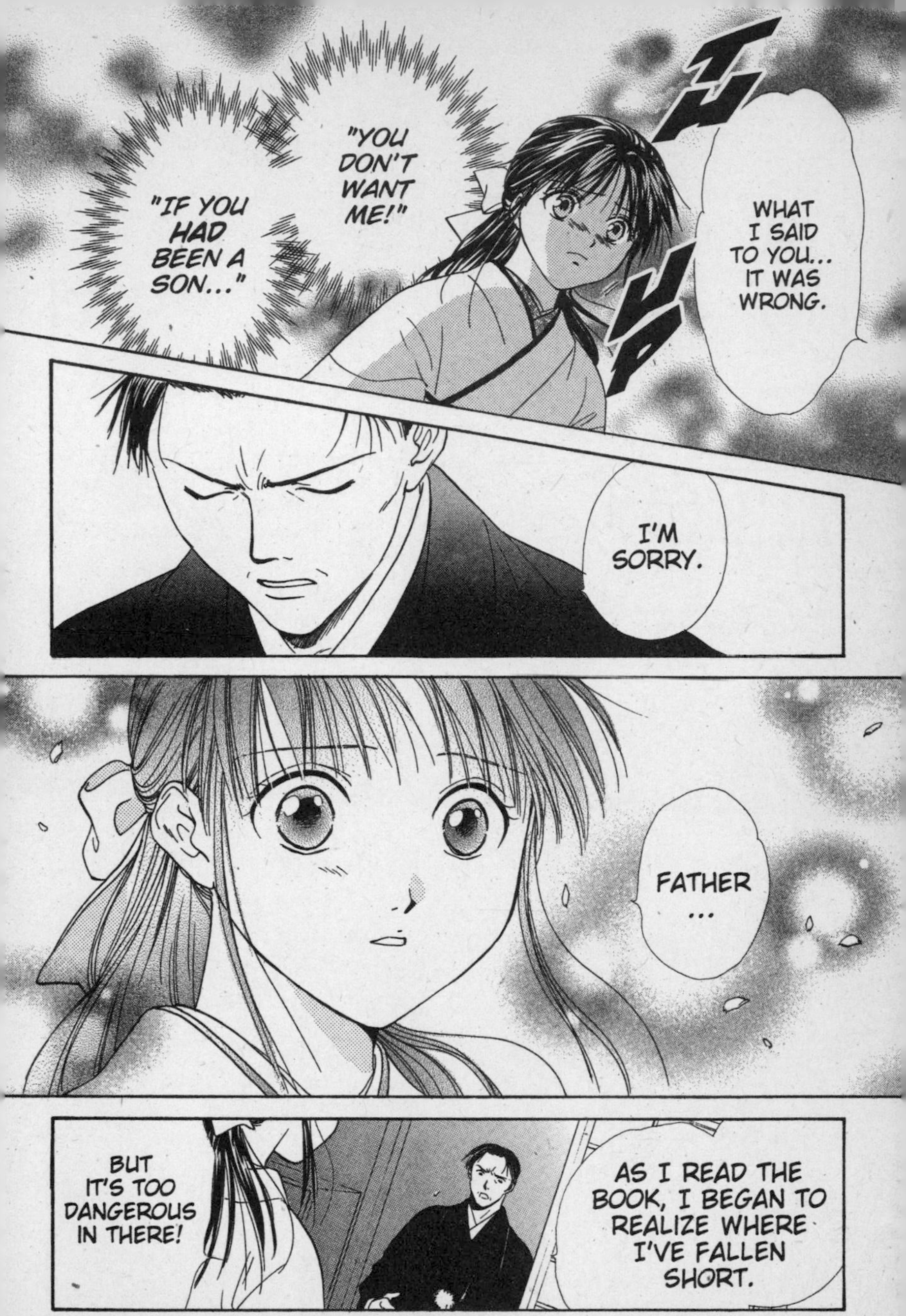
WHAT I SAID TO YOU... IT WAS WRONG.
"YOU DON'T WANT ME!"
"IF YOU HAD BEEN A SON..."
I'M SORRY.
FATHER ...
AS I READ THE BOOK, I BEGAN TO REALIZE WHERE I'VE FALLEN SHORT.
BUT IT'S TOO DANGEROUS IN THERE!

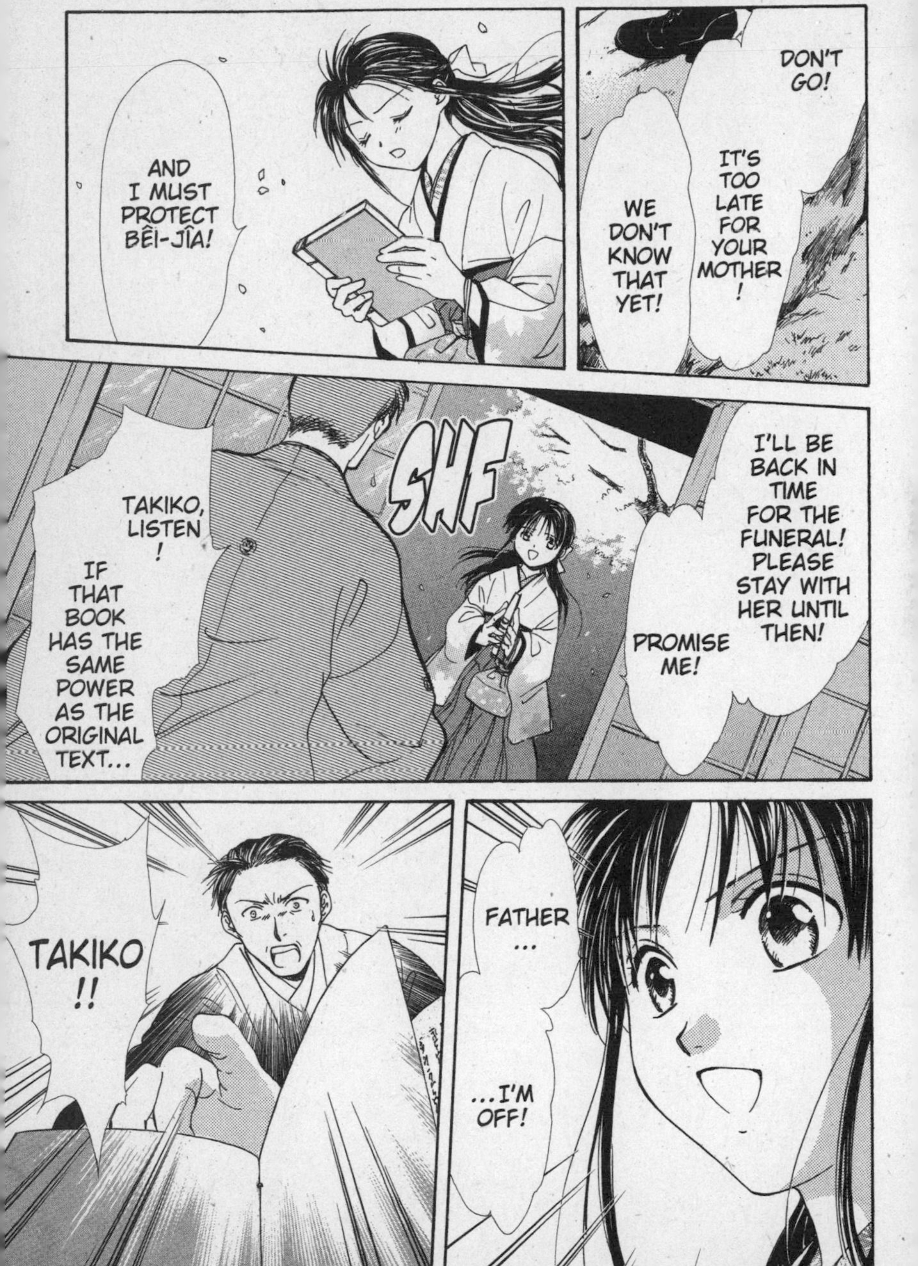
DON'T GO!
IT'S TOO LATE FOR YOUR MOTHER!
WE DON'T KNOW THAT YET!
AND I MUST PROTECT BÊI-JÎA!
I'LL BE BACK IN TIME FOR THE FUNERAL! PLEASE STAY WITH HER UNTIL THEN!
PROMISE ME!
SHF
TAKIKO, LISTEN!
IF THAT BOOK HAS THE SAME POWER AS THE ORIGINAL TEXT...
FATHER...
...I'M OFF!
TAKIKO!!

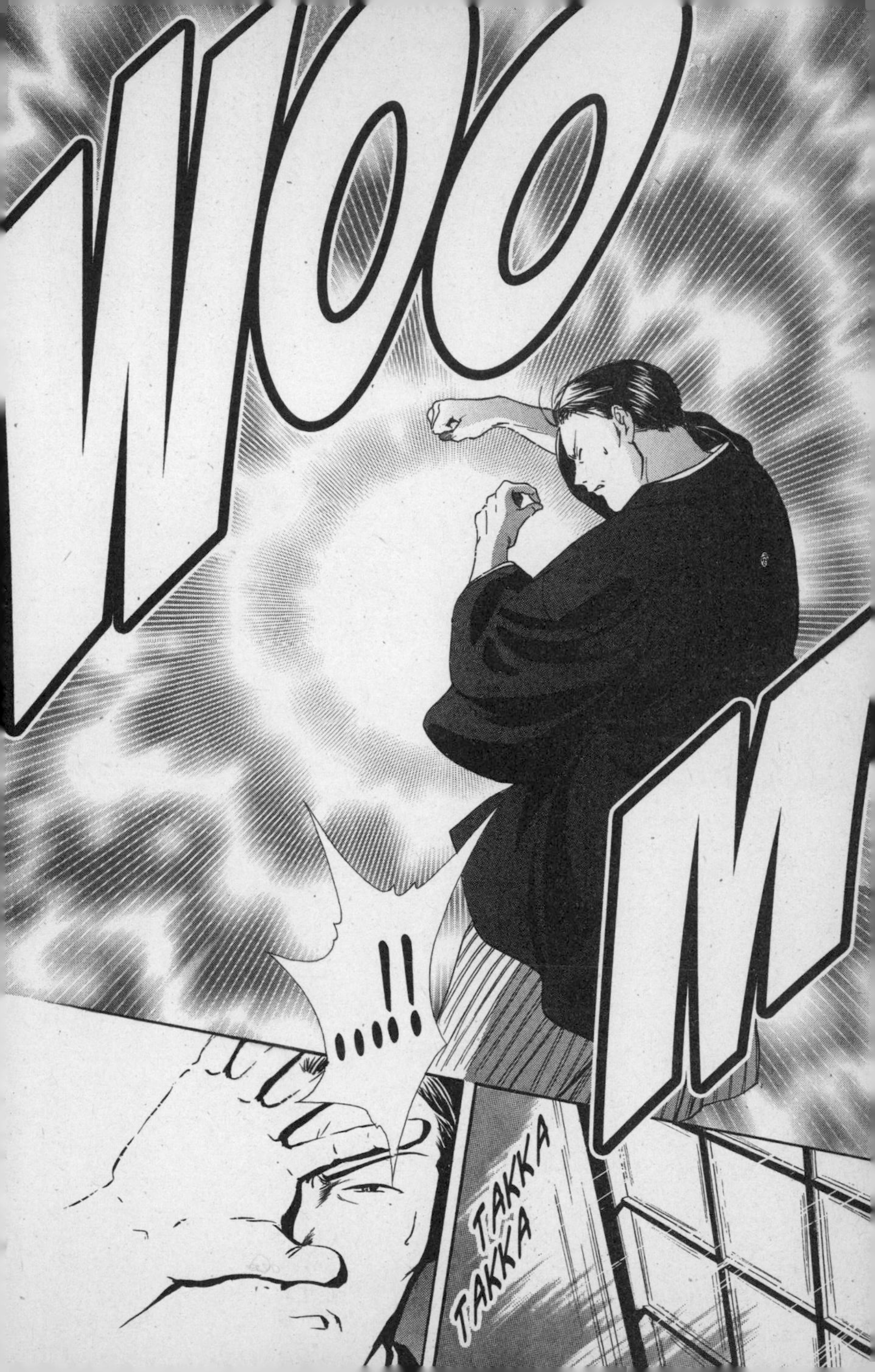
WOOM
...!!
TAKKA TAKKA

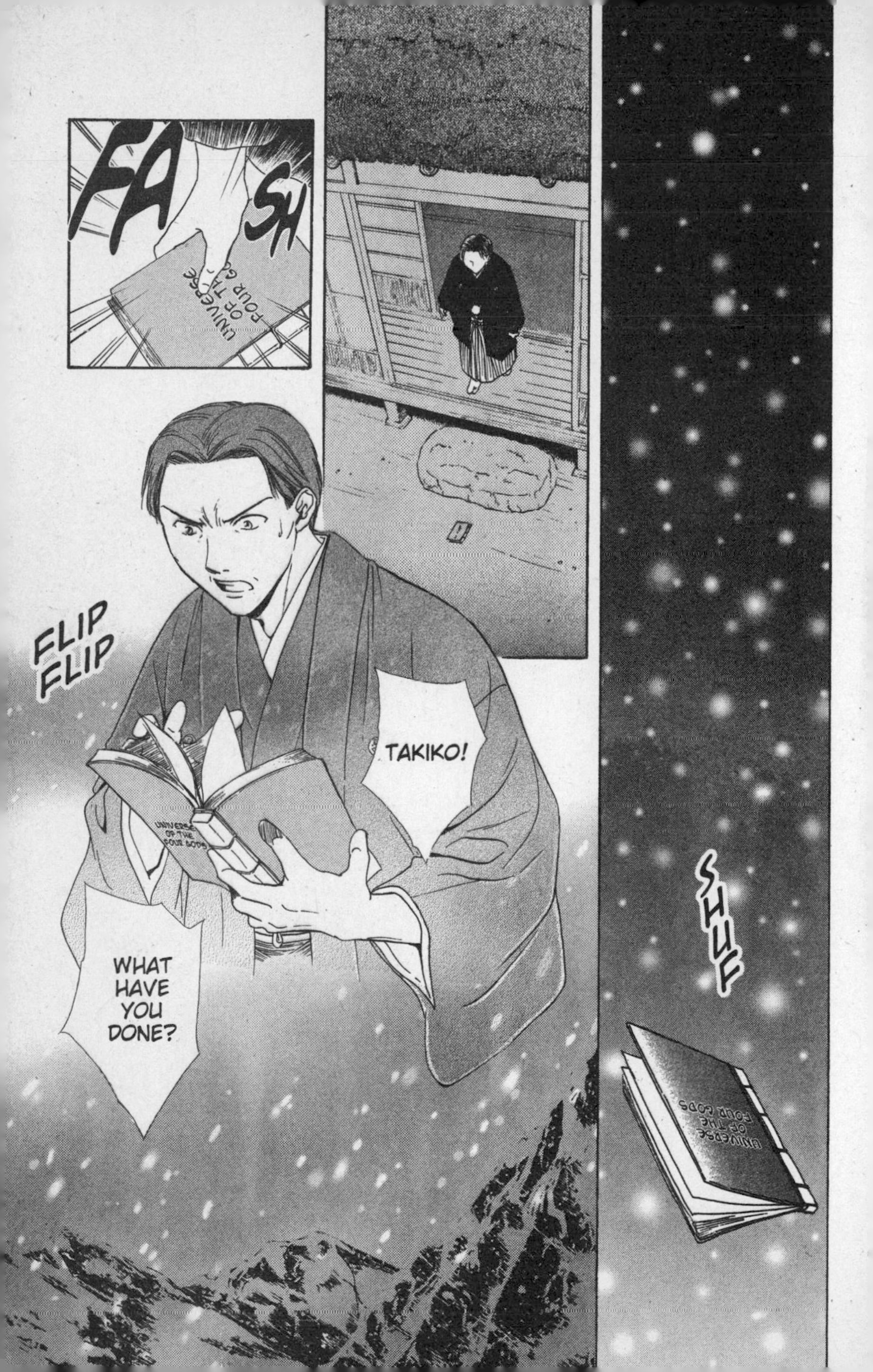
SHUFF
UNIVERSE OF THE FOUR GODS
FASH
TAKIKO!
WHAT HAVE YOU DONE?
FLIP FLIP
UNIVERSE OF THE FOUR GODS

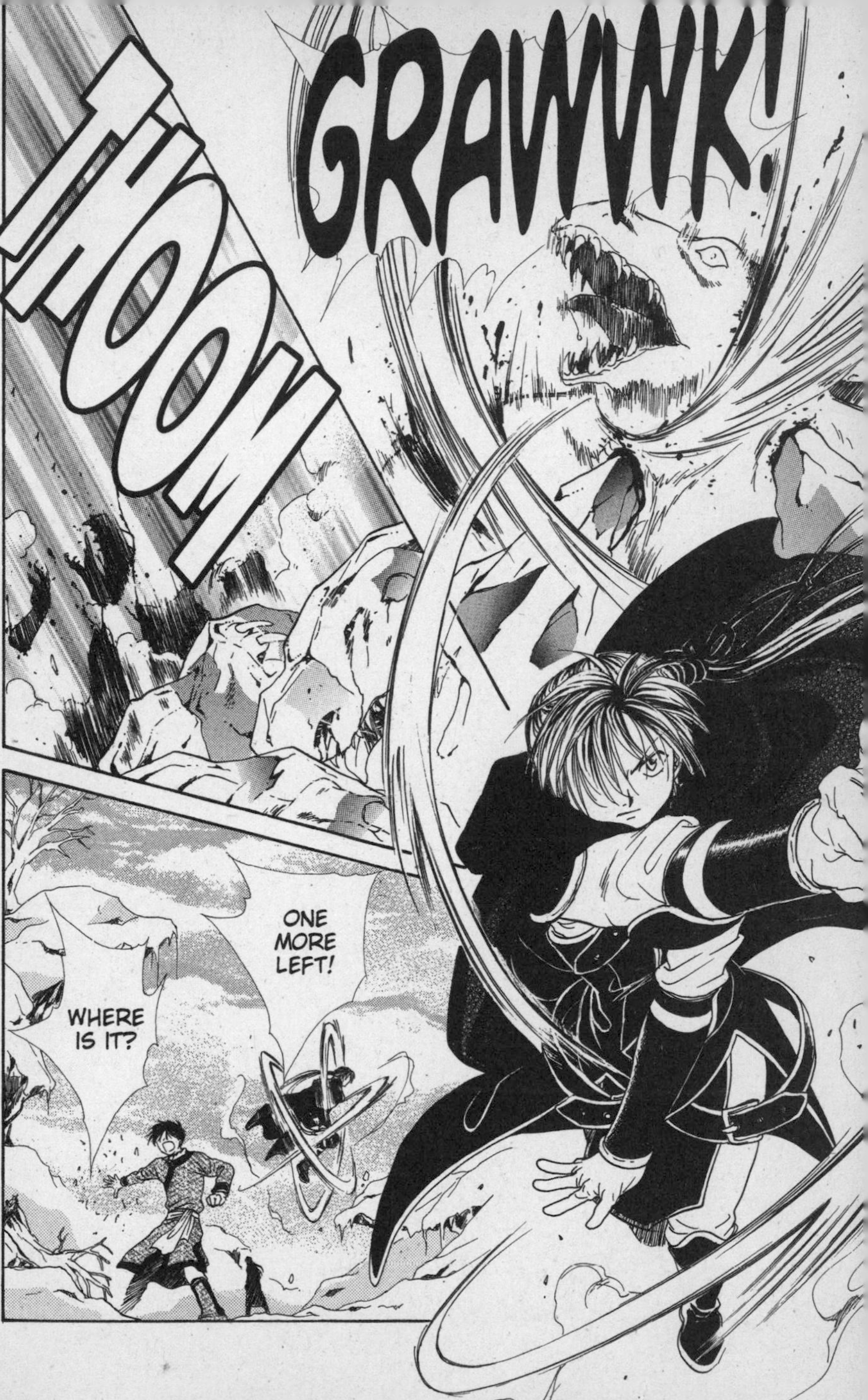
GRAWWK!
THOOM!
ONE MORE LEFT!
WHERE IS IT?

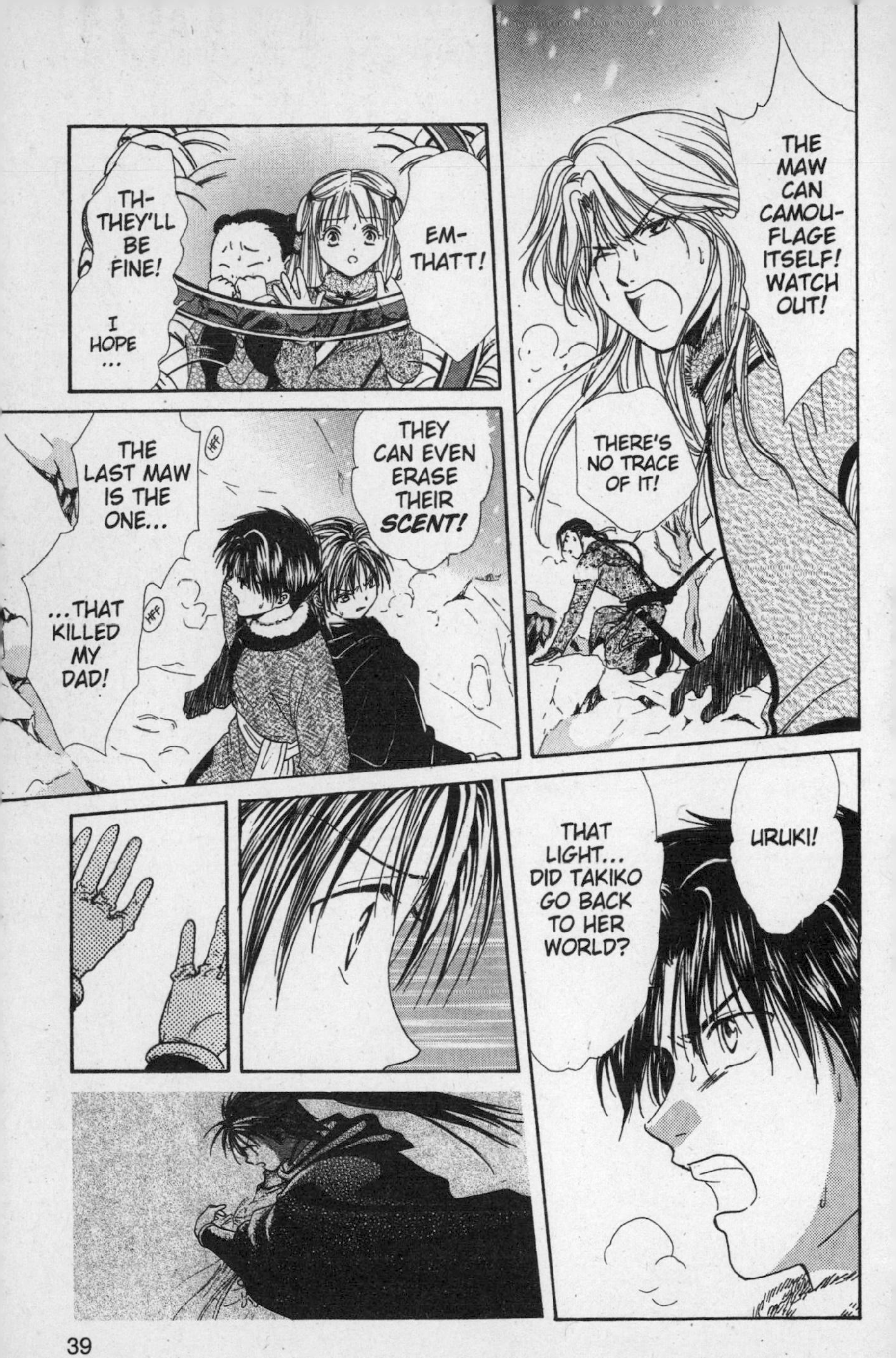
THE MAW CAN CAMOUFLAGE ITSELF! WATCH OUT!
THERE'S NO TRACE OF IT!
EM-THATT!
TH-THEY'LL BE FINE!
I HOPE ...
THEY CAN EVEN ERASE THEIR SCENT!
HFF
THE LAST MAW IS THE ONE...
HFF
...THAT KILLED MY DAD!
URUKI!
THAT LIGHT... DID TAKIKO GO BACK TO HER WORLD?

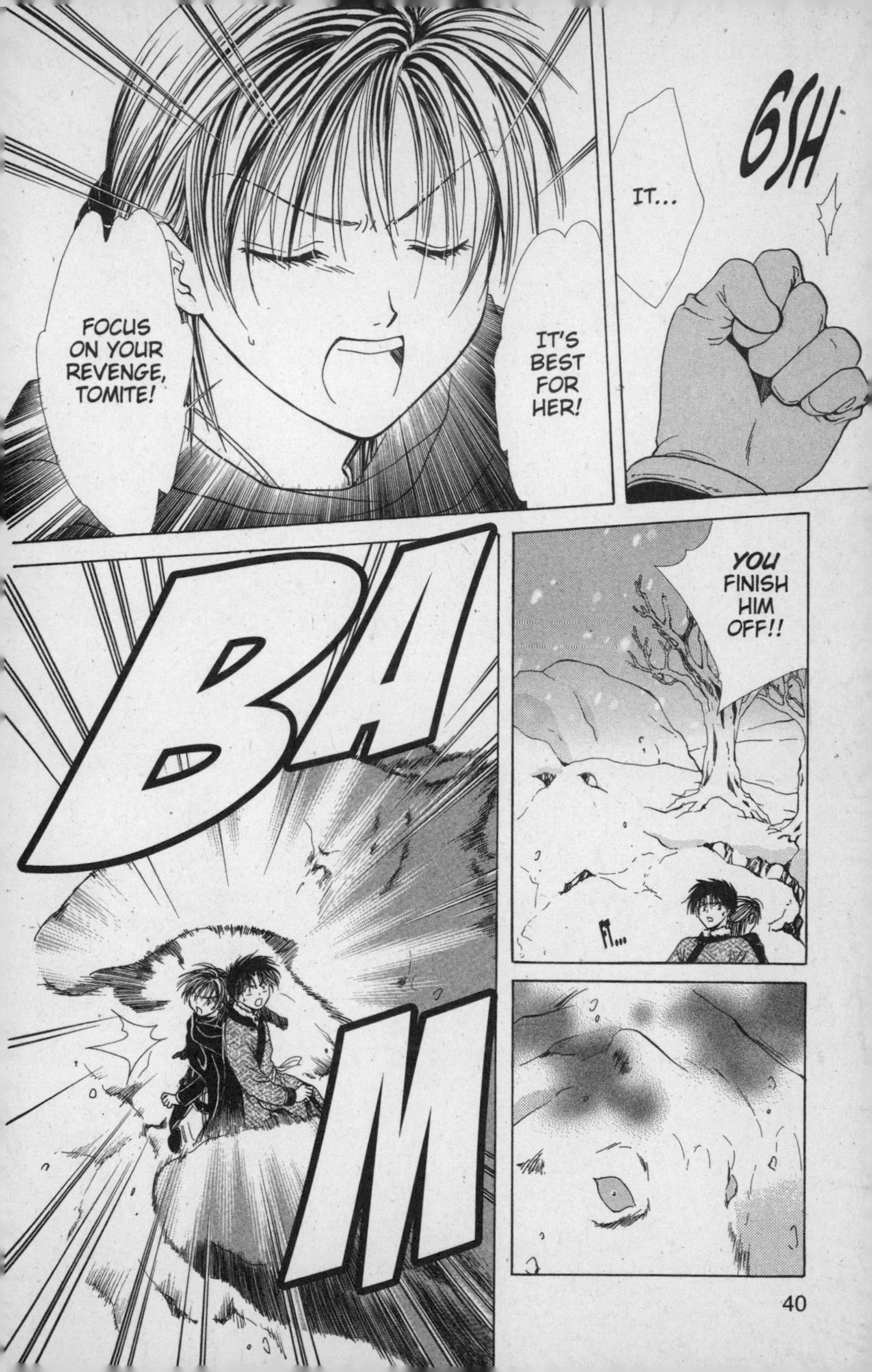
GSH
IT...
IT'S BEST FOR HER!
FOCUS ON YOUR REVENGE, TOMITE!
YOU FINISH HIM OFF!!
FT...
BAM

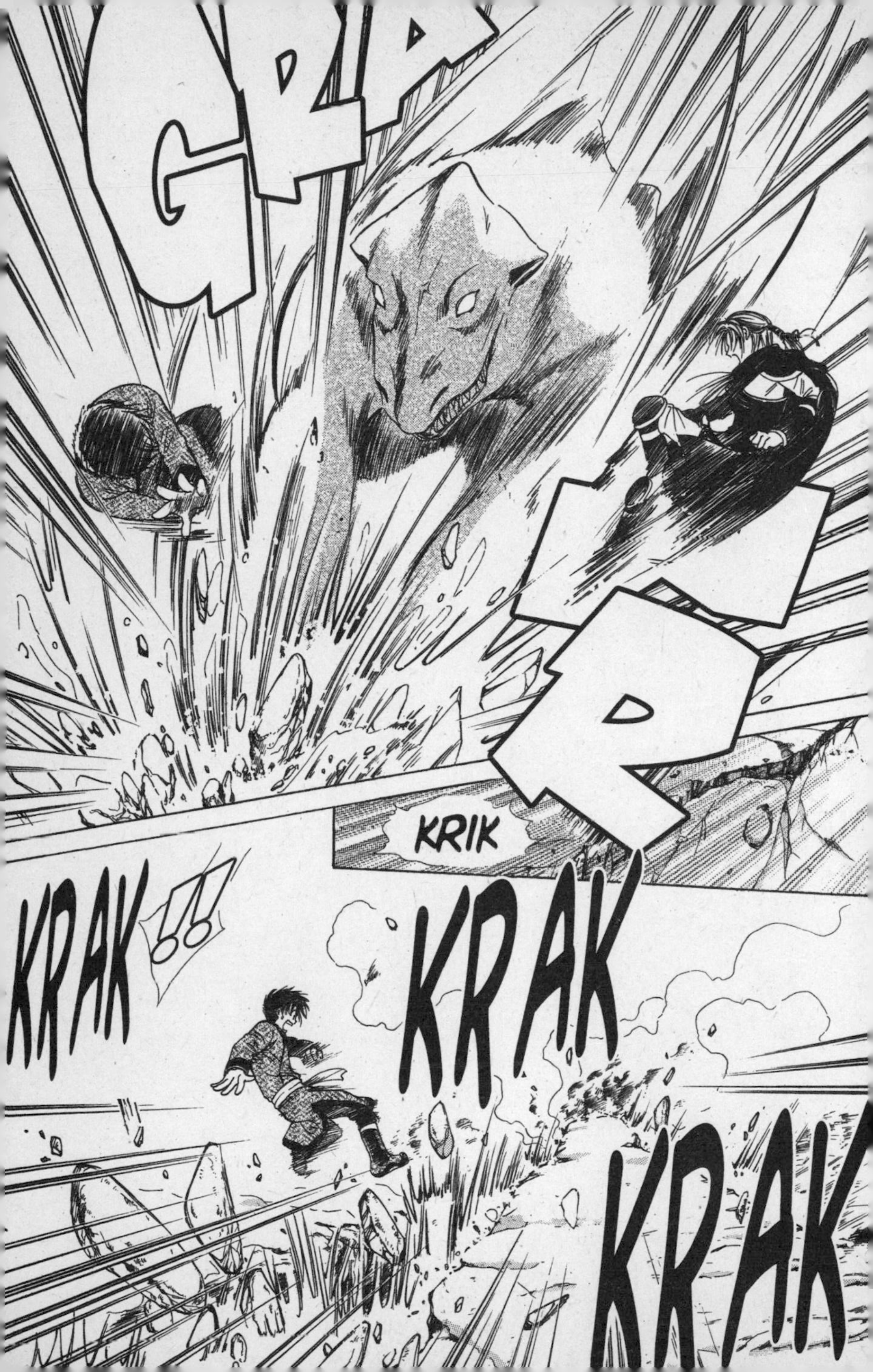
KRIK
KRAK
KRAK
KRAK!!

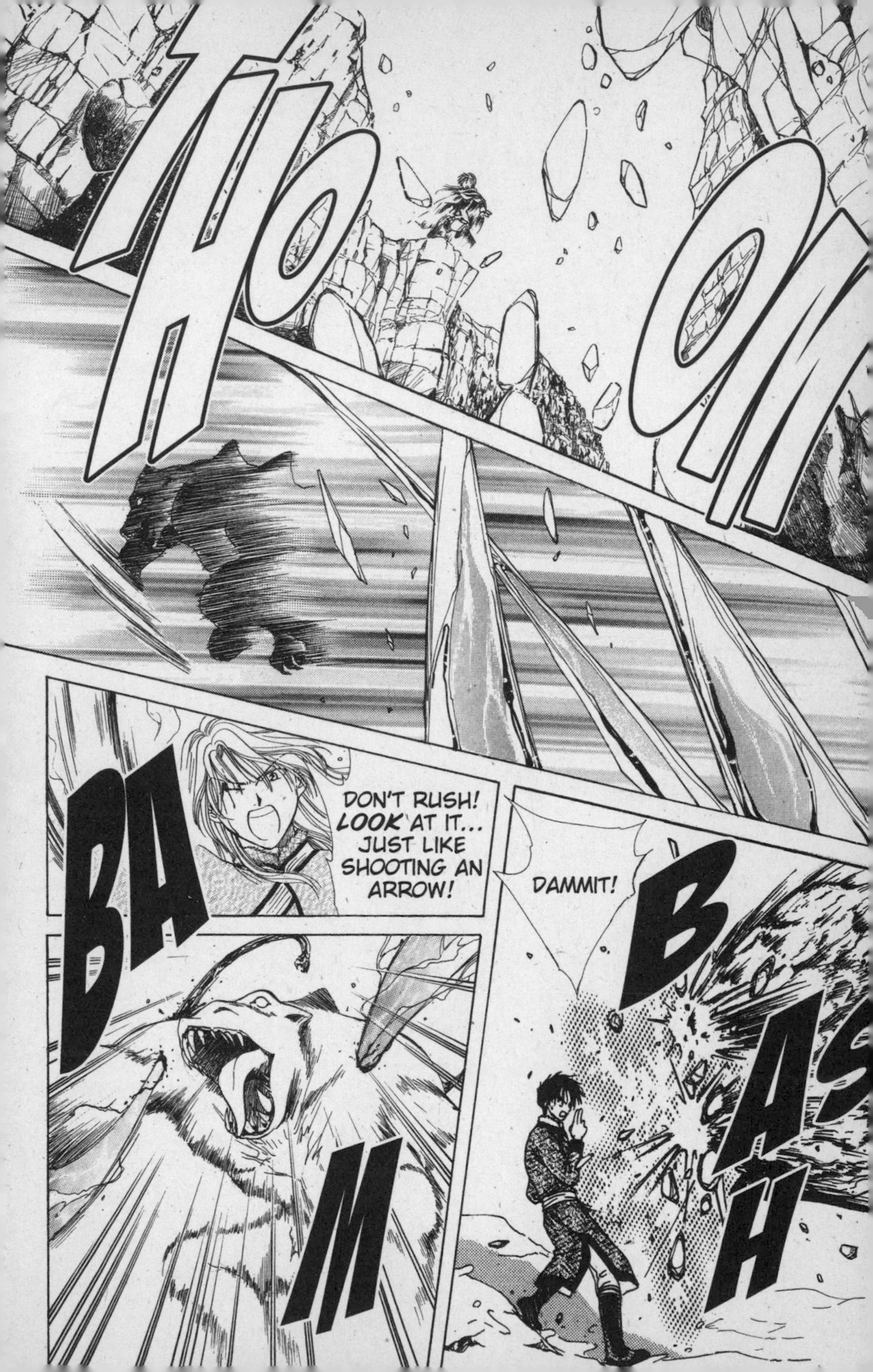
DAMMIT!
BASH
DON'T RUSH! LOOK AT IT... JUST LIKE SHOOTING AN ARROW!
BAM

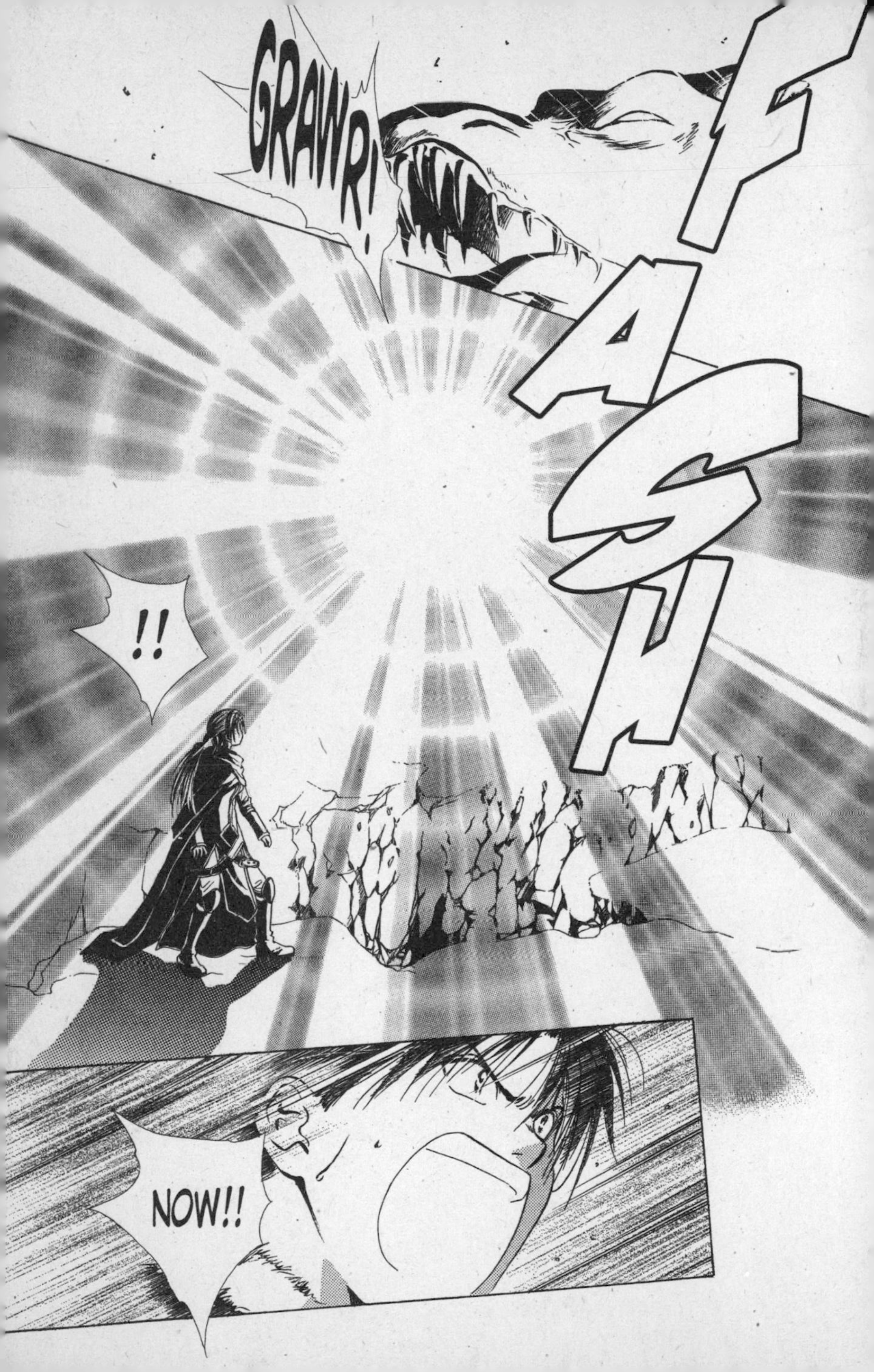
FASH
GRAWR!
!!
NOW!!

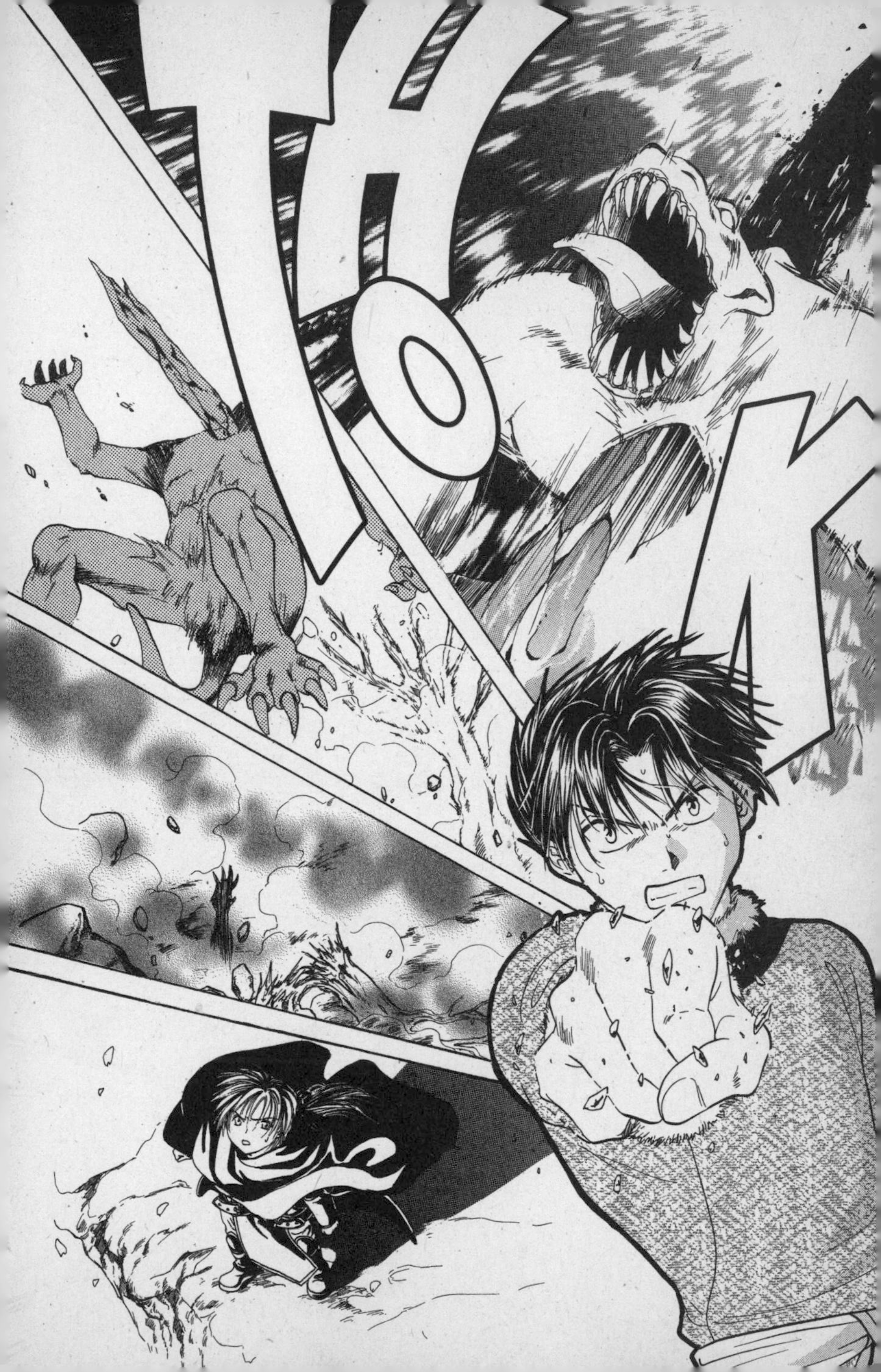

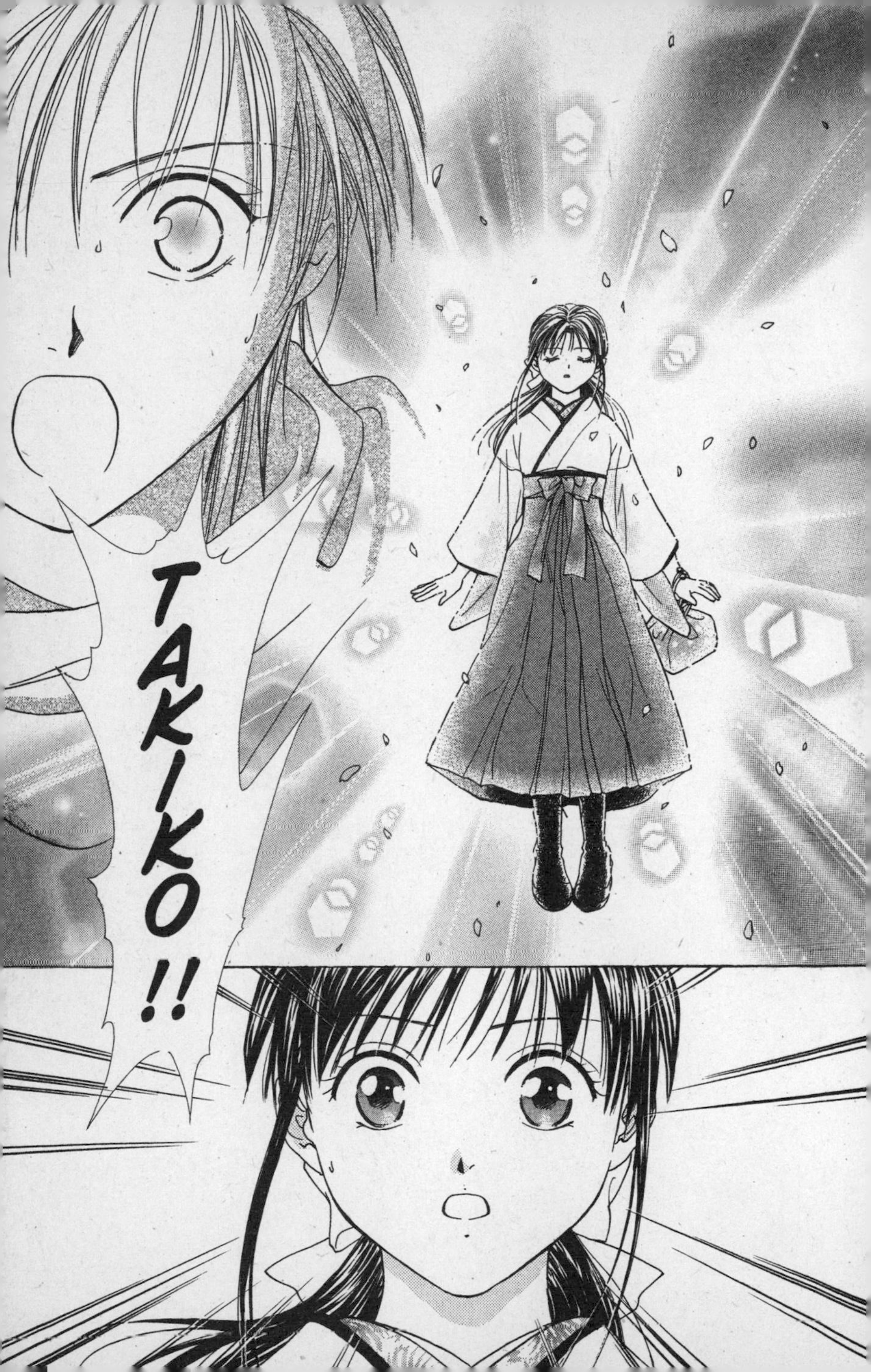
TAKIKO!!

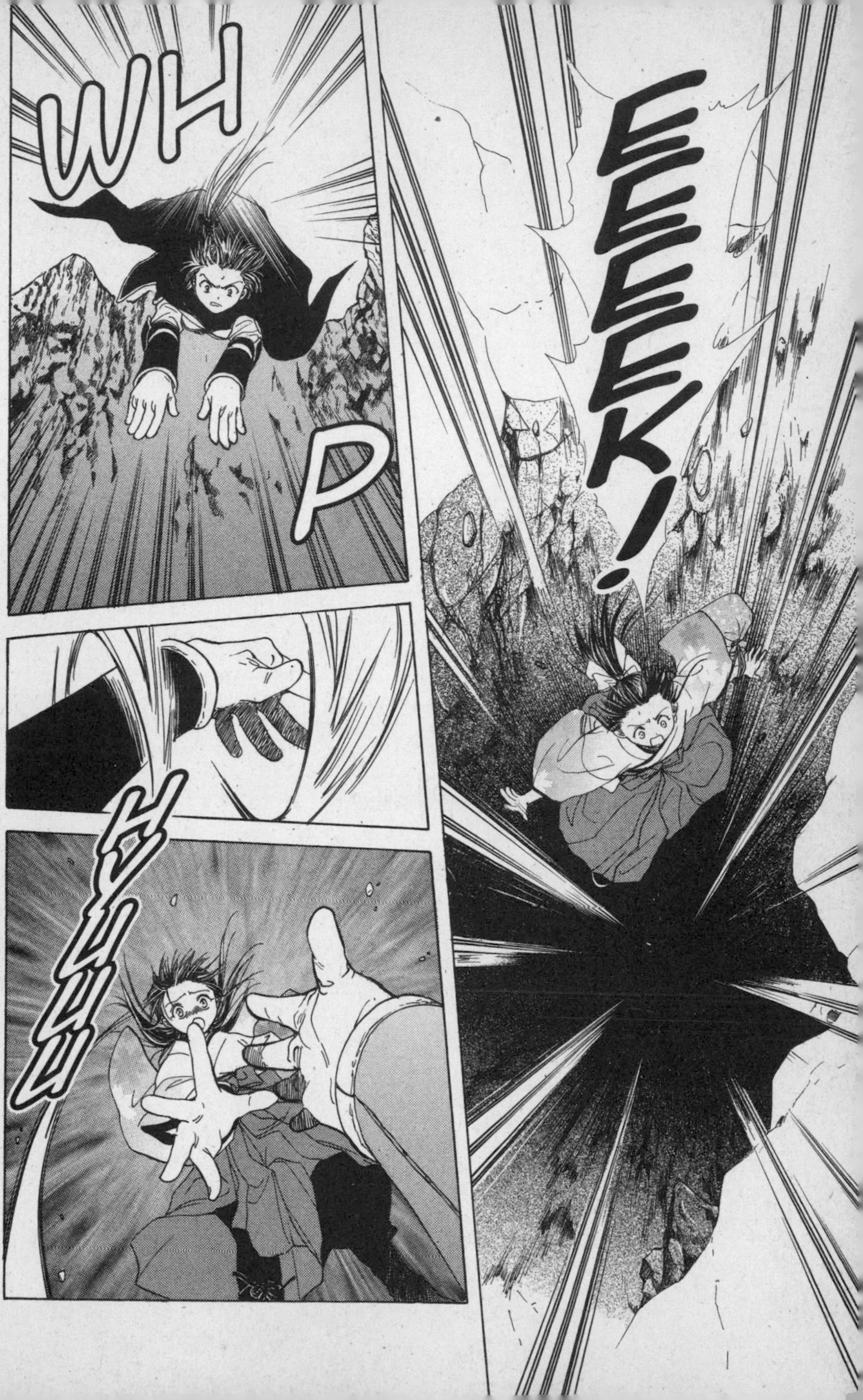
EEEEEK!
WH
P

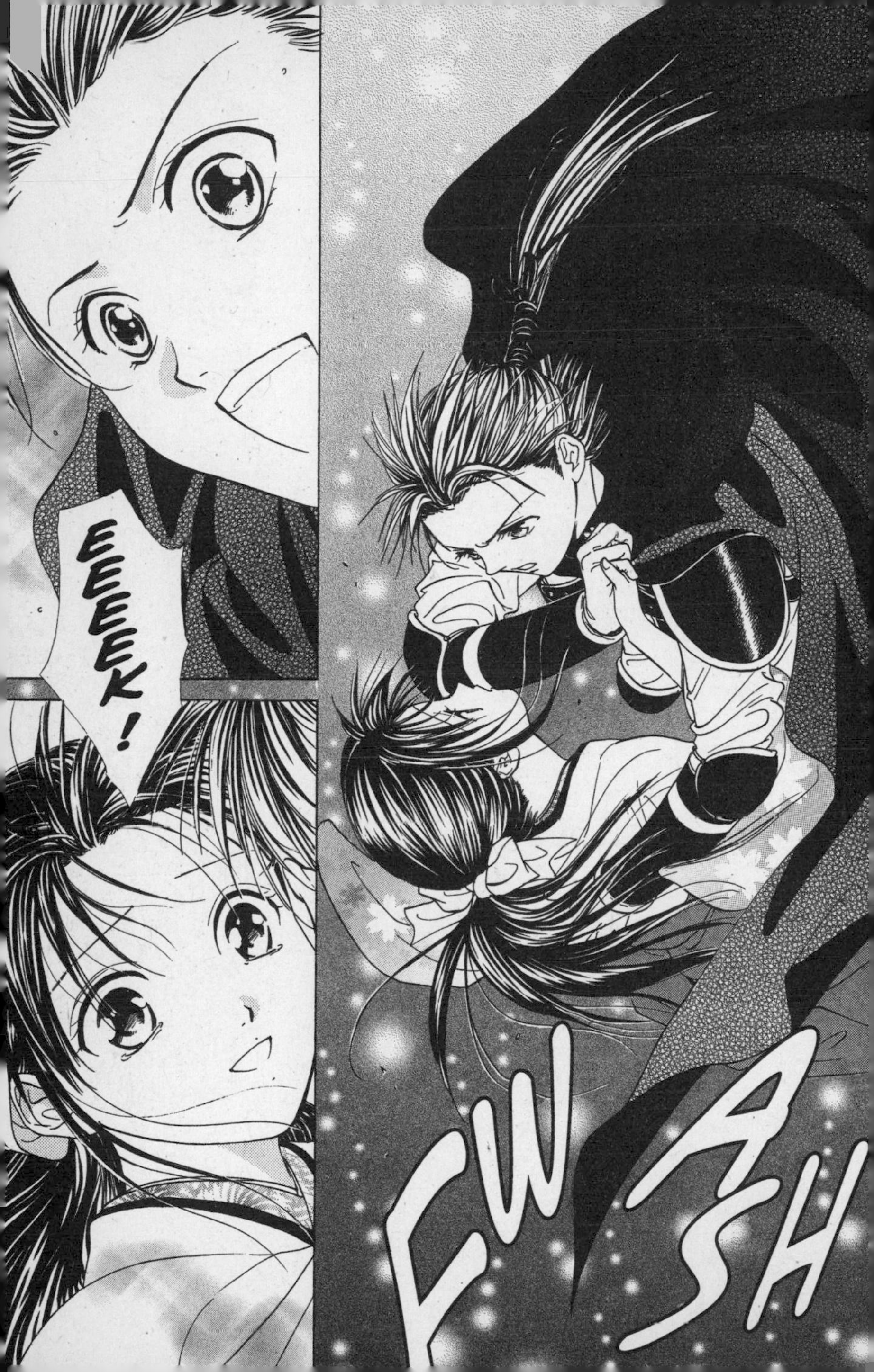
FWASH
EEEEEK!

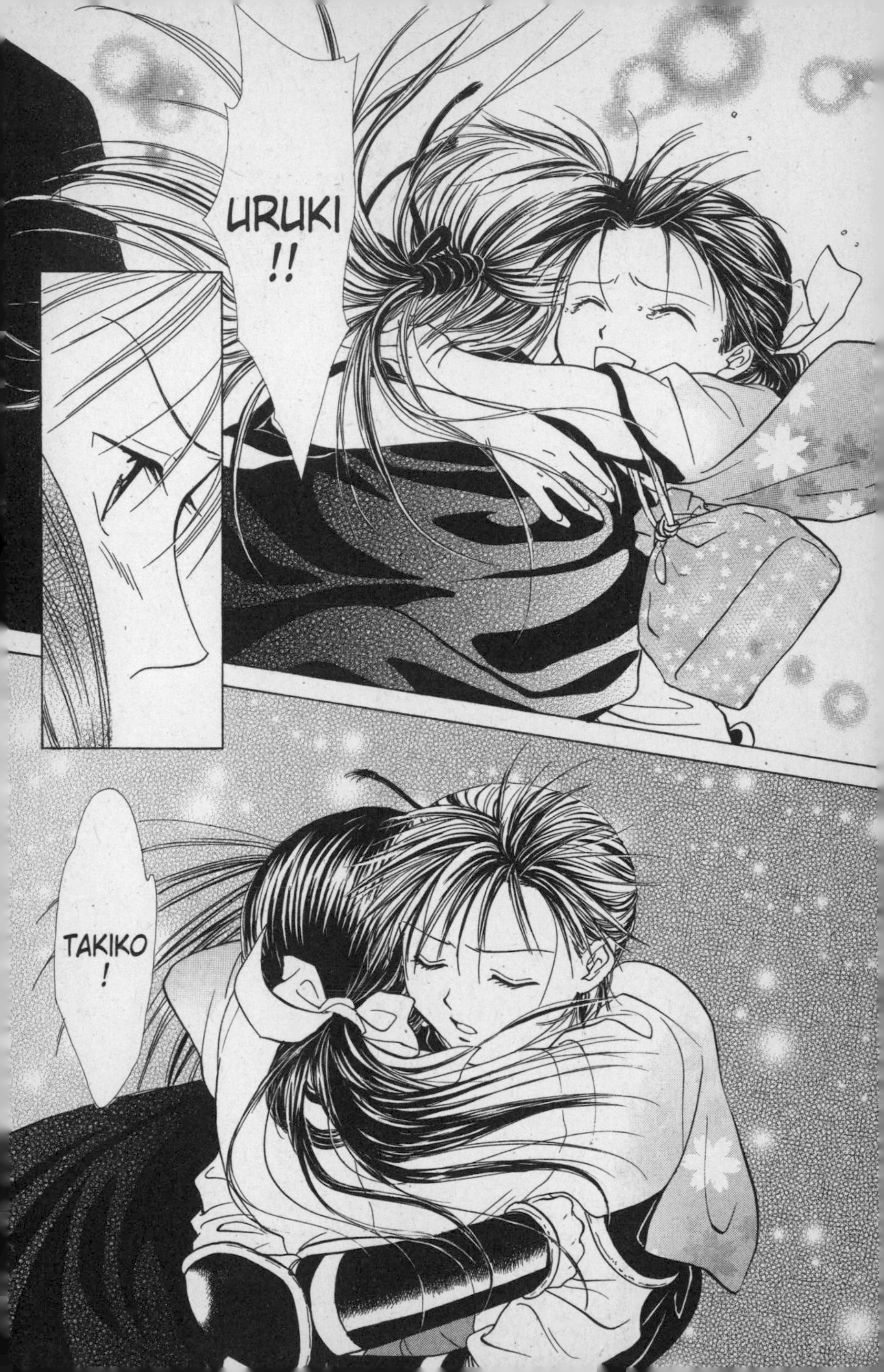
URUKI !!
TAKIKO !

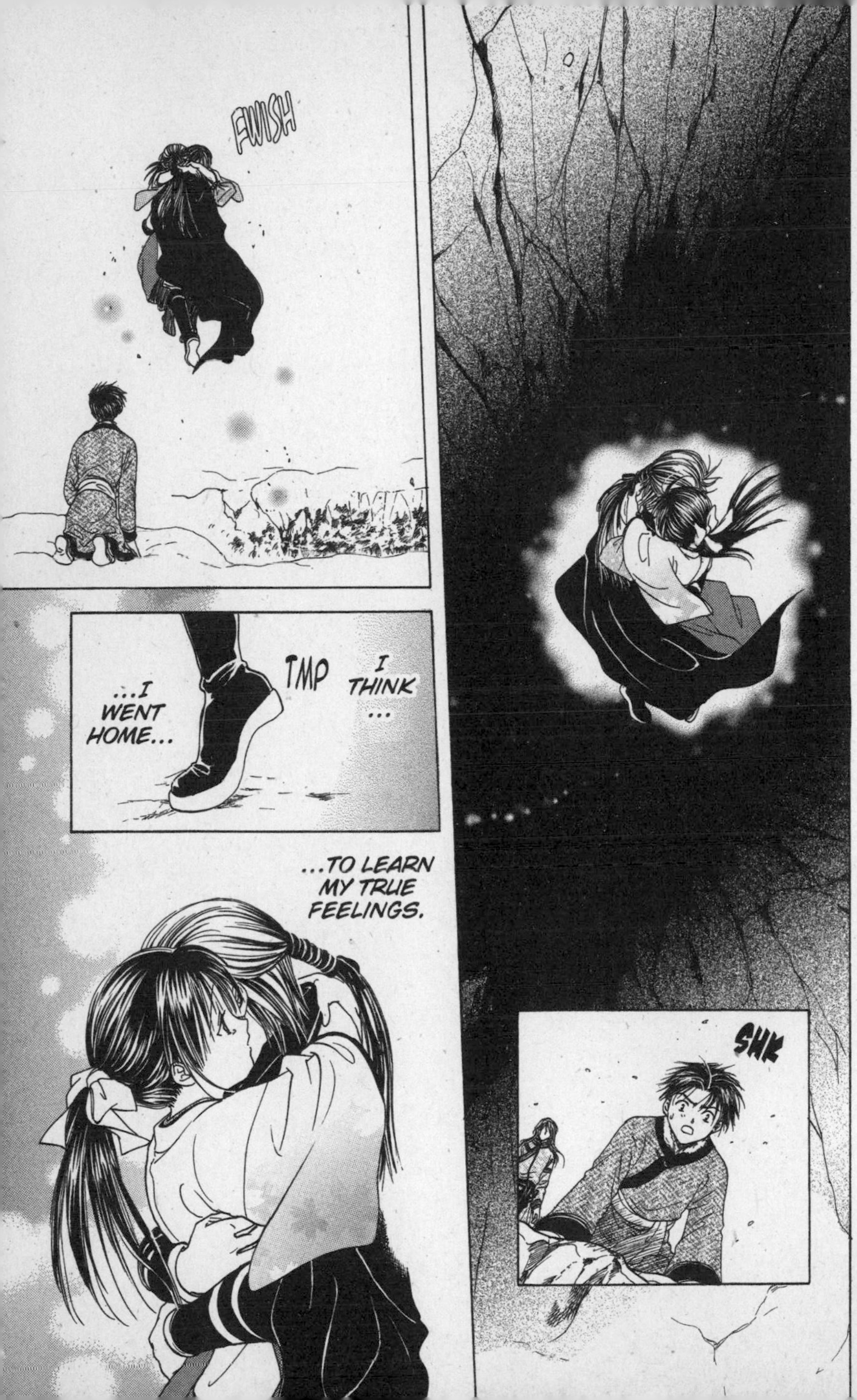
SHK
FWISH
I THINK...
TMP
...I WENT HOME...
...TO LEARN MY TRUE FEELINGS.

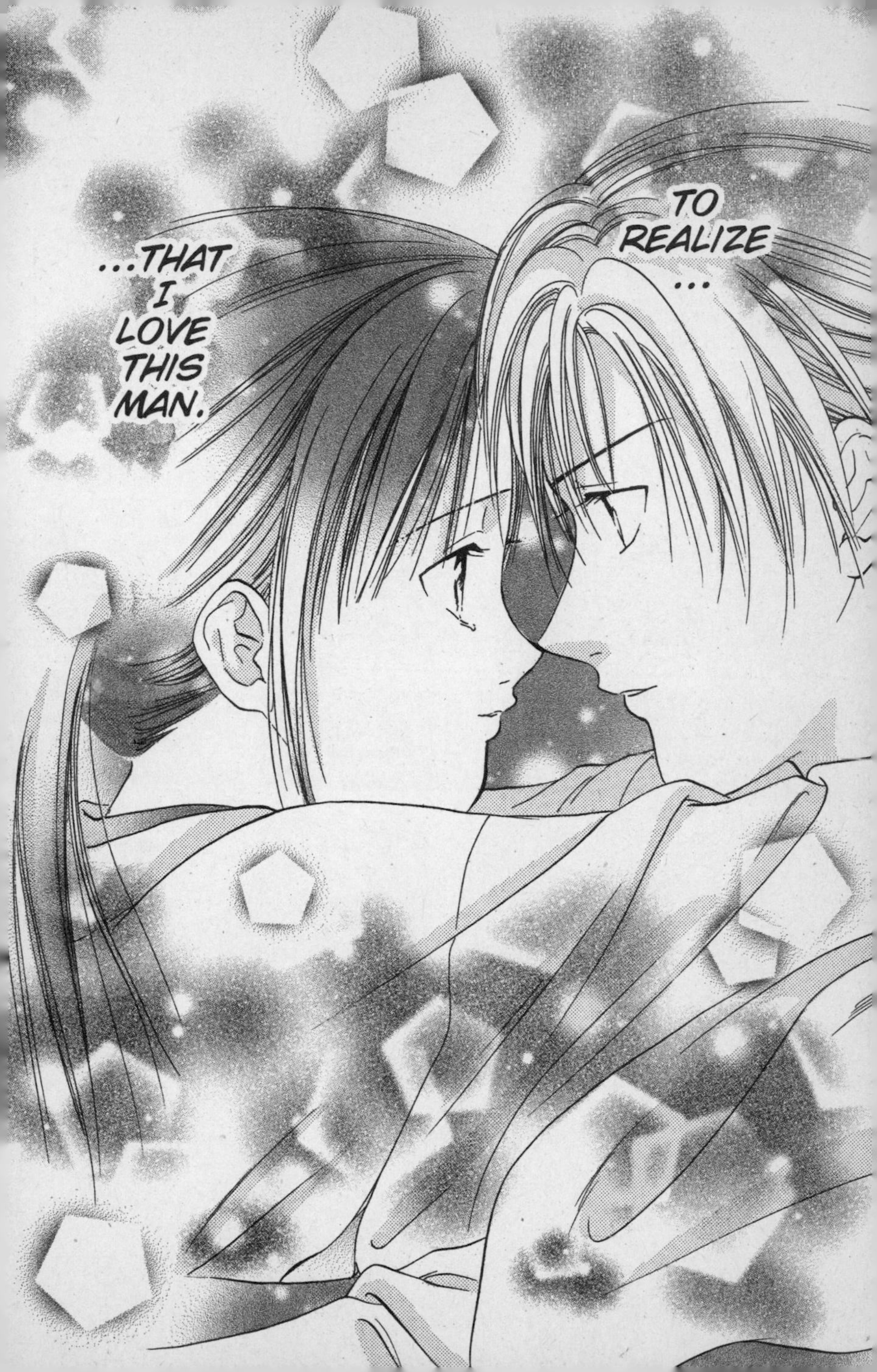
TO REALIZE ...
...THAT I LOVE THIS MAN.

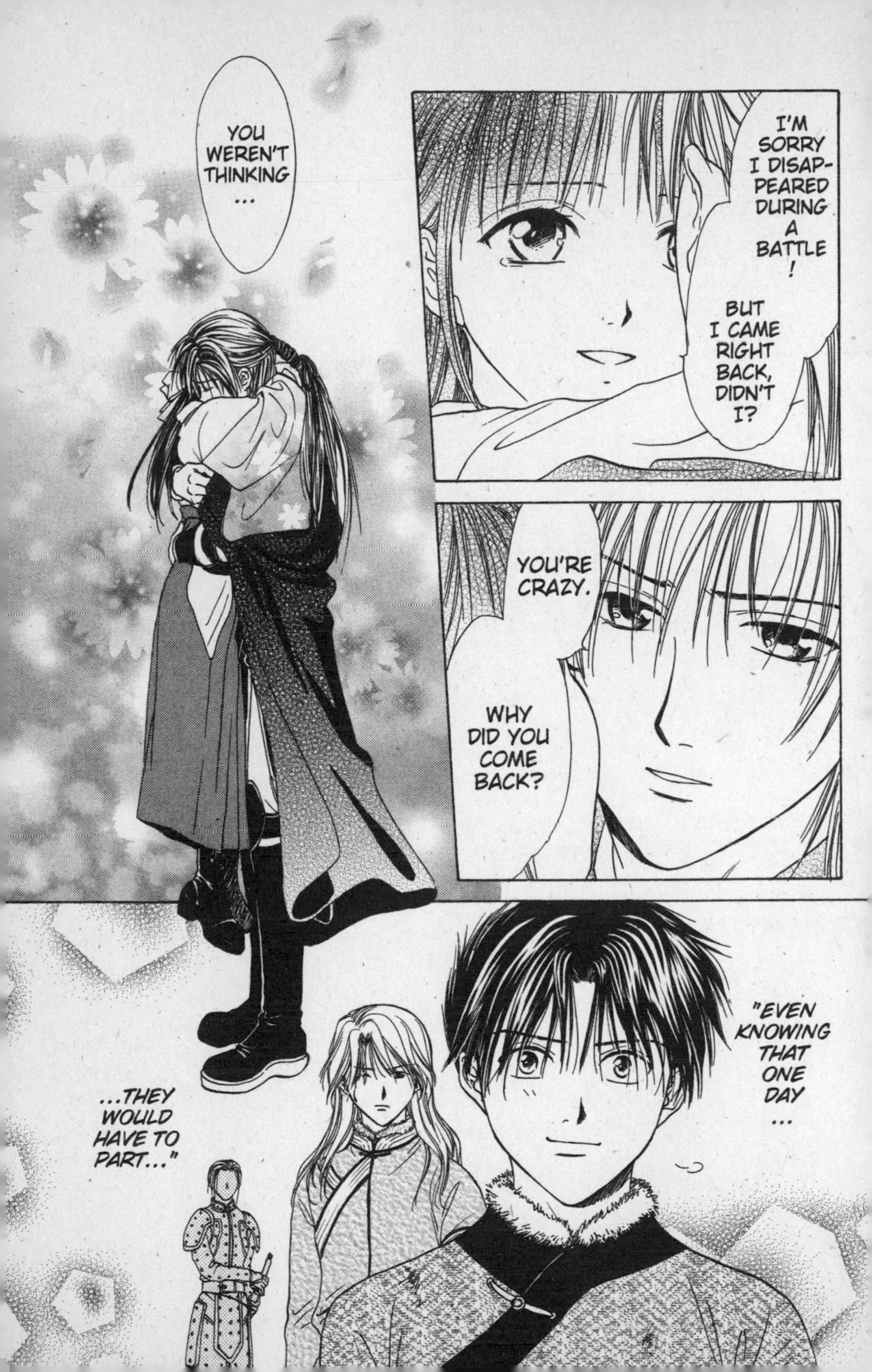
I'M SORRY I DISAPPEARED DURING A BATTLE!
BUT I CAME RIGHT BACK, DIDN'T I?
YOU'RE CRAZY.
WHY DID YOU COME BACK?
YOU WEREN'T THINKING...
"EVEN KNOWING THAT ONE DAY...
...THEY WOULD HAVE TO PART..."

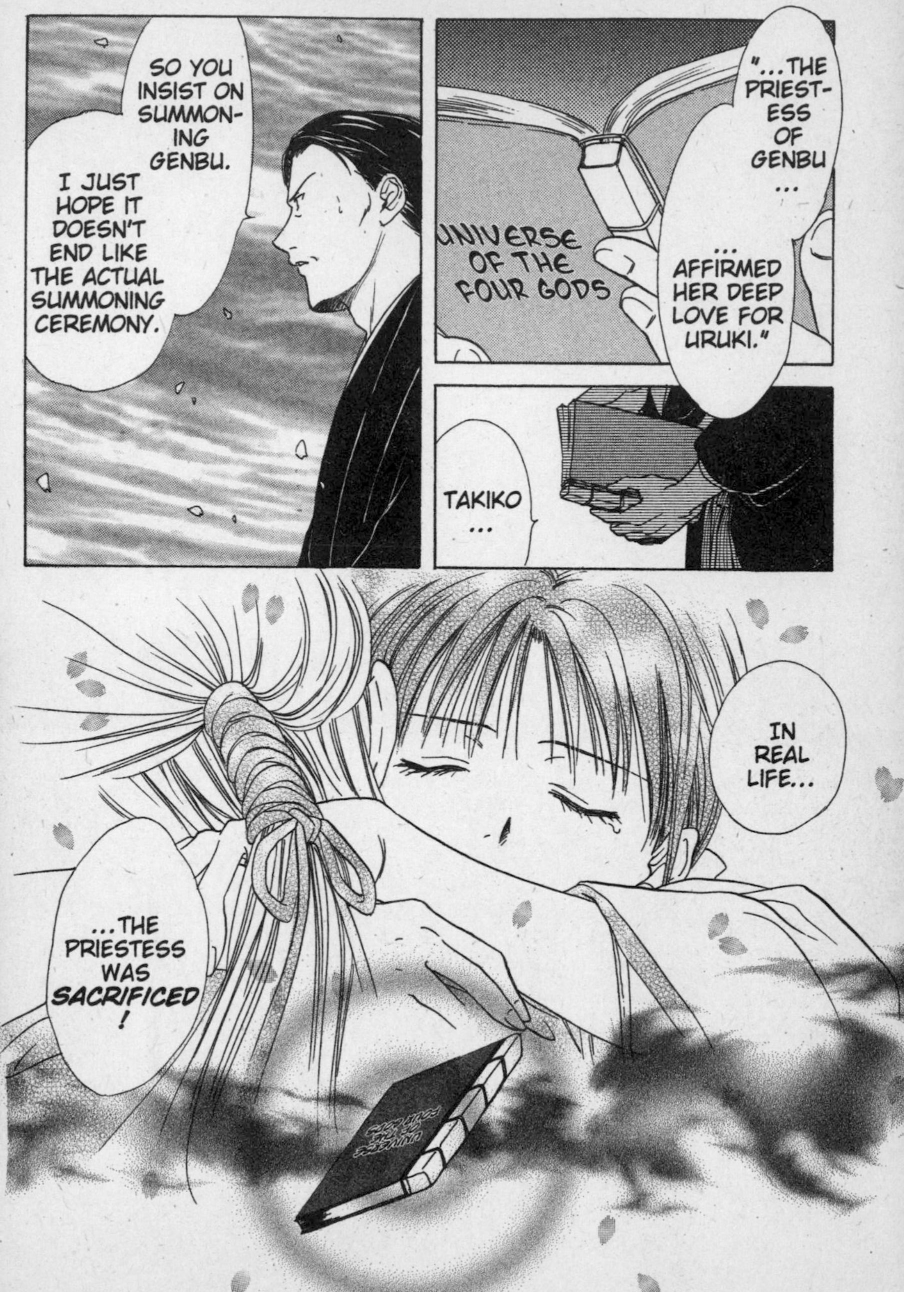
"...THE PRIESTESS OF GENBU ...
... AFFIRMED HER DEEP LOVE FOR URUKI."
UNIVERSE OF THE FOUR GODS
TAKIKO ...
SO YOU INSIST ON SUMMONING GENBU.
I JUST HOPE IT DOESN'T END LIKE THE ACTUAL SUMMONING CEREMONY.
IN REAL LIFE...
...THE PRIESTESS WAS **SACRIFICED**!

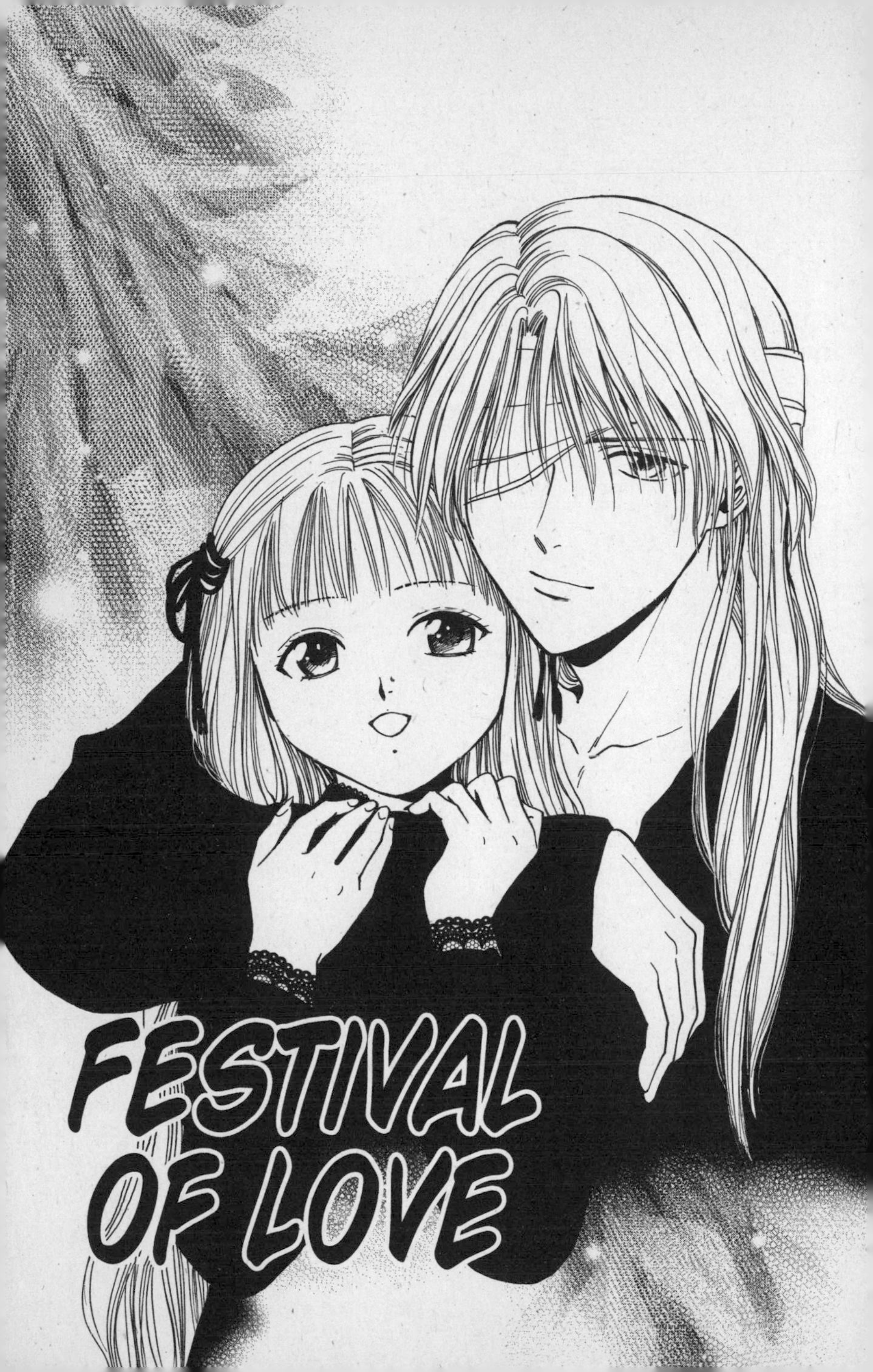
FESTIVAL
OF LOVE

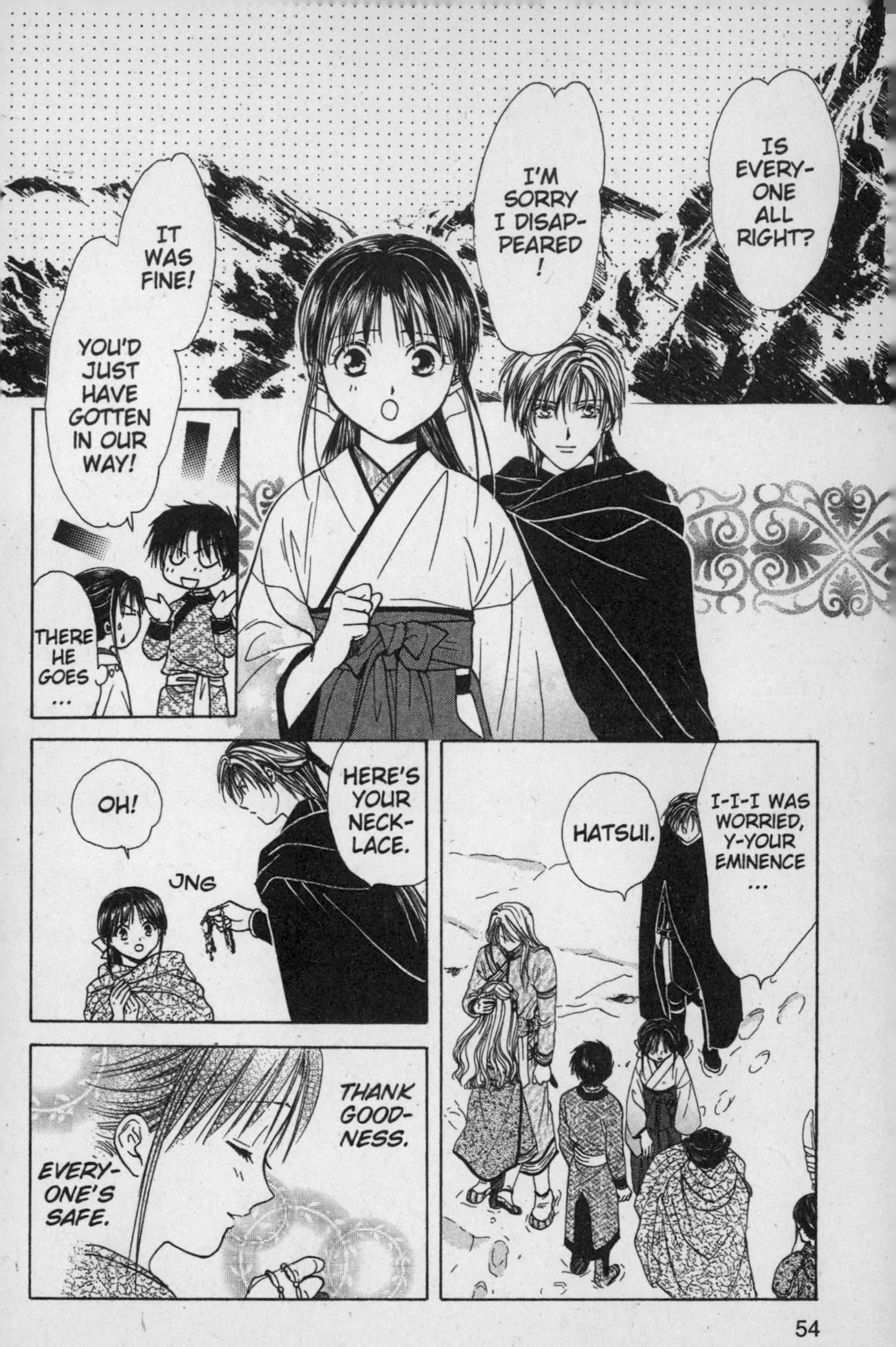
IS EVERY-ONE ALL RIGHT?
I'M SORRY I DISAP-PEARED!
IT WAS FINE! YOU'D JUST HAVE GOTTEN IN OUR WAY!
THERE HE GOES...
I-I-I WAS WORRIED, Y-YOUR EMINENCE...
HATSUI.
HERE'S YOUR NECK-LACE.
OH!
JNG
THANK GOOD-NESS.
EVERY-ONE'S SAFE.

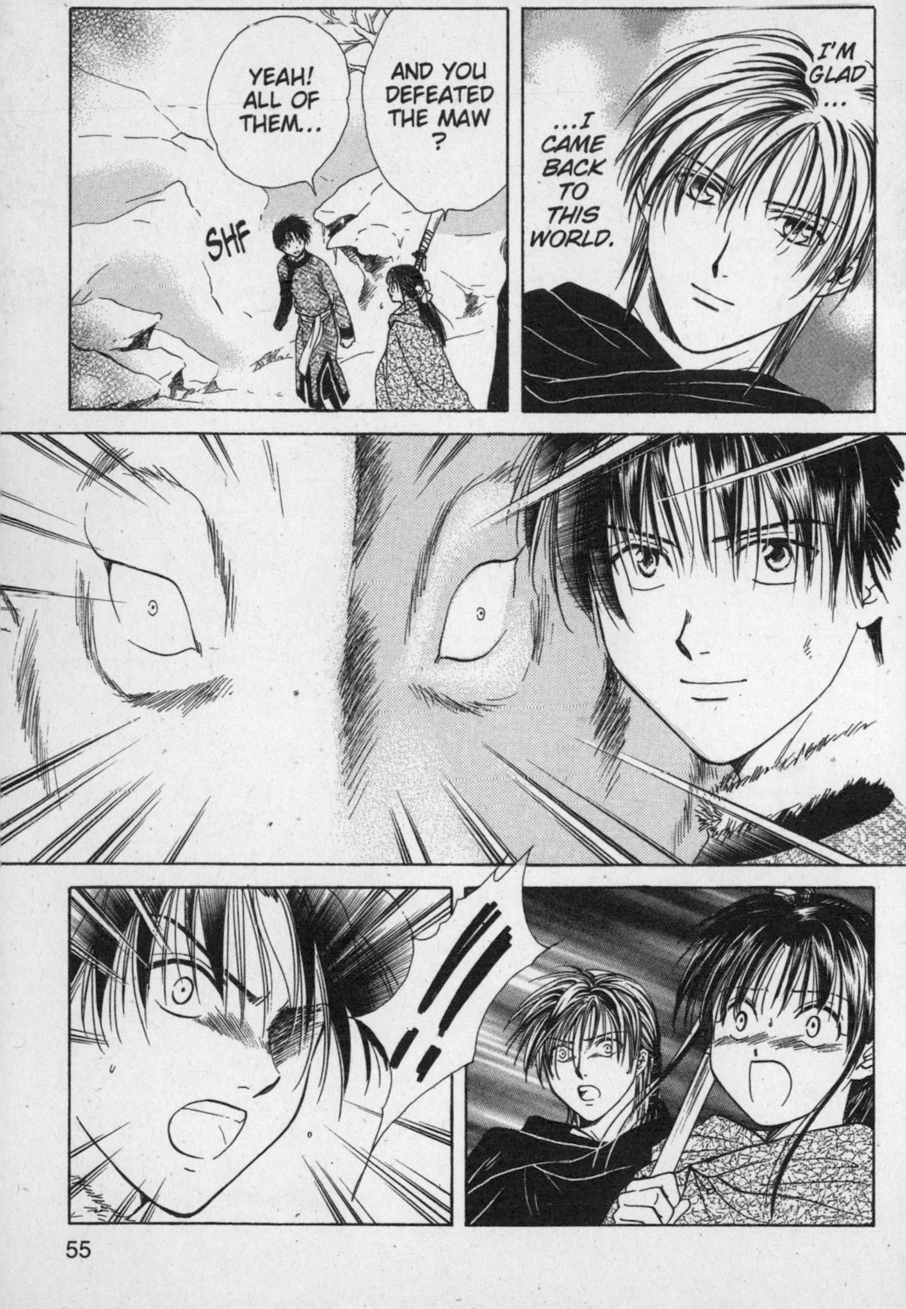
I'M GLAD...
...I CAME BACK TO THIS WORLD.
AND YOU DEFEATED THE MAW?
YEAH! ALL OF THEM...
SHF

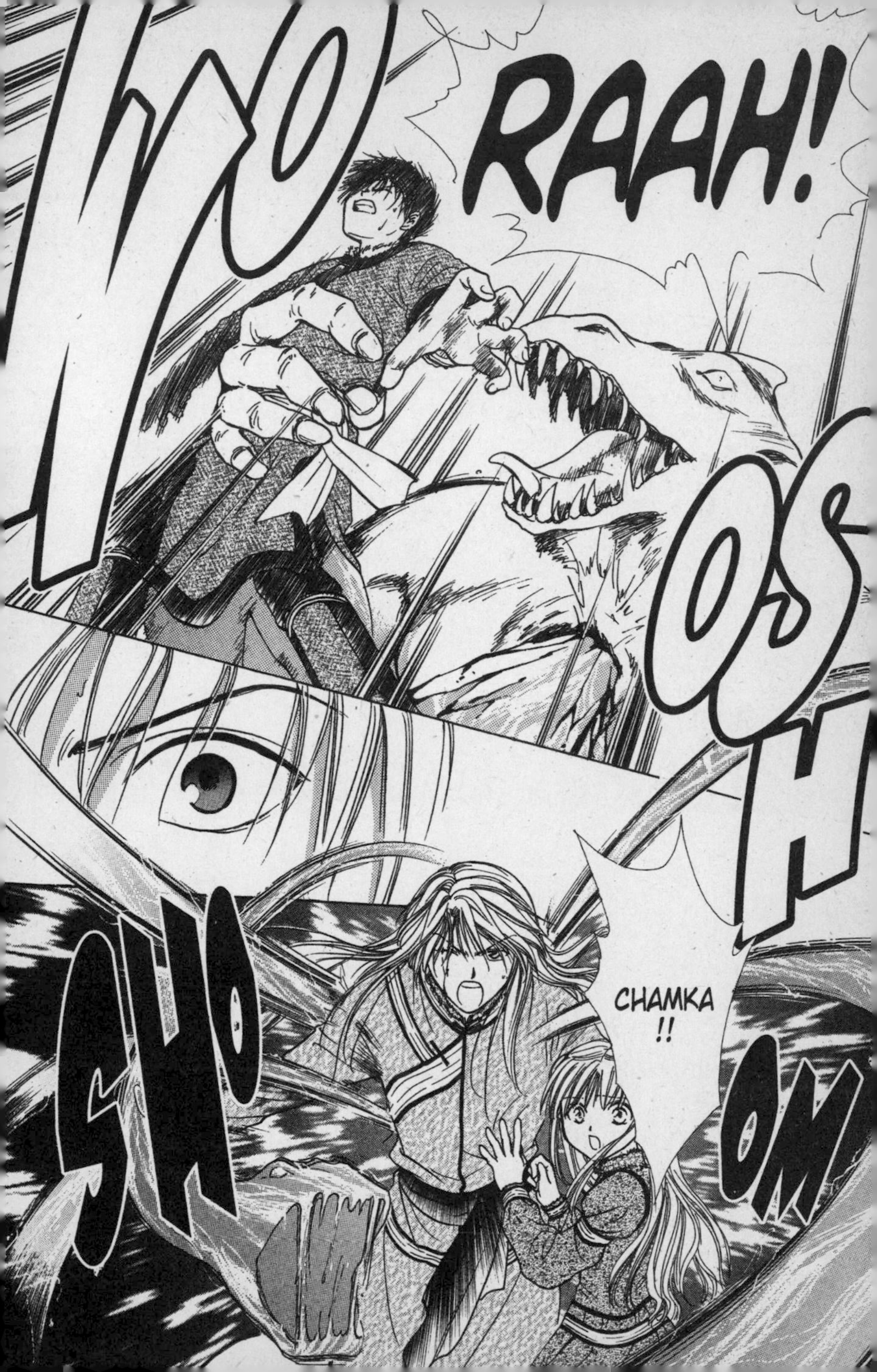
WHO RAAH!
CHAMKA !!
SHO OM

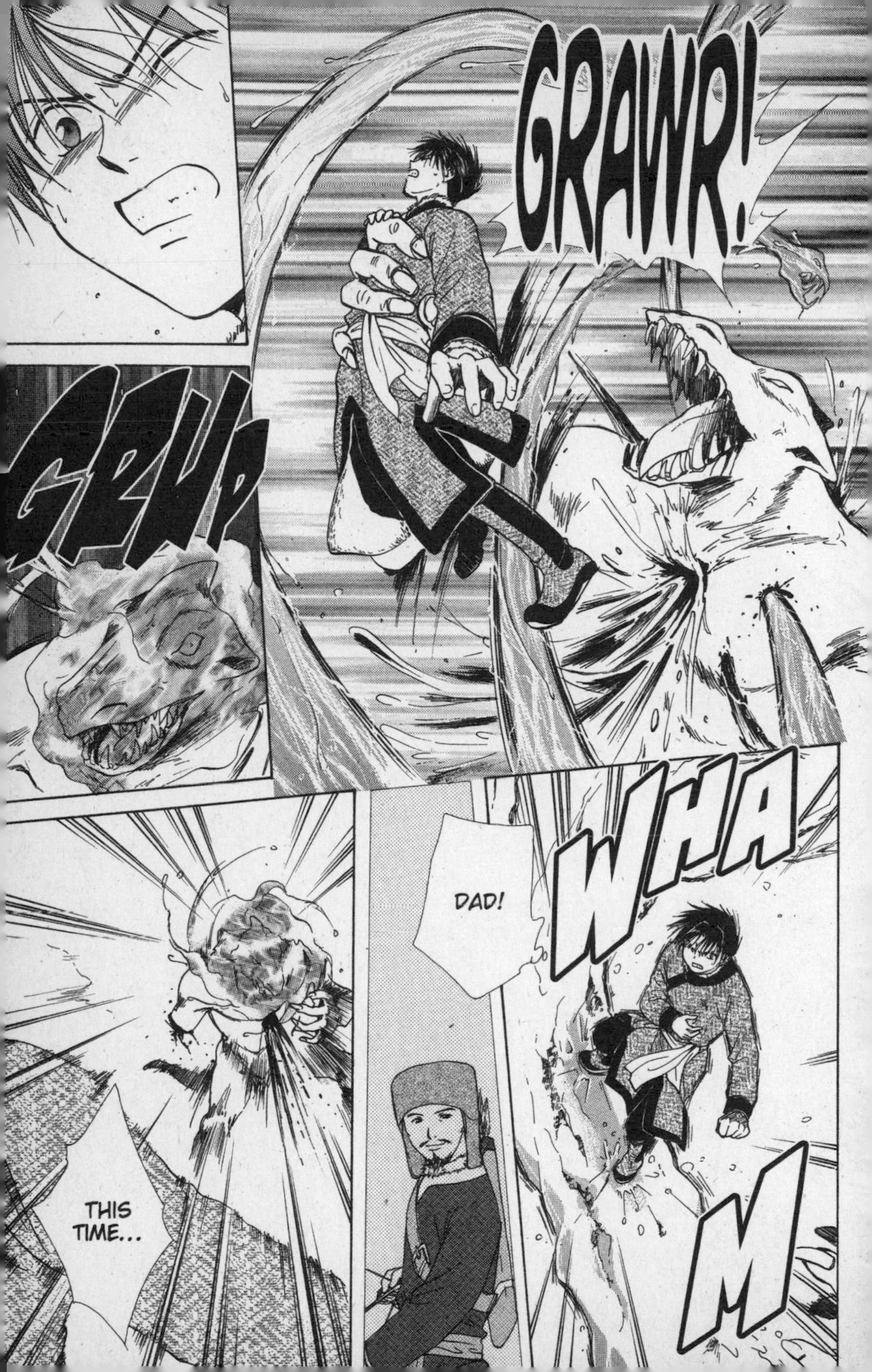
GRAWR!
GRUP
WHAM
DAD!
THIS TIME...

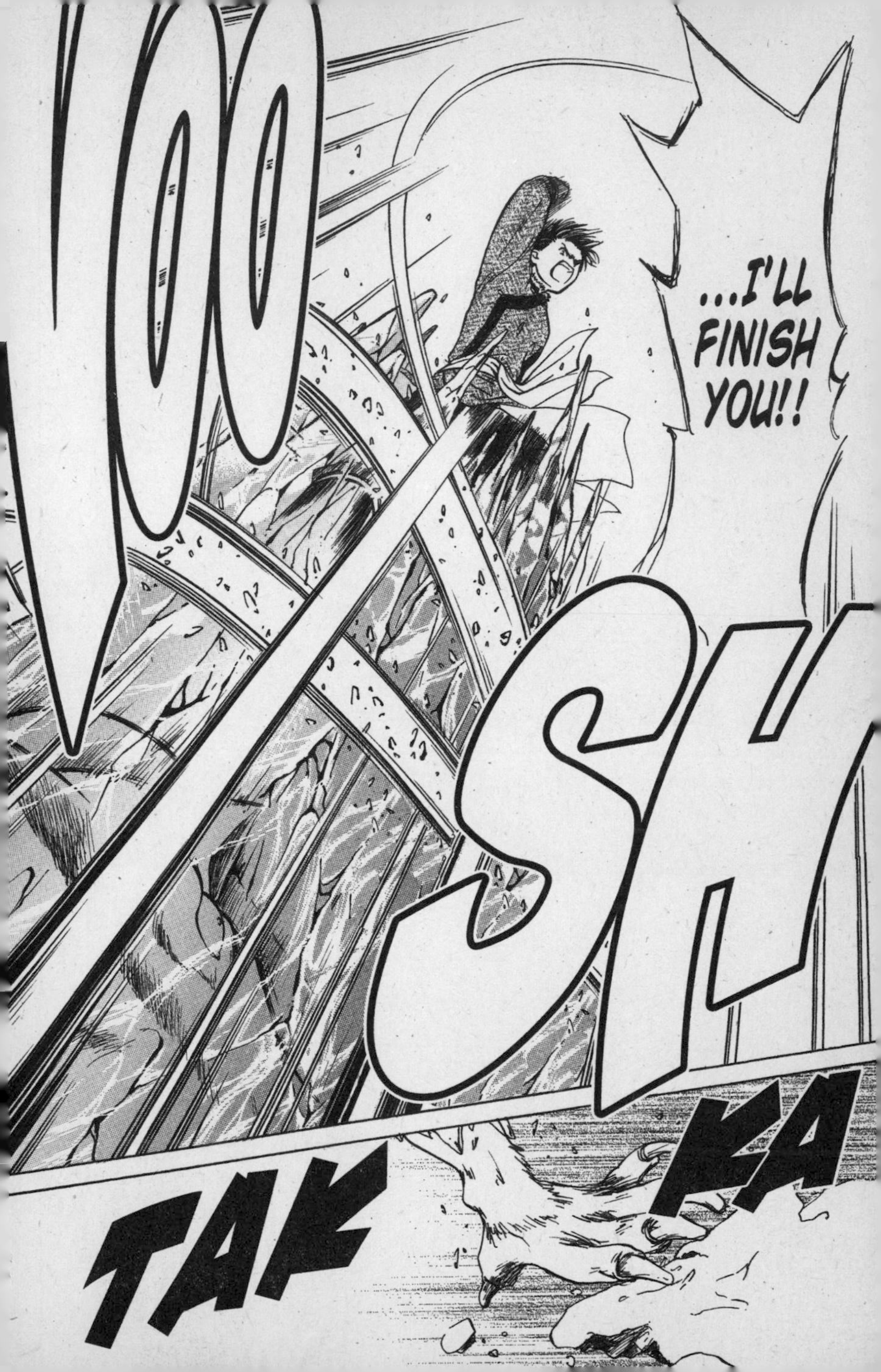
...I'LL FINISH YOU!!
VOO
SH
TAK
KA

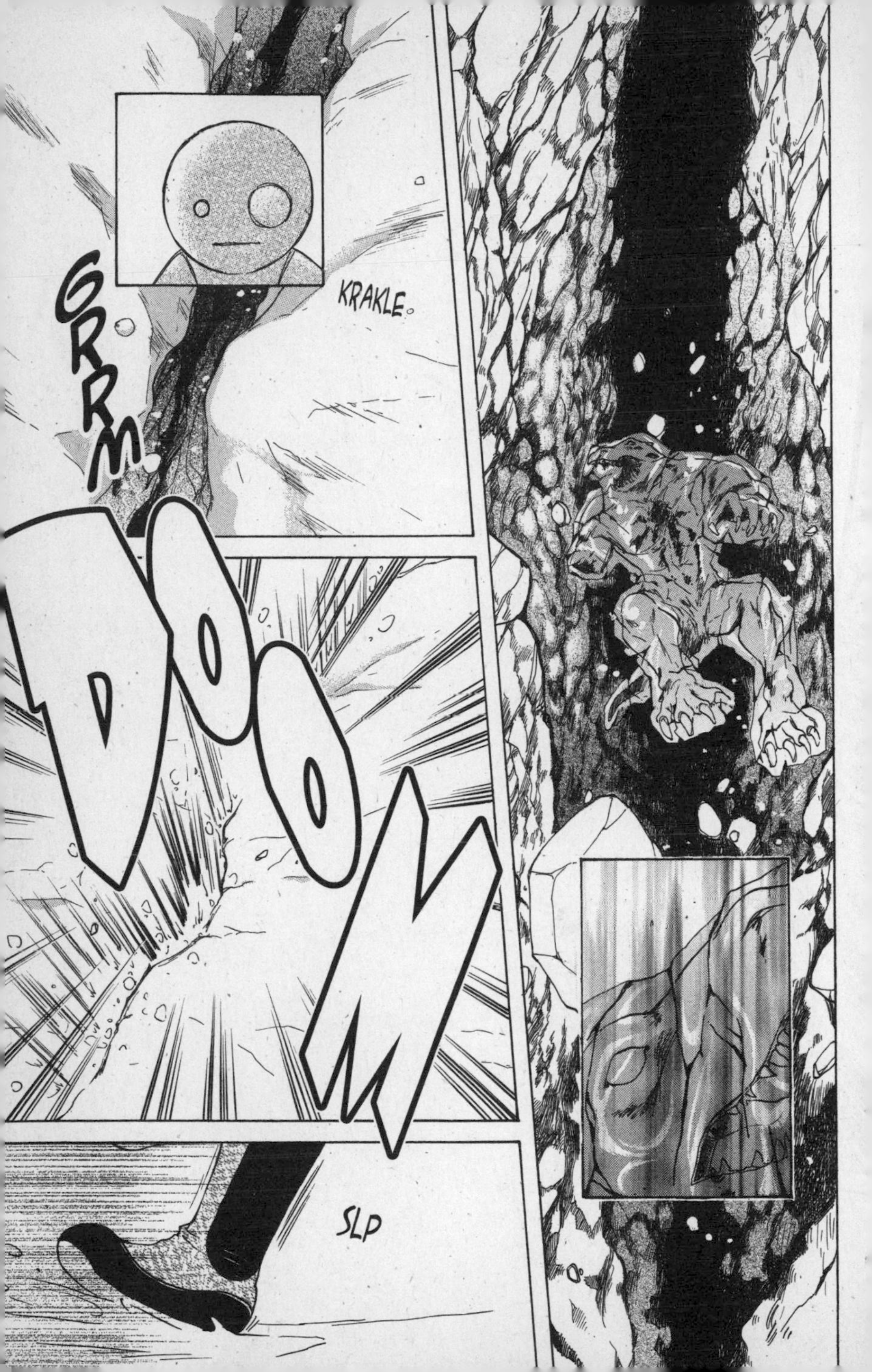
KRAKLE
GRRM
DOOM
SLP

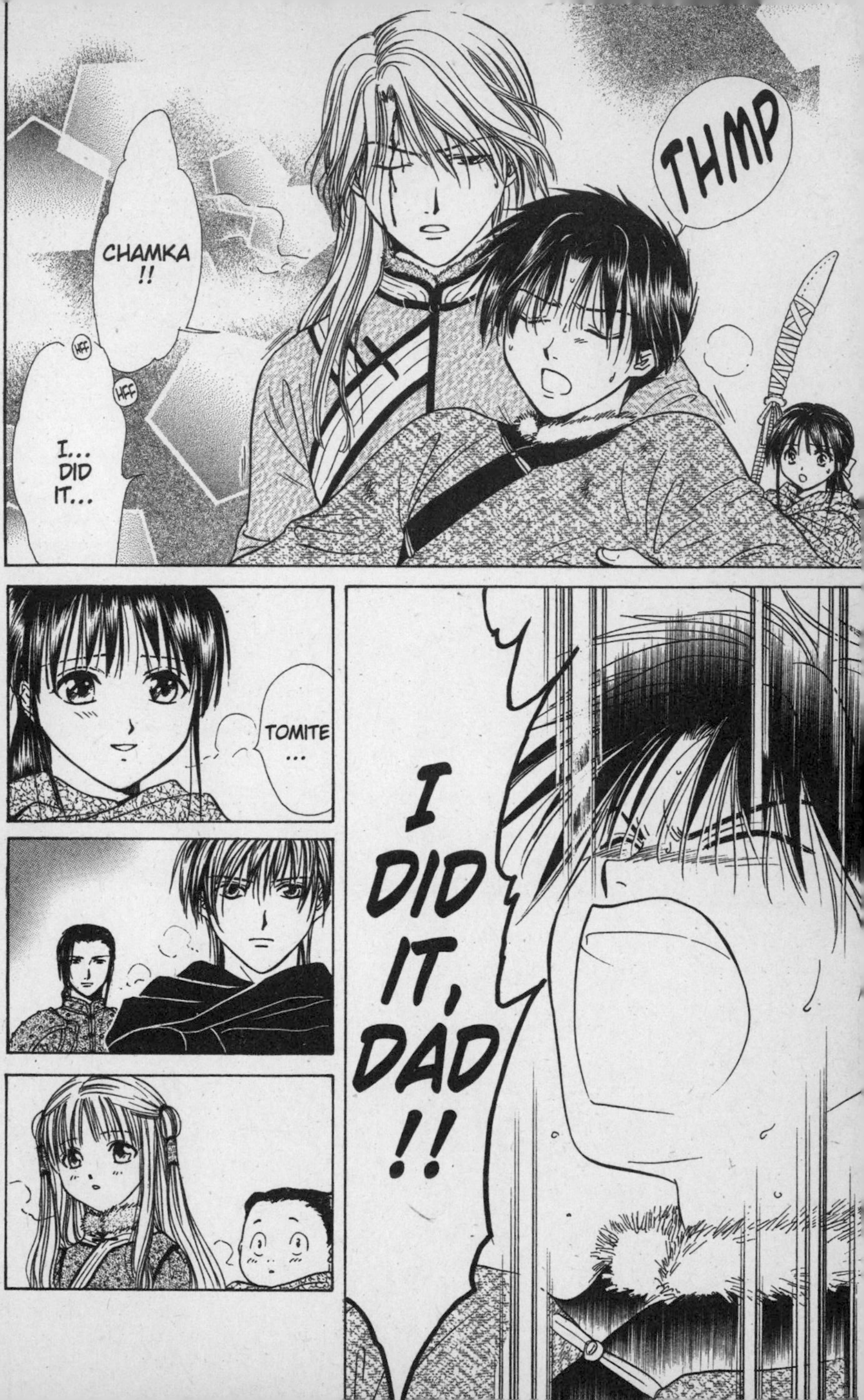
THMP
CHAMKA !!
HFF
HFF
I... DID IT...
I DID IT, DAD !!
TOMITE ...

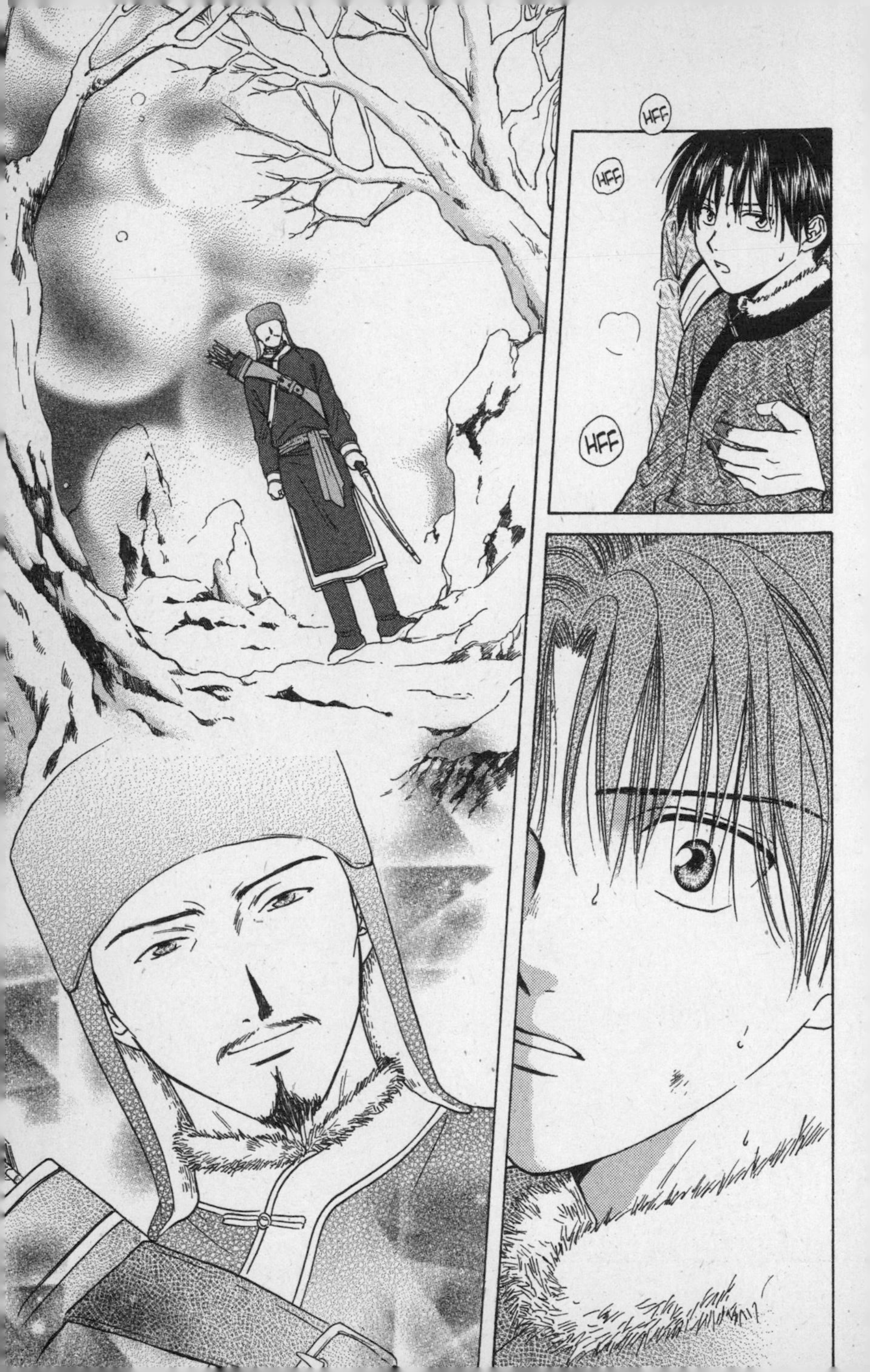
HFF
HFF
HFF

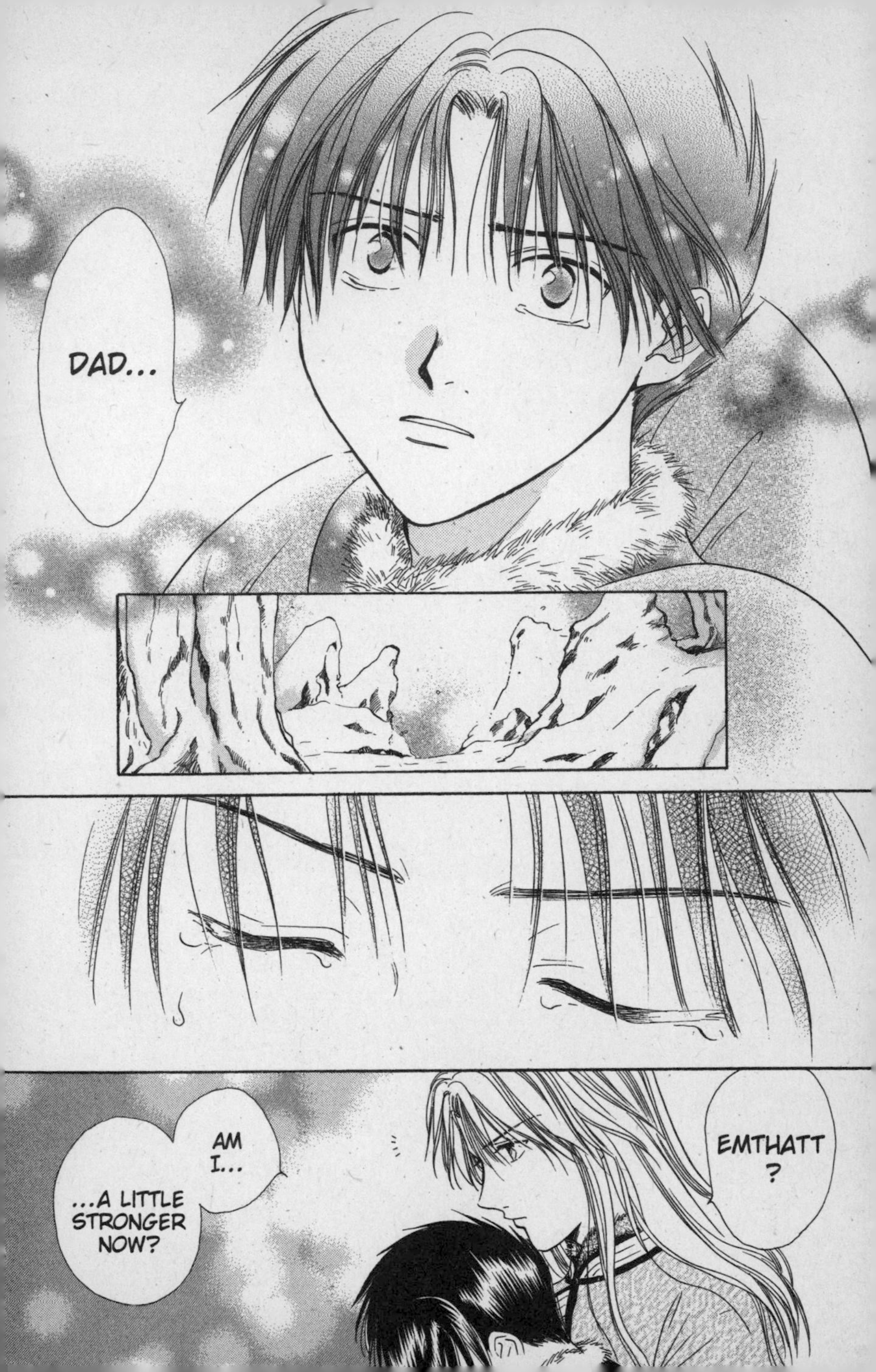
DAD...
EMTHATT ?
AM I...
...A LITTLE STRONGER NOW?

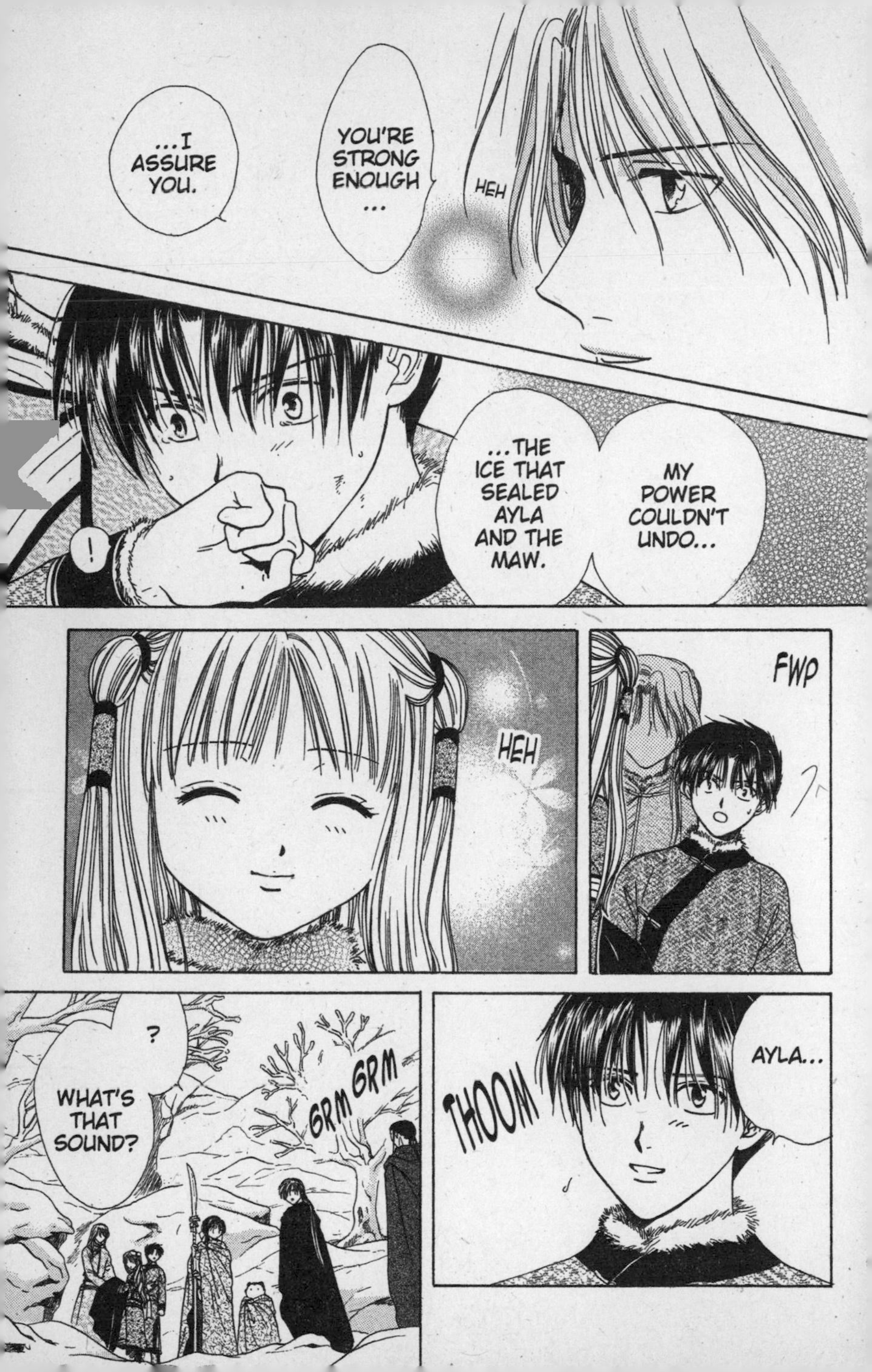
HEH
YOU'RE STRONG ENOUGH ...
...I ASSURE YOU.
MY POWER COULDN'T UNDO...
...THE ICE THAT SEALED AYLA AND THE MAW.
!
FWP
HEH
AYLA...
THOOM
GRM GRM
?
WHAT'S THAT SOUND?

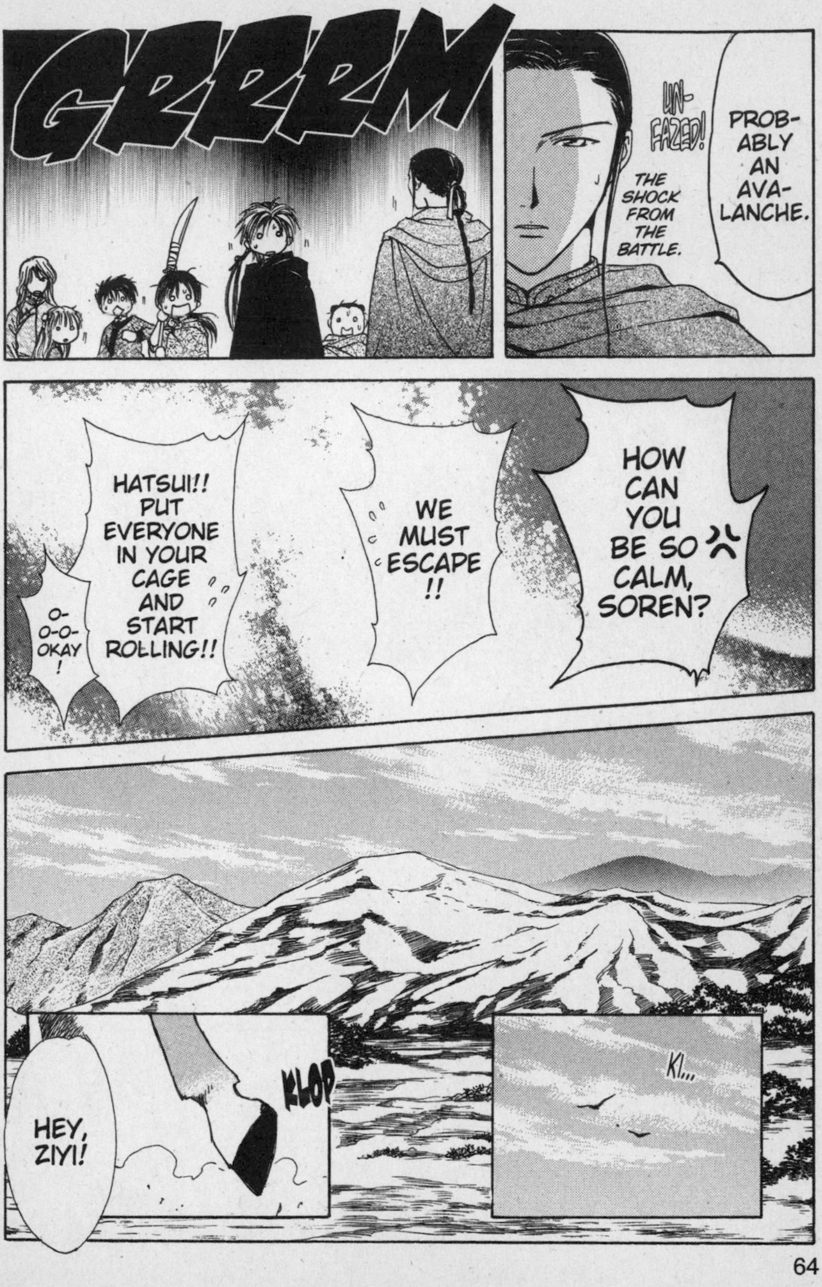
PROB-ABLY AN AVA-LANCHE.
UN-FAZED!
THE SHOCK FROM THE BATTLE.
GRRRM
HOW CAN YOU BE SO CALM, SOREN?
WE MUST ESCAPE!!
HATSUI!! PUT EVERYONE IN YOUR CAGE AND START ROLLING!!
O-O-O-OKAY!
KI...
KLOP
HEY, ZIYI!

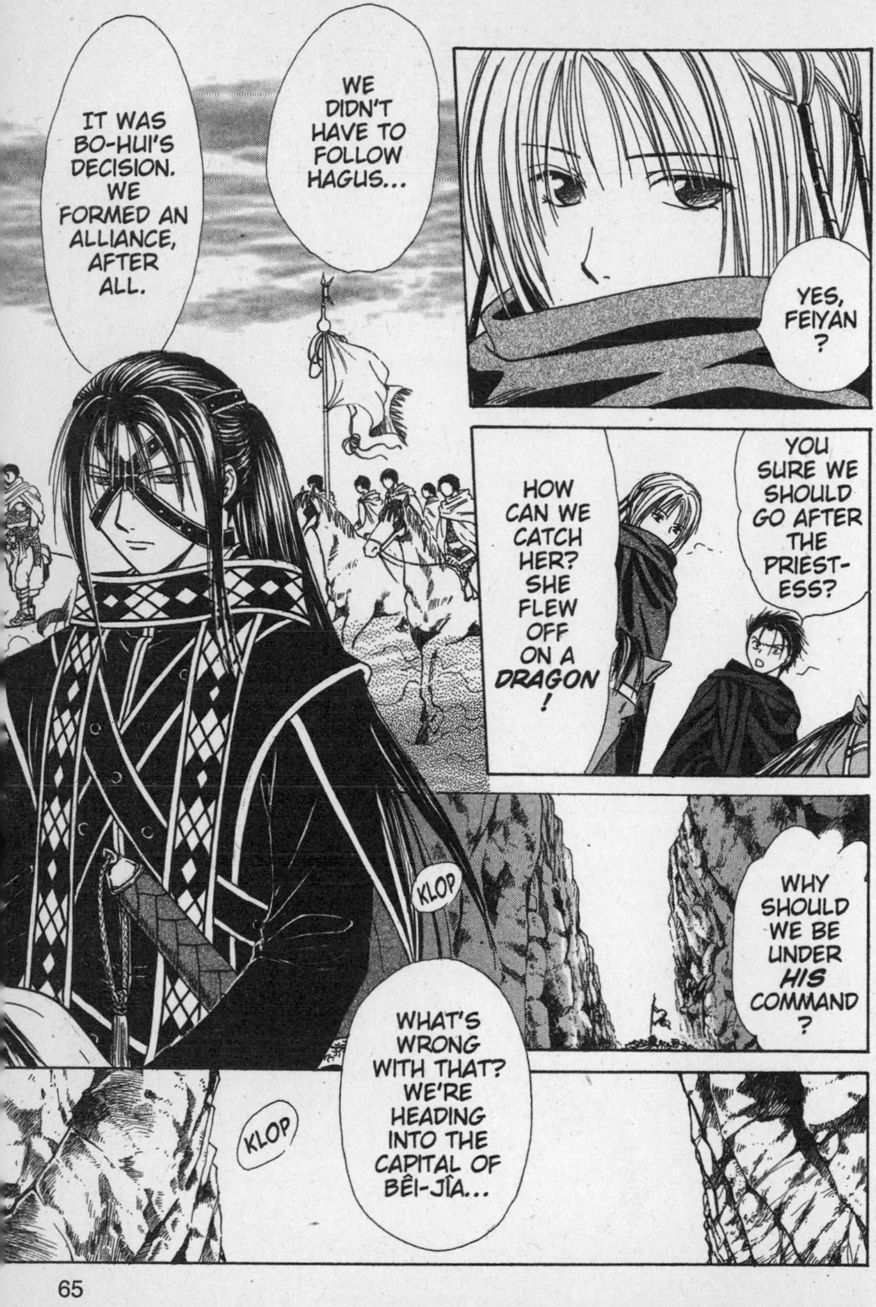
YES, FEIYAN?
YOU SURE WE SHOULD GO AFTER THE PRIEST-ESS?
HOW CAN WE CATCH HER? SHE FLEW OFF ON A *DRAGON*!
WE DIDN'T HAVE TO FOLLOW HAGUS...
IT WAS BO-HUI'S DECISION. WE FORMED AN ALLIANCE, AFTER ALL.
WHY SHOULD WE BE UNDER *HIS* COMMAND?
KLOP
WHAT'S WRONG WITH THAT? WE'RE HEADING INTO THE CAPITAL OF BÊI-JÎA...
KLOP

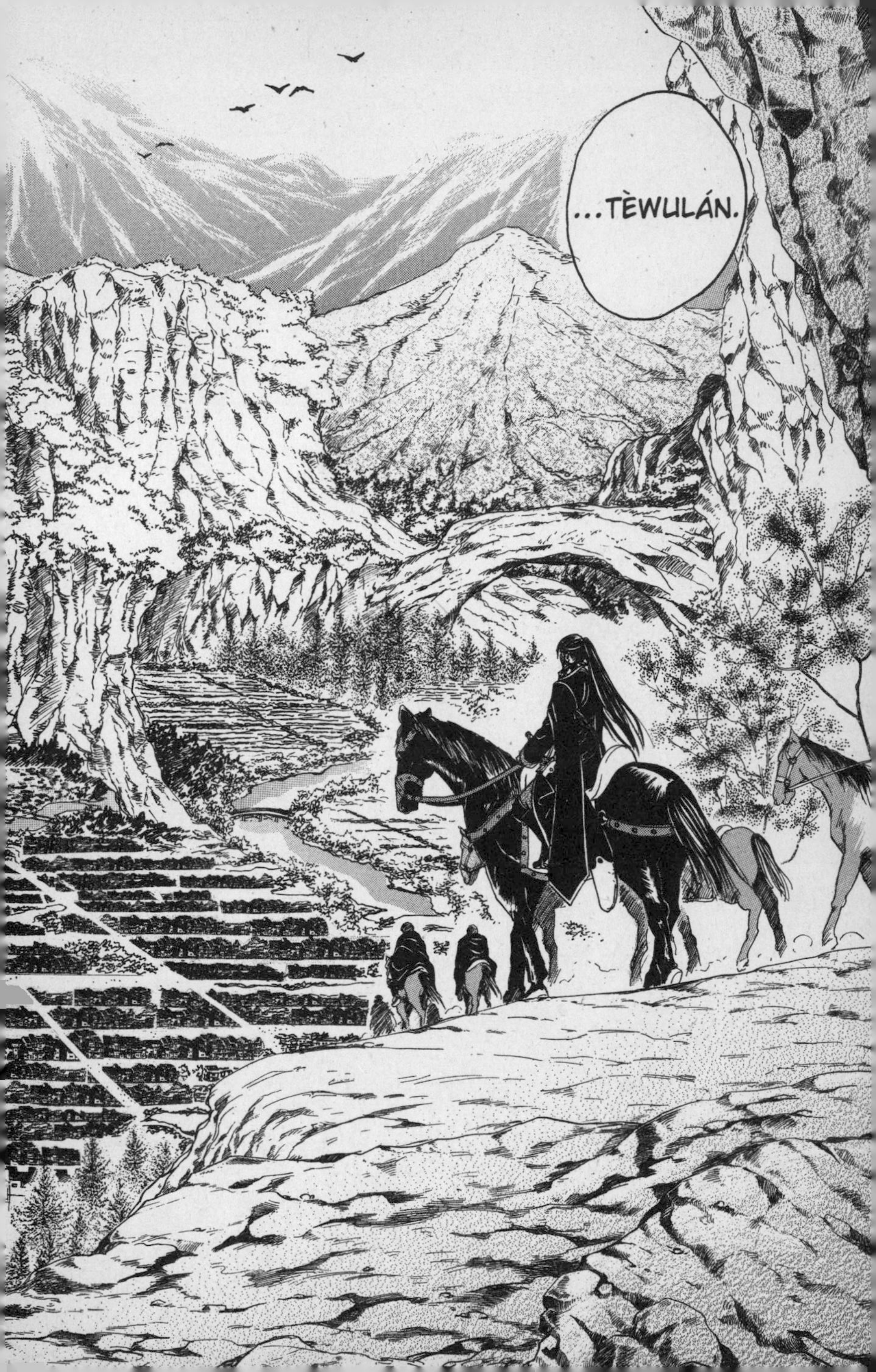
...TÈWULÁN.

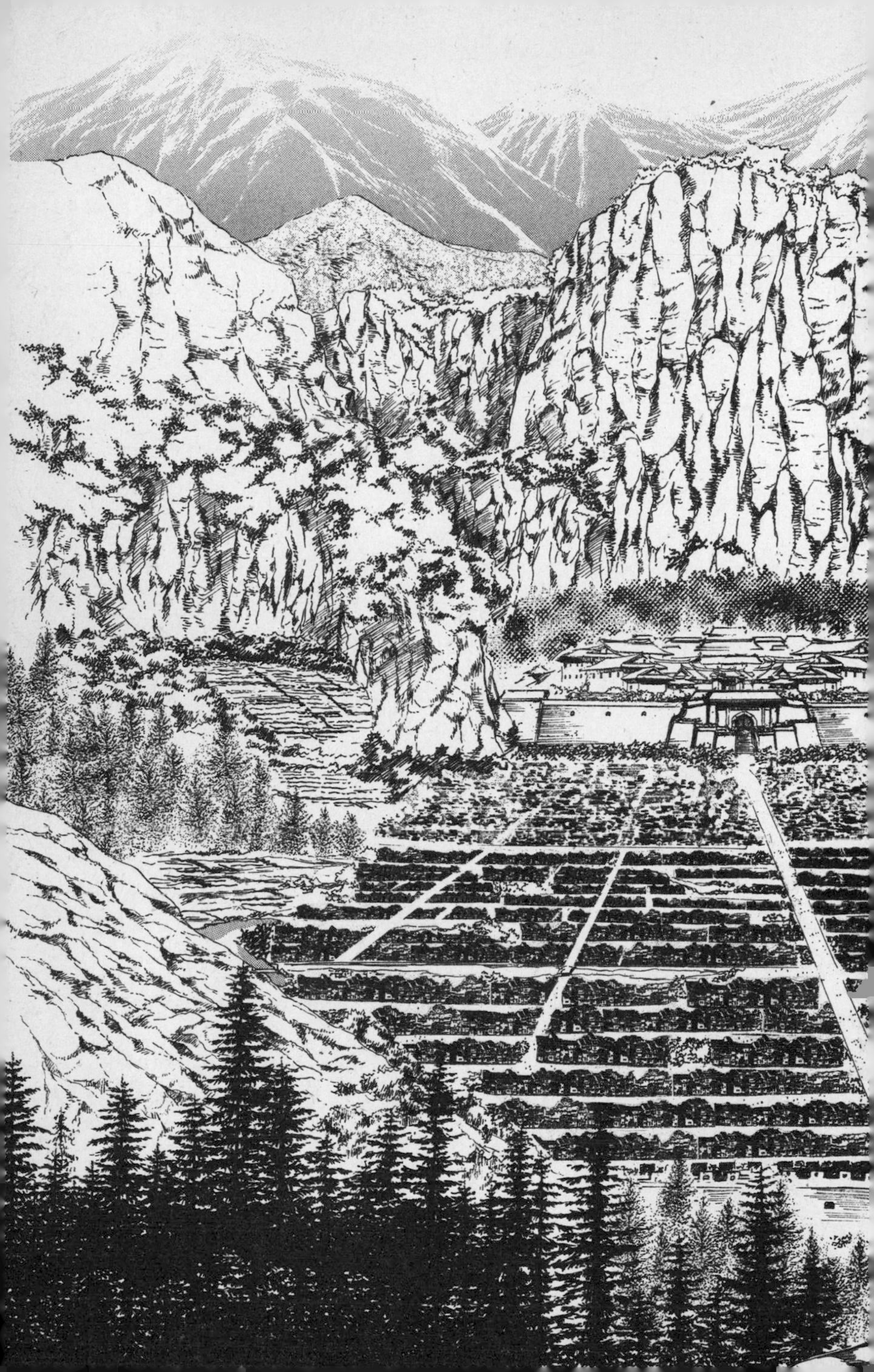

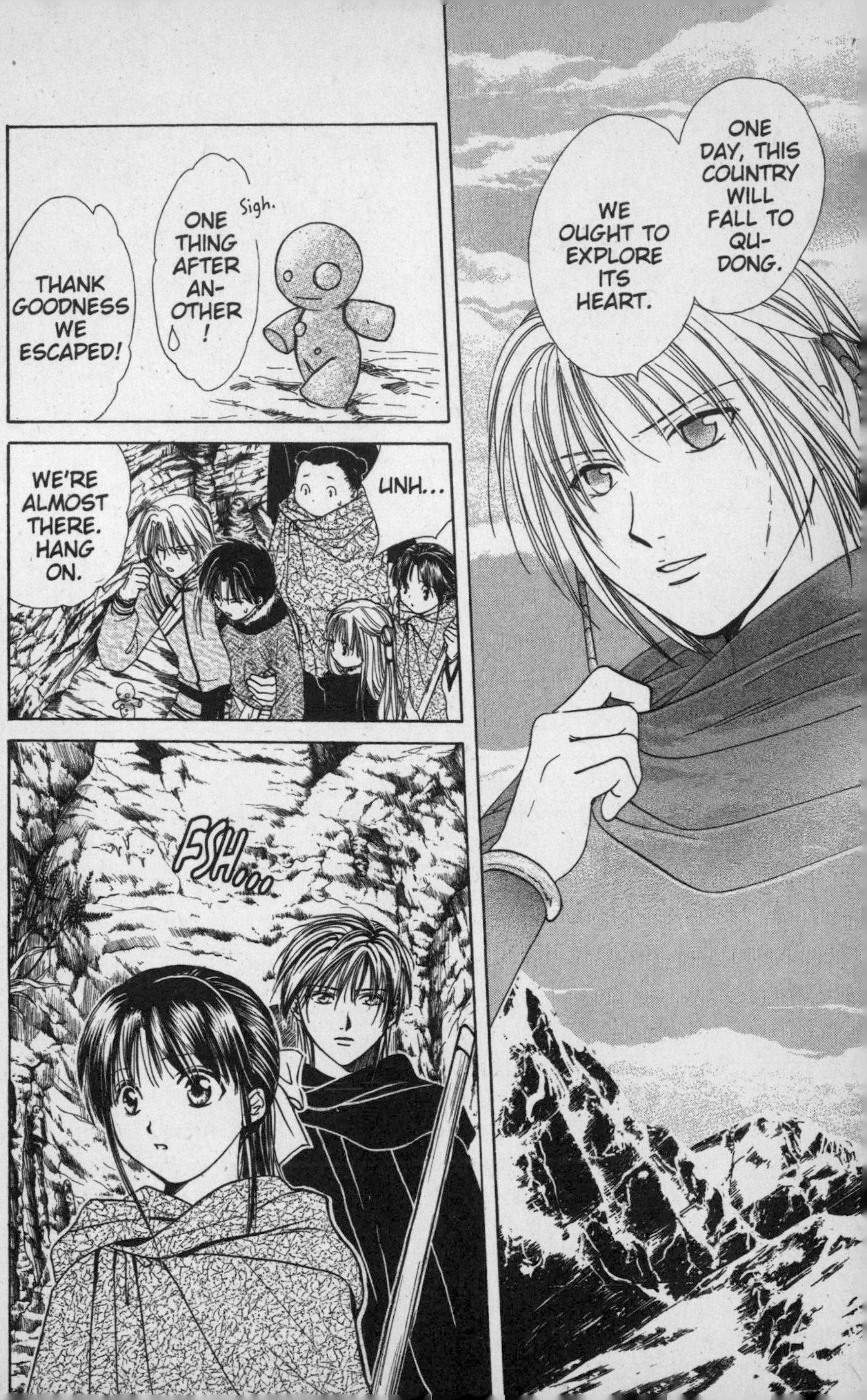
ONE DAY, THIS COUNTRY WILL FALL TO QU-DONG.
WE OUGHT TO EXPLORE ITS HEART.
Sigh.
ONE THING AFTER AN-OTHER!
THANK GOODNESS WE ESCAPED!
UNH...
WE'RE ALMOST THERE. HANG ON.
FSHooo

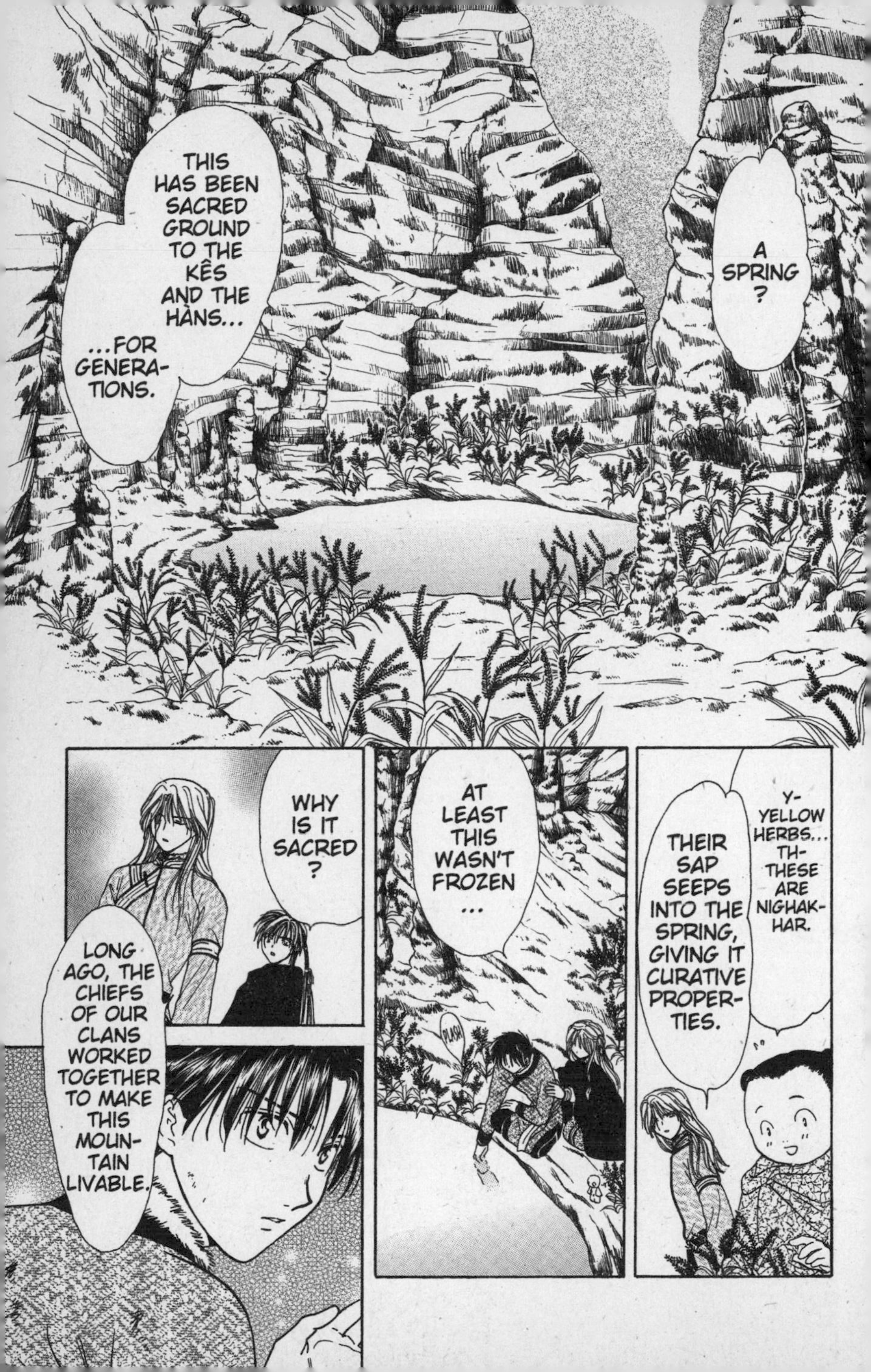
A SPRING?
THIS HAS BEEN SACRED GROUND TO THE KÊS AND THE HÀNS...
...FOR GENERATIONS.
Y-YELLOW HERBS... TH-THESE ARE NIGHAKHAR.
THEIR SAP SEEPS INTO THE SPRING, GIVING IT CURATIVE PROPERTIES.
AT LEAST THIS WASN'T FROZEN...
PLASH
WHY IS IT SACRED?
LONG AGO, THE CHIEFS OF OUR CLANS WORKED TOGETHER TO MAKE THIS MOUNTAIN LIVABLE.

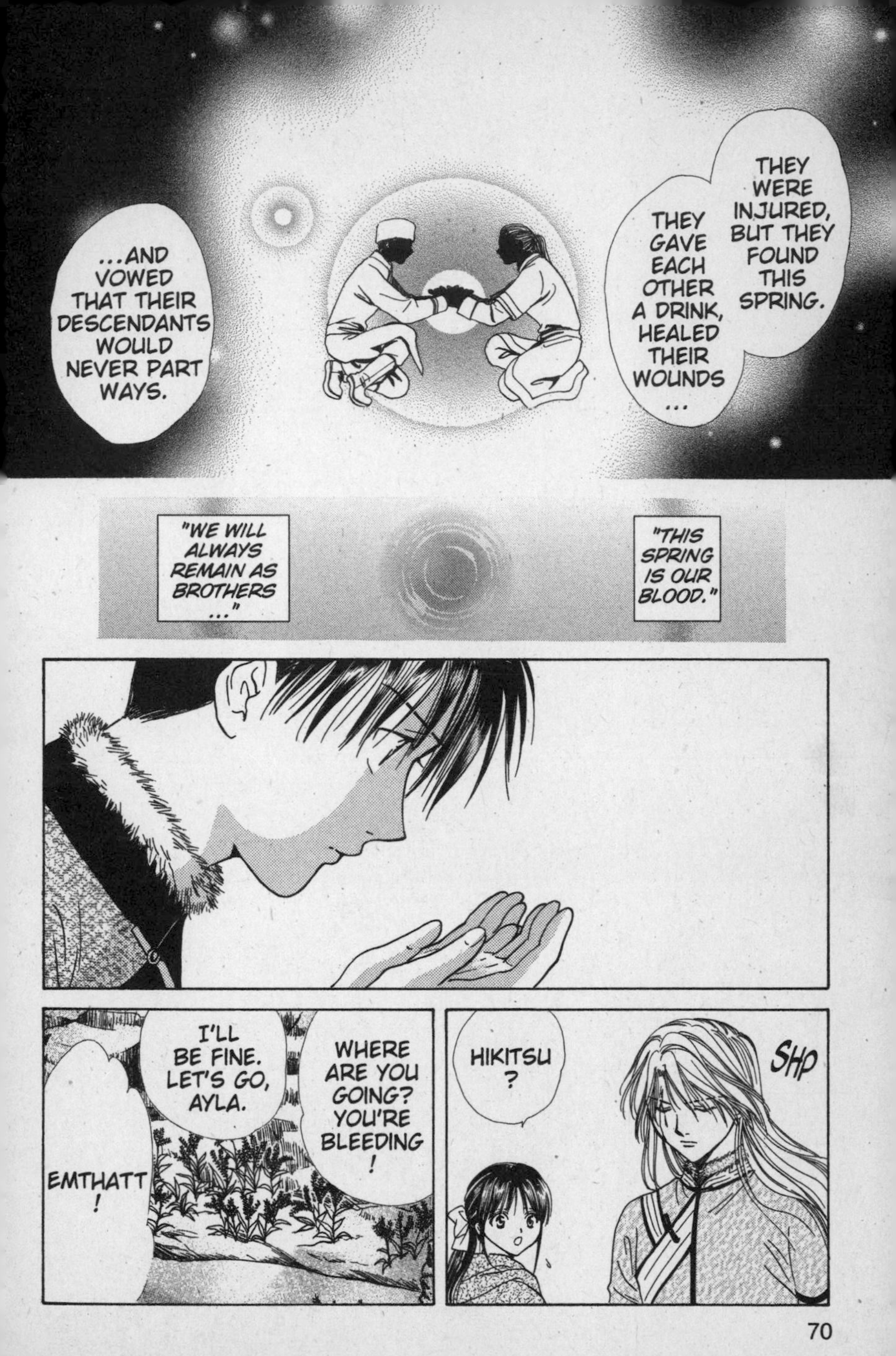
THEY WERE INJURED, BUT THEY FOUND THIS SPRING.
THEY GAVE EACH OTHER A DRINK, HEALED THEIR WOUNDS ...
...AND VOWED THAT THEIR DESCENDANTS WOULD NEVER PART WAYS.
"THIS SPRING IS OUR BLOOD."
"WE WILL ALWAYS REMAIN AS BROTHERS ..."
SHP
HIKITSU ?
WHERE ARE YOU GOING? YOU'RE BLEEDING !
I'LL BE FINE. LET'S GO, AYLA.
EMTHATT !

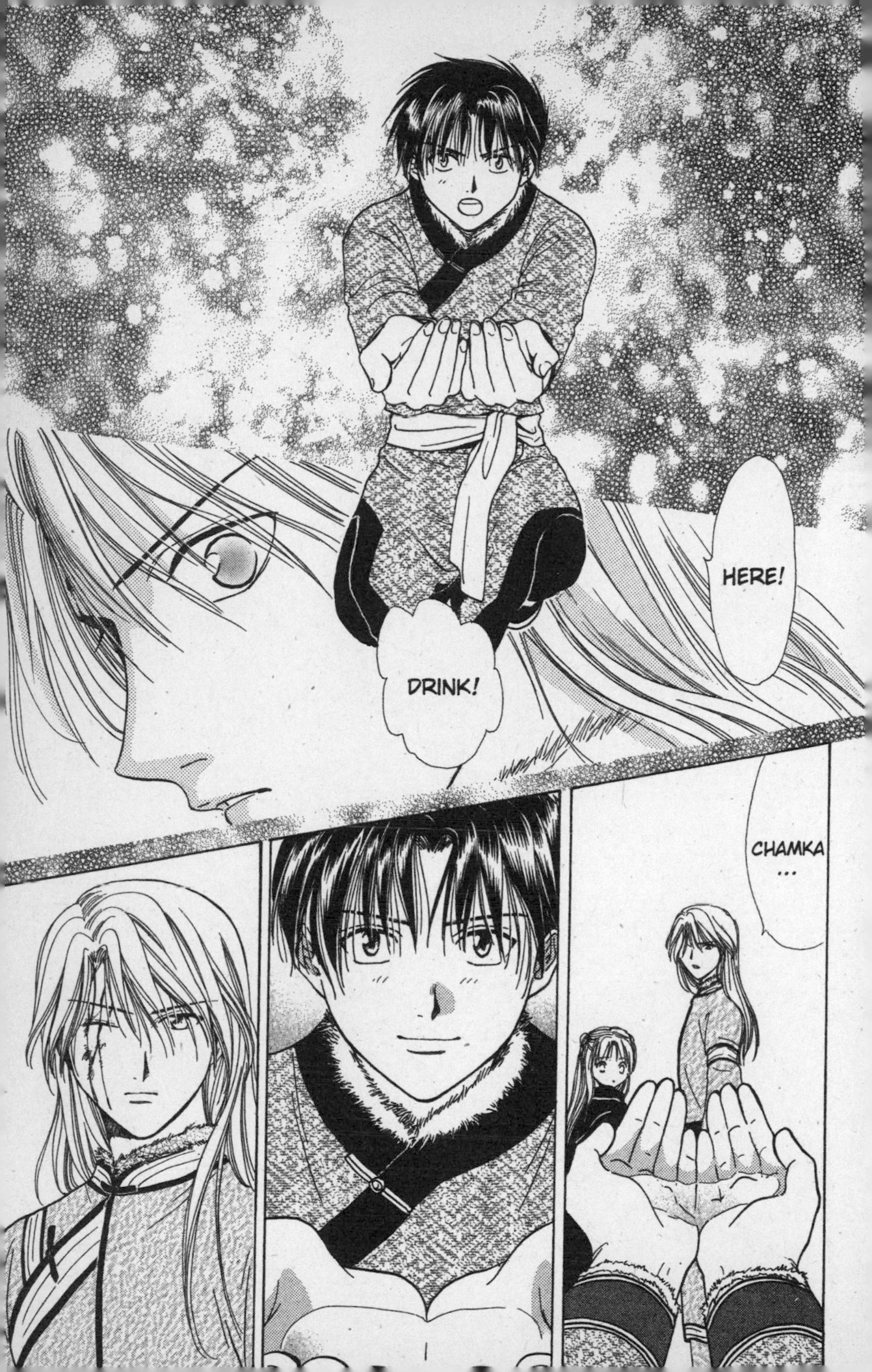
HERE!
DRINK!
CHAMKA ...

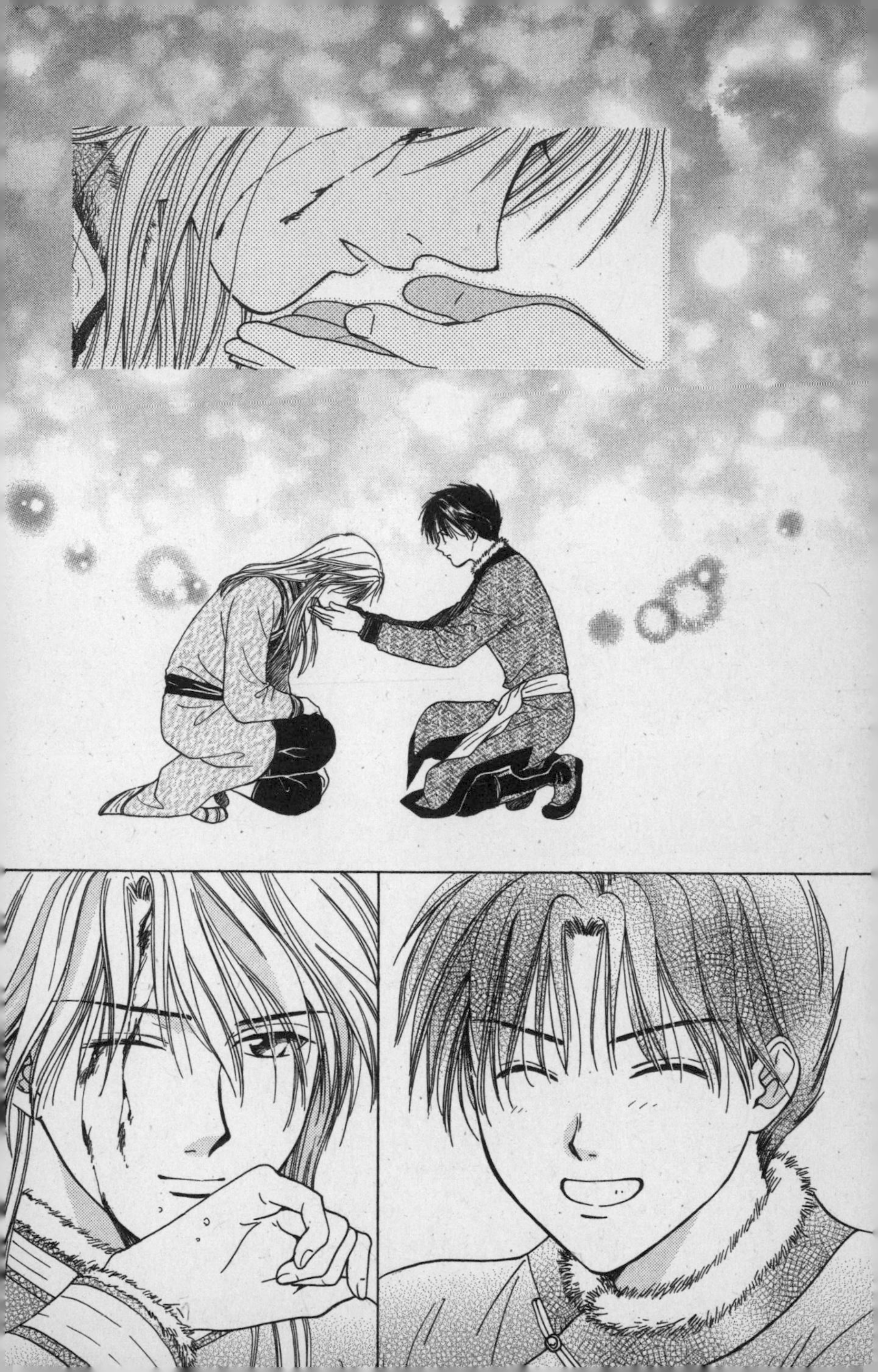

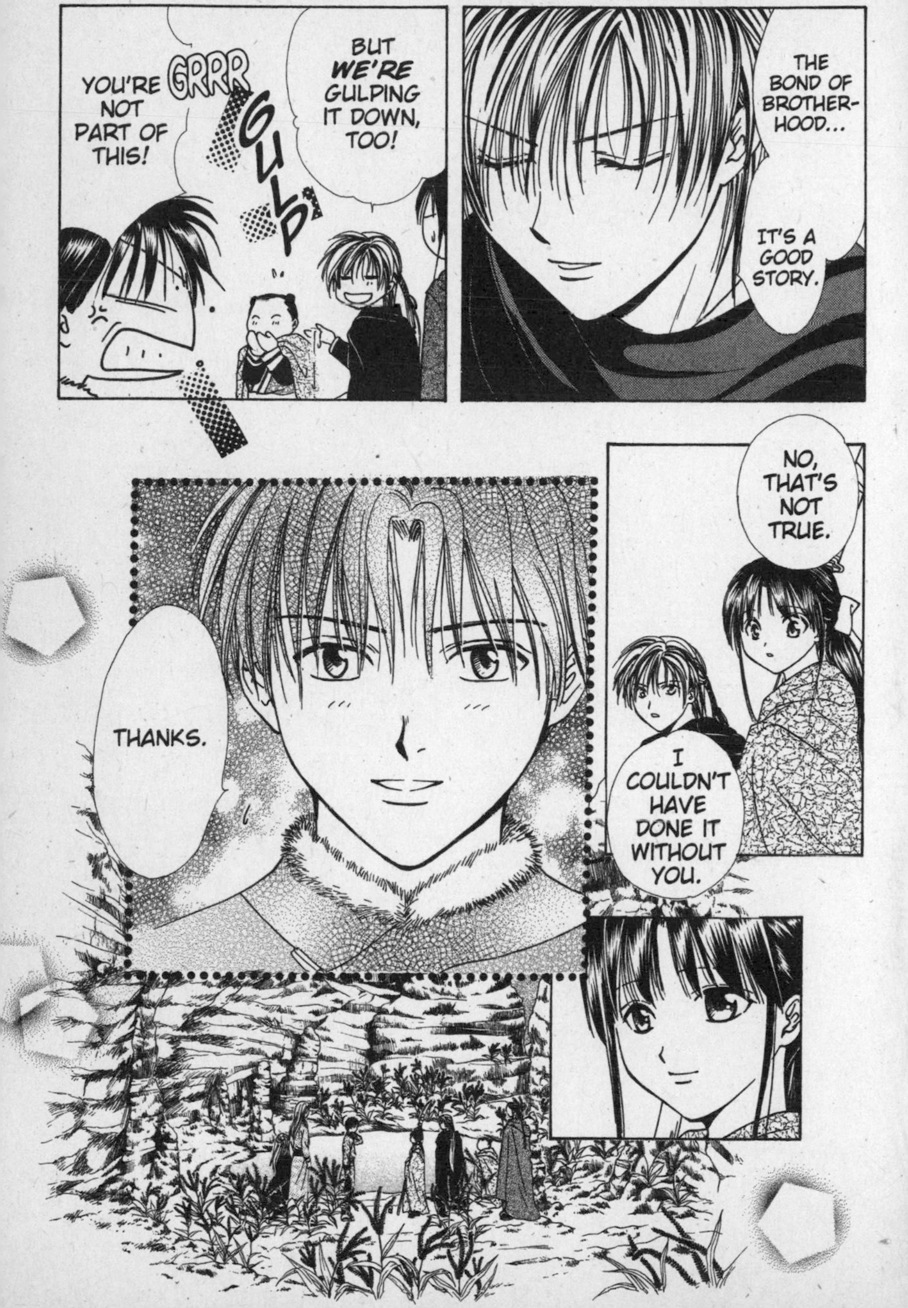
THE BOND OF BROTHER-HOOD...
IT'S A GOOD STORY.
BUT *WE'RE* GULPING IT DOWN, TOO!
GRRR
YOU'RE NOT PART OF THIS!
GULP
NO, THAT'S NOT TRUE.
I COULDN'T HAVE DONE IT WITHOUT YOU.
THANKS.

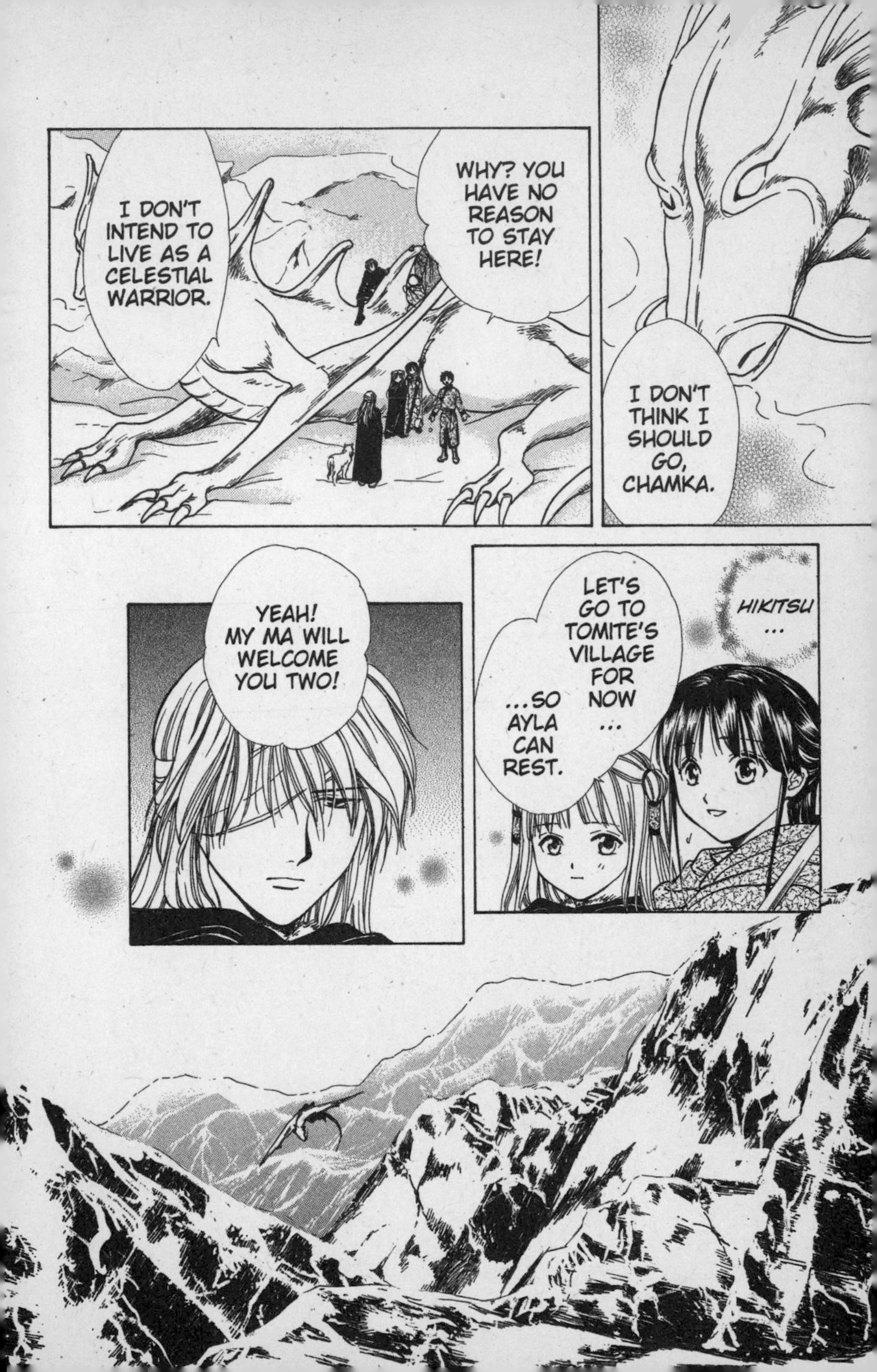
I DON'T THINK I SHOULD GO, CHAMKA.
WHY? YOU HAVE NO REASON TO STAY HERE!
I DON'T INTEND TO LIVE AS A CELESTIAL WARRIOR.
HIKITSU ...
LET'S GO TO TOMITE'S VILLAGE FOR NOW ...
...SO AYLA CAN REST.
YEAH! MY MA WILL WELCOME YOU TWO!

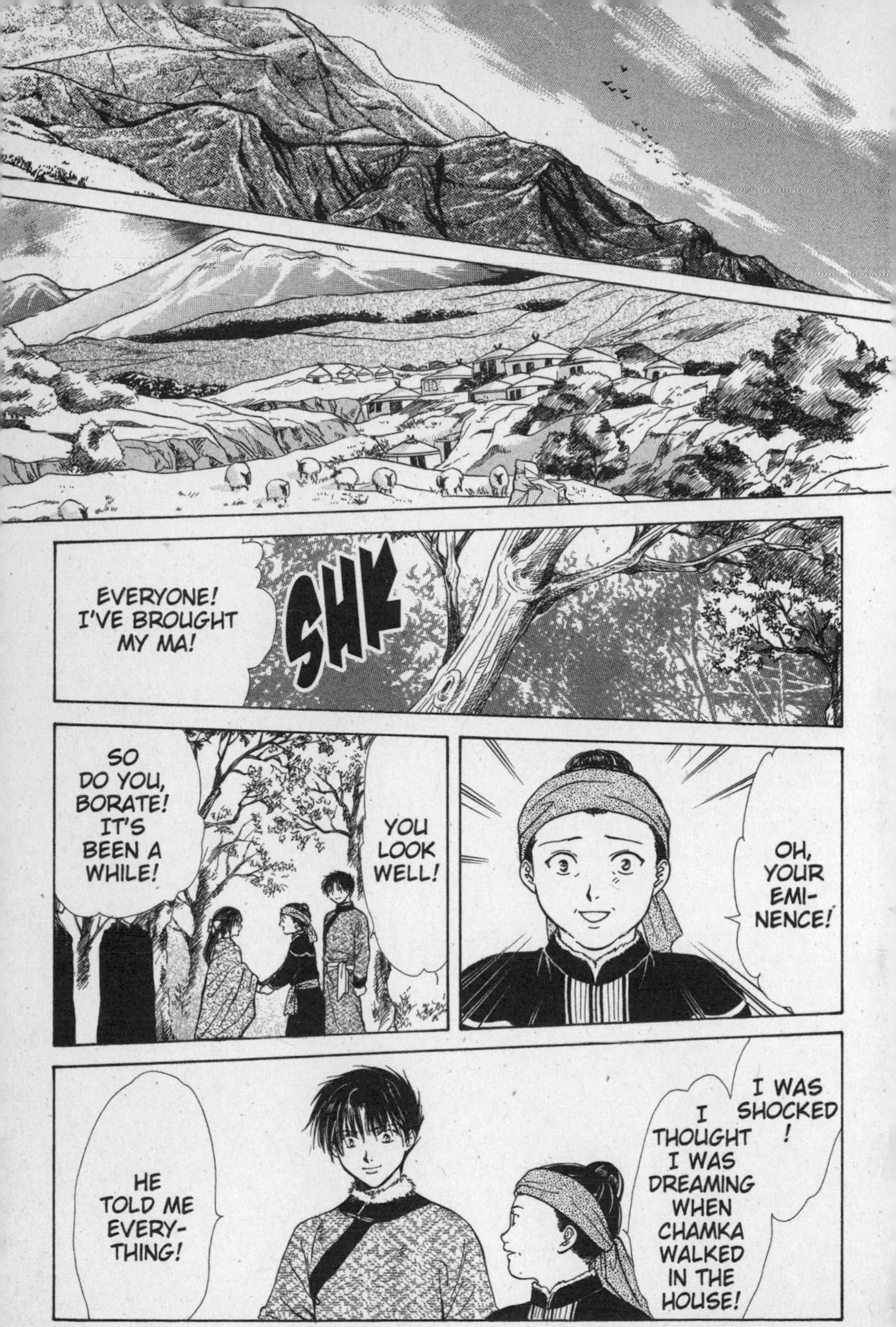
SHK
EVERYONE! I'VE BROUGHT MY MA!
OH, YOUR EMINENCE!
YOU LOOK WELL!
SO DO YOU, BORATE! IT'S BEEN A WHILE!
I WAS SHOCKED!
I THOUGHT I WAS DREAMING WHEN CHAMKA WALKED IN THE HOUSE!
HE TOLD ME EVERY-THING!

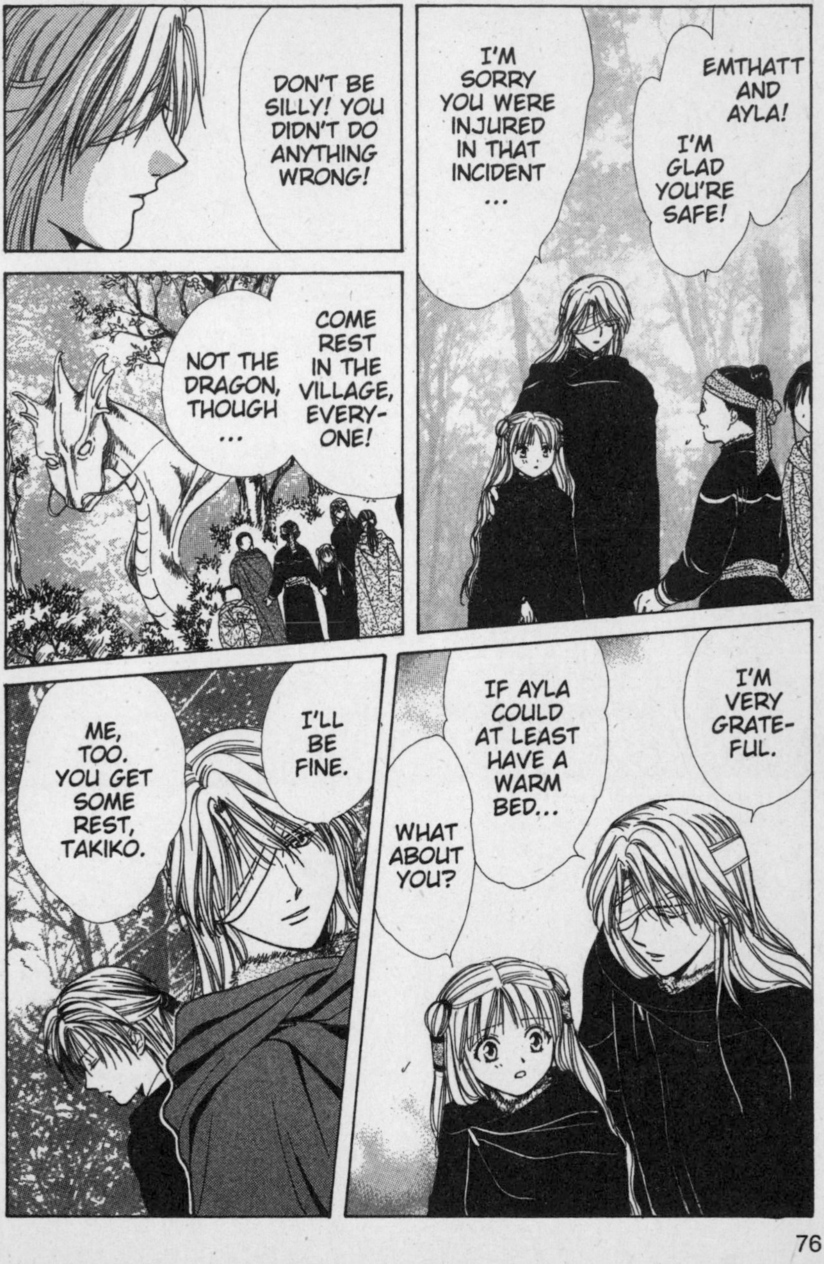
EMTHATT AND AYLA!
I'M GLAD YOU'RE SAFE!
I'M SORRY YOU WERE INJURED IN THAT INCIDENT ...
DON'T BE SILLY! YOU DIDN'T DO ANYTHING WRONG!
COME REST IN THE VILLAGE, EVERY-ONE!
NOT THE DRAGON, THOUGH ...
I'M VERY GRATE-FUL.
IF AYLA COULD AT LEAST HAVE A WARM BED...
WHAT ABOUT YOU?
I'LL BE FINE.
ME, TOO. YOU GET SOME REST, TAKIKO.

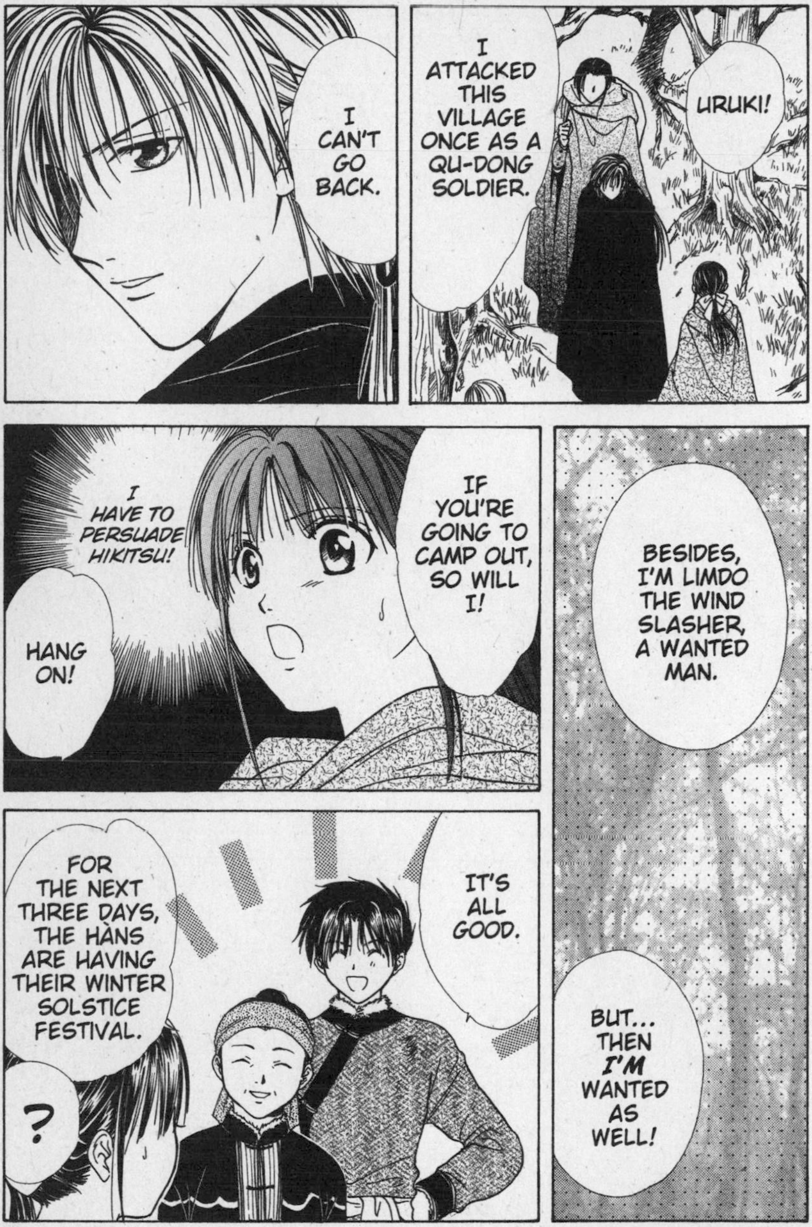
URUKI!
I ATTACKED THIS VILLAGE ONCE AS A QU-DONG SOLDIER.
I CAN'T GO BACK.
BESIDES, I'M LIMDO THE WIND SLASHER, A WANTED MAN.
BUT... THEN *I'M* WANTED AS WELL!
IF YOU'RE GOING TO CAMP OUT, SO WILL I!
I HAVE TO PERSUADE HIKITSU!
HANG ON!
IT'S ALL GOOD.
FOR THE NEXT THREE DAYS, THE HÀNS ARE HAVING THEIR WINTER SOLSTICE FESTIVAL.
?

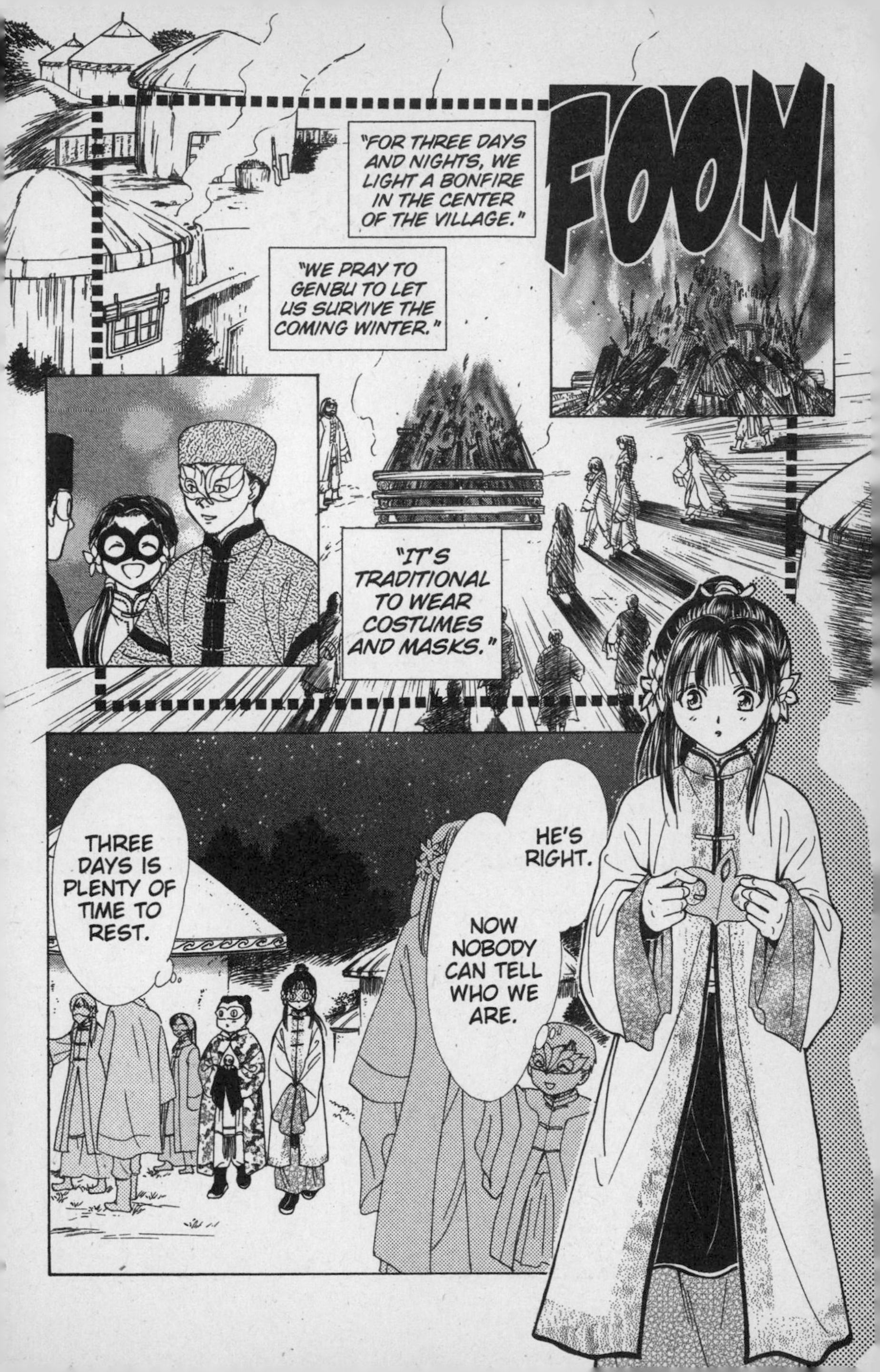
FOOM
"FOR THREE DAYS AND NIGHTS, WE LIGHT A BONFIRE IN THE CENTER OF THE VILLAGE."
"WE PRAY TO GENBU TO LET US SURVIVE THE COMING WINTER."
"IT'S TRADITIONAL TO WEAR COSTUMES AND MASKS."
HE'S RIGHT.
NOW NOBODY CAN TELL WHO WE ARE.
THREE DAYS IS PLENTY OF TIME TO REST.

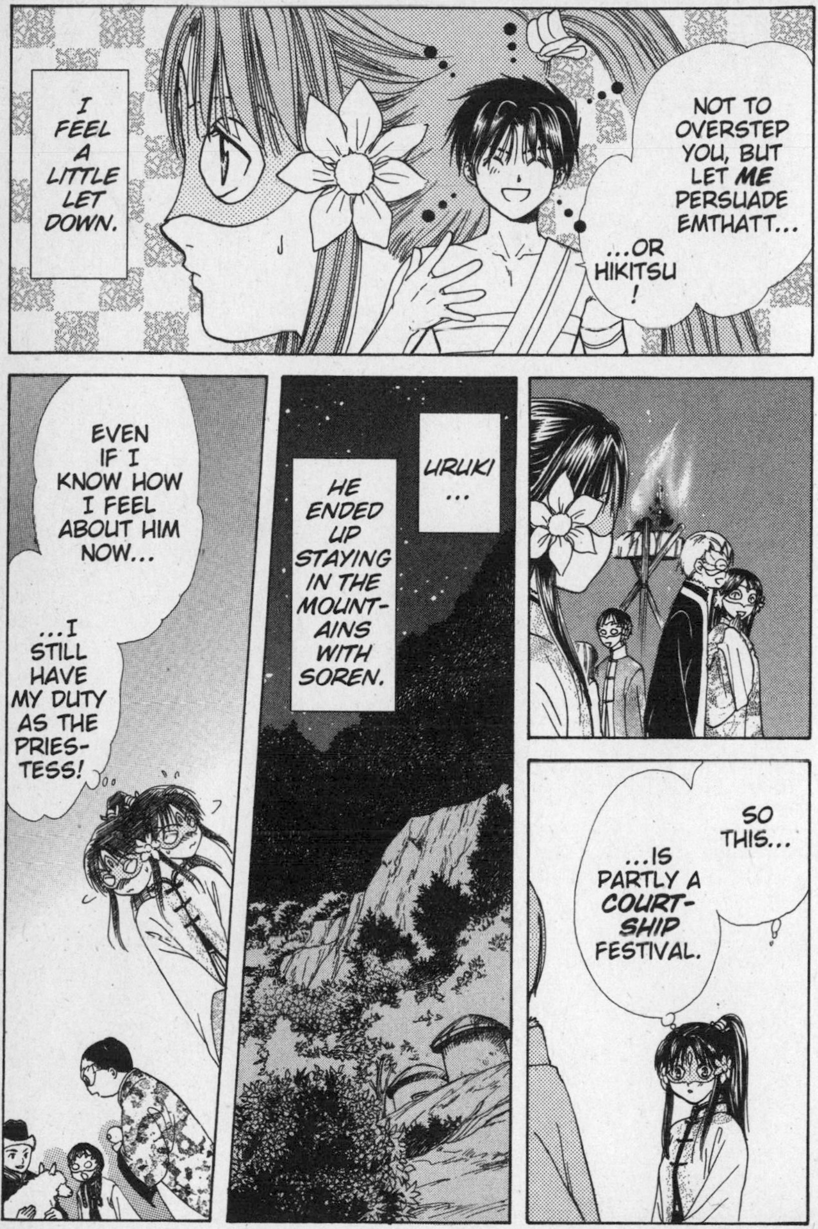
NOT TO OVERSTEP YOU, BUT LET ME PERSUADE EMTHATT...
...OR HIKITSU!
I FEEL A LITTLE LET DOWN.
SO THIS...
...IS PARTLY A COURTSHIP FESTIVAL.
URUKI...
HE ENDED UP STAYING IN THE MOUNTAINS WITH SOREN.
EVEN IF I KNOW HOW I FEEL ABOUT HIM NOW...
...I STILL HAVE MY DUTY AS THE PRIESTESS!

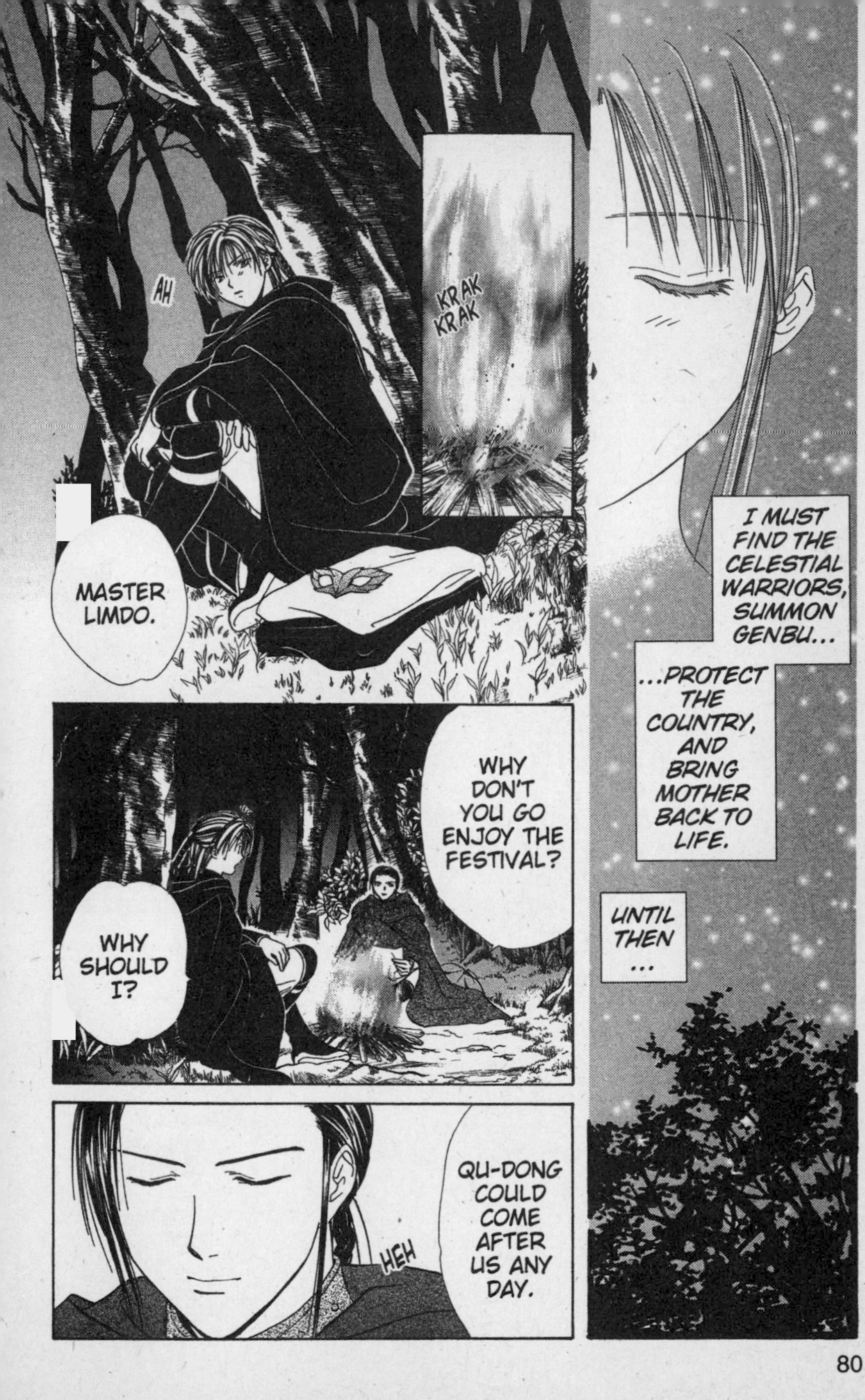
I MUST FIND THE CELESTIAL WARRIORS, SUMMON GENBU...
...PROTECT THE COUNTRY, AND BRING MOTHER BACK TO LIFE.
UNTIL THEN ...
KRAK KRAK
AH
MASTER LIMDO.
WHY DON'T YOU GO ENJOY THE FESTIVAL?
WHY SHOULD I?
QU-DONG COULD COME AFTER US ANY DAY.
HEH

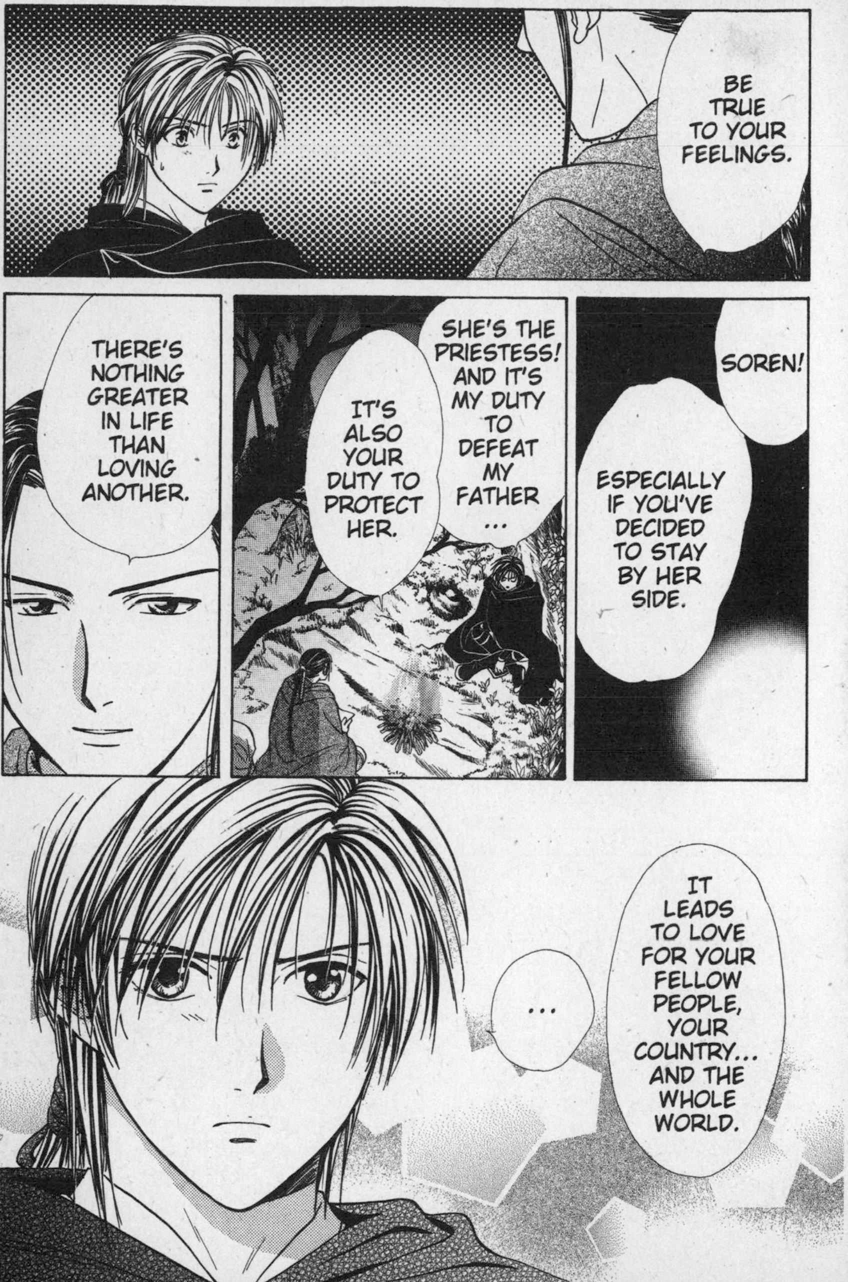
BE TRUE TO YOUR FEELINGS.
SOREN!
ESPECIALLY IF YOU'VE DECIDED TO STAY BY HER SIDE.
SHE'S THE PRIESTESS! AND IT'S MY DUTY TO DEFEAT MY FATHER ...
IT'S ALSO YOUR DUTY TO PROTECT HER.
THERE'S NOTHING GREATER IN LIFE THAN LOVING ANOTHER.
IT LEADS TO LOVE FOR YOUR FELLOW PEOPLE, YOUR COUNTRY... AND THE WHOLE WORLD.
...

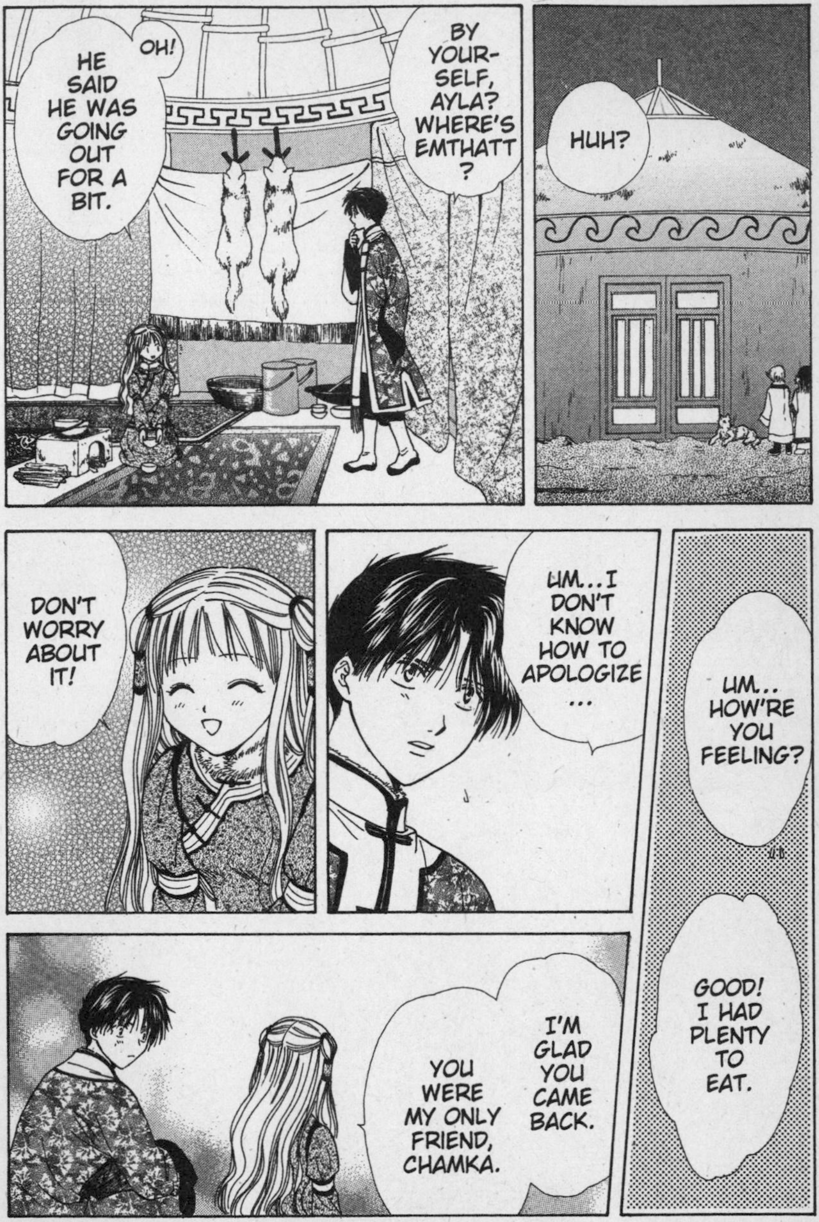
HUH?
BY YOURSELF, AYLA? WHERE'S EMTHATT?
OH!
HE SAID HE WAS GOING OUT FOR A BIT.
UM... HOW'RE YOU FEELING?
GOOD! I HAD PLENTY TO EAT.
UM...I DON'T KNOW HOW TO APOLOGIZE...
DON'T WORRY ABOUT IT!
I'M GLAD YOU CAME BACK.
YOU WERE MY ONLY FRIEND, CHAMKA.

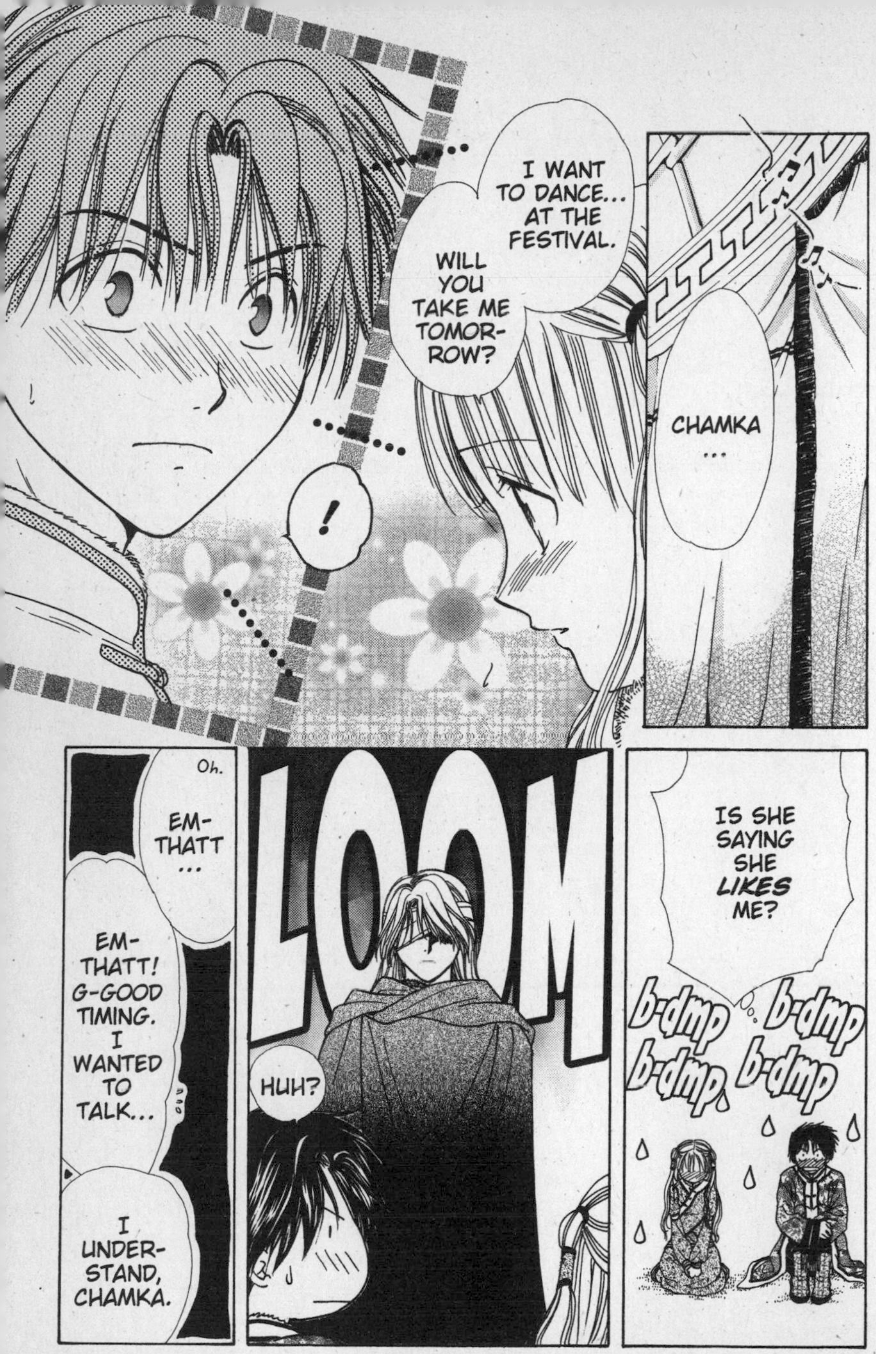
CHAMKA ...
I WANT TO DANCE... AT THE FESTIVAL.
WILL YOU TAKE ME TOMORROW?
!
IS SHE SAYING SHE LIKES ME?
b-dmp b-dmp
b-dmp b-dmp
LOOM
HUH?
Oh.
EM-THATT ...
EM-THATT! G-GOOD TIMING. I WANTED TO TALK...
I UNDERSTAND, CHAMKA.

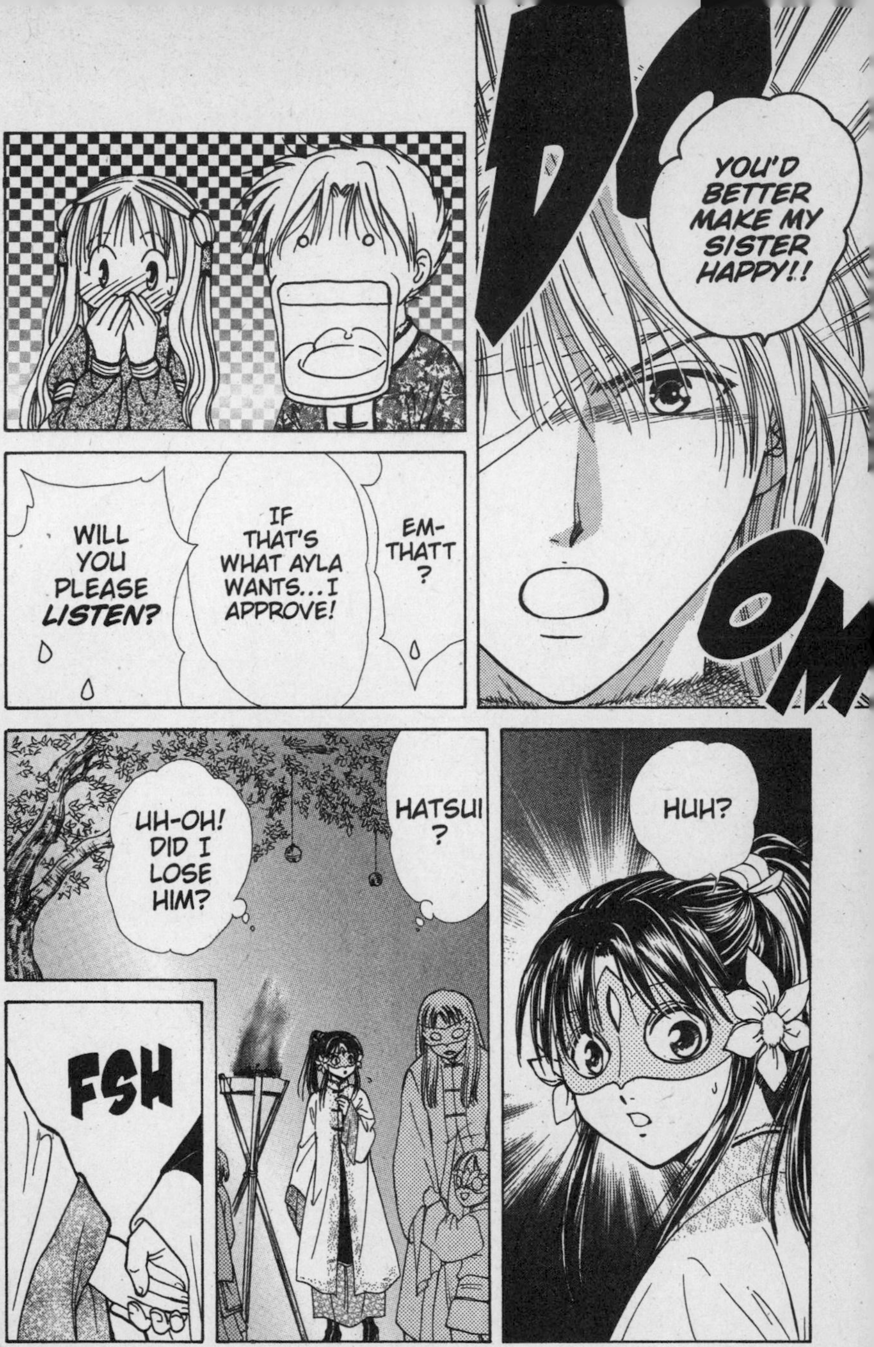
DOOM
YOU'D BETTER MAKE MY SISTER HAPPY!!
EM-THATT?
IF THAT'S WHAT AYLA WANTS...I APPROVE!
WILL YOU PLEASE LISTEN?
HUH?
HATSUI?
UH-OH! DID I LOSE HIM?
FSH

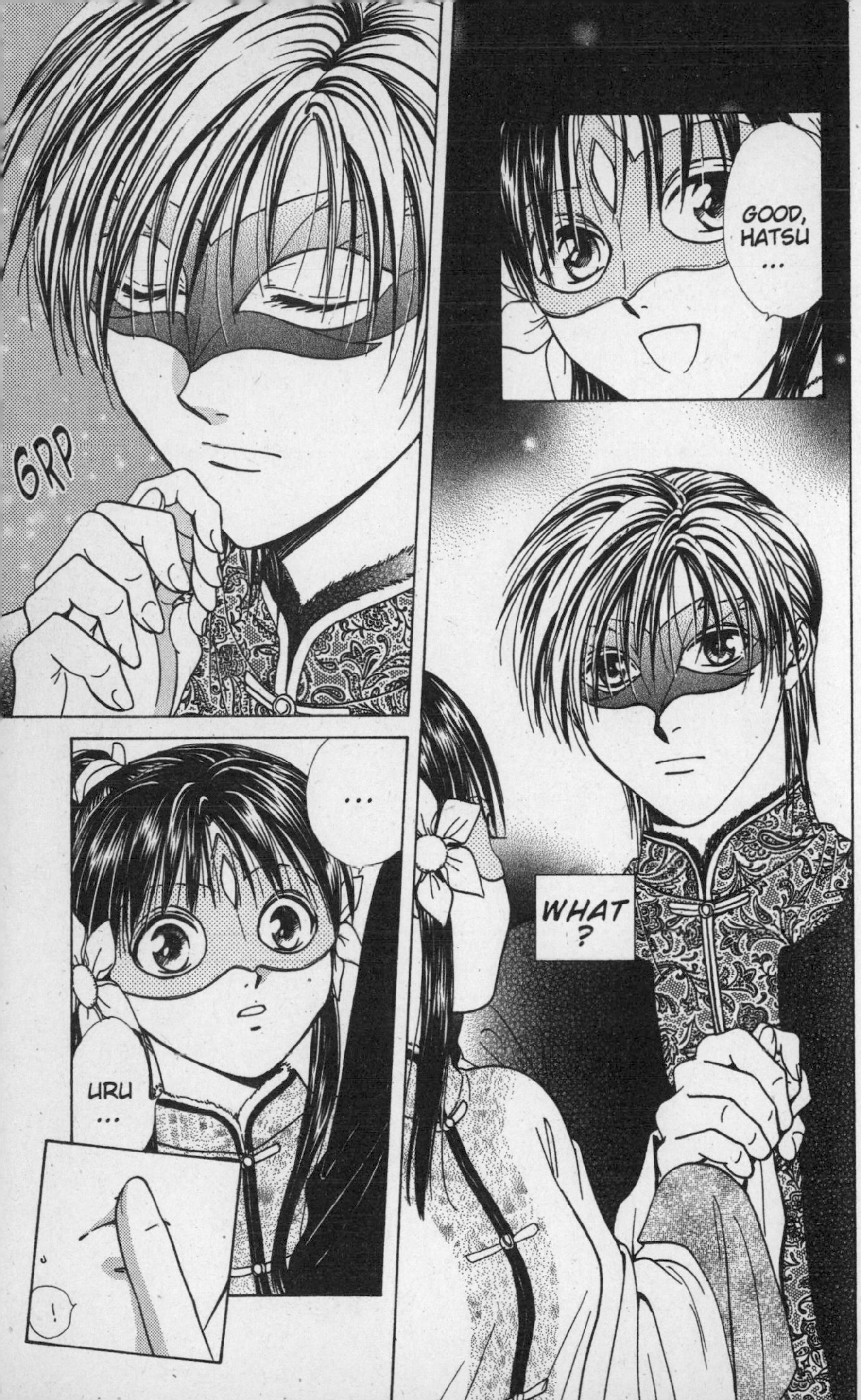
GOOD, HATSU ...
GRP
WHAT?
...
URU ...
!

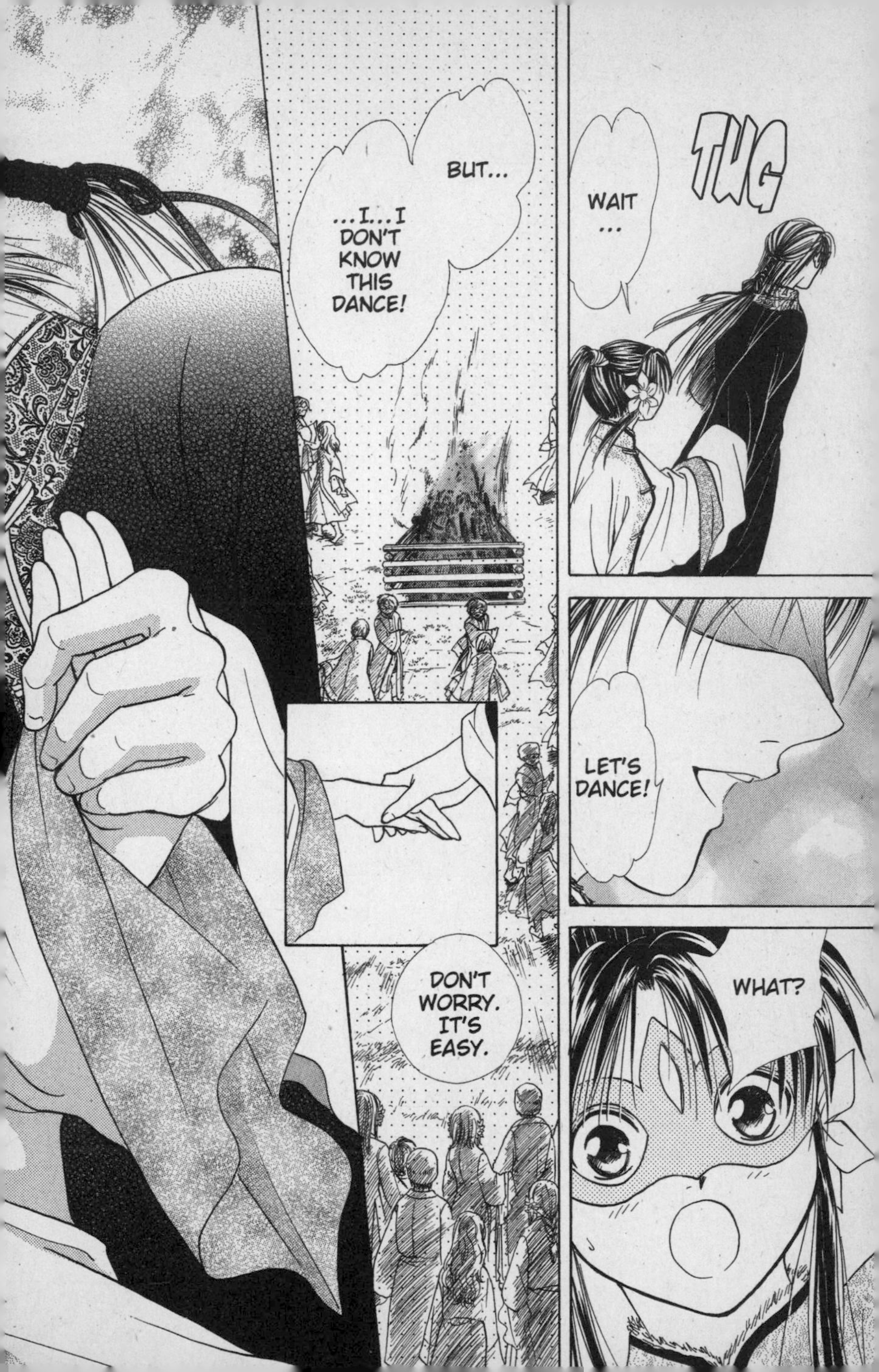
TUG
WAIT ...
LET'S DANCE!
WHAT?
BUT...
...I...I DON'T KNOW THIS DANCE!
DON'T WORRY. IT'S EASY.

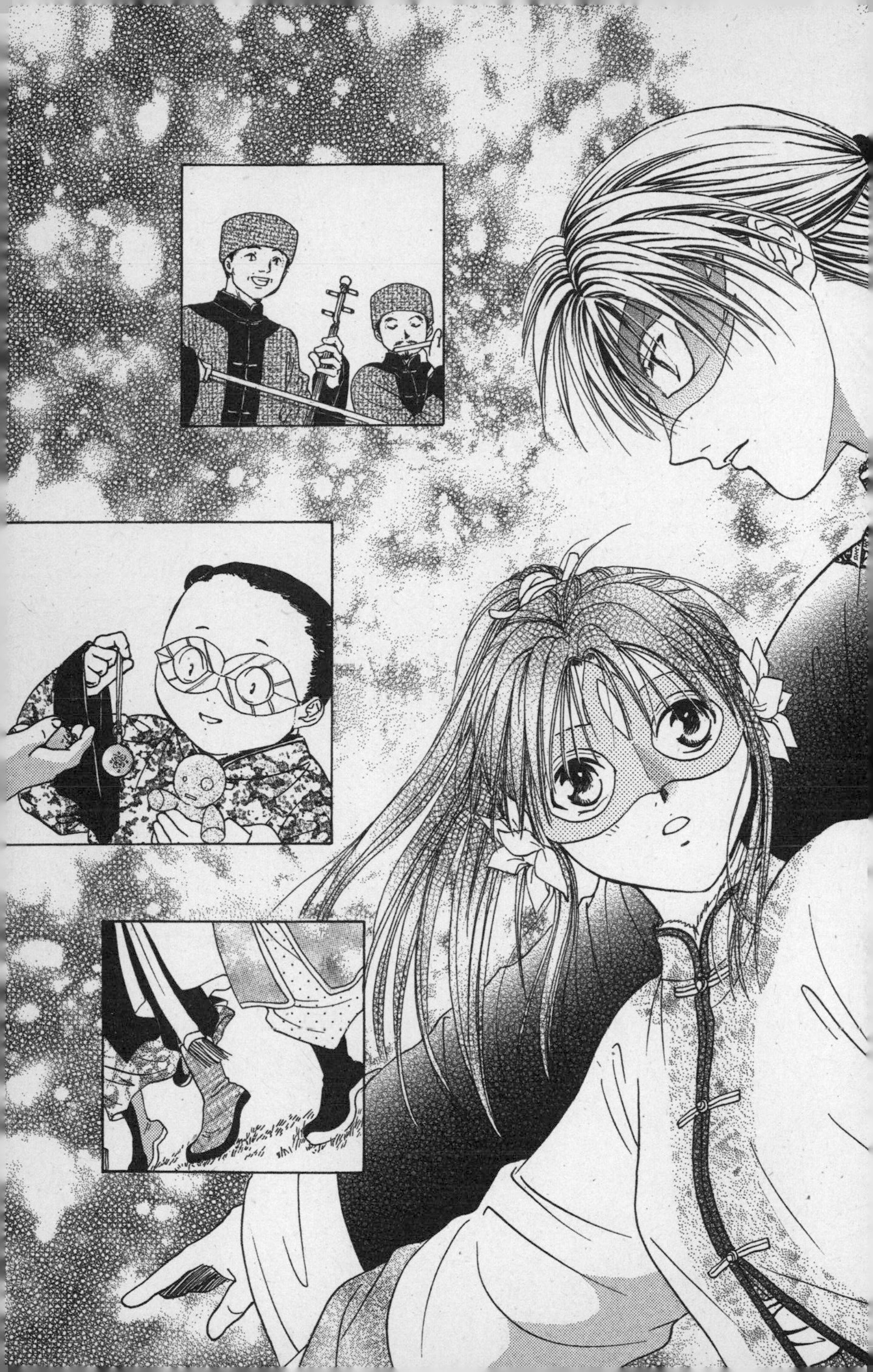

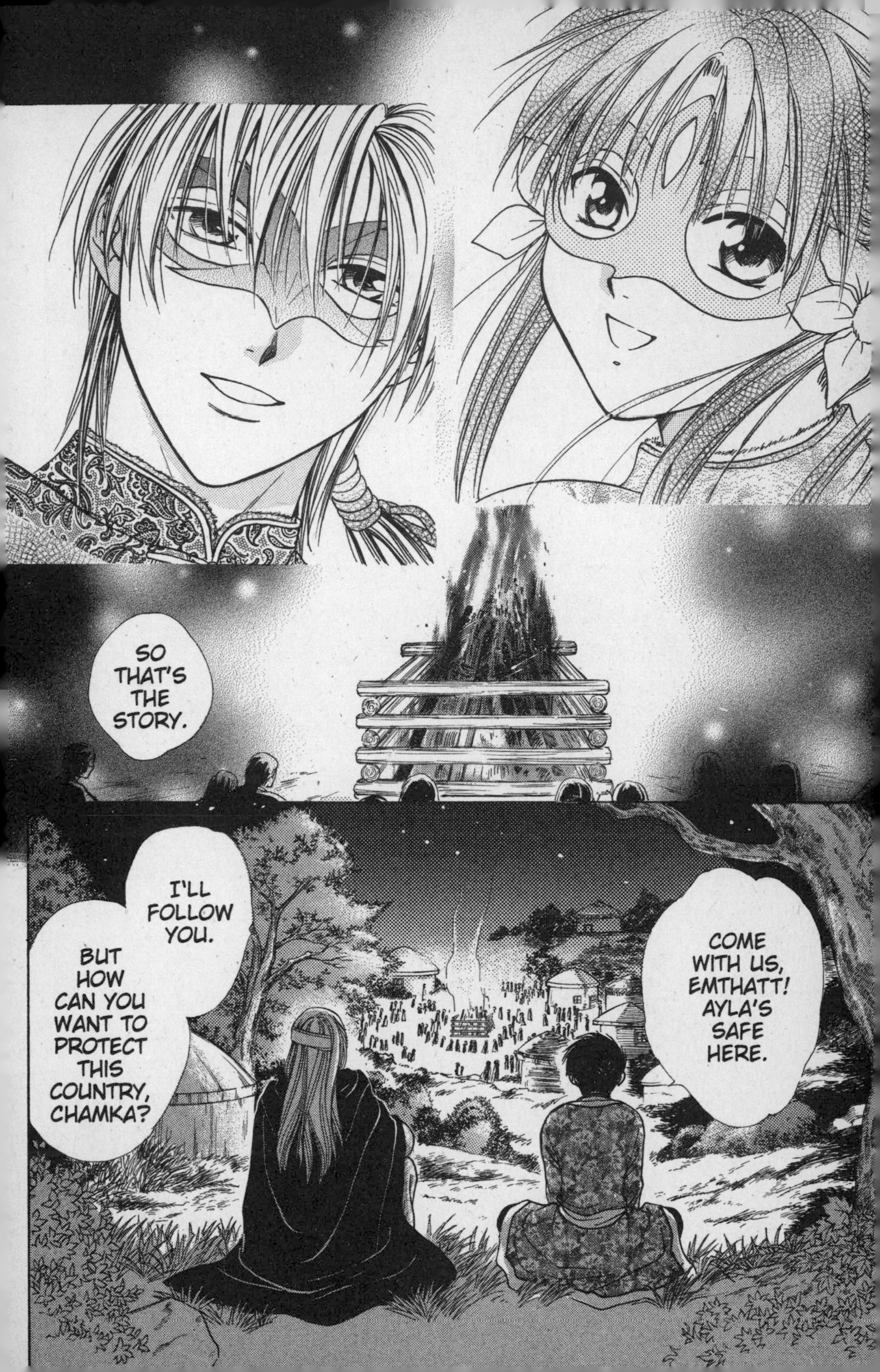
SO THAT'S THE STORY.
COME WITH US, EMTHATT! AYLA'S SAFE HERE.
I'LL FOLLOW YOU.
BUT HOW CAN YOU WANT TO PROTECT THIS COUNTRY, CHAMKA?

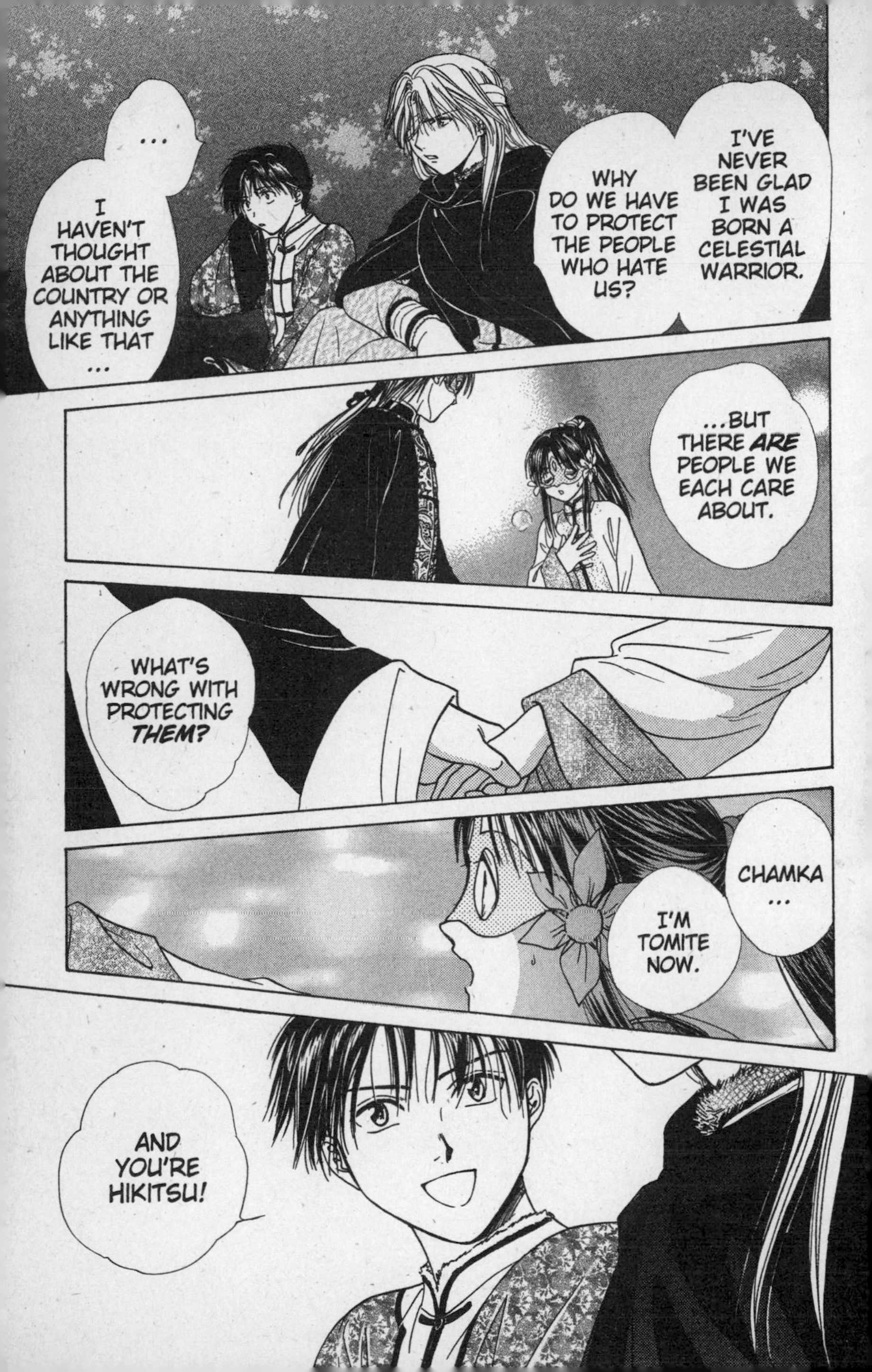
I'VE NEVER BEEN GLAD I WAS BORN A CELESTIAL WARRIOR.
WHY DO WE HAVE TO PROTECT THE PEOPLE WHO HATE US?
...
I HAVEN'T THOUGHT ABOUT THE COUNTRY OR ANYTHING LIKE THAT ...
...BUT THERE *ARE* PEOPLE WE EACH CARE ABOUT.
WHAT'S WRONG WITH PROTECTING *THEM?*
CHAMKA ...
I'M TOMITE NOW.
AND YOU'RE HIKITSU!

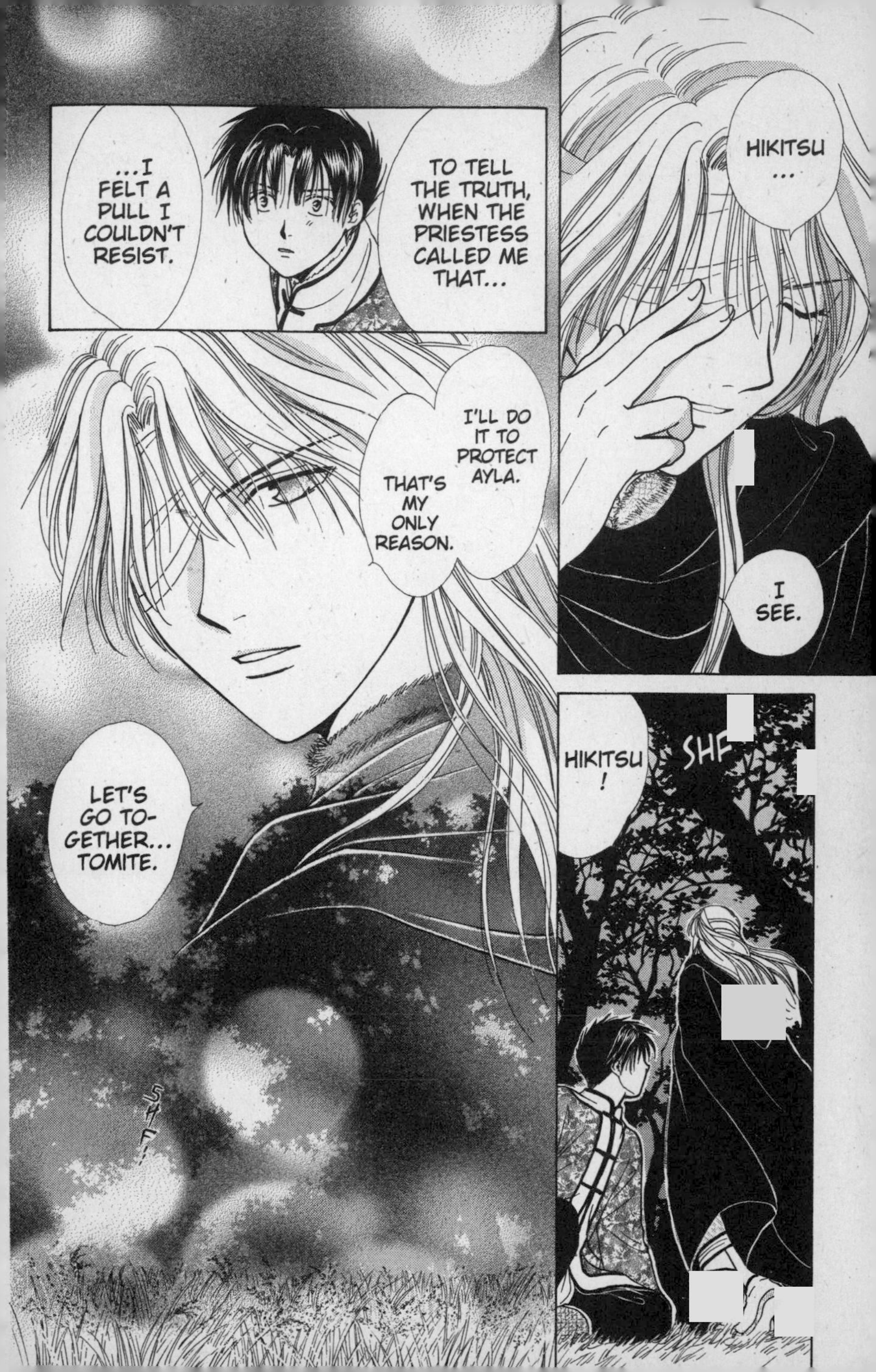
HIKITSU...
I SEE.
HIKITSU!
SHF
TO TELL THE TRUTH, WHEN THE PRIESTESS CALLED ME THAT...
...I FELT A PULL I COULDN'T RESIST.
I'LL DO IT TO PROTECT AYLA.
THAT'S MY ONLY REASON.
LET'S GO TO-GETHER... TOMITE.
SHF!

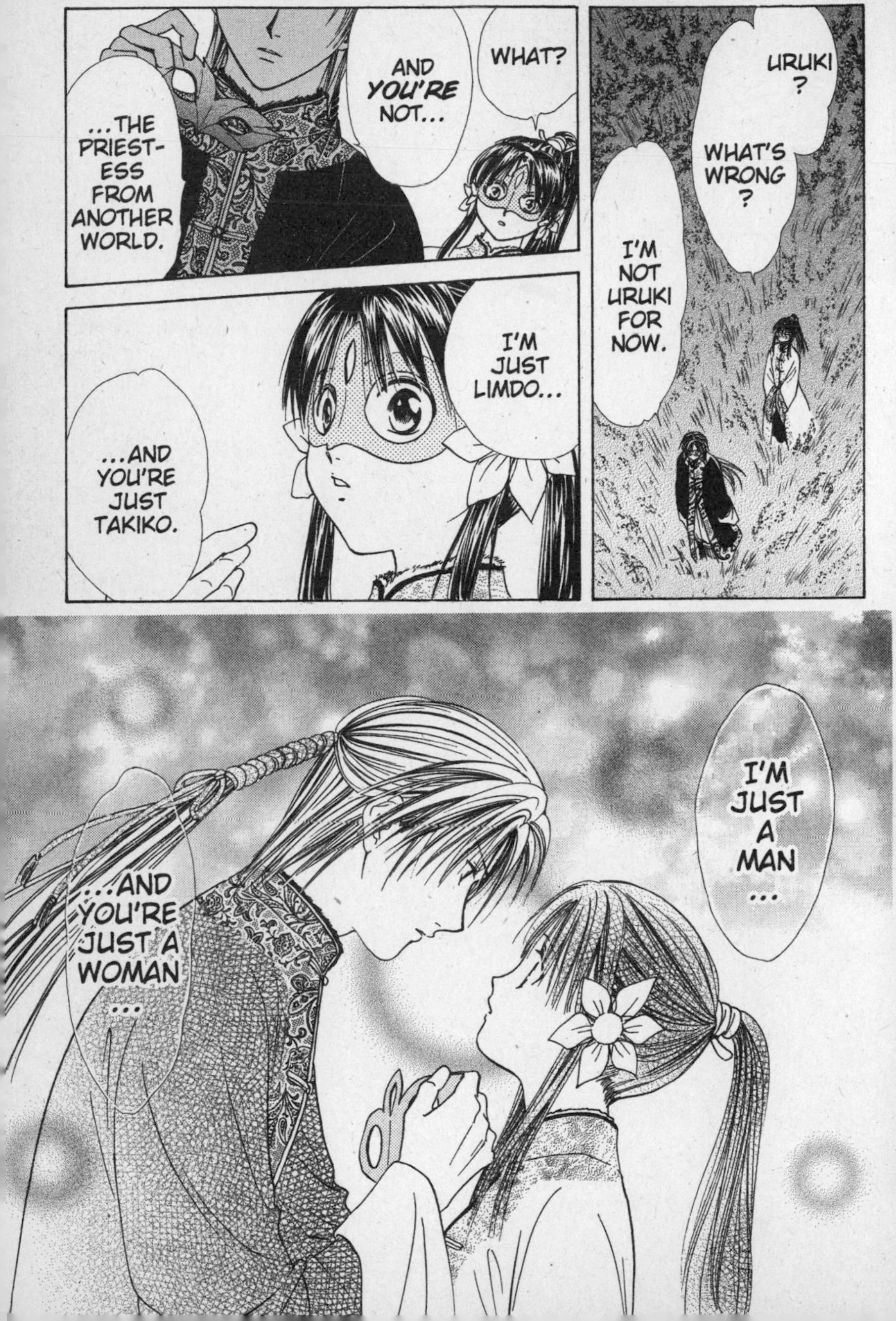
URUKI ?
WHAT'S WRONG ?
I'M NOT URUKI FOR NOW.
WHAT?
AND *YOU'RE* NOT...
...THE PRIEST-ESS FROM ANOTHER WORLD.
I'M JUST LIMDO...
...AND YOU'RE JUST TAKIKO.
I'M JUST A MAN ...
...AND YOU'RE JUST A WOMAN ...

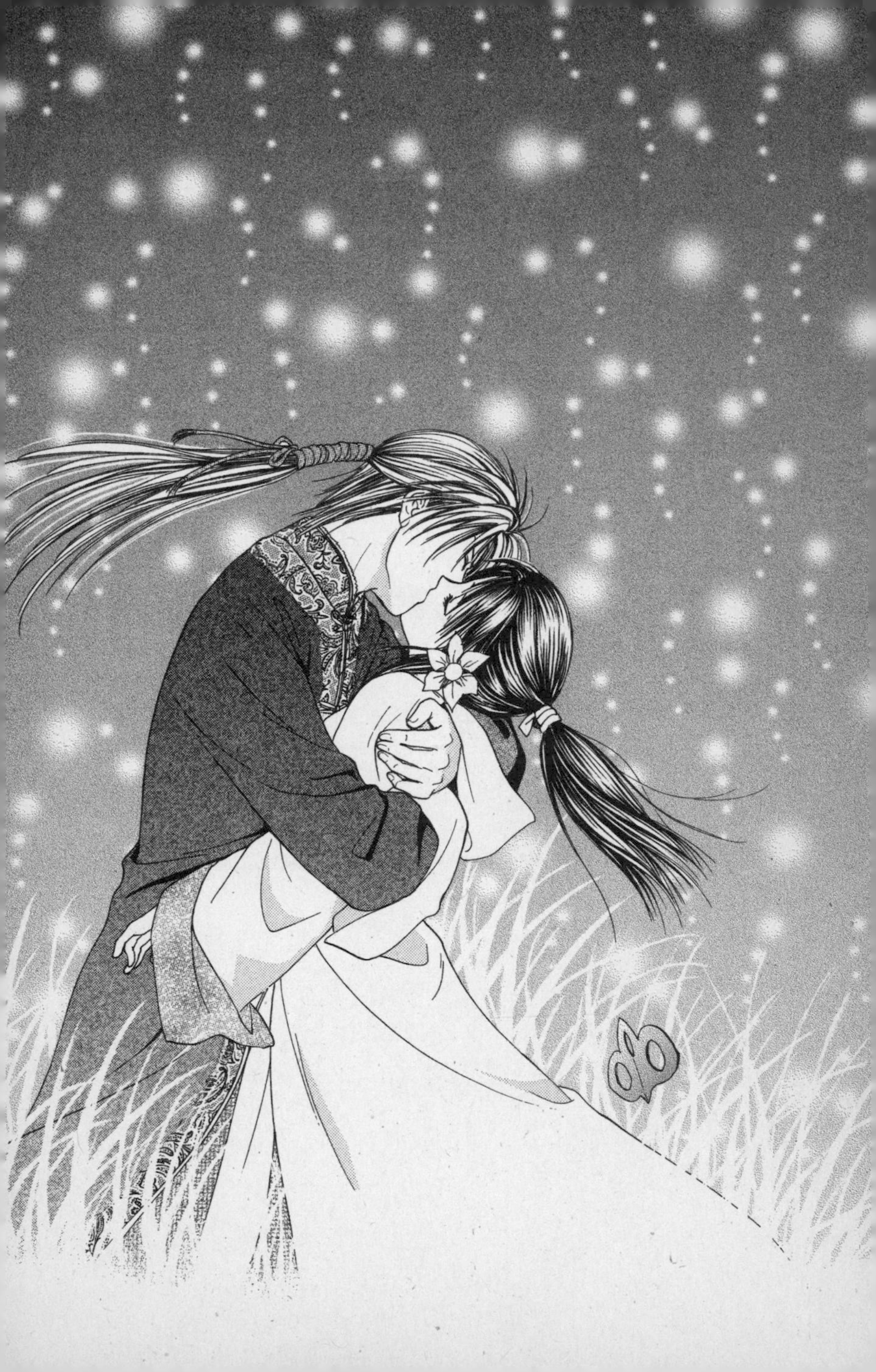

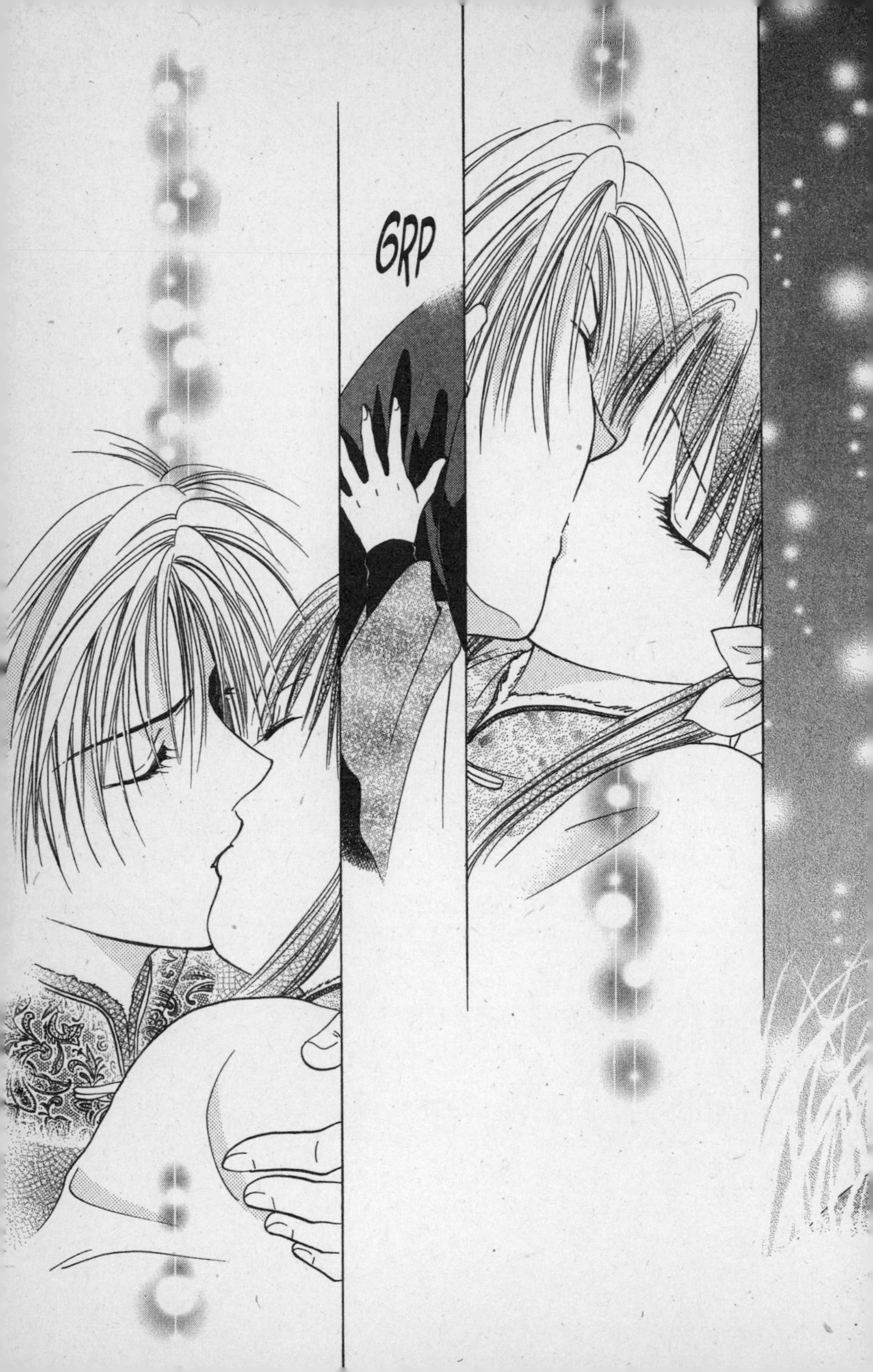
GRP

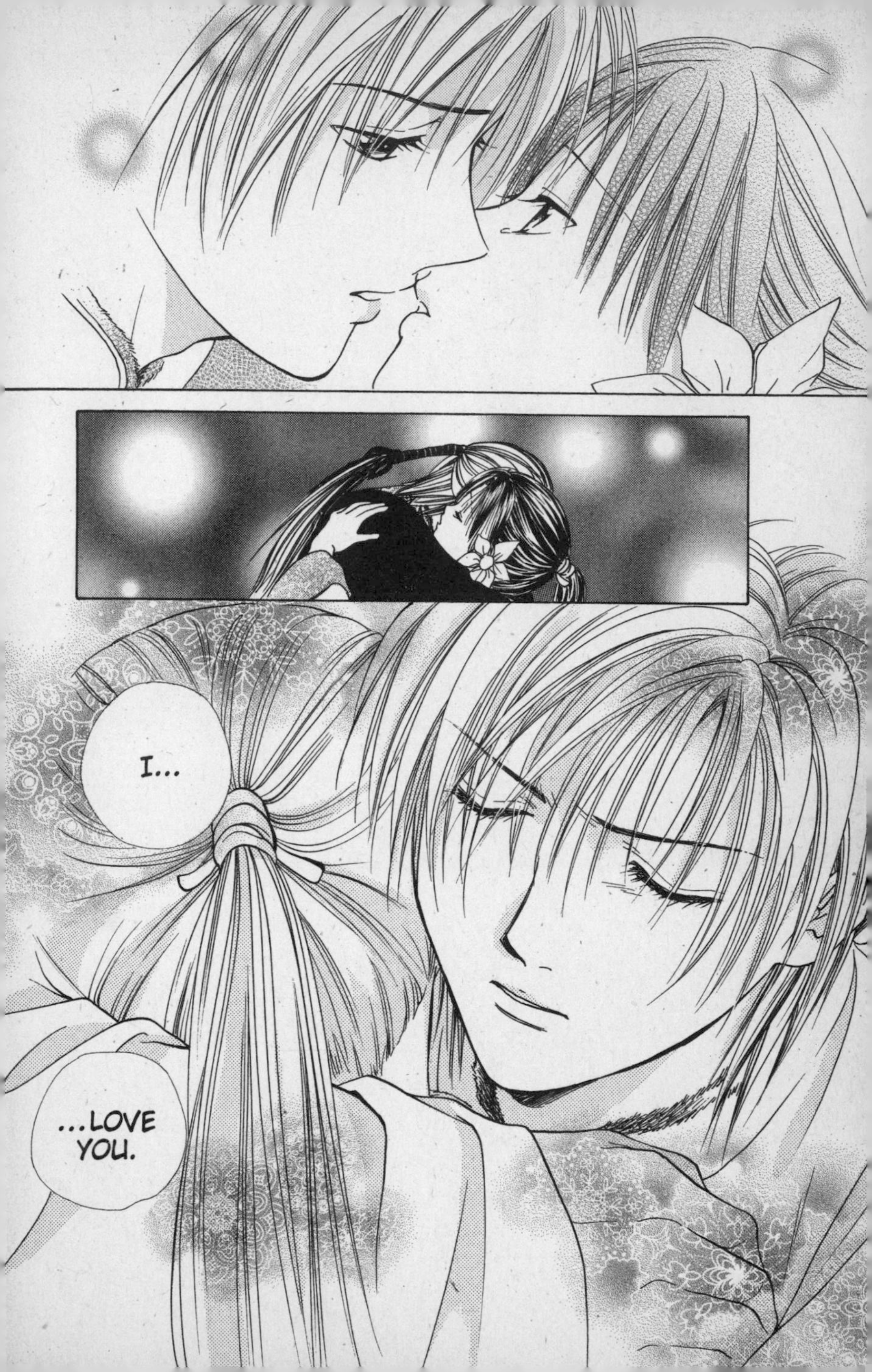
I...
...LOVE YOU.

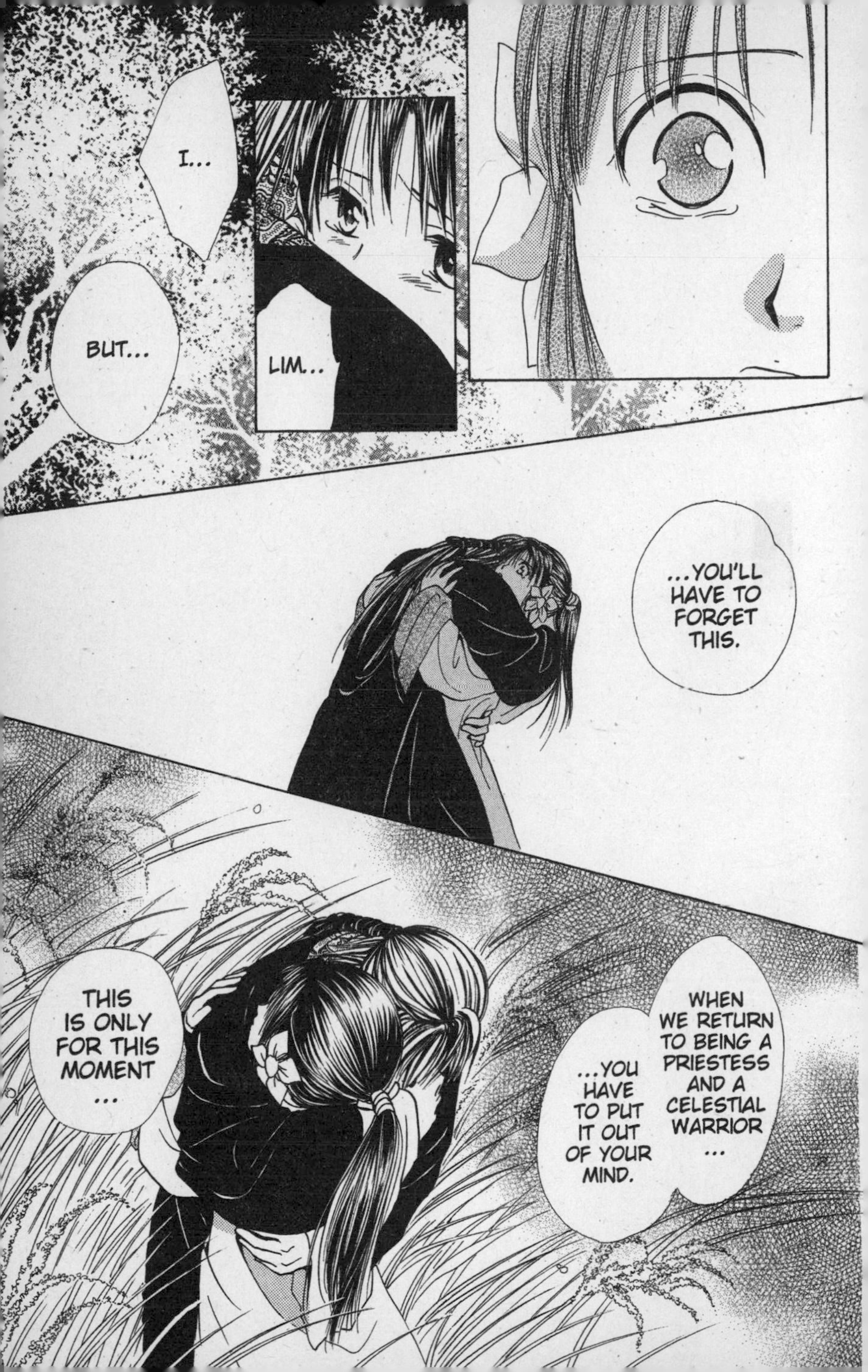
LIM...
I...
BUT...
...YOU'LL HAVE TO FORGET THIS.
WHEN WE RETURN TO BEING A PRIESTESS AND A CELESTIAL WARRIOR...
...YOU HAVE TO PUT IT OUT OF YOUR MIND.
THIS IS ONLY FOR THIS MOMENT...

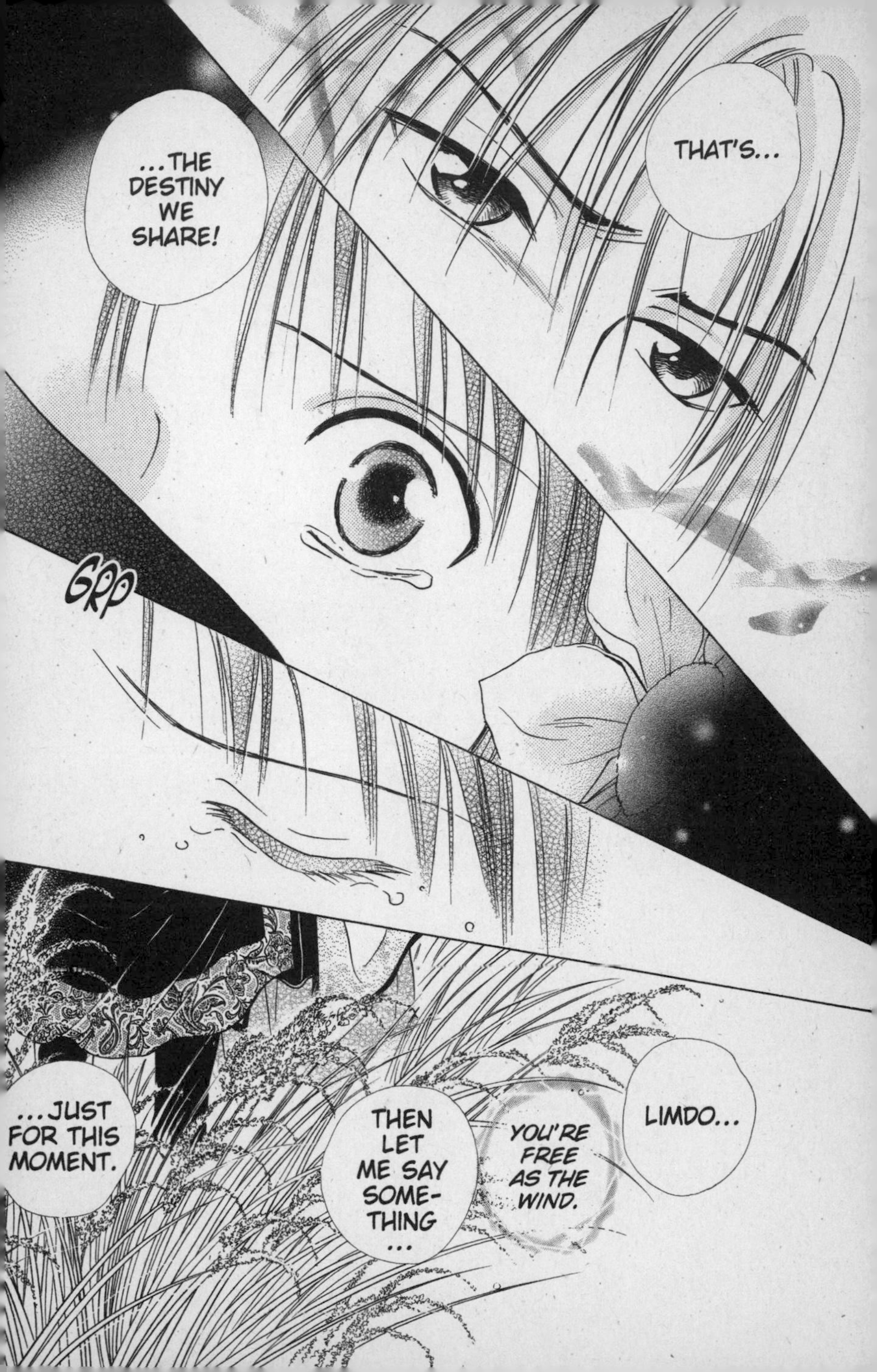
THAT'S...
...THE DESTINY WE SHARE!
GRP
LIMDO...
YOU'RE FREE AS THE WIND.
THEN LET ME SAY SOME-THING...
...JUST FOR THIS MOMENT.

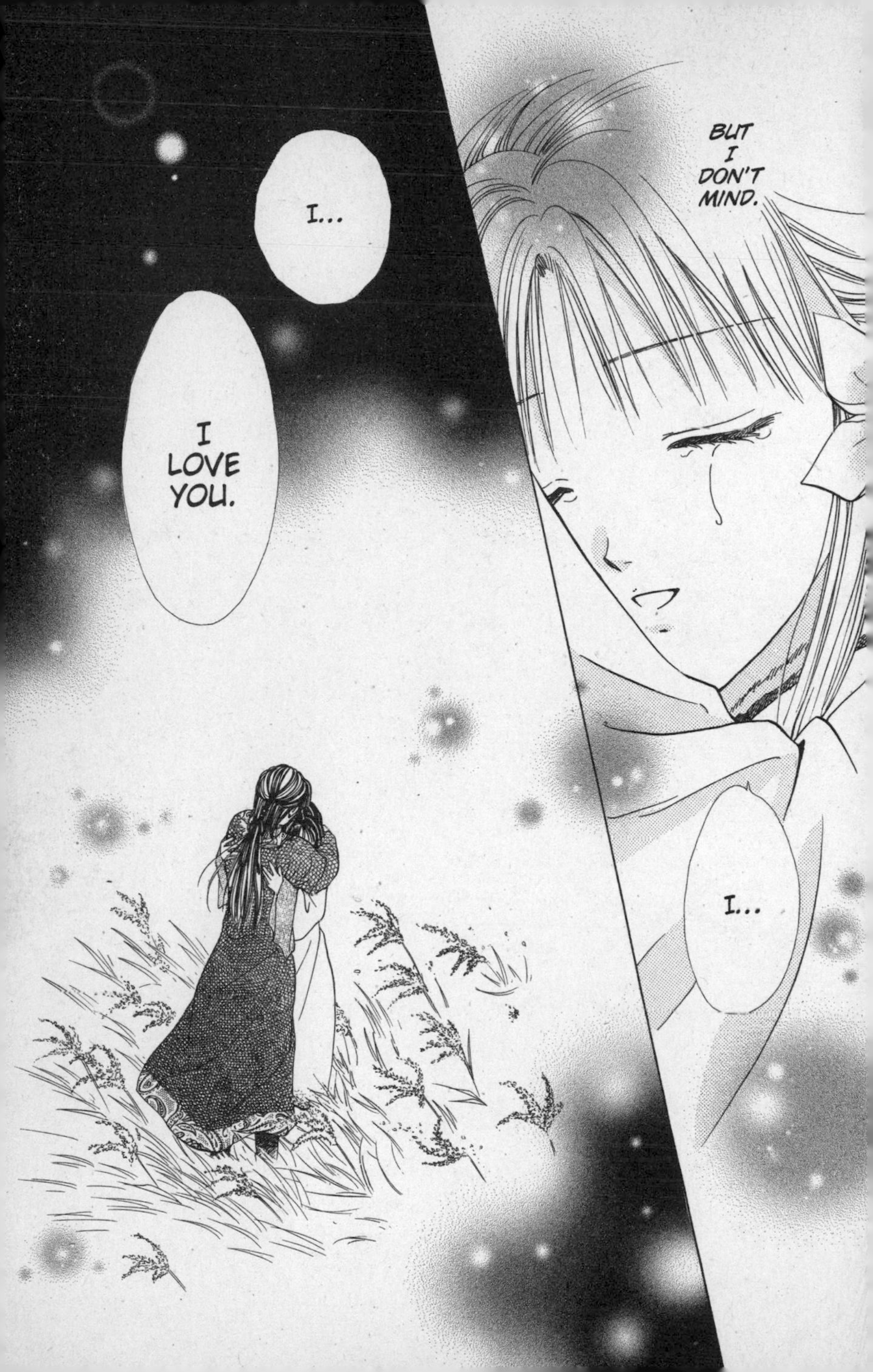
BUT I DON'T MIND.
I...
I...
I LOVE YOU.

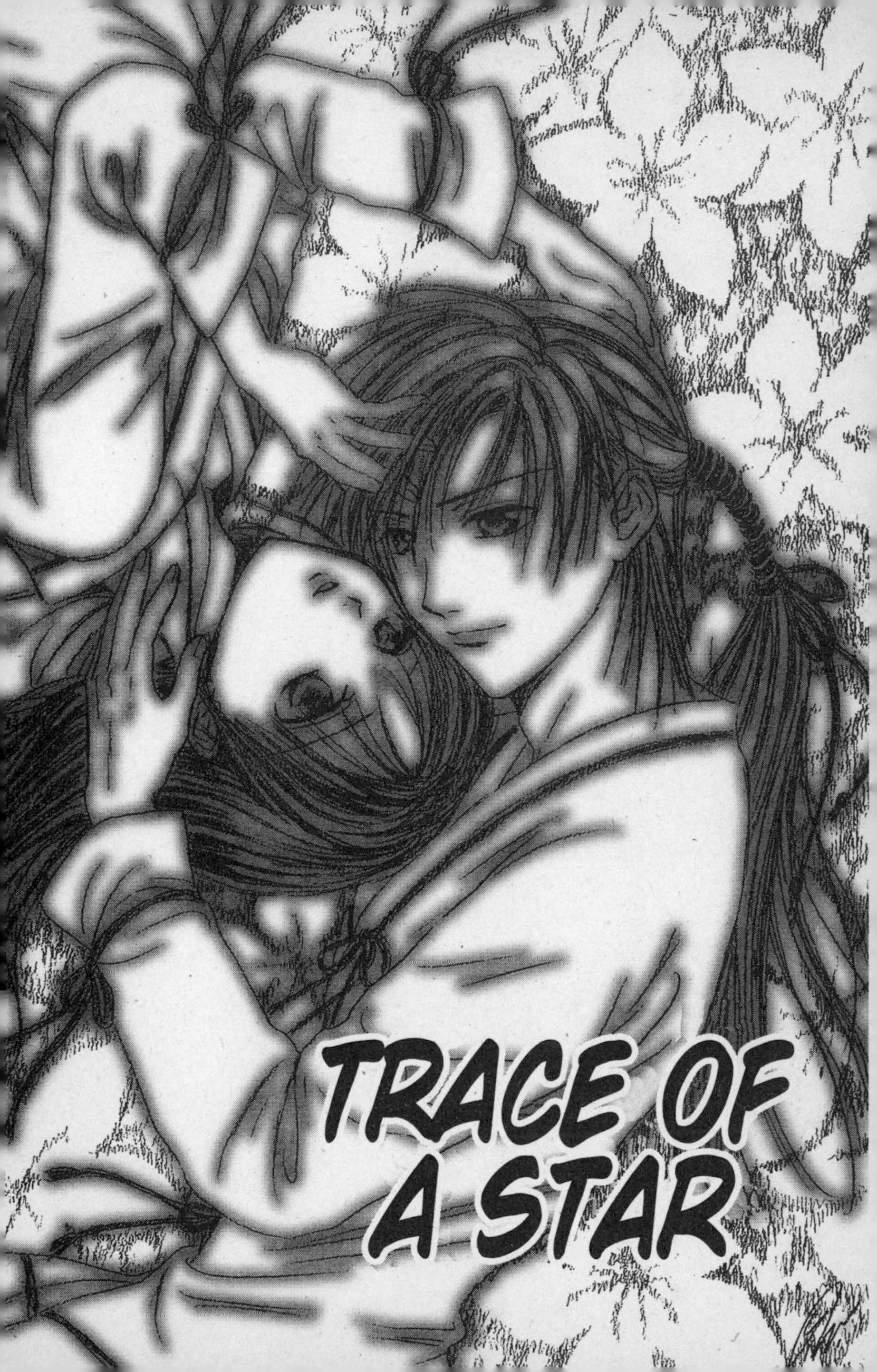
TRACE OF
A STAR

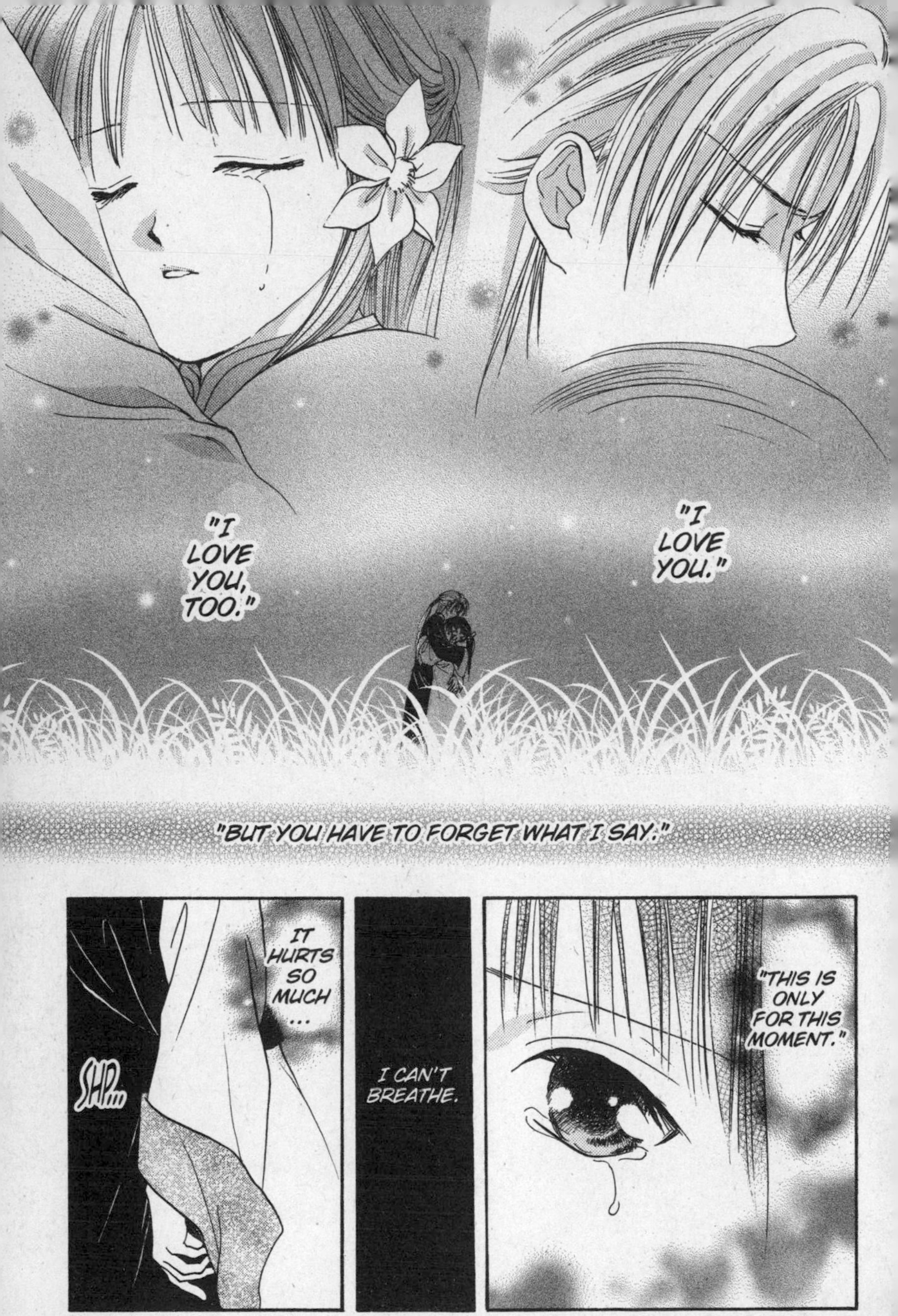
"I LOVE YOU."
"I LOVE YOU, TOO."
"BUT YOU HAVE TO FORGET WHAT I SAY."
"THIS IS ONLY FOR THIS MOMENT."
I CAN'T BREATHE.
IT HURTS SO MUCH...
SHP...

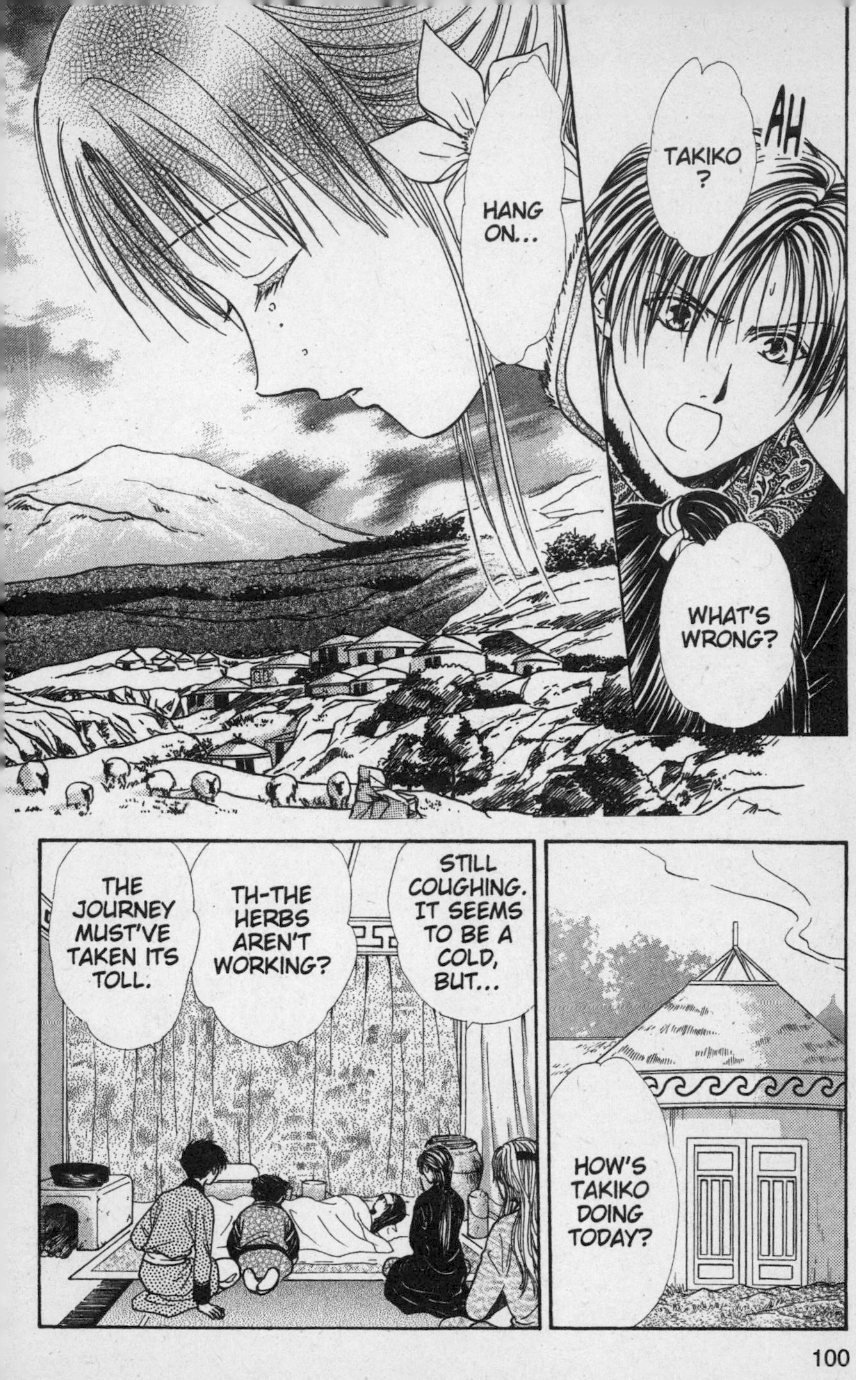
AH
TAKIKO?
WHAT'S WRONG?
HANG ON...
HOW'S TAKIKO DOING TODAY?
STILL COUGHING. IT SEEMS TO BE A COLD, BUT...
TH-THE HERBS AREN'T WORKING?
THE JOURNEY MUST'VE TAKEN ITS TOLL.

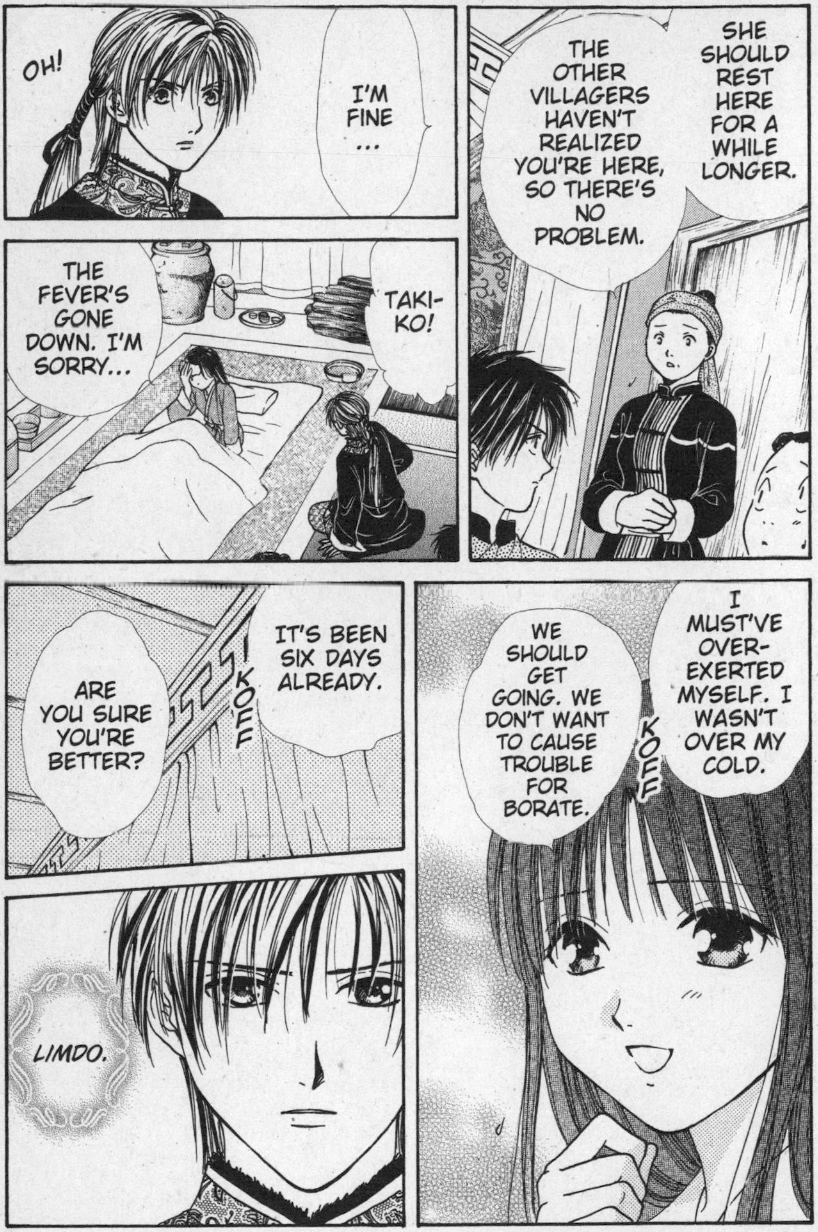
SHE SHOULD REST HERE FOR A WHILE LONGER.
THE OTHER VILLAGERS HAVEN'T REALIZED YOU'RE HERE, SO THERE'S NO PROBLEM.
I'M FINE ...
OH!
TAKI-KO!
THE FEVER'S GONE DOWN. I'M SORRY...
I MUST'VE OVER-EXERTED MYSELF. I WASN'T OVER MY COLD.
KOFF
WE SHOULD GET GOING. WE DON'T WANT TO CAUSE TROUBLE FOR BORATE.
IT'S BEEN SIX DAYS ALREADY.
KOFF
ARE YOU SURE YOU'RE BETTER?
LIMDO.

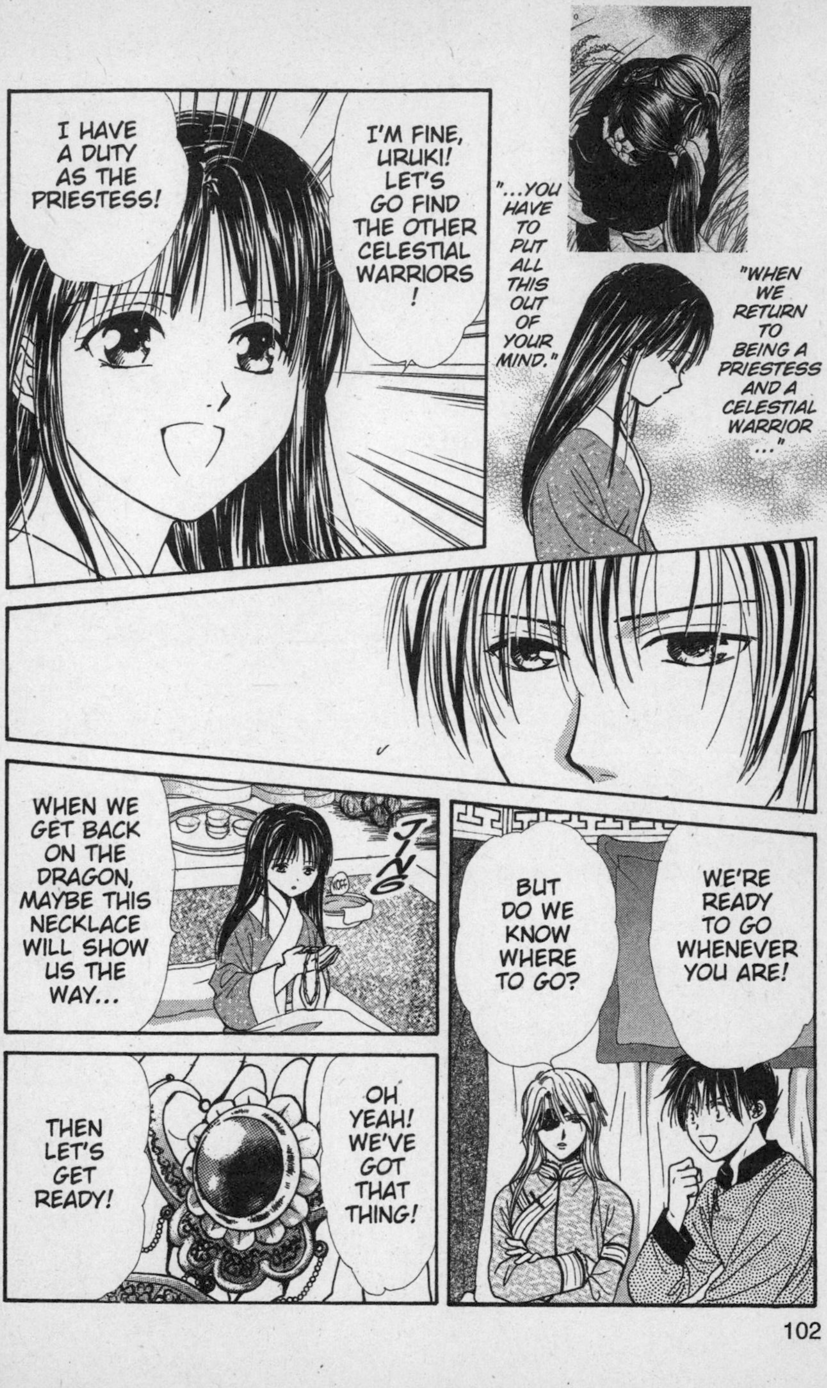
"WHEN WE RETURN TO BEING A PRIESTESS AND A CELESTIAL WARRIOR..."
"...YOU HAVE TO PUT ALL THIS OUT OF YOUR MIND."
I'M FINE, URUKI! LET'S GO FIND THE OTHER CELESTIAL WARRIORS!
I HAVE A DUTY AS THE PRIESTESS!
WE'RE READY TO GO WHENEVER YOU ARE!
BUT DO WE KNOW WHERE TO GO?
WHEN WE GET BACK ON THE DRAGON, MAYBE THIS NECKLACE WILL SHOW US THE WAY...
JING
KOFF
OH YEAH! WE'VE GOT THAT THING!
THEN LET'S GET READY!

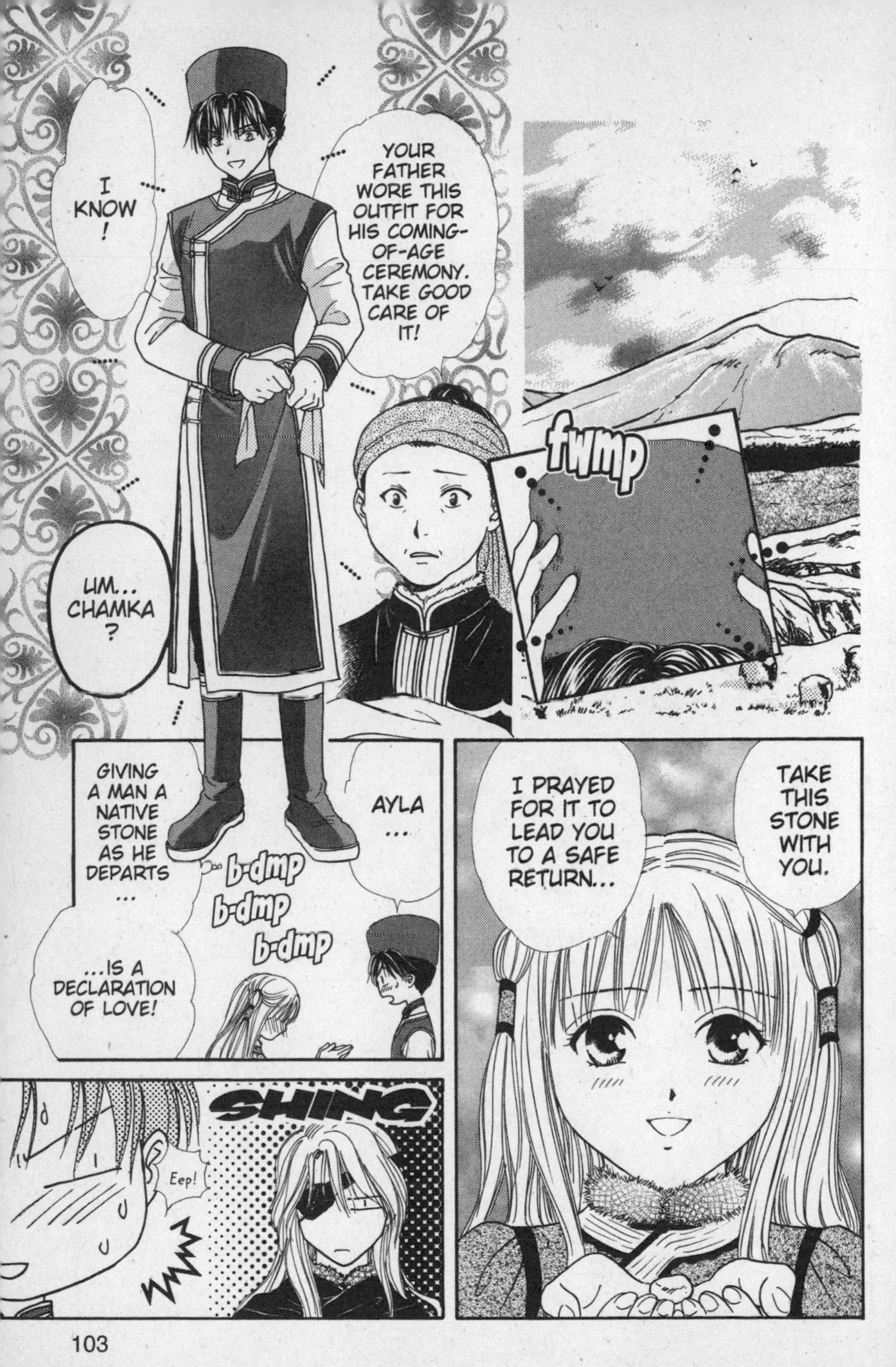

fwmp
YOUR FATHER WORE THIS OUTFIT FOR HIS COMING-OF-AGE CEREMONY. TAKE GOOD CARE OF IT!
I KNOW!
UM... CHAMKA?
TAKE THIS STONE WITH YOU.
I PRAYED FOR IT TO LEAD YOU TO A SAFE RETURN...
AYLA...
b-dmp
b-dmp
b-dmp
GIVING A MAN A NATIVE STONE AS HE DEPARTS...
...IS A DECLARATION OF LOVE!
SHING
Eep!

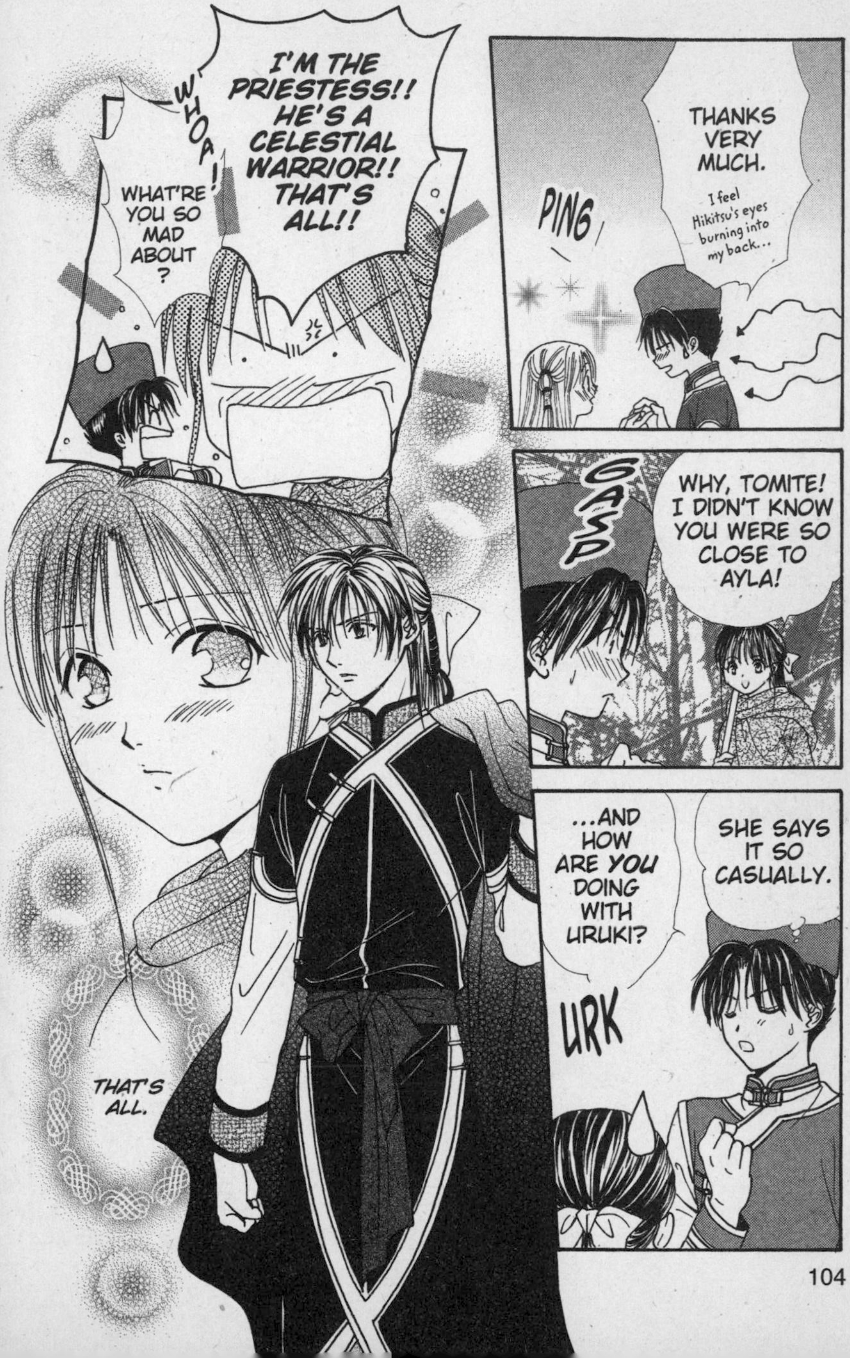
THANKS VERY MUCH.
I feel Hikitsu's eyes burning into my back...
PING
WHY, TOMITE! I DIDN'T KNOW YOU WERE SO CLOSE TO AYLA!
GASP
SHE SAYS IT SO CASUALLY.
...AND HOW ARE *YOU* DOING WITH URUKI?
URK
I'M THE PRIESTESS!! HE'S A CELESTIAL WARRIOR!! THAT'S ALL!!
WHOA!
WHAT'RE YOU SO MAD ABOUT?
THAT'S ALL.

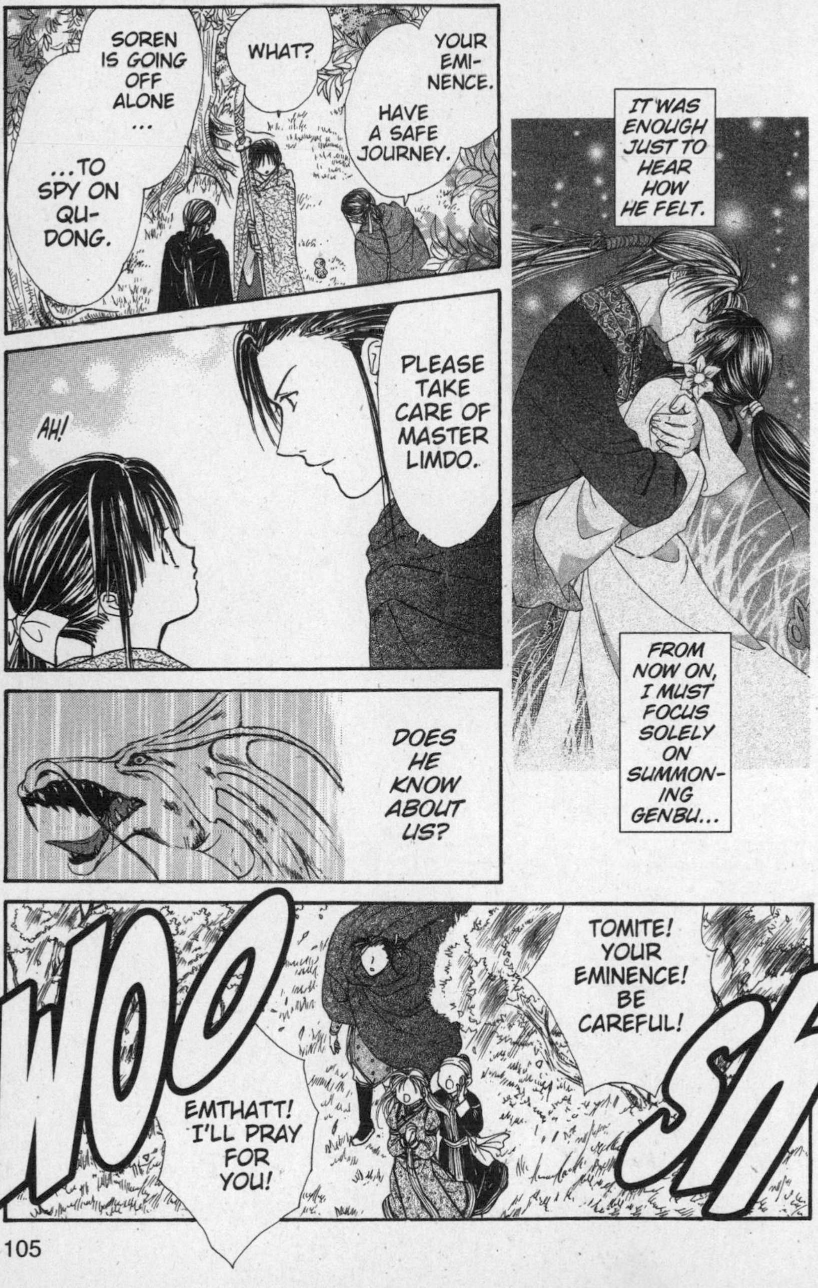
IT WAS ENOUGH JUST TO HEAR HOW HE FELT.
FROM NOW ON, I MUST FOCUS SOLELY ON SUMMONING GENBU...
YOUR EMINENCE.
HAVE A SAFE JOURNEY.
WHAT?
SOREN IS GOING OFF ALONE ...
...TO SPY ON QU-DONG.
PLEASE TAKE CARE OF MASTER LIMDO.
AH!
DOES HE KNOW ABOUT US?
TOMITE! YOUR EMINENCE! BE CAREFUL!
SH
EMTHATT! I'LL PRAY FOR YOU!
WHOO

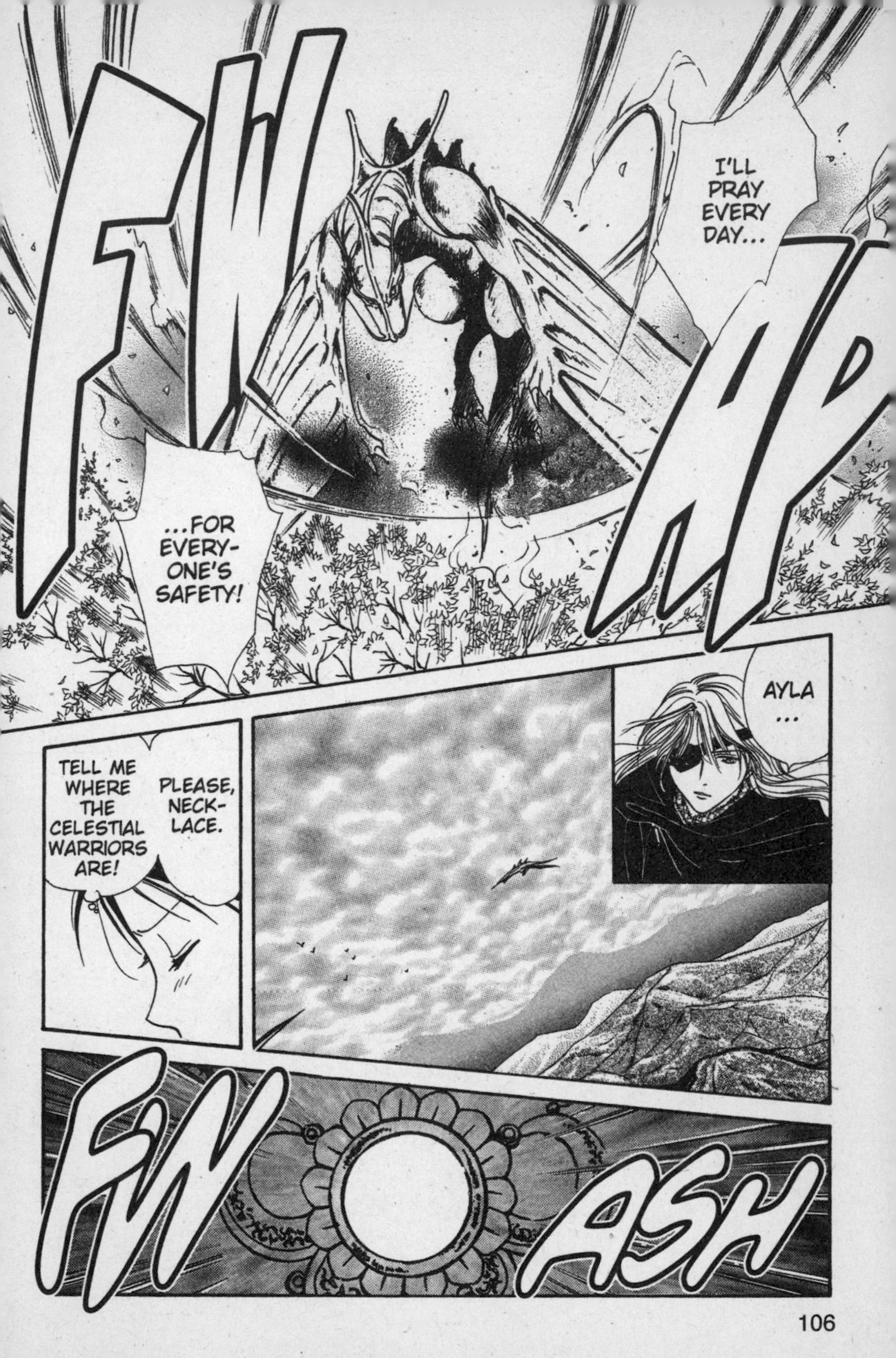
FWAP
I'LL PRAY EVERY DAY...
...FOR EVERY-ONE'S SAFETY!
AYLA ...
PLEASE, NECK-LACE.
TELL ME WHERE THE CELESTIAL WARRIORS ARE!
FWASH

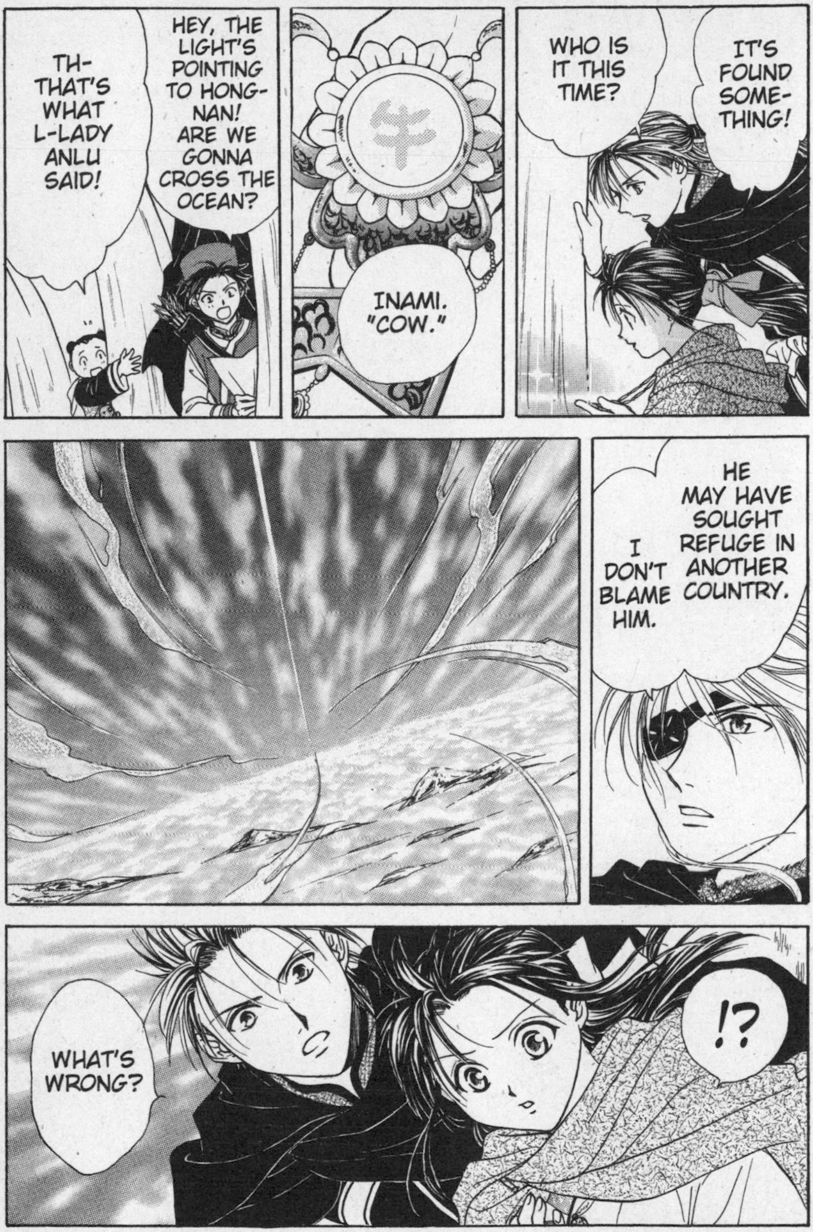
IT'S FOUND SOME-THING!
WHO IS IT THIS TIME?
牛
INAMI. "COW."
HEY, THE LIGHT'S POINTING TO HONG-NAN! ARE WE GONNA CROSS THE OCEAN?
TH-THAT'S WHAT L-LADY ANLU SAID!
HE MAY HAVE SOUGHT REFUGE IN ANOTHER COUNTRY.
I DON'T BLAME HIM.
!?
WHAT'S WRONG?

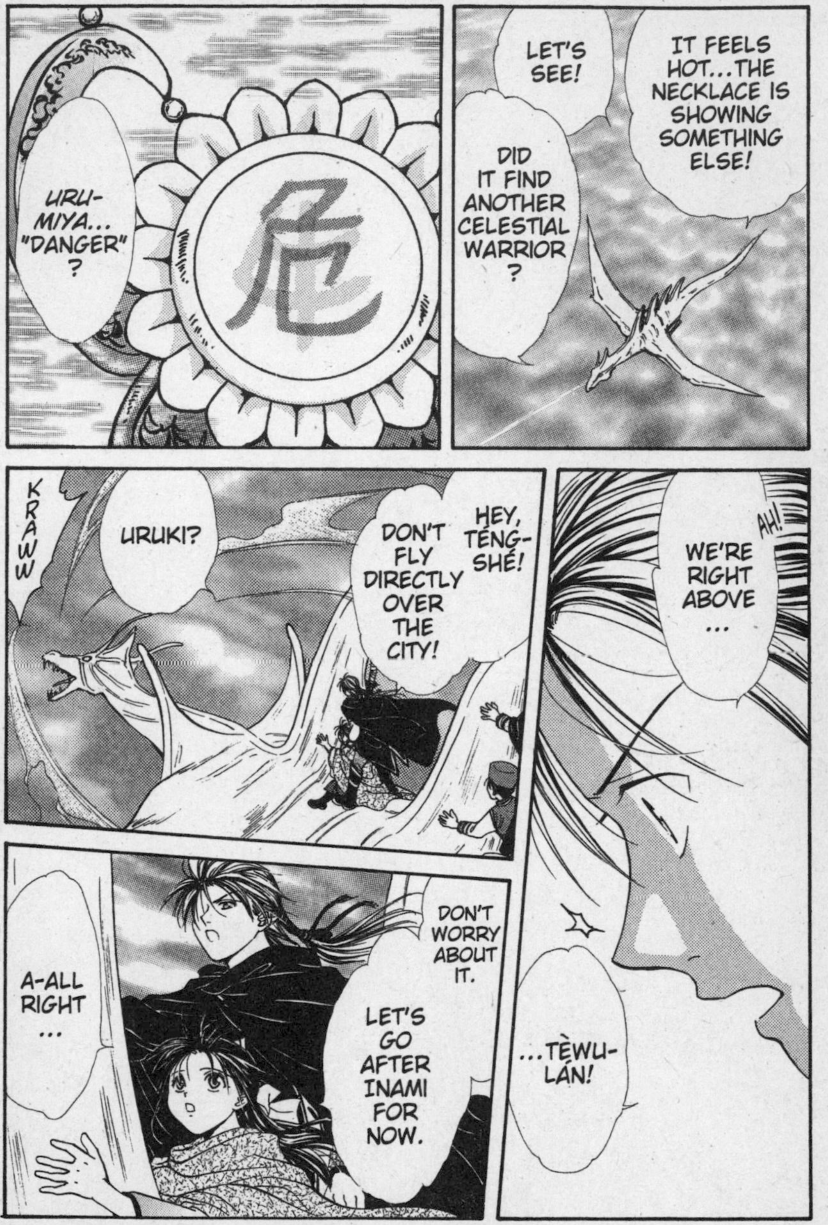
IT FEELS HOT...THE NECKLACE IS SHOWING SOMETHING ELSE!
LET'S SEE!
DID IT FIND ANOTHER CELESTIAL WARRIOR?
危
URU-MIYA... "DANGER"?
AH!
WE'RE RIGHT ABOVE...
...TÈWULÁN!
HEY, TÉNG-SHÉ!
DON'T FLY DIRECTLY OVER THE CITY!
URUKI?
KRAWW
DON'T WORRY ABOUT IT.
LET'S GO AFTER INAMI FOR NOW.
A-ALL RIGHT...

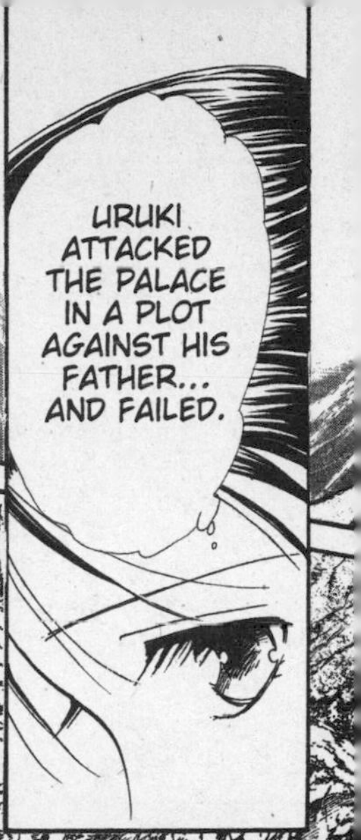
URUKI ATTACKED THE PALACE IN A PLOT AGAINST HIS FATHER... AND FAILED.

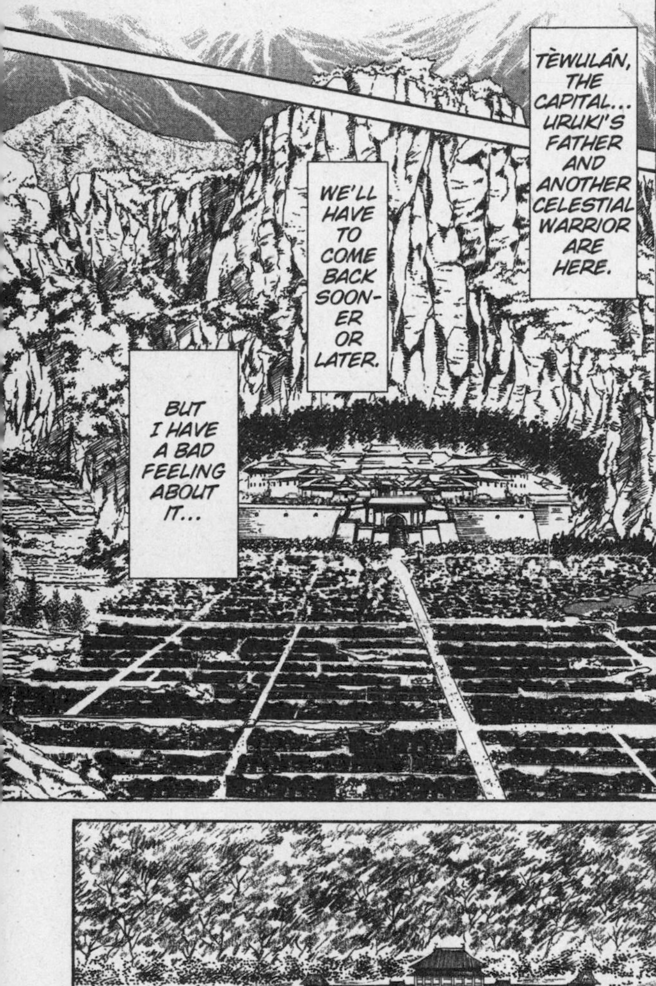
TÈWULÁN, THE CAPITAL... URUKI'S FATHER AND ANOTHER CELESTIAL WARRIOR ARE HERE.
WE'LL HAVE TO COME BACK SOONER OR LATER.
BUT I HAVE A BAD FEELING ABOUT IT...

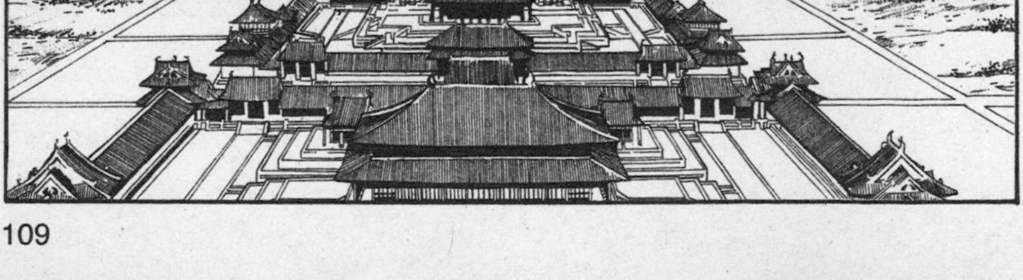

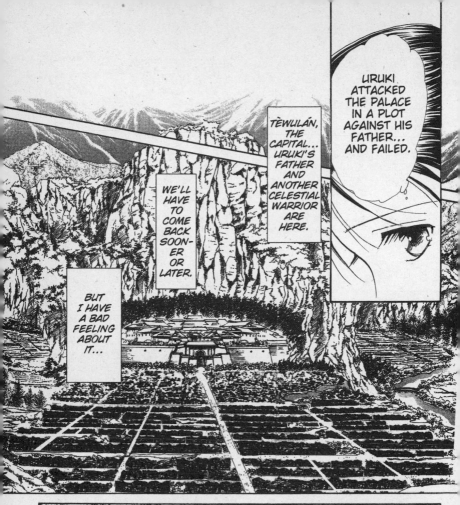

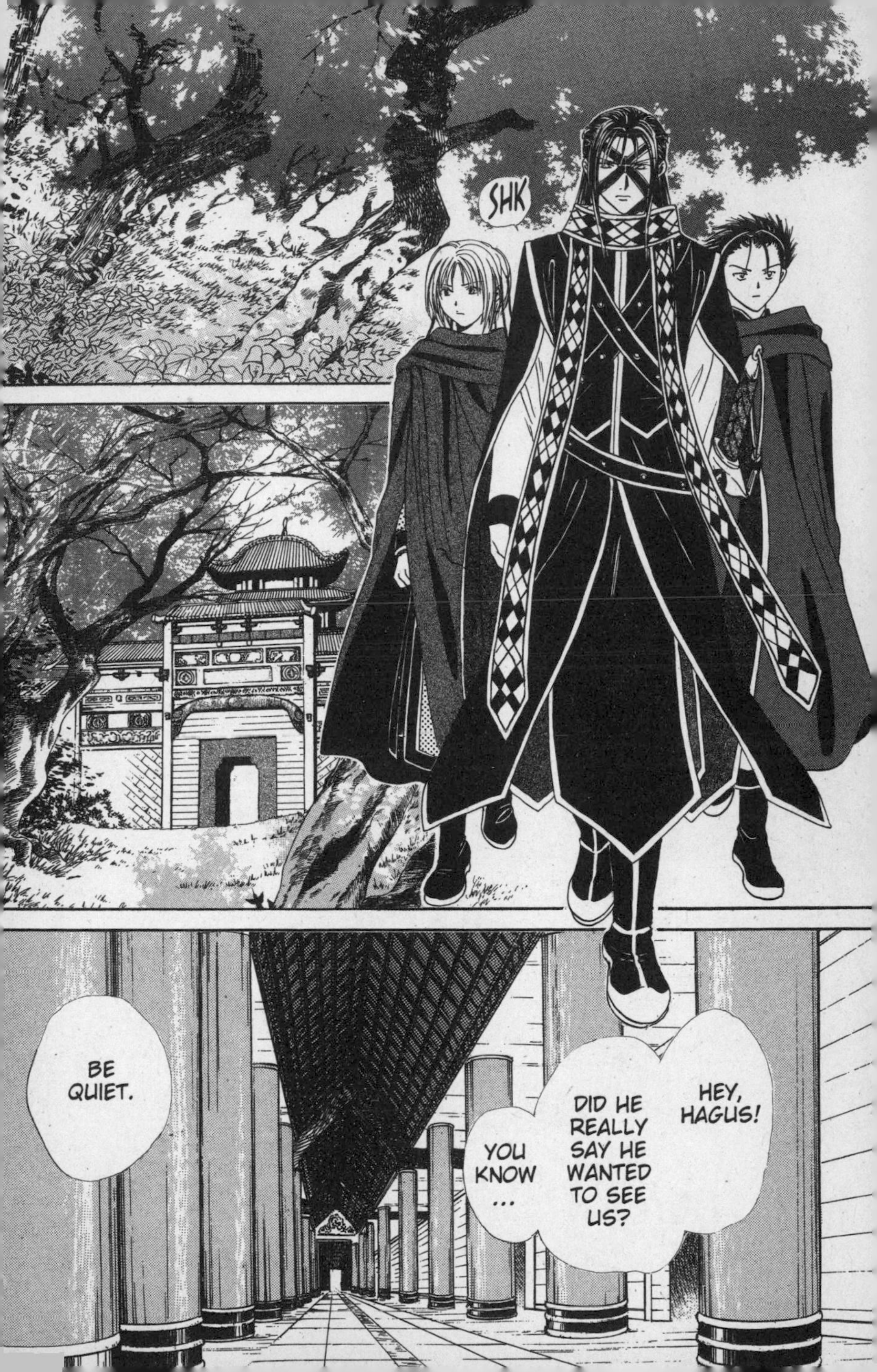
SHK
HEY, HAGUS!
DID HE REALLY SAY HE WANTED TO SEE US?
YOU KNOW ...
BE QUIET.

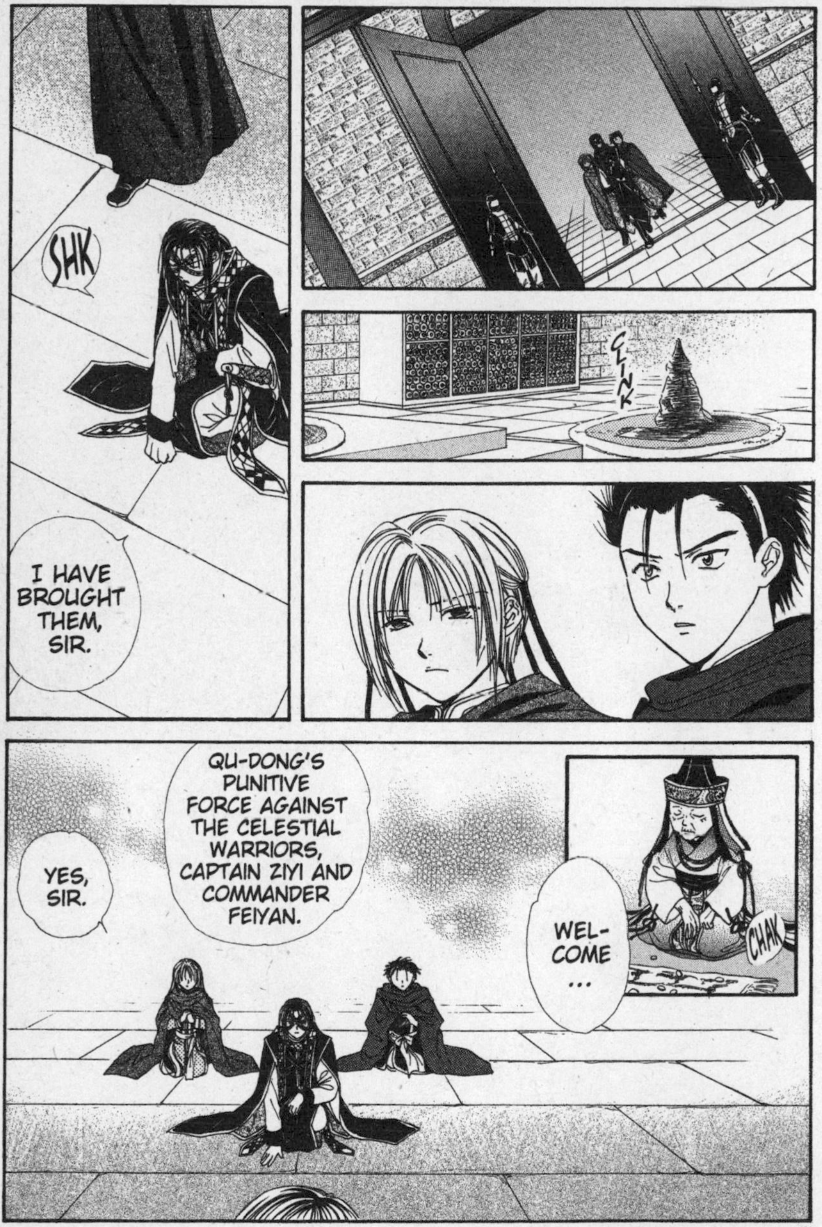
CLINK
SHK
I HAVE BROUGHT THEM, SIR.
CHAK
WEL-COME ...
QU-DONG'S PUNITIVE FORCE AGAINST THE CELESTIAL WARRIORS, CAPTAIN ZIYI AND COMMANDER FEIYAN.
YES, SIR.

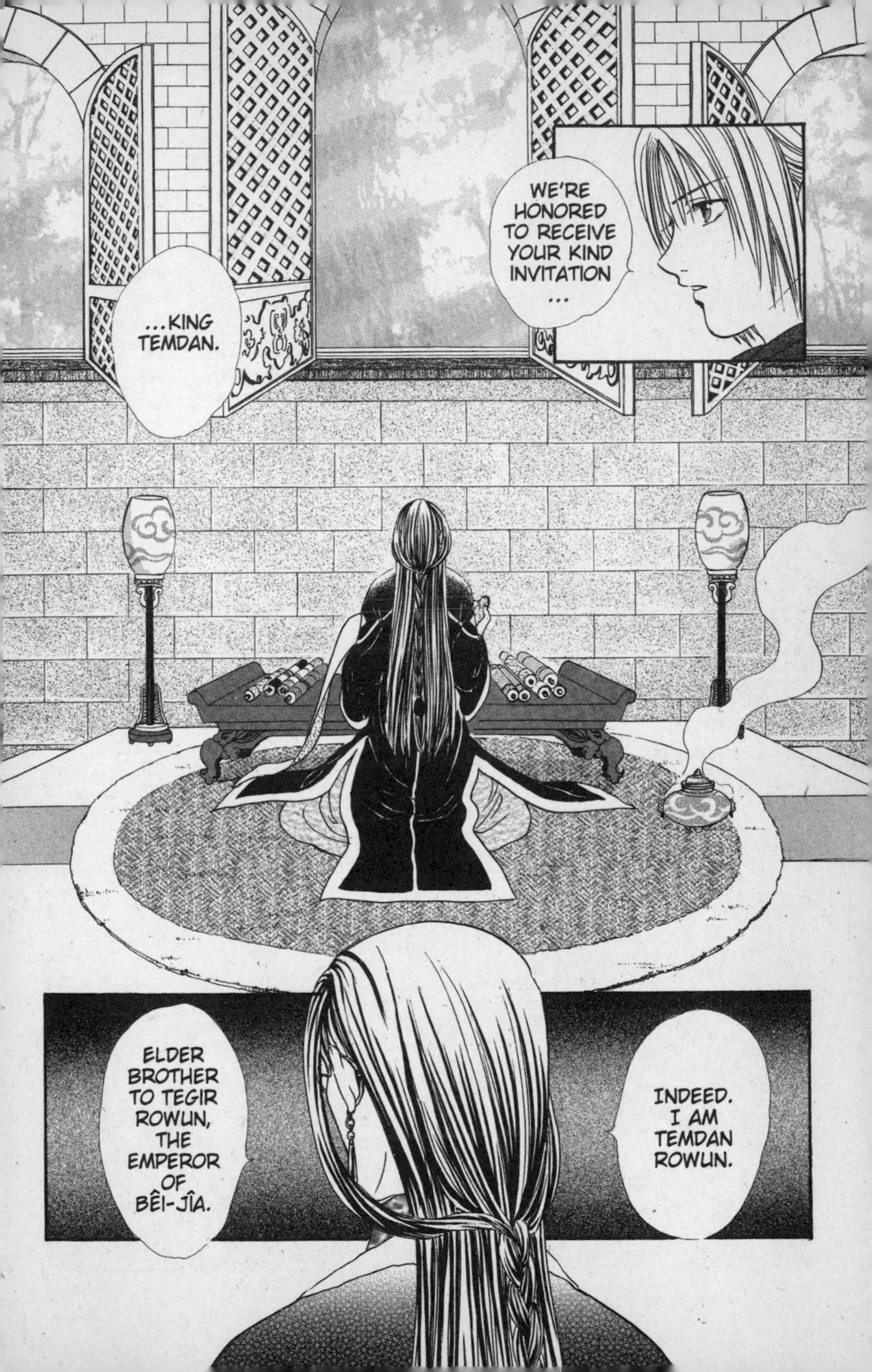
WE'RE HONORED TO RECEIVE YOUR KIND INVITATION ...
...KING TEMDAN.
INDEED. I AM TEMDAN ROWUN.
ELDER BROTHER TO TEGIR ROWUN, THE EMPEROR OF BÊI-JÎA.

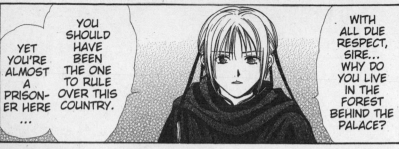

WITH ALL DUE RESPECT, SIRE... WHY DO YOU LIVE IN THE FOREST BEHIND THE PALACE?
YOU SHOULD HAVE BEEN THE ONE TO RULE OVER THIS COUNTRY.
YET YOU'RE ALMOST A PRISON-ER HERE...
HEH...
LORD FEIYAN... HOW DO YOU LIKE YOUR NEW ARM?
THE IRON AND LEAD INDUS-TRIES THRIVE IN THIS REGION.
THERE ARE MANY SKILLED ARTISANS.
SLP...
!?
MY OWN ARM, LONG SINCE SLOUGHED OFF, HAS LIKEWISE BEEN REPAIRED.
CH-CHK...

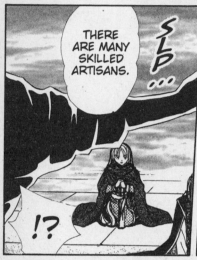

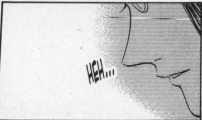

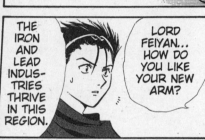

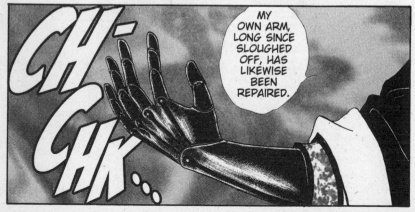

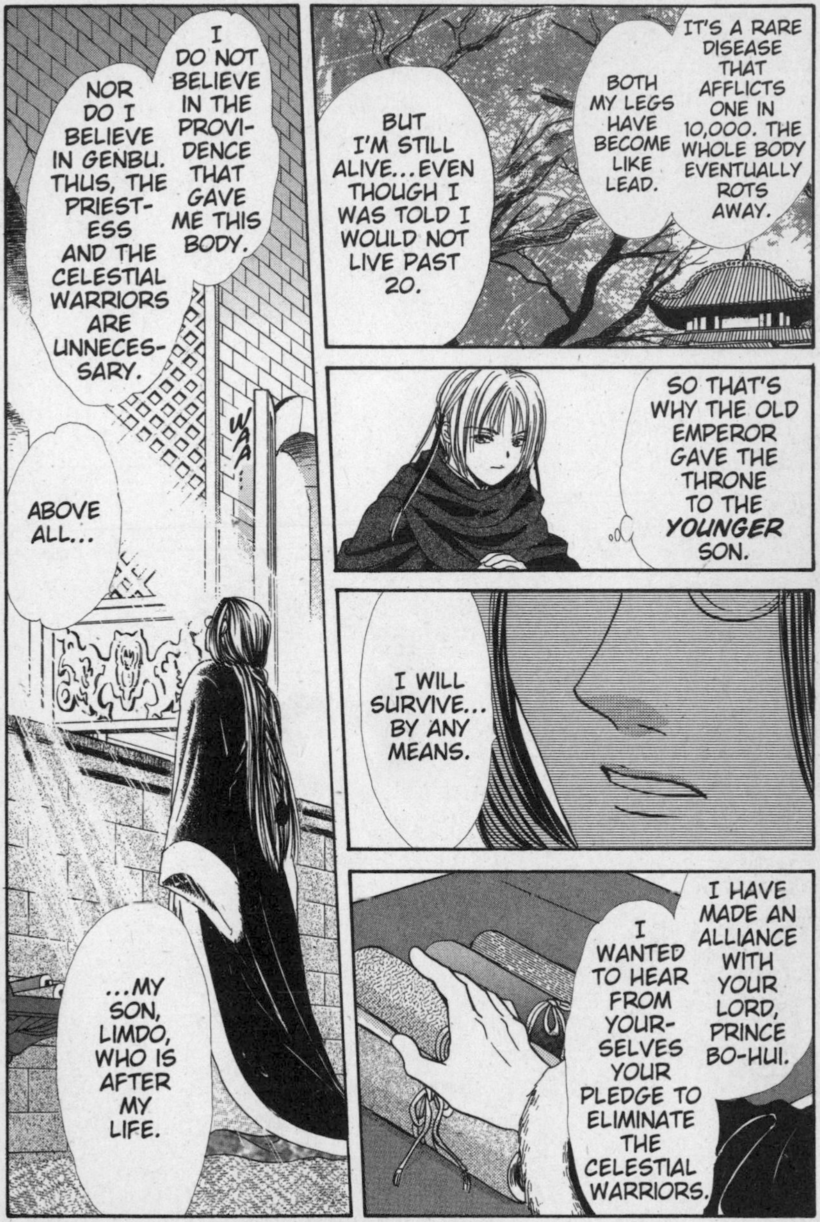
IT'S A RARE DISEASE THAT AFFLICTS ONE IN 10,000. THE WHOLE BODY EVENTUALLY ROTS AWAY.
BOTH MY LEGS HAVE BECOME LIKE LEAD.
BUT I'M STILL ALIVE...EVEN THOUGH I WAS TOLD I WOULD NOT LIVE PAST 20.
SO THAT'S WHY THE OLD EMPEROR GAVE THE THRONE TO THE *YOUNGER* SON.
I WILL SURVIVE... BY ANY MEANS.
I HAVE MADE AN ALLIANCE WITH YOUR LORD, PRINCE BO-HUI.
I WANTED TO HEAR FROM YOUR-SELVES YOUR PLEDGE TO ELIMINATE THE CELESTIAL WARRIORS.
I DO NOT BELIEVE IN THE PROVI-DENCE THAT GAVE ME THIS BODY.
NOR DO I BELIEVE IN GENBU. THUS, THE PRIEST-ESS AND THE CELESTIAL WARRIORS ARE UNNECES-SARY.
ABOVE ALL...
...MY SON, LIMDO, WHO IS AFTER MY LIFE.

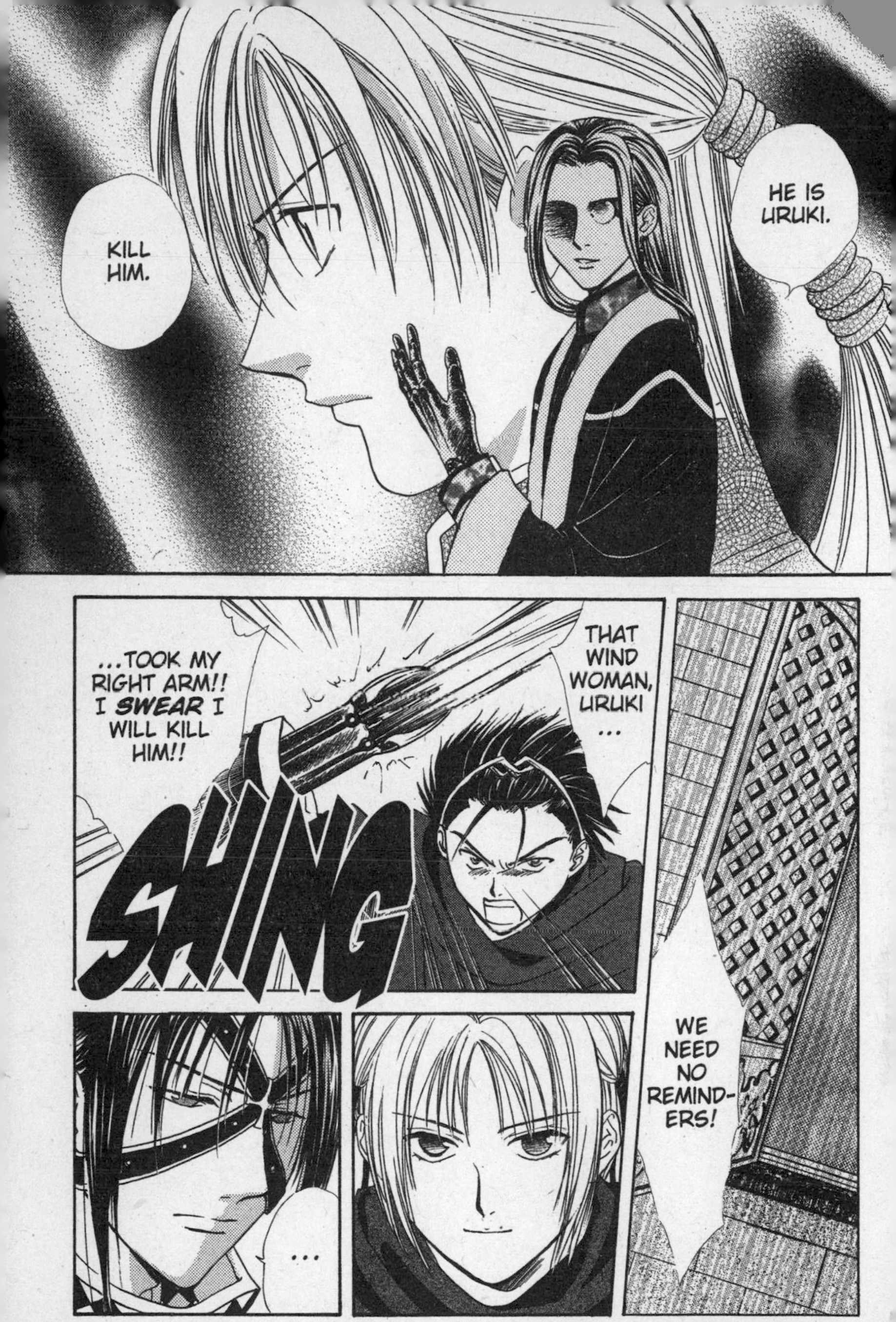
HE IS URUKI.
KILL HIM.
WE NEED NO REMINDERS!
THAT WIND WOMAN, URUKI ...
...TOOK MY RIGHT ARM!! I *SWEAR* I WILL KILL HIM!!
SHING
...

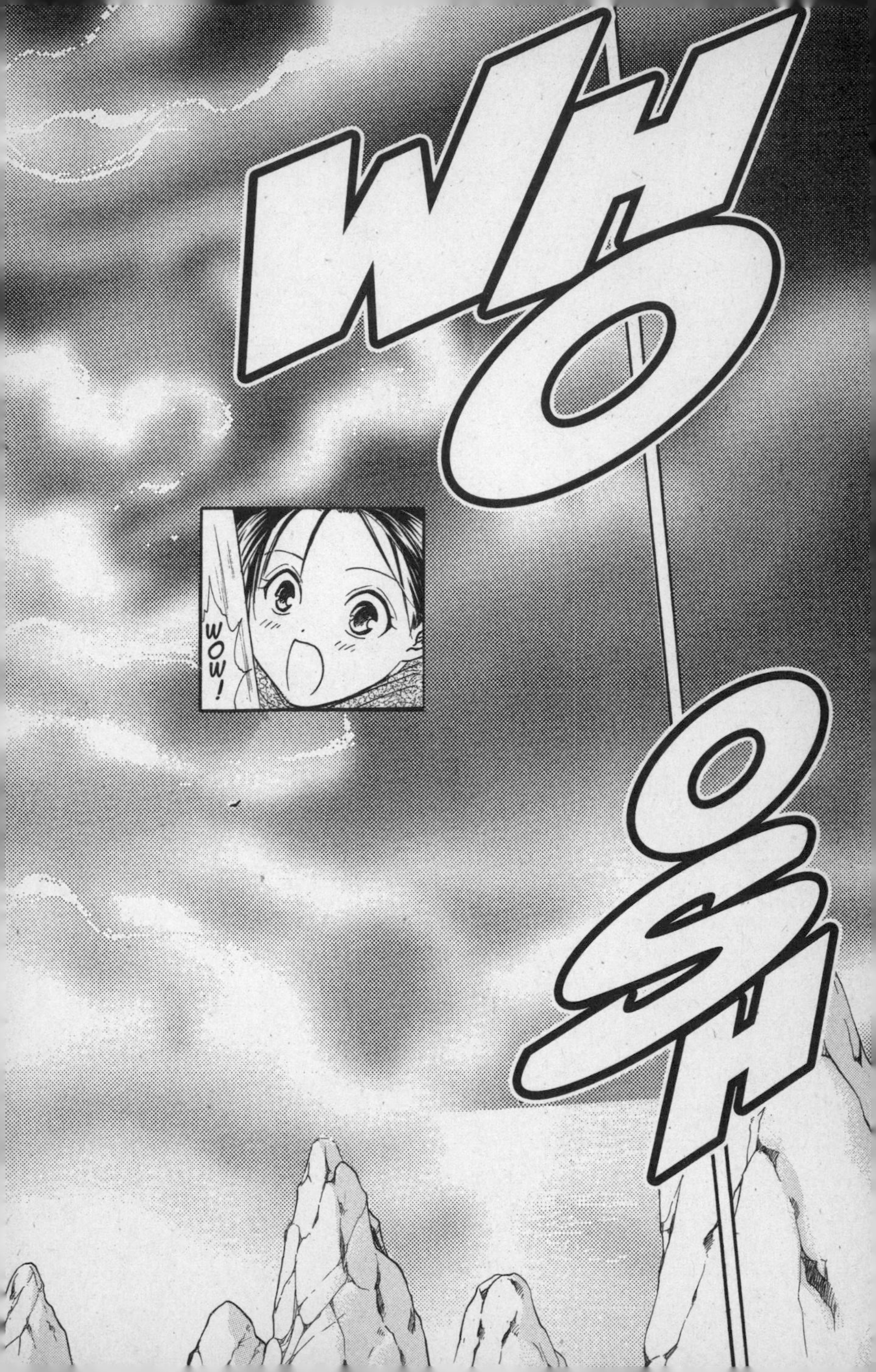
WHOOOSH
WOW!

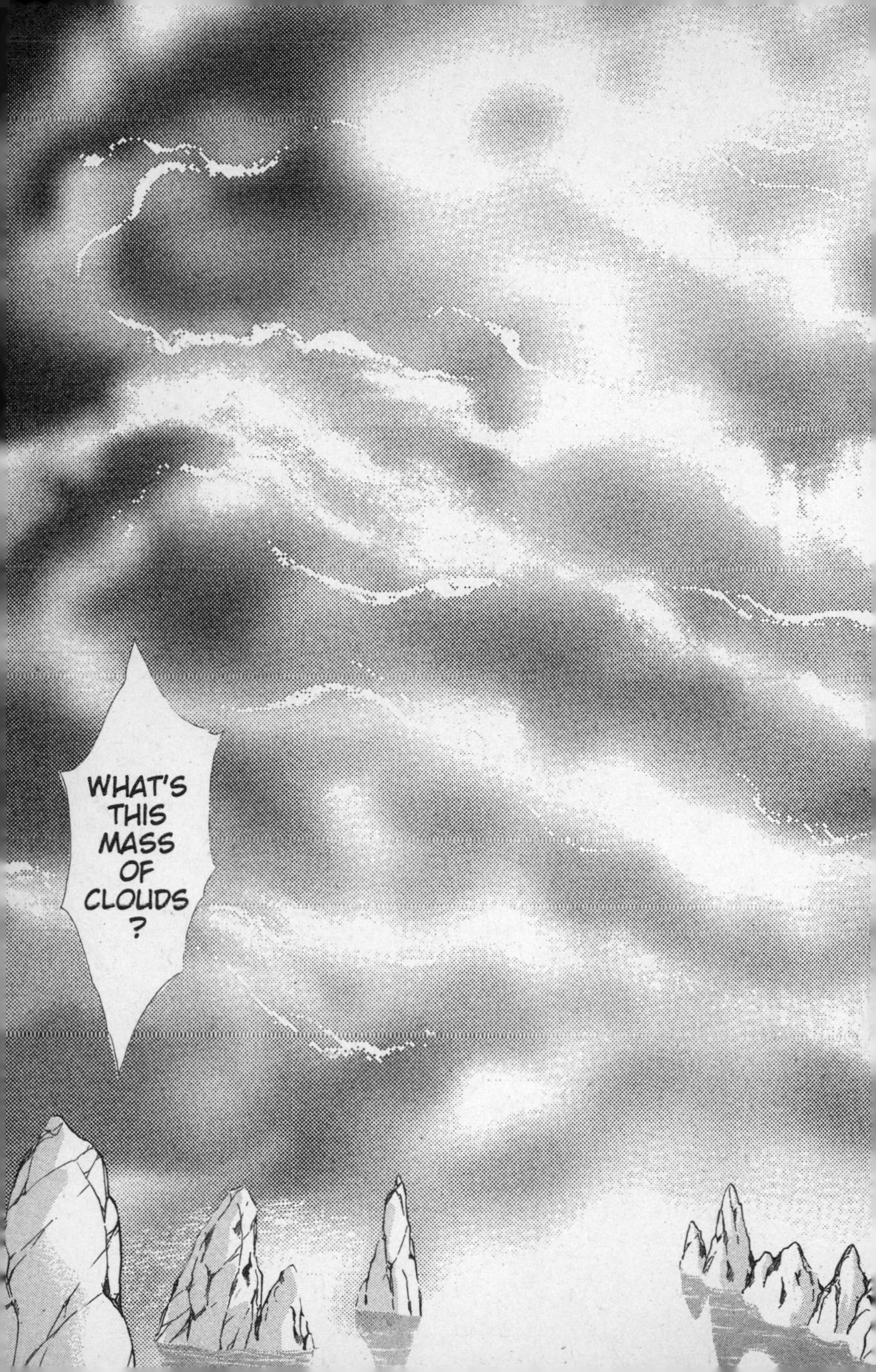
WHAT'S THIS MASS OF CLOUDS ?

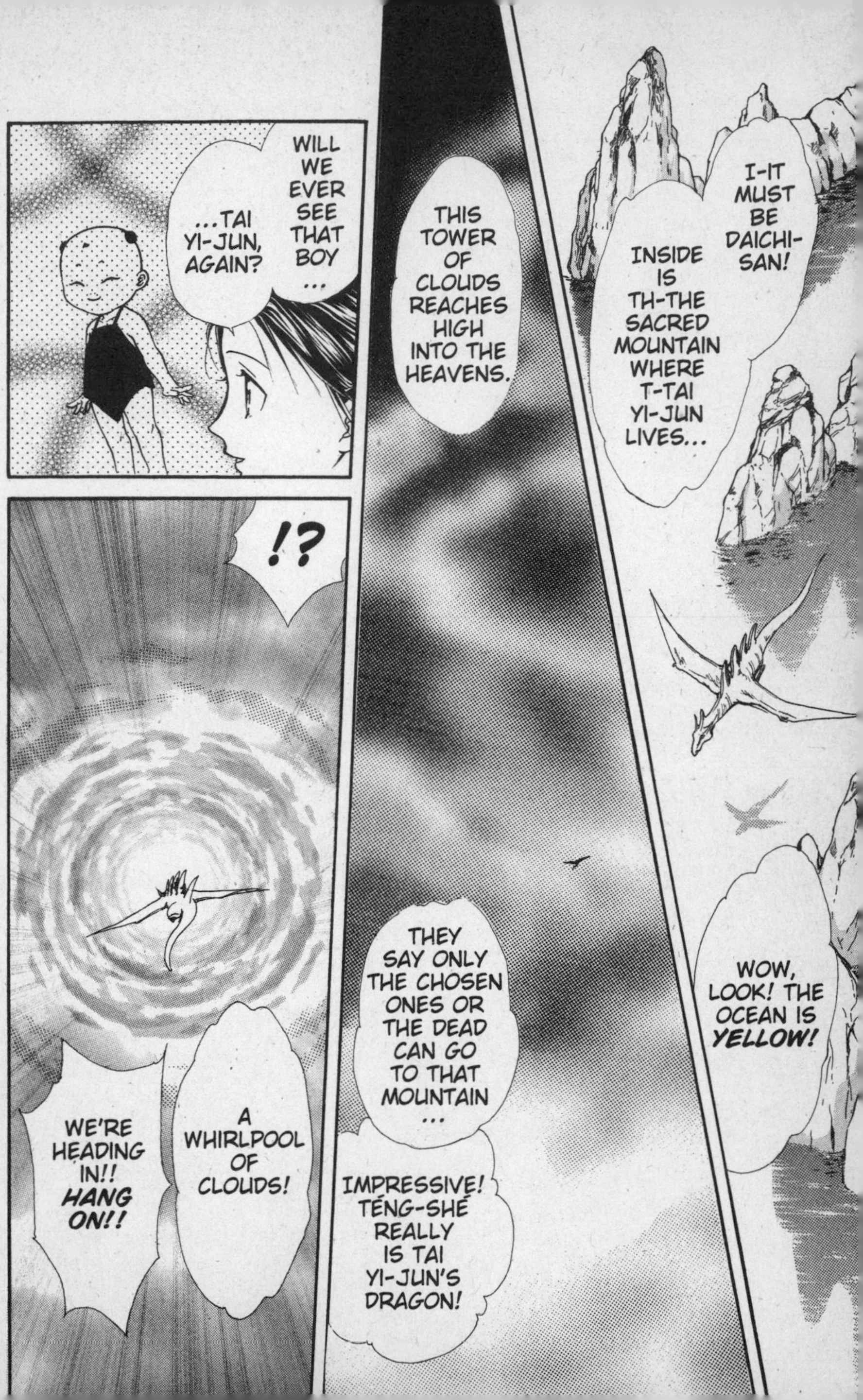
I-IT MUST BE DAICHI-SAN!
INSIDE IS TH-THE SACRED MOUNTAIN WHERE T-TAI YI-JUN LIVES...
WOW, LOOK! THE OCEAN IS *YELLOW!*
THIS TOWER OF CLOUDS REACHES HIGH INTO THE HEAVENS.
THEY SAY ONLY THE CHOSEN ONES OR THE DEAD CAN GO TO THAT MOUNTAIN...
IMPRESSIVE! TÉNG-SHÉ REALLY IS TAI YI-JUN'S DRAGON!
WILL WE EVER SEE THAT BOY...
...TAI YI-JUN, AGAIN?
!?
A WHIRLPOOL OF CLOUDS!
WE'RE HEADING IN!! *HANG ON!!*

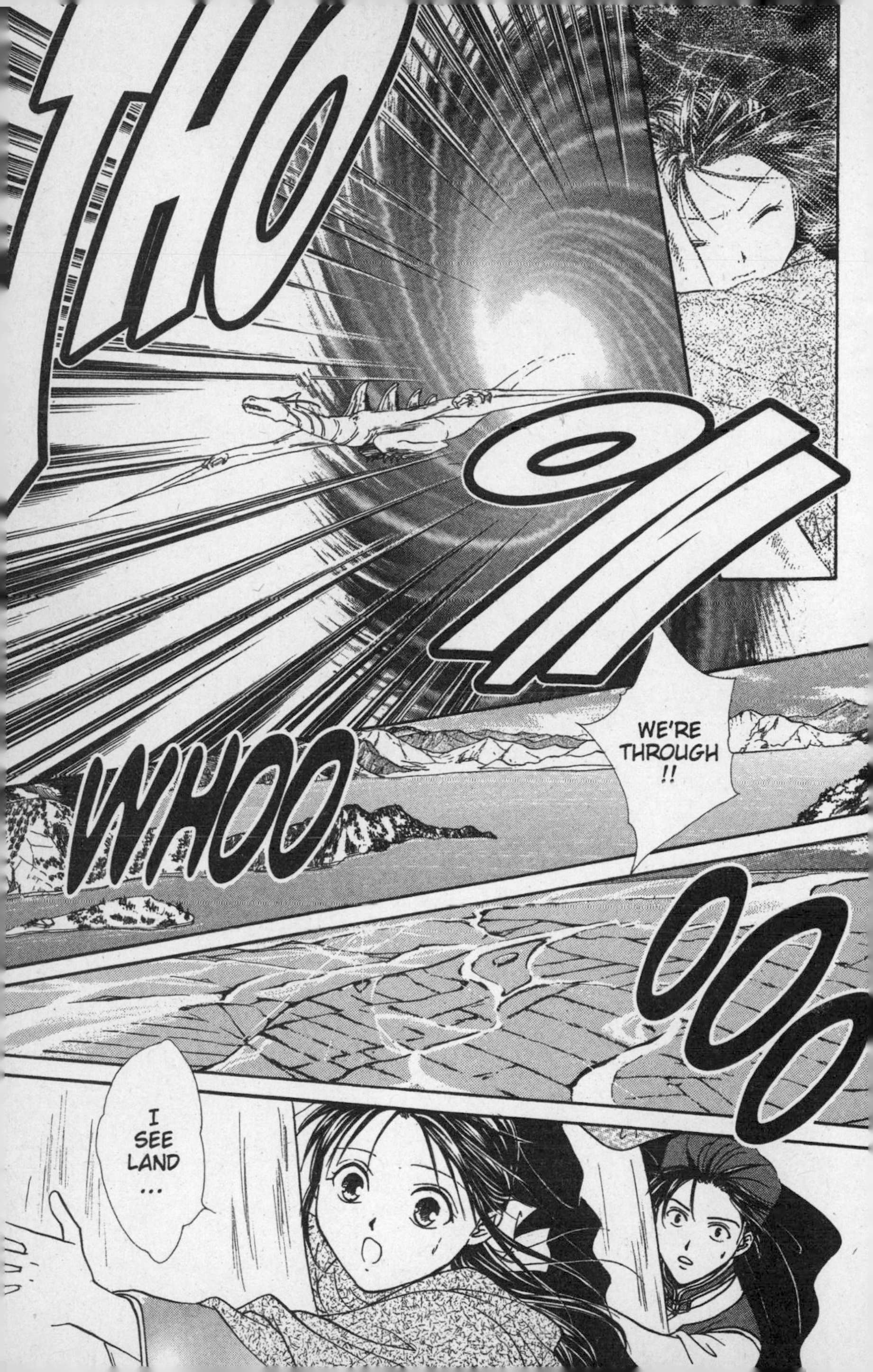
THO
WE'RE THROUGH !!
WHOOOOO
I SEE LAND ...

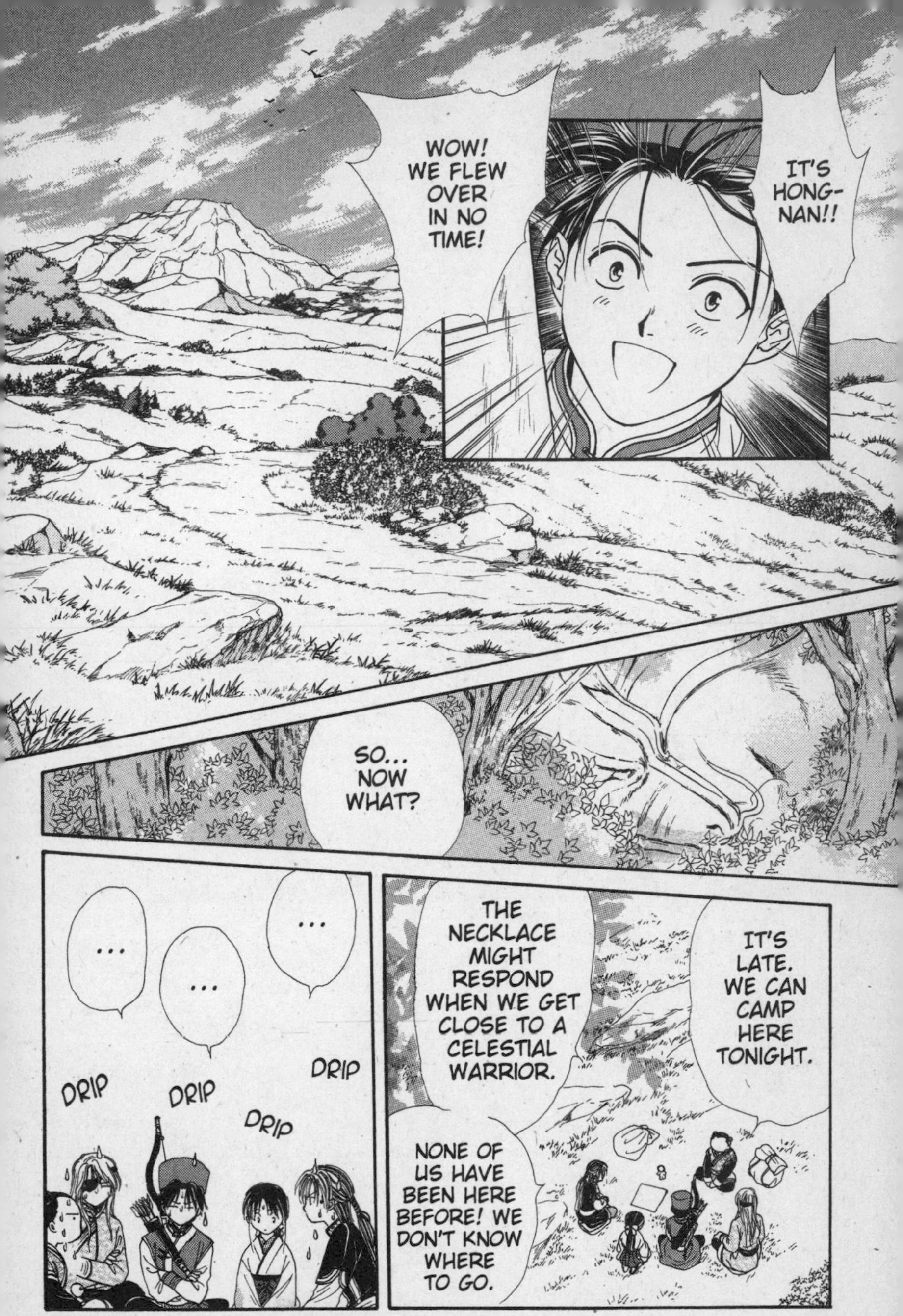
IT'S HONG-NAN!!
WOW! WE FLEW OVER IN NO TIME!
SO... NOW WHAT?
IT'S LATE. WE CAN CAMP HERE TONIGHT.
THE NECKLACE MIGHT RESPOND WHEN WE GET CLOSE TO A CELESTIAL WARRIOR.
NONE OF US HAVE BEEN HERE BEFORE! WE DON'T KNOW WHERE TO GO.
...
...
...
DRIP
DRIP
DRIP
DRIP

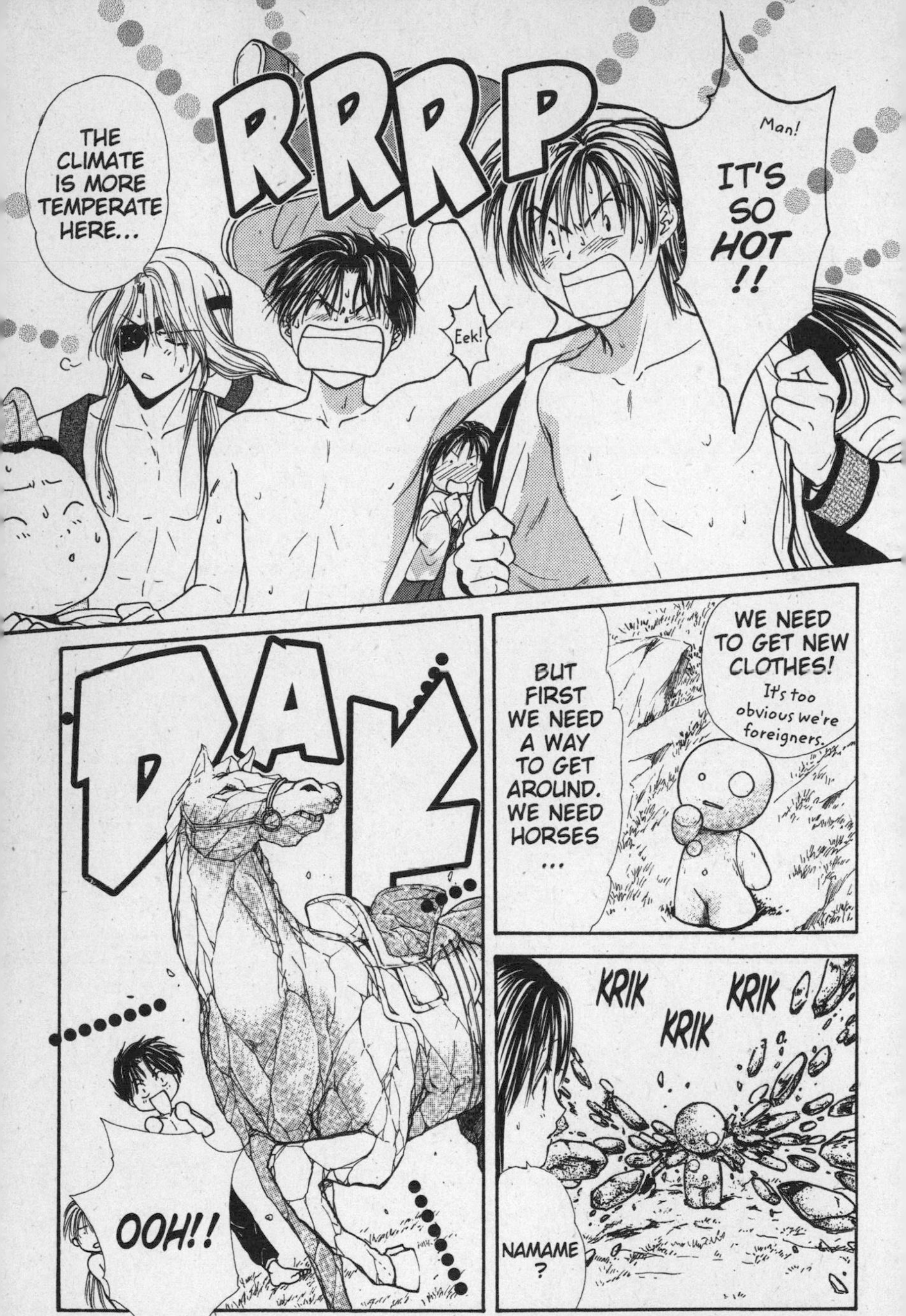
Man!
IT'S SO HOT!!
RRRP
Eek!
THE CLIMATE IS MORE TEMPERATE HERE...
WE NEED TO GET NEW CLOTHES! It's too obvious we're foreigners.
BUT FIRST WE NEED A WAY TO GET AROUND. WE NEED HORSES ...
KRIK
KRIK
KRIK
NAMAME ?
DAK
OOH!!

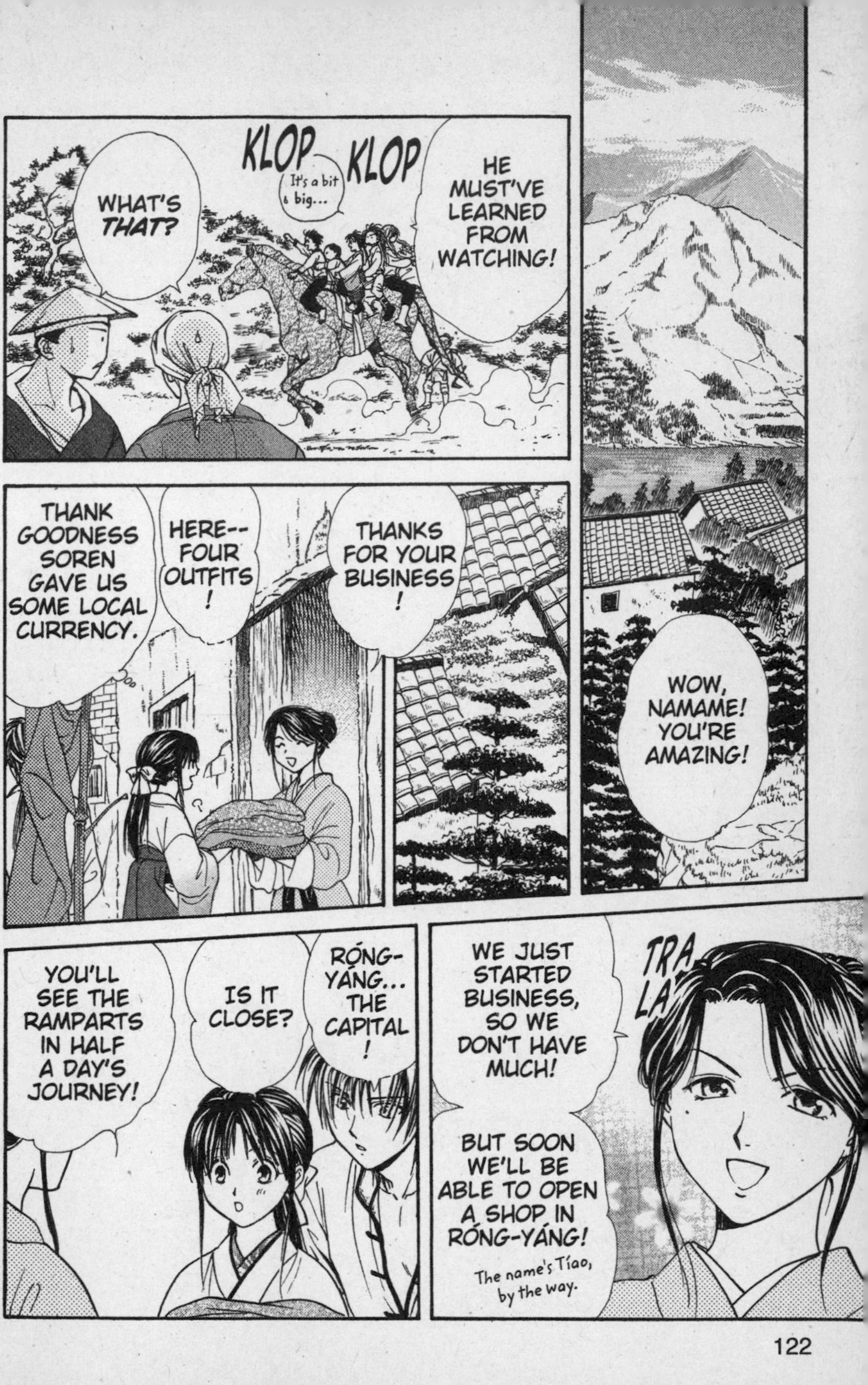
WOW, NAMAME! YOU'RE AMAZING!
HE MUST'VE LEARNED FROM WATCHING!
KLOP KLOP
It's a bit big...
WHAT'S *THAT?*
THANKS FOR YOUR BUSINESS!
HERE--FOUR OUTFITS!
THANK GOODNESS SOREN GAVE US SOME LOCAL CURRENCY.
TRA LA
WE JUST STARTED BUSINESS, SO WE DON'T HAVE MUCH!
BUT SOON WE'LL BE ABLE TO OPEN A SHOP IN RÓNG-YÁNG!
The name's Tíao, by the way.
RÓNG-YÁNG... THE CAPITAL!
IS IT CLOSE?
YOU'LL SEE THE RAMPARTS IN HALF A DAY'S JOURNEY!

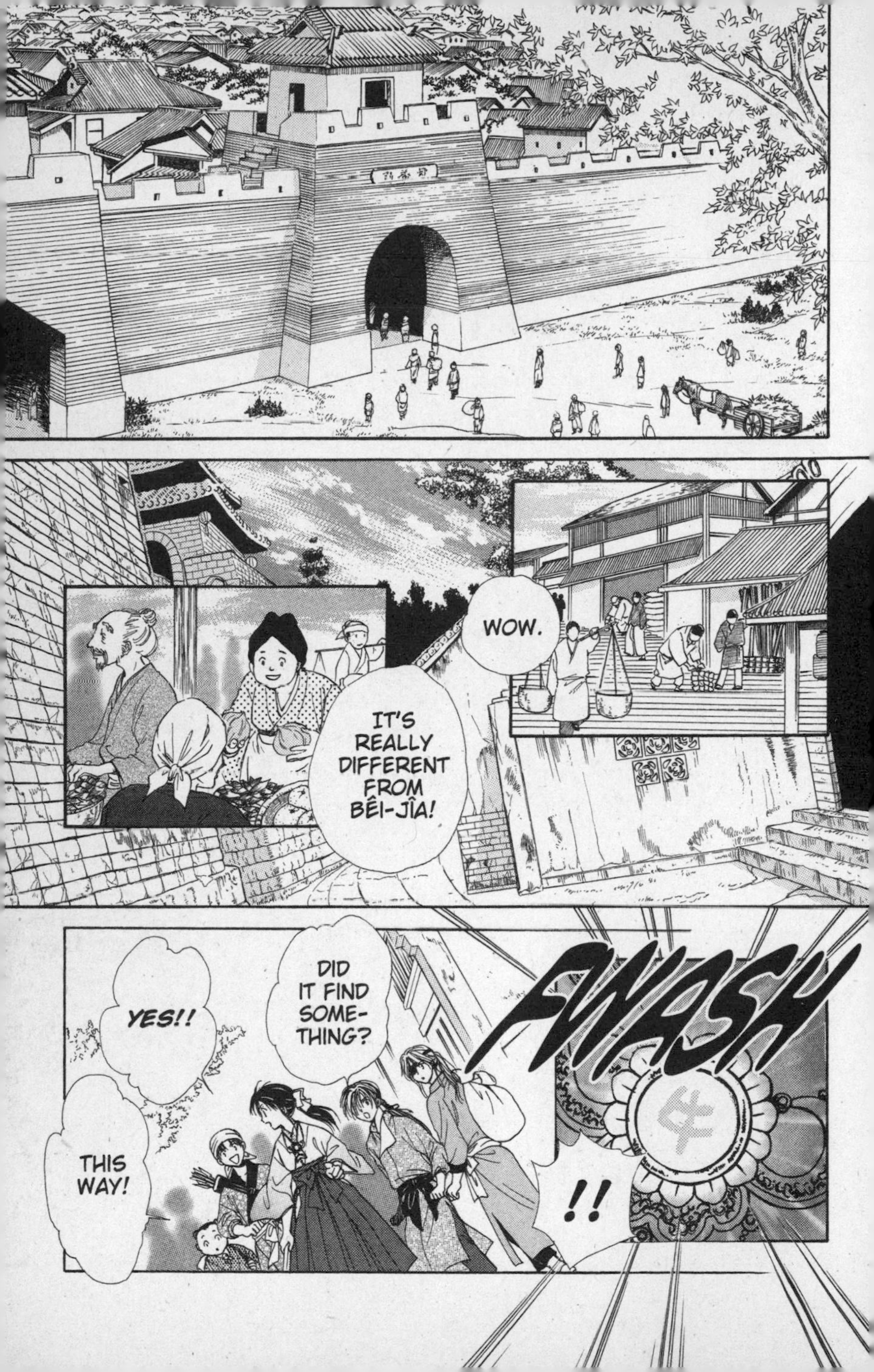
WOW.
IT'S REALLY DIFFERENT FROM BÊI-JÎA!
FWASH
!!
DID IT FIND SOME-THING?
YES!!
THIS WAY!

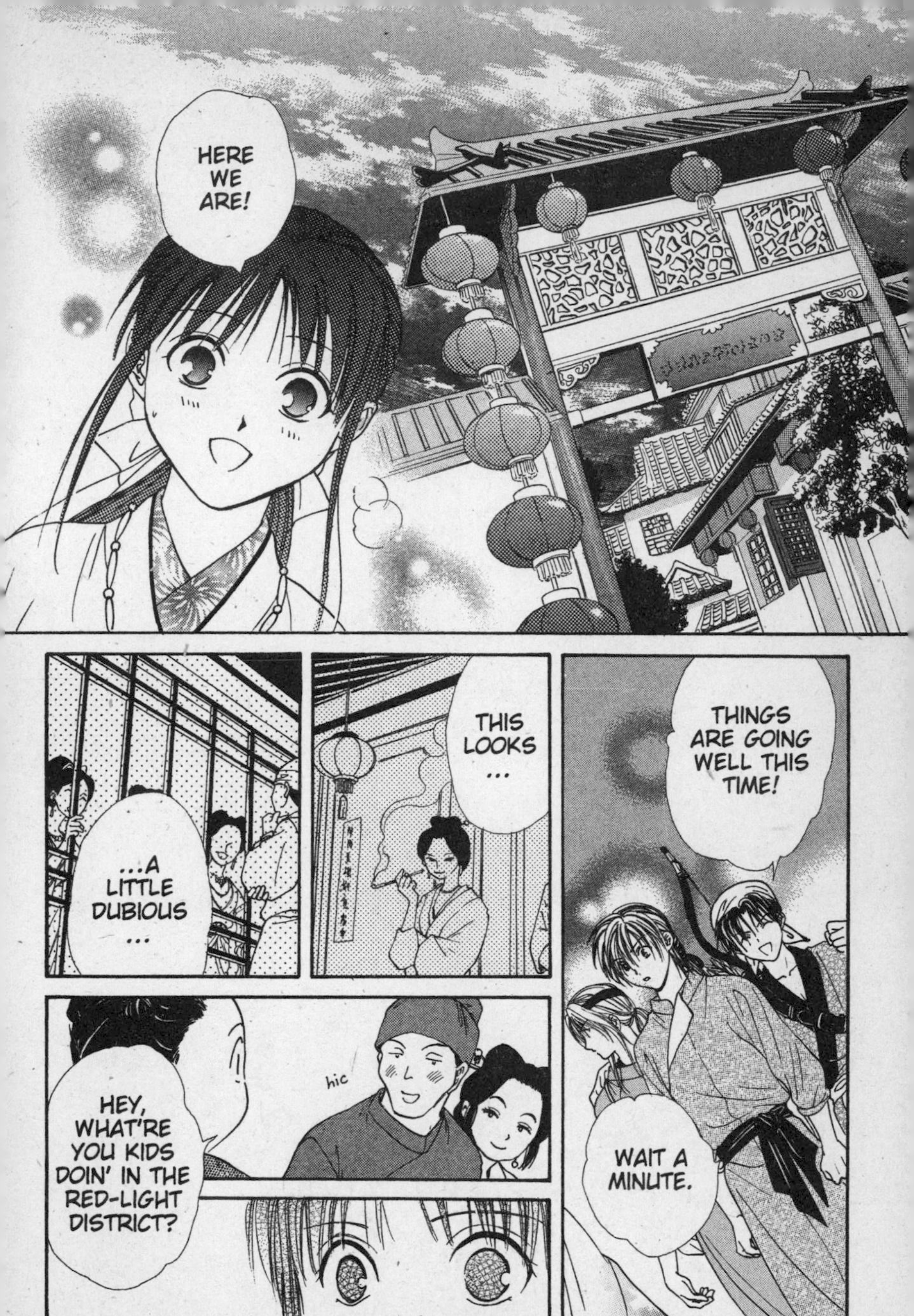
HERE WE ARE!
THINGS ARE GOING WELL THIS TIME!
WAIT A MINUTE.
THIS LOOKS ...
...A LITTLE DUBIOUS ...
hic
HEY, WHAT'RE YOU KIDS DOIN' IN THE RED-LIGHT DISTRICT?

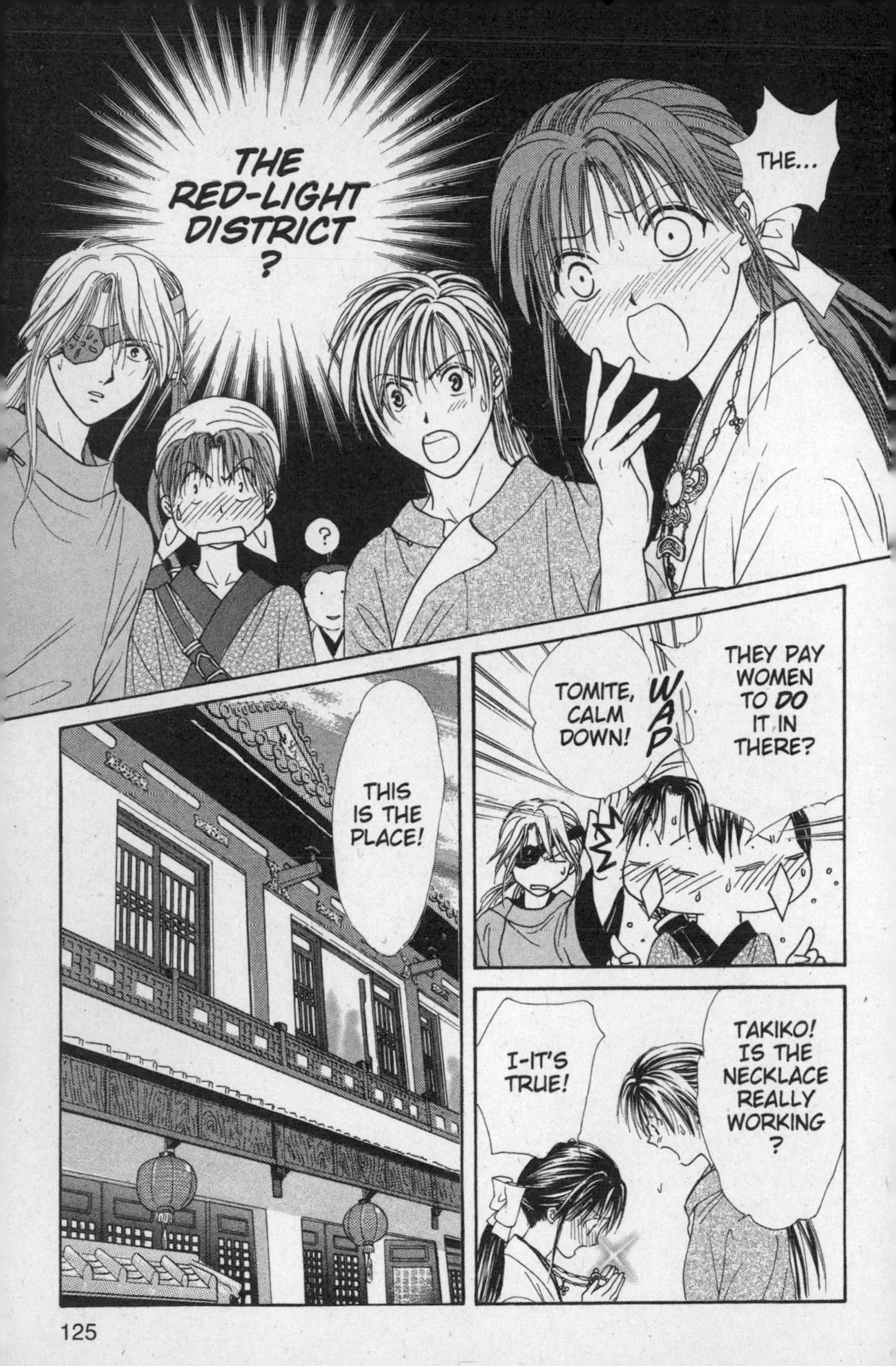
THE...
THE RED-LIGHT DISTRICT?
?
THEY PAY WOMEN TO *DO* IT IN THERE?
WAP
TOMITE, CALM DOWN!
TAKIKO! IS THE NECKLACE REALLY WORKING?
I-IT'S TRUE!
THIS IS THE PLACE!

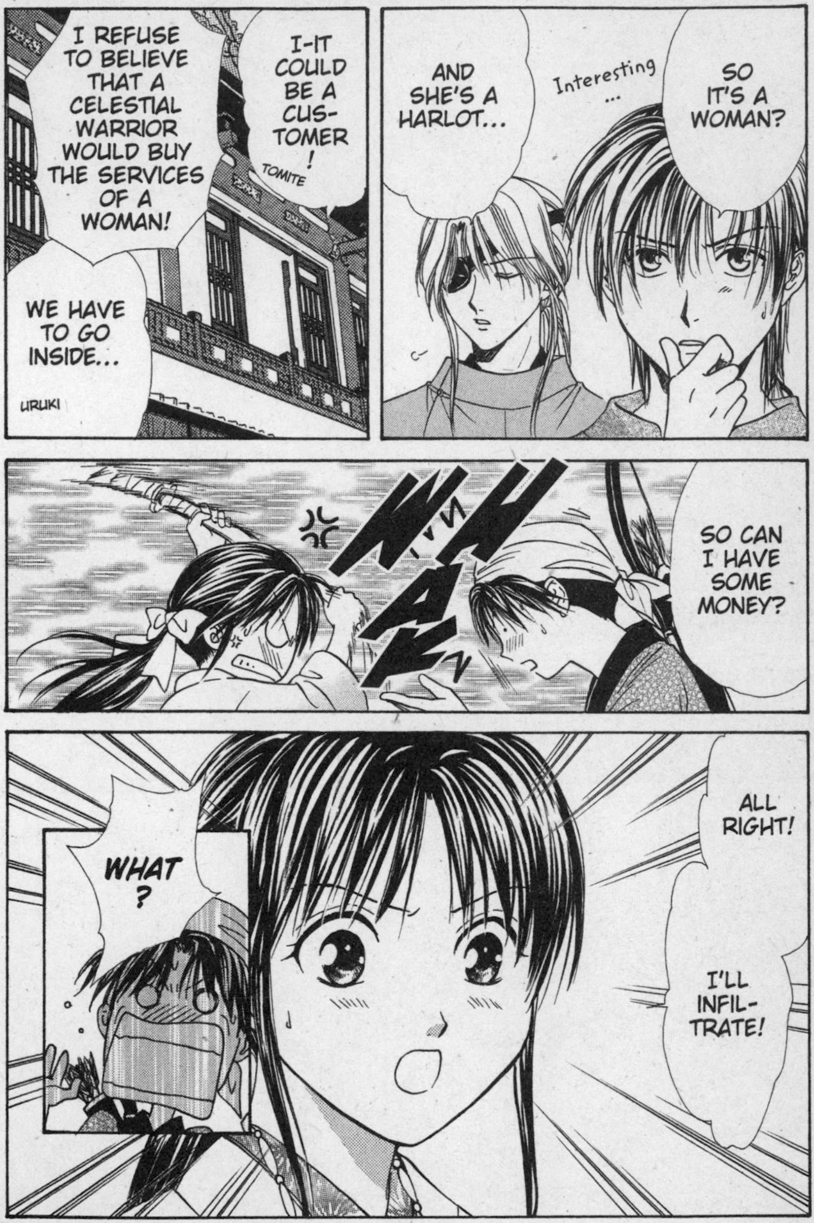
SO IT'S A WOMAN?
Interesting ...
AND SHE'S A HARLOT...
I-IT COULD BE A CUS-TOMER!
TOMITE
I REFUSE TO BELIEVE THAT A CELESTIAL WARRIOR WOULD BUY THE SERVICES OF A WOMAN!
WE HAVE TO GO INSIDE...
URUKI
SO CAN I HAVE SOME MONEY?
WHAM
ALL RIGHT!
I'LL INFIL-TRATE!
WHAT?

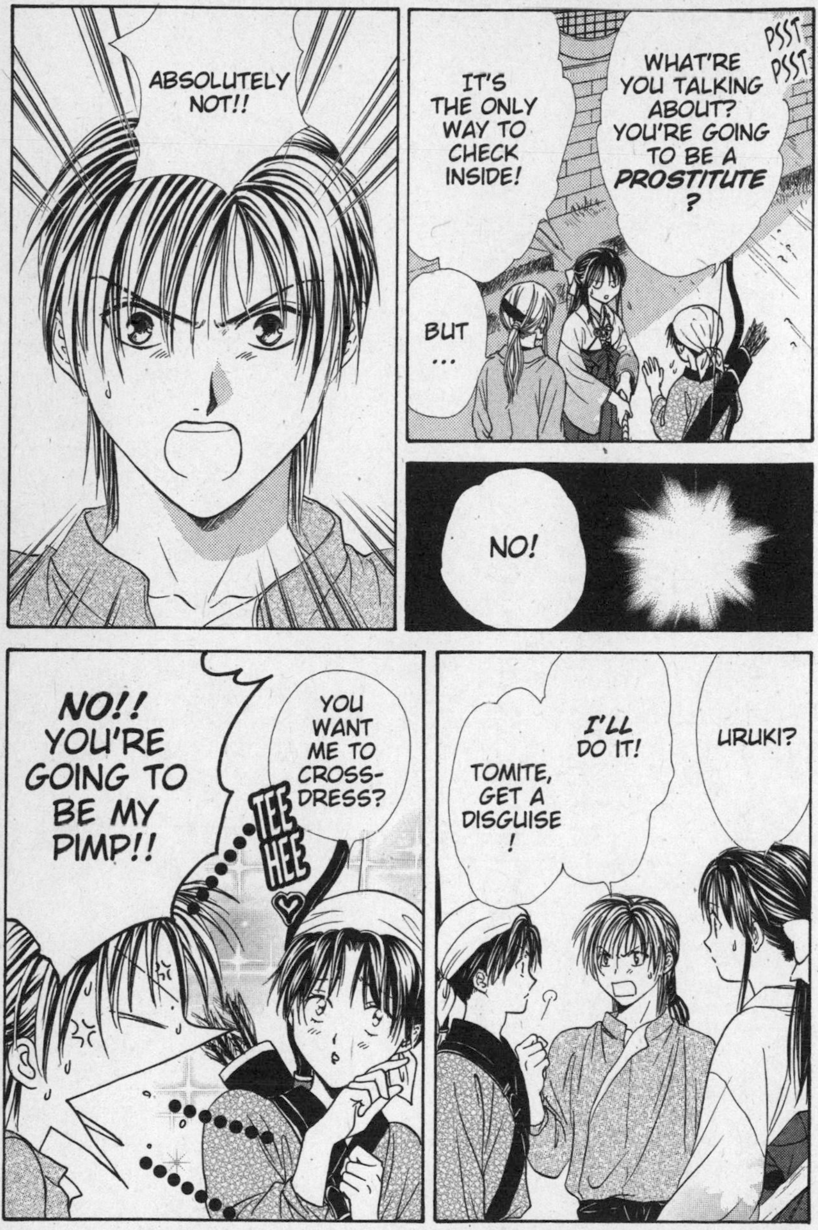
PSST PSST
WHAT'RE YOU TALKING ABOUT? YOU'RE GOING TO BE A PROSTITUTE?
IT'S THE ONLY WAY TO CHECK INSIDE!
BUT...
NO!
ABSOLUTELY NOT!!
URUKI?
I'LL DO IT!
TOMITE, GET A DISGUISE!
YOU WANT ME TO CROSS-DRESS?
TEE HEE
NO!! YOU'RE GOING TO BE MY PIMP!!

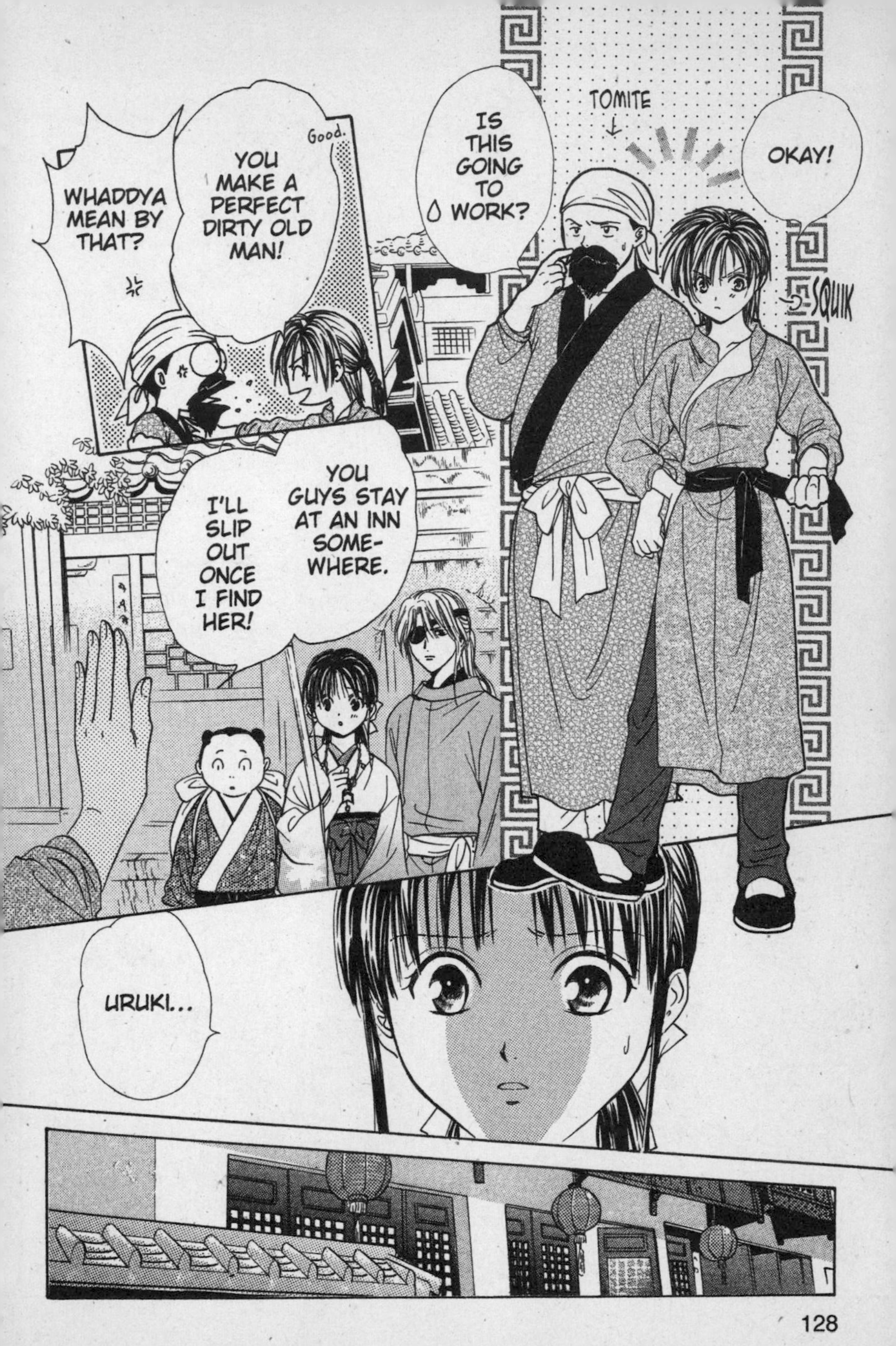
OKAY!
SQUIK
TOMITE
IS THIS GOING TO WORK?
YOU MAKE A PERFECT DIRTY OLD MAN!
Good.
WHADDYA MEAN BY THAT?
YOU GUYS STAY AT AN INN SOMEWHERE.
I'LL SLIP OUT ONCE I FIND HER!
URUKI...

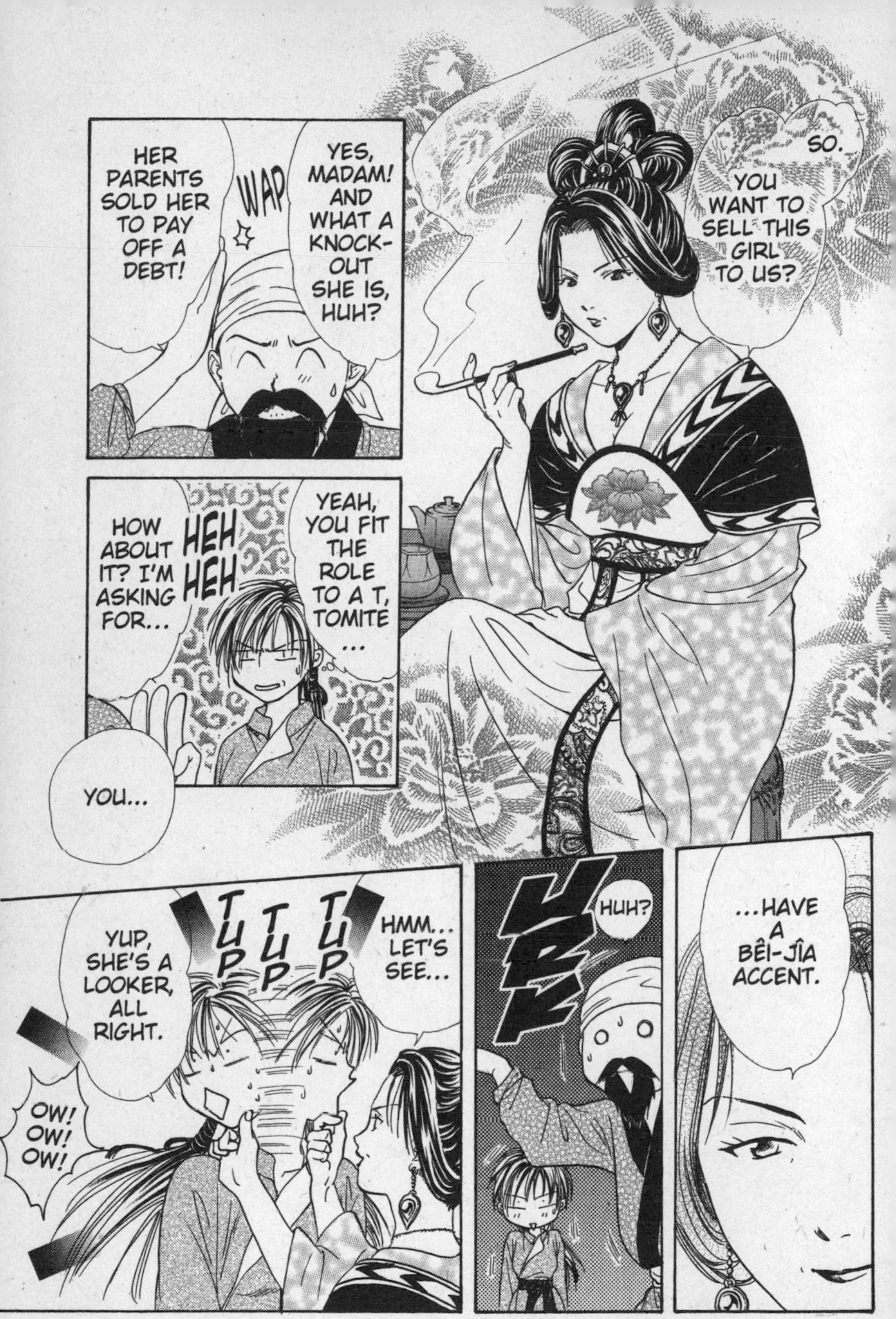
SO.
YOU WANT TO SELL THIS GIRL TO US?
YES, MADAM! AND WHAT A KNOCKOUT SHE IS, HUH?
WAP
HER PARENTS SOLD HER TO PAY OFF A DEBT!
YEAH, YOU FIT THE ROLE TO A T, TOMITE...
HEH HEH
HOW ABOUT IT? I'M ASKING FOR...
YOU...
...HAVE A BÊI-JÎA ACCENT.
HUH?
HMM... LET'S SEE...
TUP TUP TUP
YUP, SHE'S A LOOKER, ALL RIGHT.
OW! OW! OW!

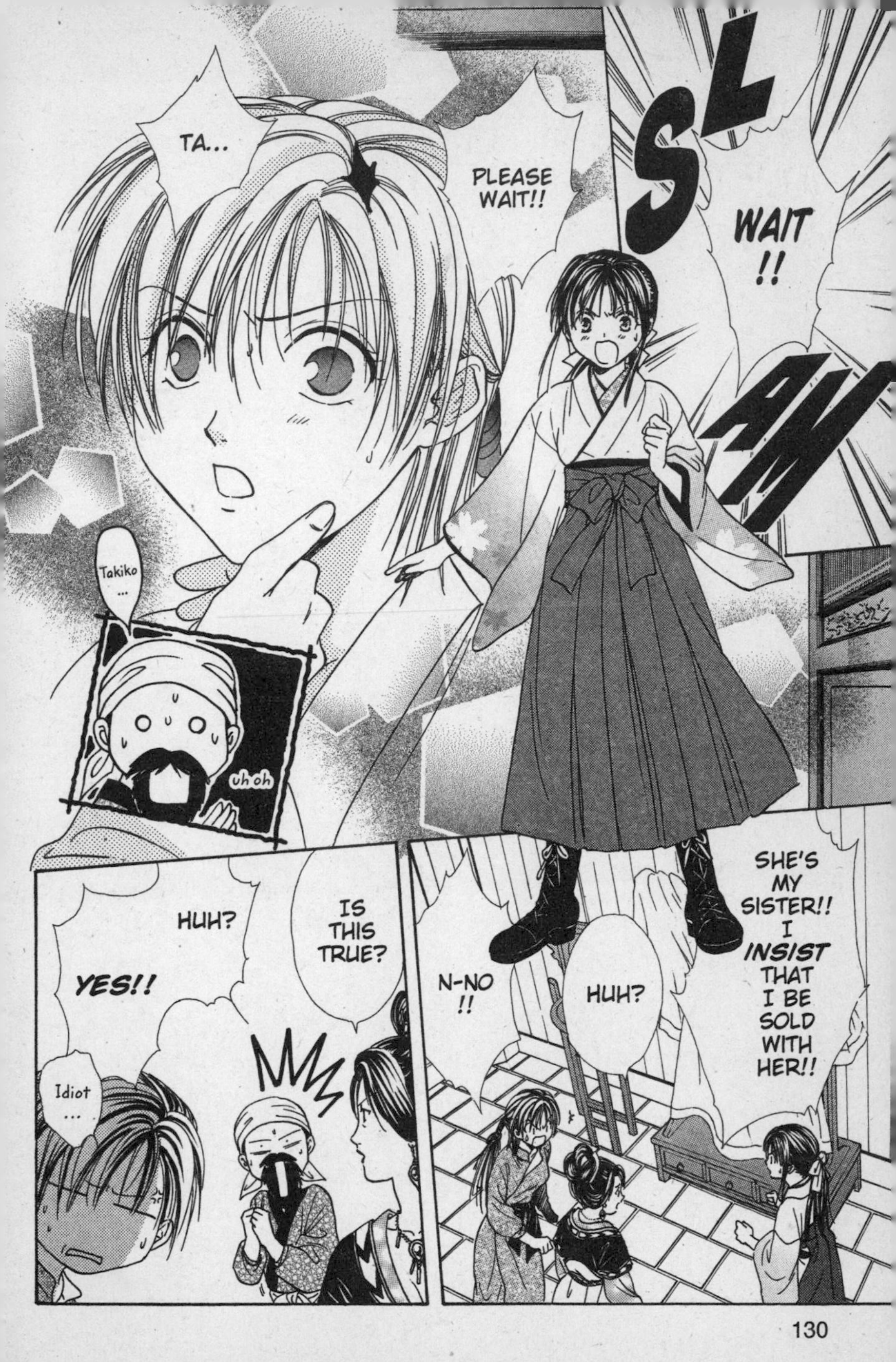
SL
AM
WAIT!!
PLEASE WAIT!!
TA...
Takiko...
uh oh
SHE'S MY SISTER!! I *INSIST* THAT I BE SOLD WITH HER!!
HUH?
N-NO!!
IS THIS TRUE?
HUH?
YES!!
Idiot...

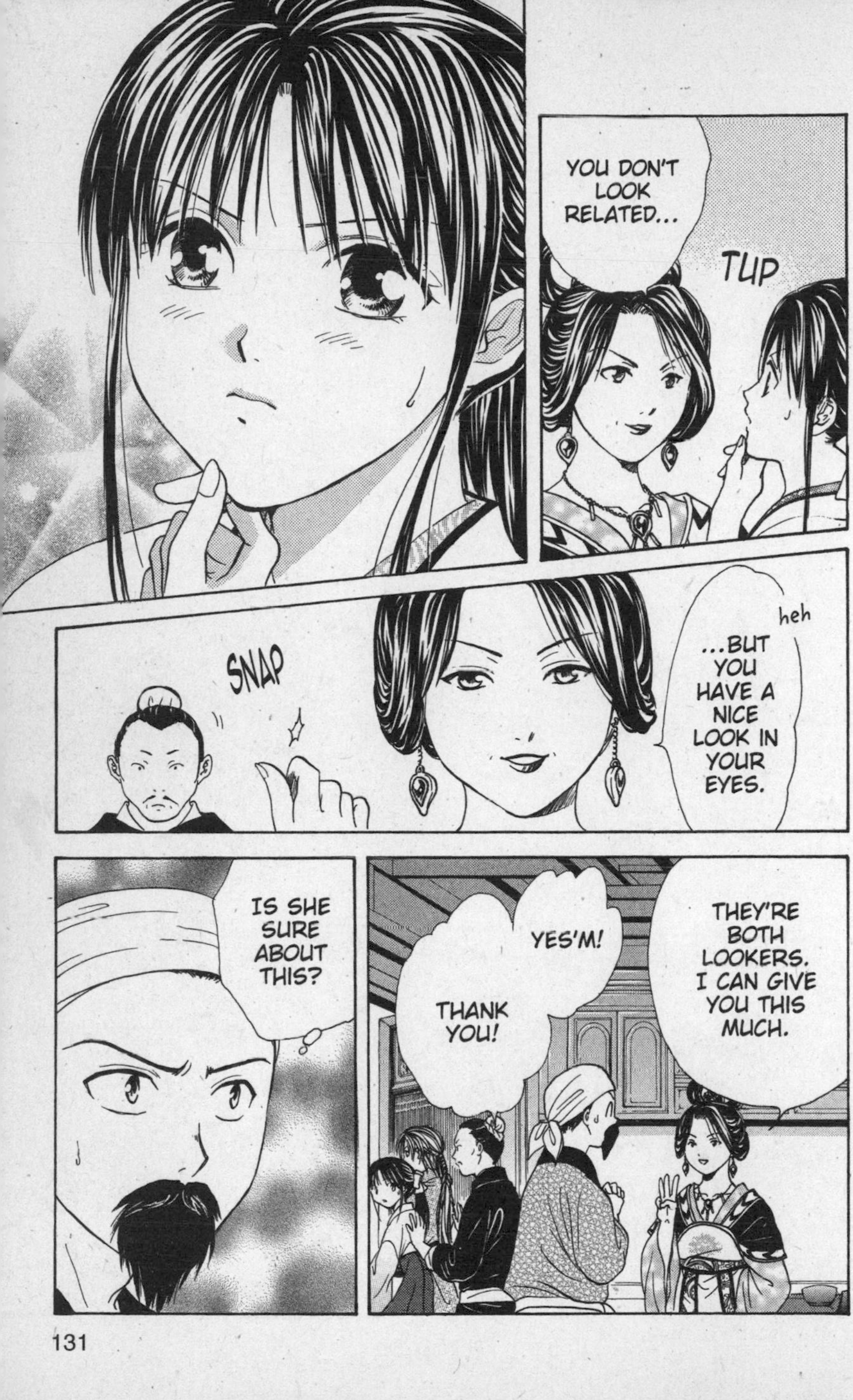
YOU DON'T LOOK RELATED...
TUP
heh
...BUT YOU HAVE A NICE LOOK IN YOUR EYES.
SNAP
THEY'RE BOTH LOOKERS. I CAN GIVE YOU THIS MUCH.
YES'M!
THANK YOU!
IS SHE SURE ABOUT THIS?

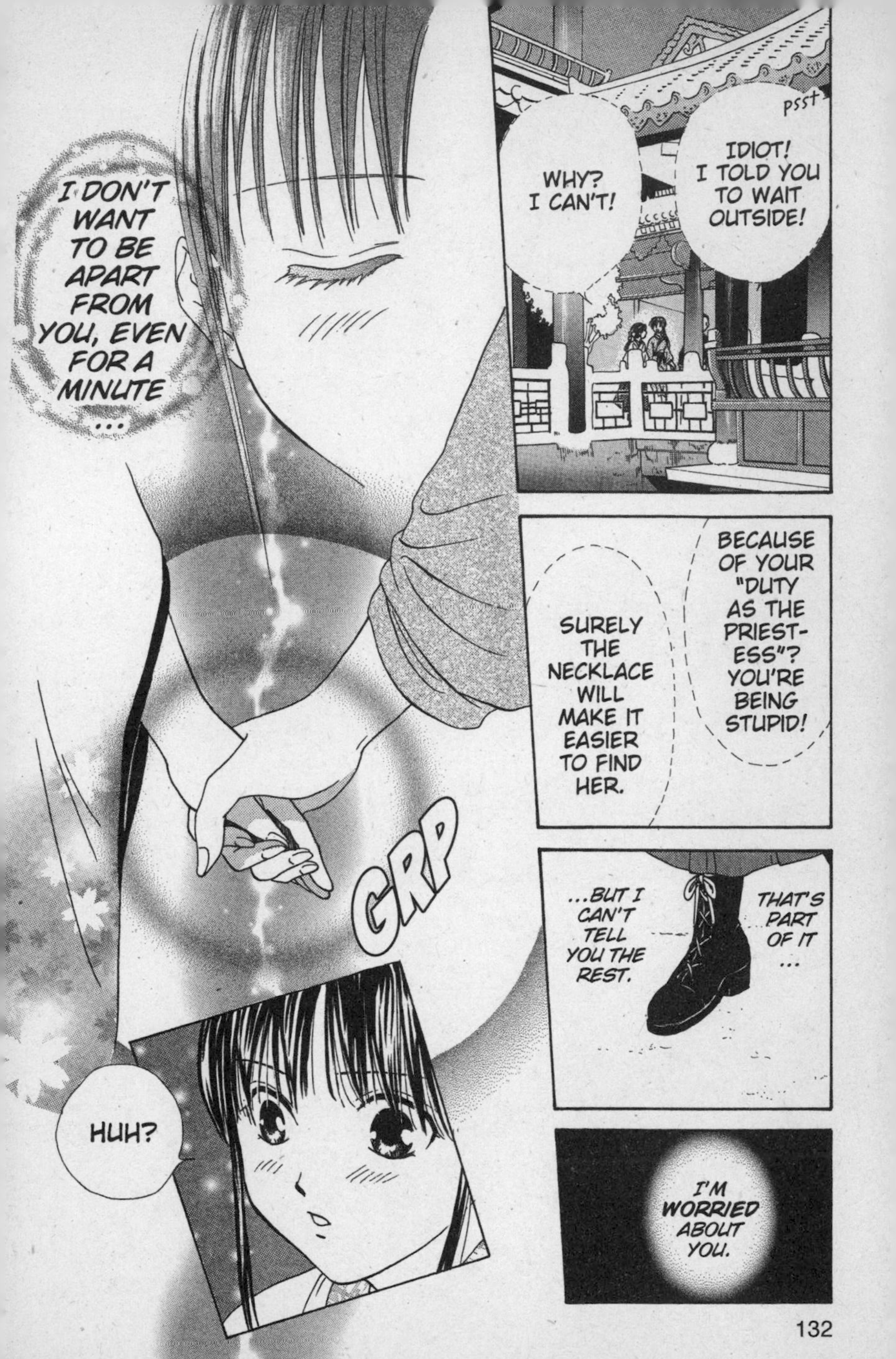
psst
IDIOT! I TOLD YOU TO WAIT OUTSIDE!
WHY? I CAN'T!
BECAUSE OF YOUR "DUTY AS THE PRIEST-ESS"? YOU'RE BEING STUPID!
SURELY THE NECKLACE WILL MAKE IT EASIER TO FIND HER.
THAT'S PART OF IT...
...BUT I CAN'T TELL YOU THE REST.
I'M WORRIED ABOUT YOU.
I DON'T WANT TO BE APART FROM YOU, EVEN FOR A MINUTE...
GRP
HUH?

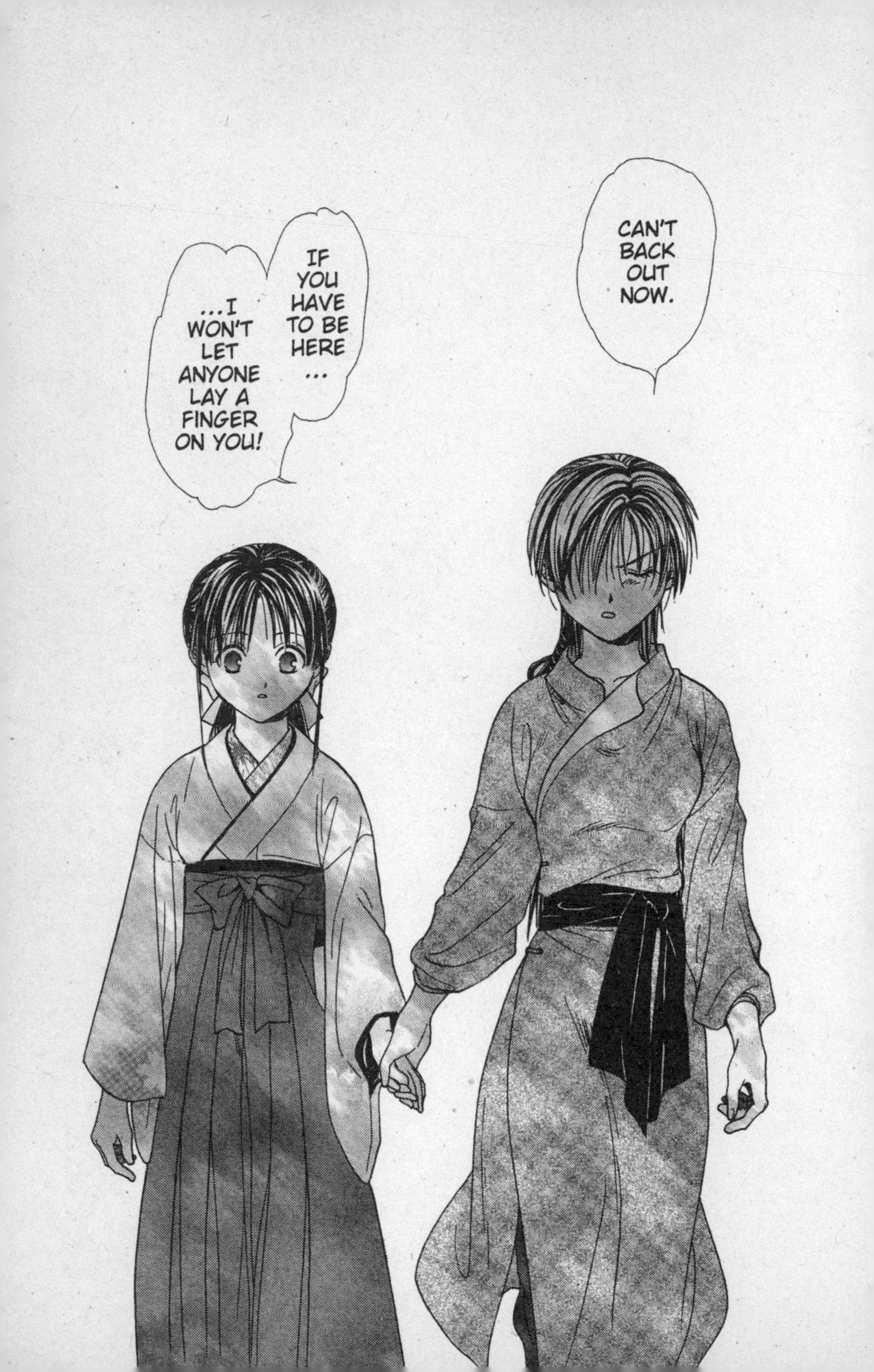
CAN'T BACK OUT NOW.
IF YOU HAVE TO BE HERE ...
...I WON'T LET ANYONE LAY A FINGER ON YOU!

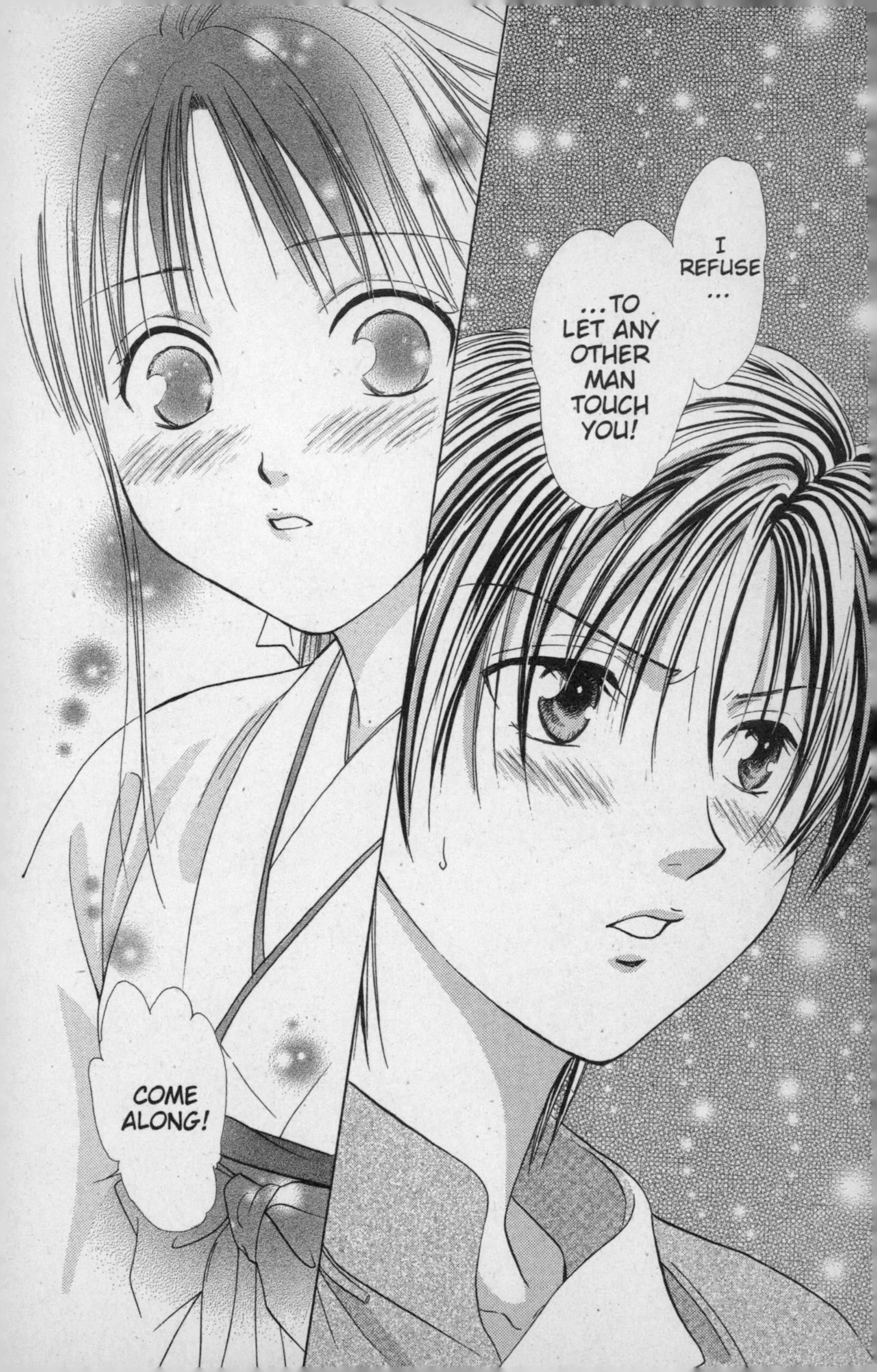
I REFUSE ...
...TO LET ANY OTHER MAN TOUCH YOU!
COME ALONG!

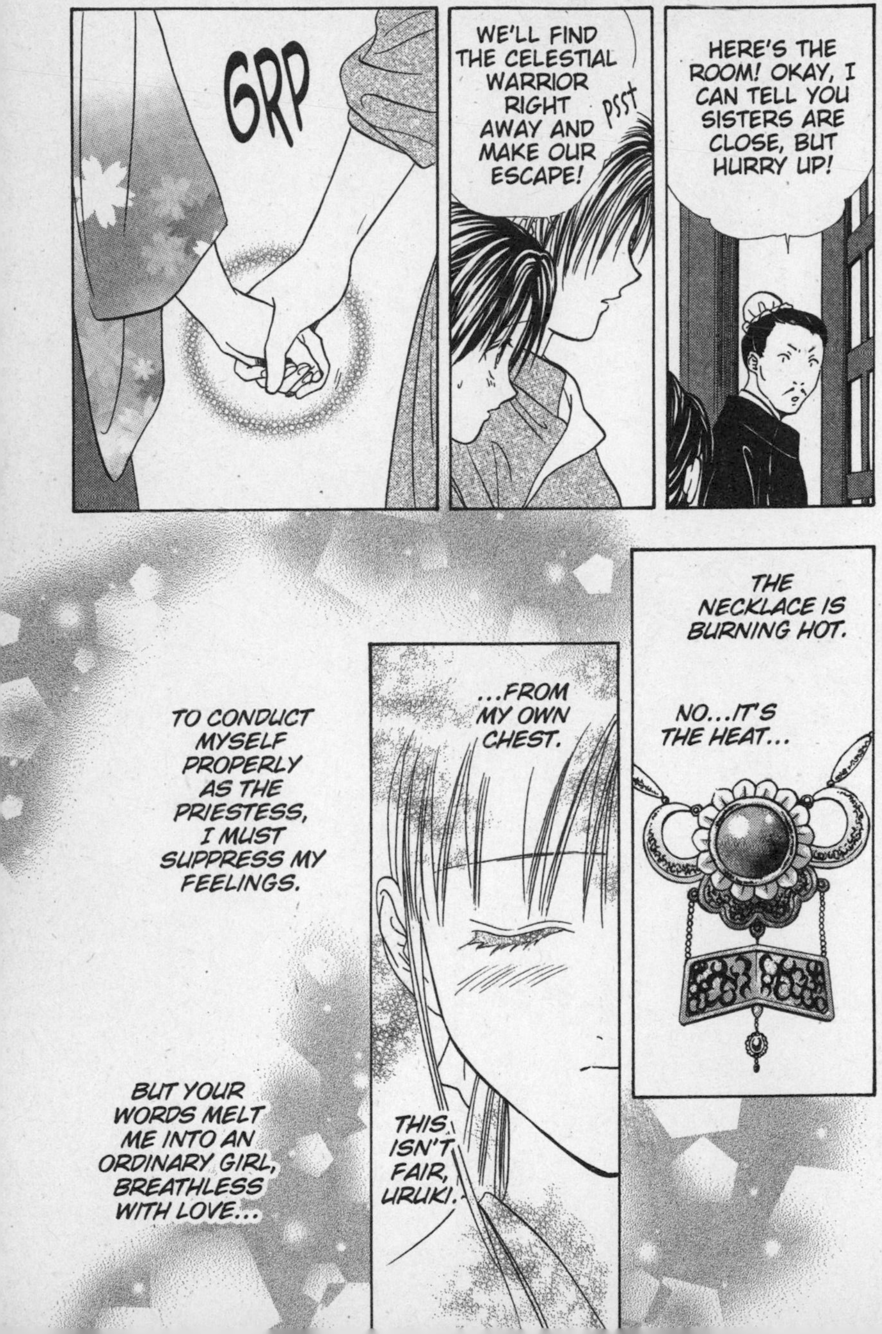
HERE'S THE ROOM! OKAY, I CAN TELL YOU SISTERS ARE CLOSE, BUT HURRY UP!
WE'LL FIND THE CELESTIAL WARRIOR RIGHT AWAY AND MAKE OUR ESCAPE!
psst
GRP
THE NECKLACE IS BURNING HOT.
NO...IT'S THE HEAT...
...FROM MY OWN CHEST.
THIS ISN'T FAIR, URUKI.
TO CONDUCT MYSELF PROPERLY AS THE PRIESTESS, I MUST SUPPRESS MY FEELINGS.
BUT YOUR WORDS MELT ME INTO AN ORDINARY GIRL, BREATHLESS WITH LOVE...

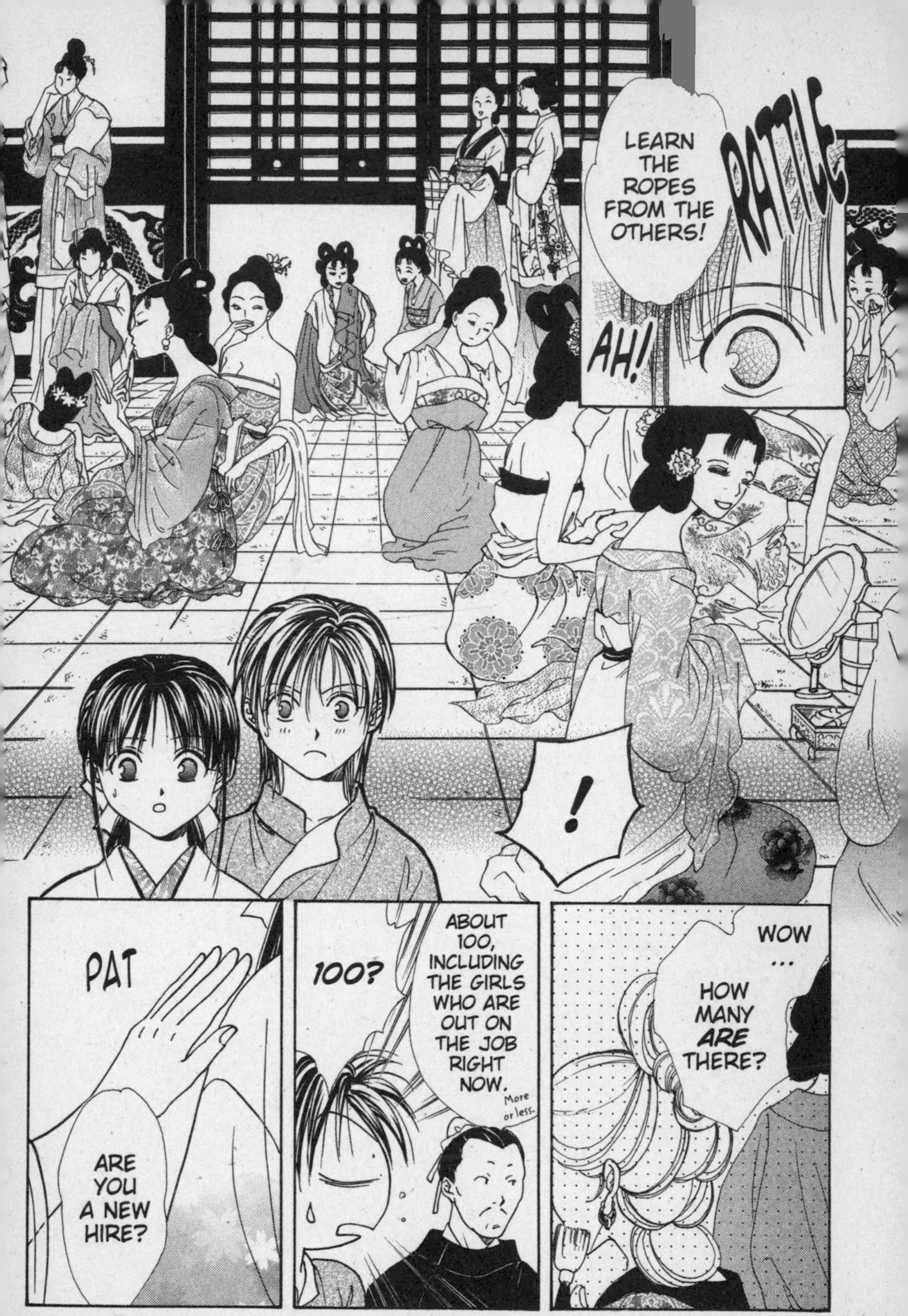
LEARN THE ROPES FROM THE OTHERS!
RATTLE
AH!
!
WOW ...
HOW MANY *ARE* THERE?
ABOUT 100, INCLUDING THE GIRLS WHO ARE OUT ON THE JOB RIGHT NOW.
More or less.
100?
PAT
ARE YOU A NEW HIRE?

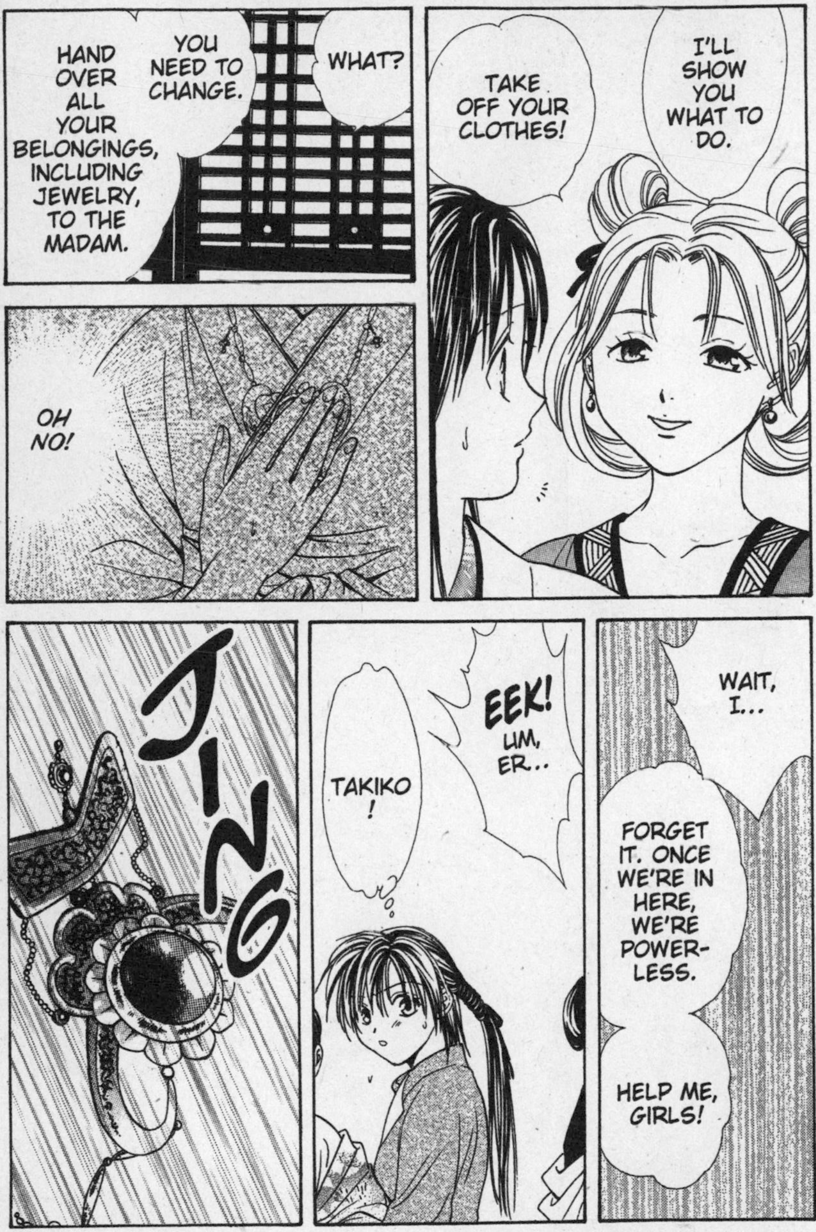
I'LL SHOW YOU WHAT TO DO.
TAKE OFF YOUR CLOTHES!
WHAT?
YOU NEED TO CHANGE.
HAND OVER ALL YOUR BELONGINGS, INCLUDING JEWELRY, TO THE MADAM.
OH NO!
WAIT, I...
FORGET IT. ONCE WE'RE IN HERE, WE'RE POWERLESS.
HELP ME, GIRLS!
EEK!
UM, ER...
TAKIKO!
JING

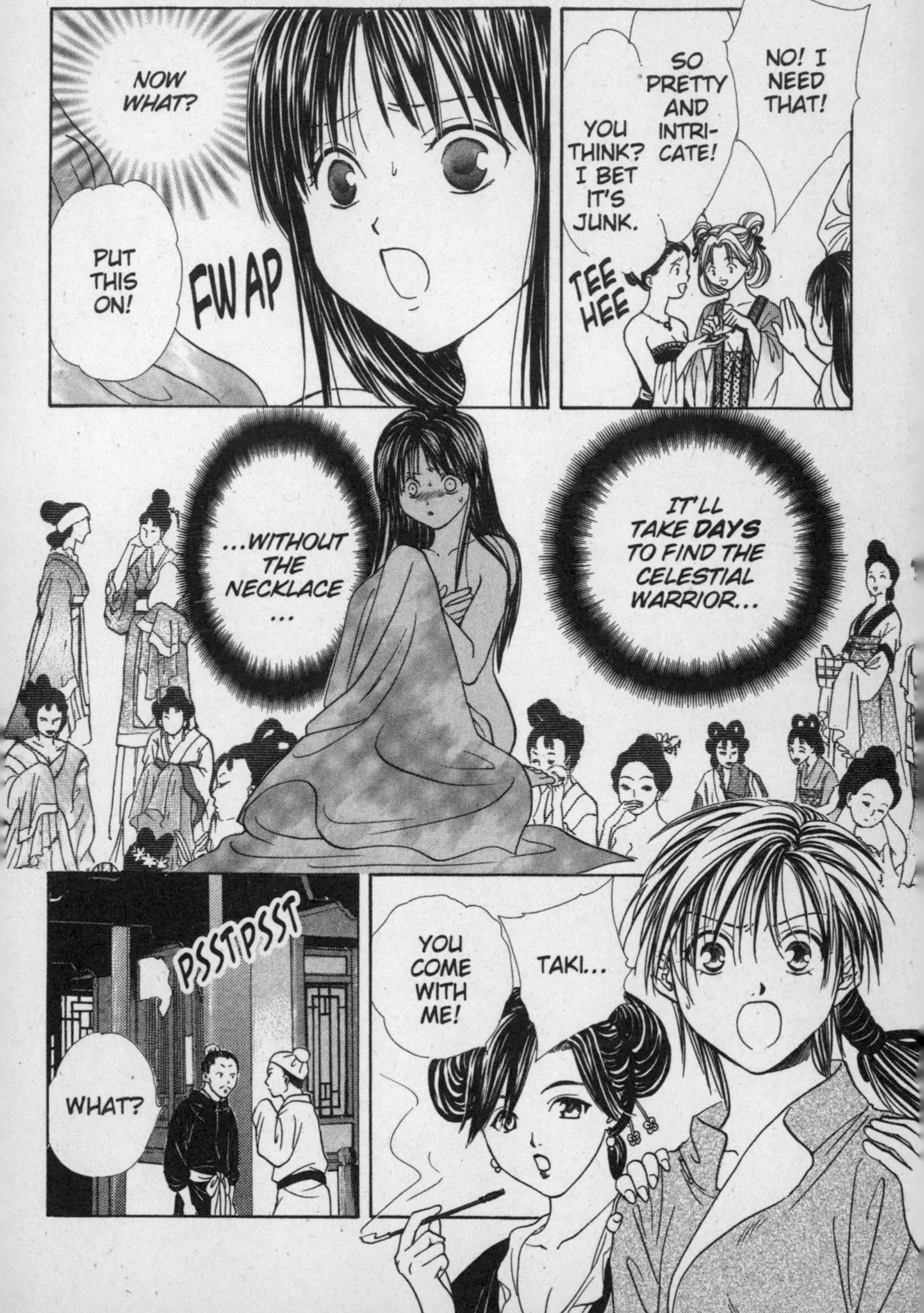
NO! I NEED THAT!
SO PRETTY AND INTRICATE!
YOU THINK? I BET IT'S JUNK.
TEE HEE
NOW WHAT?
FWAP
PUT THIS ON!
IT'LL TAKE DAYS TO FIND THE CELESTIAL WARRIOR...
...WITHOUT THE NECKLACE ...
TAKI...
YOU COME WITH ME!
PSSTPSST
WHAT?

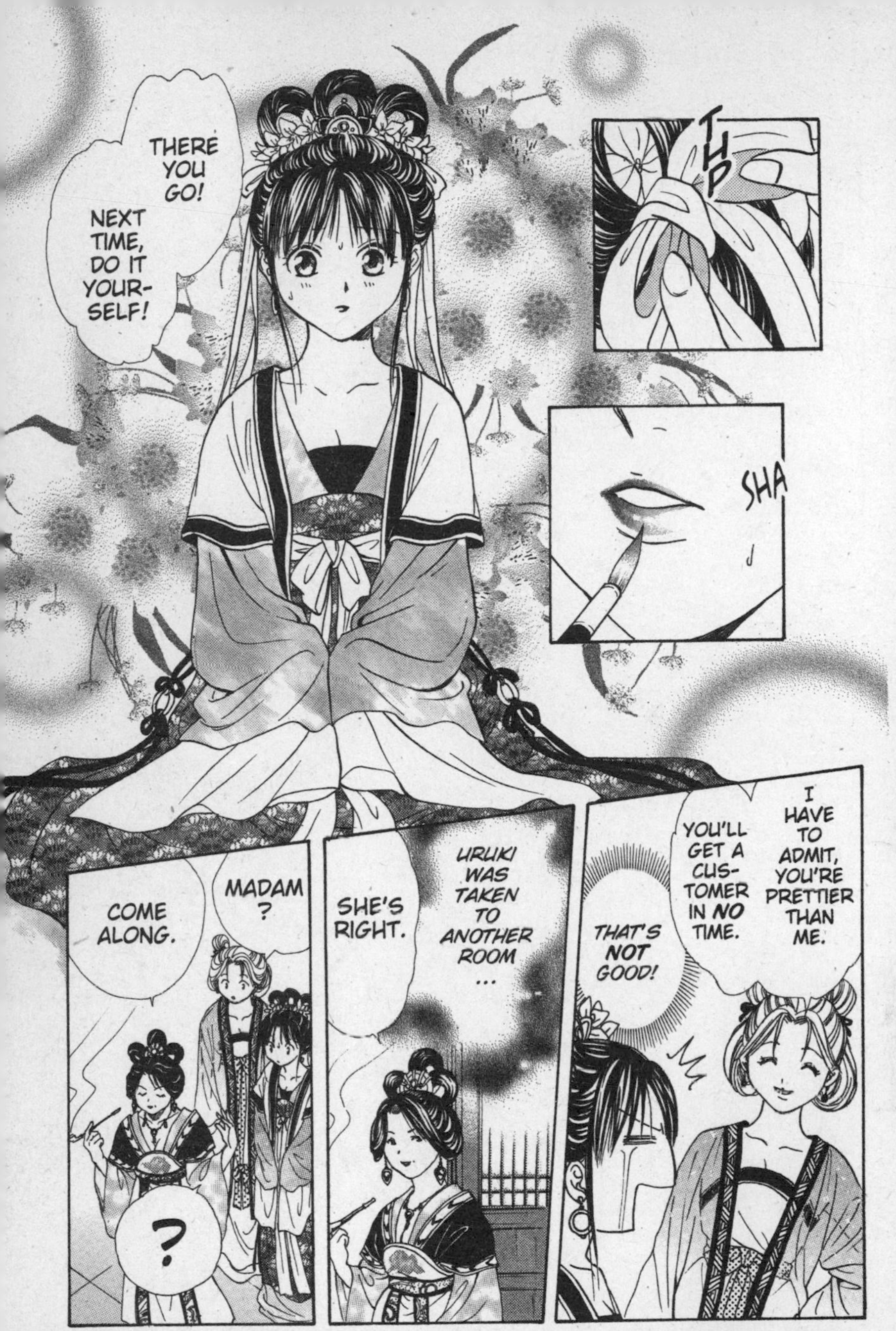
THP
SHA
THERE YOU GO!
NEXT TIME, DO IT YOURSELF!
I HAVE TO ADMIT, YOU'RE PRETTIER THAN ME.
YOU'LL GET A CUSTOMER IN *NO* TIME.
THAT'S NOT GOOD!
URUKI WAS TAKEN TO ANOTHER ROOM ...
SHE'S RIGHT.
MADAM ?
COME ALONG.
?

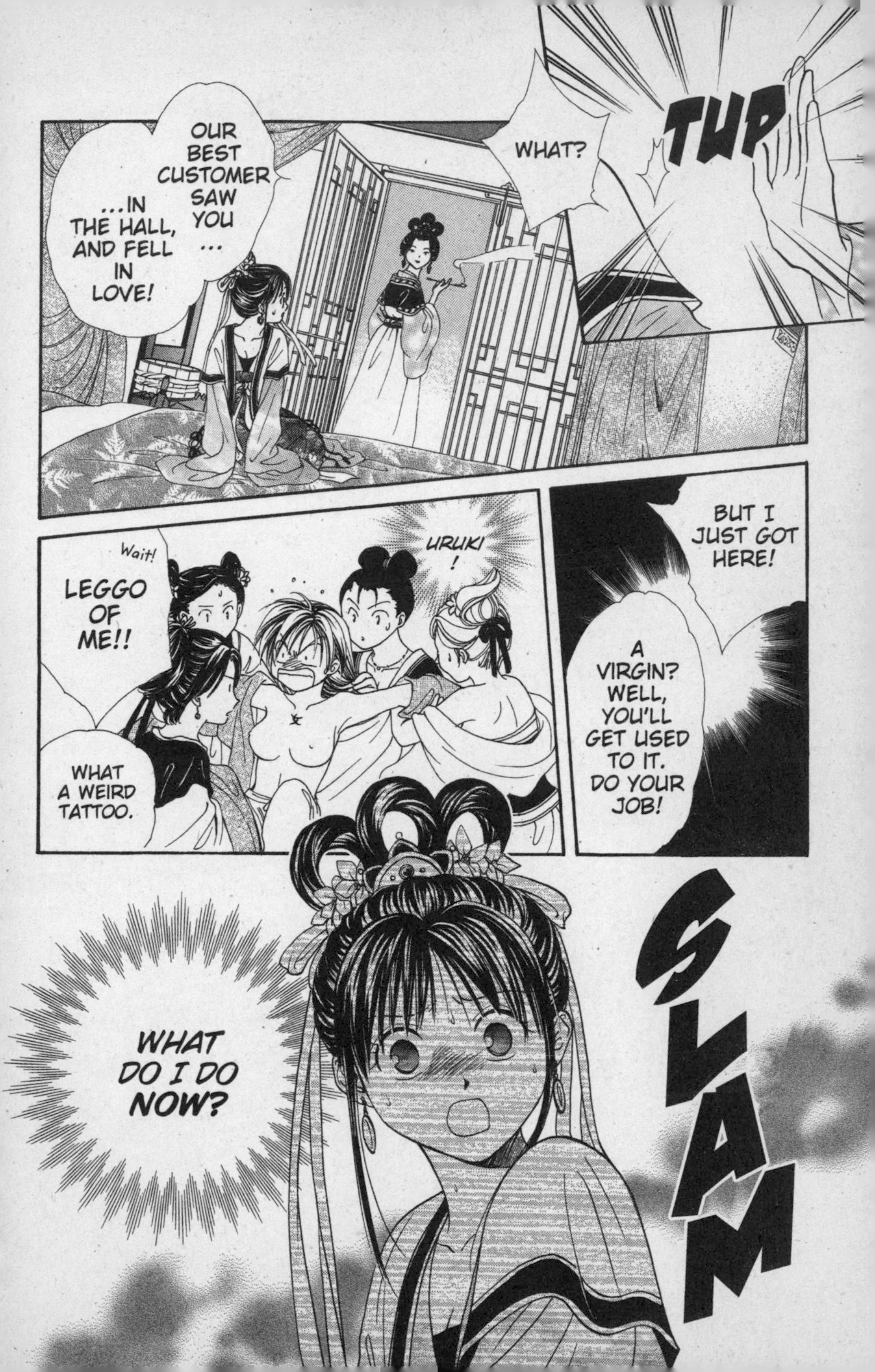
TUP
WHAT?
OUR BEST CUSTOMER SAW YOU ...
...IN THE HALL, AND FELL IN LOVE!
BUT I JUST GOT HERE!
A VIRGIN? WELL, YOU'LL GET USED TO IT. DO YOUR JOB!
URUKI!
Wait!
LEGGO OF ME!!
WHAT A WEIRD TATTOO.
SLAM
WHAT DO I DO NOW?

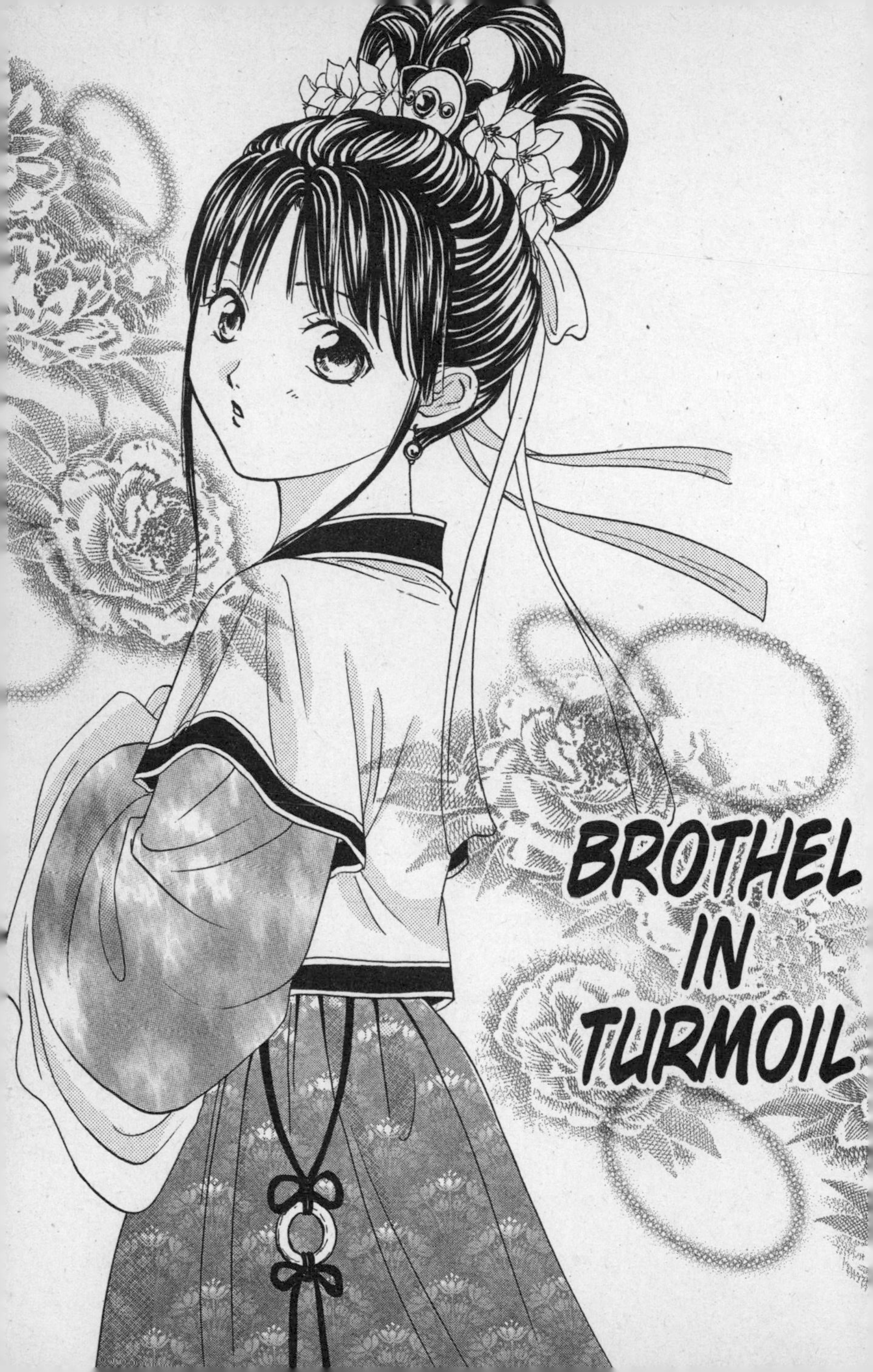
BROTHEL IN TURMOIL

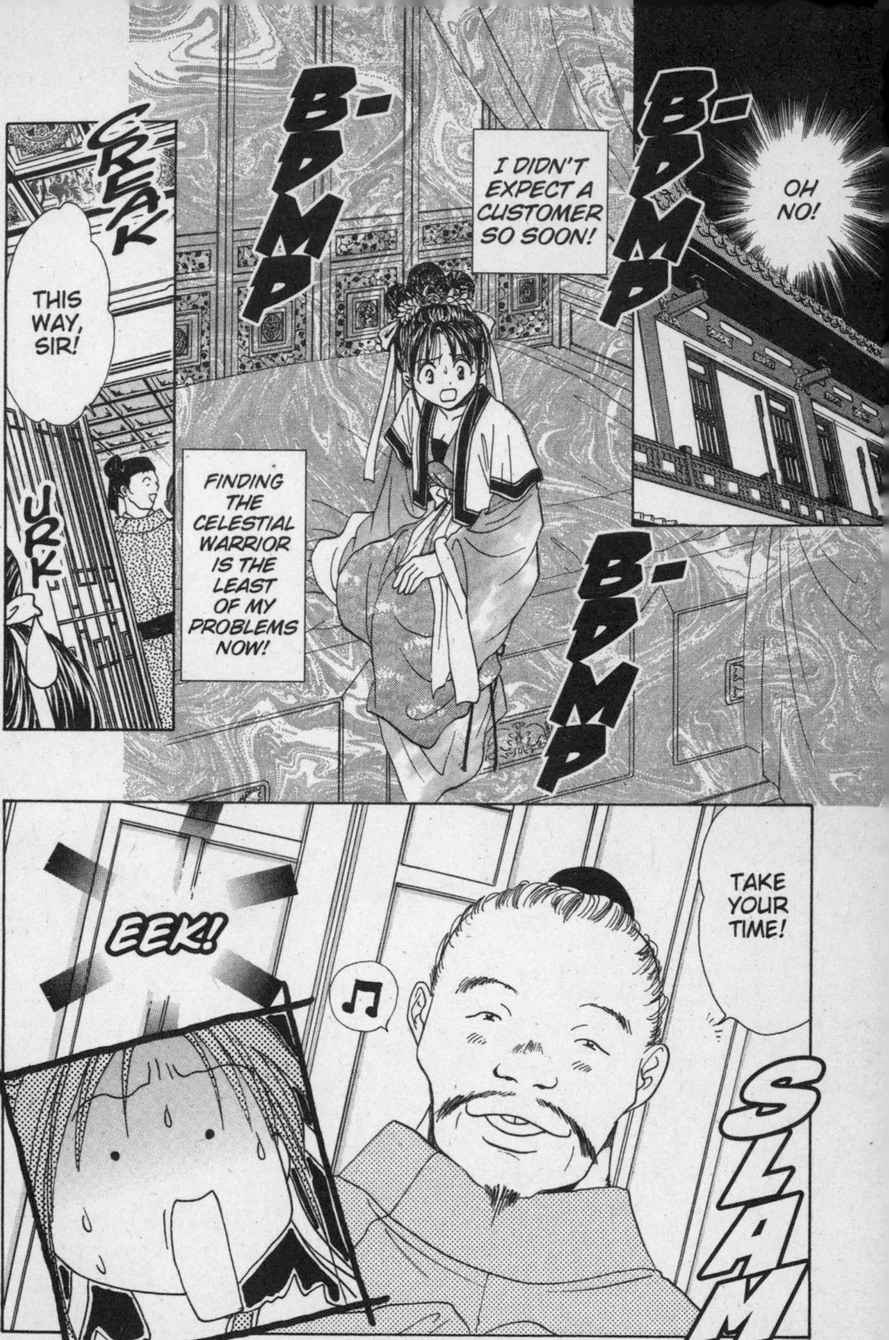
OH NO!
B-BDMP
I DIDN'T EXPECT A CUSTOMER SO SOON!
B-BDMP
FINDING THE CELESTIAL WARRIOR IS THE LEAST OF MY PROBLEMS NOW!
B-BDMP
CREAK
THIS WAY, SIR!
URK
TAKE YOUR TIME!
SLAM
♫
EEK!

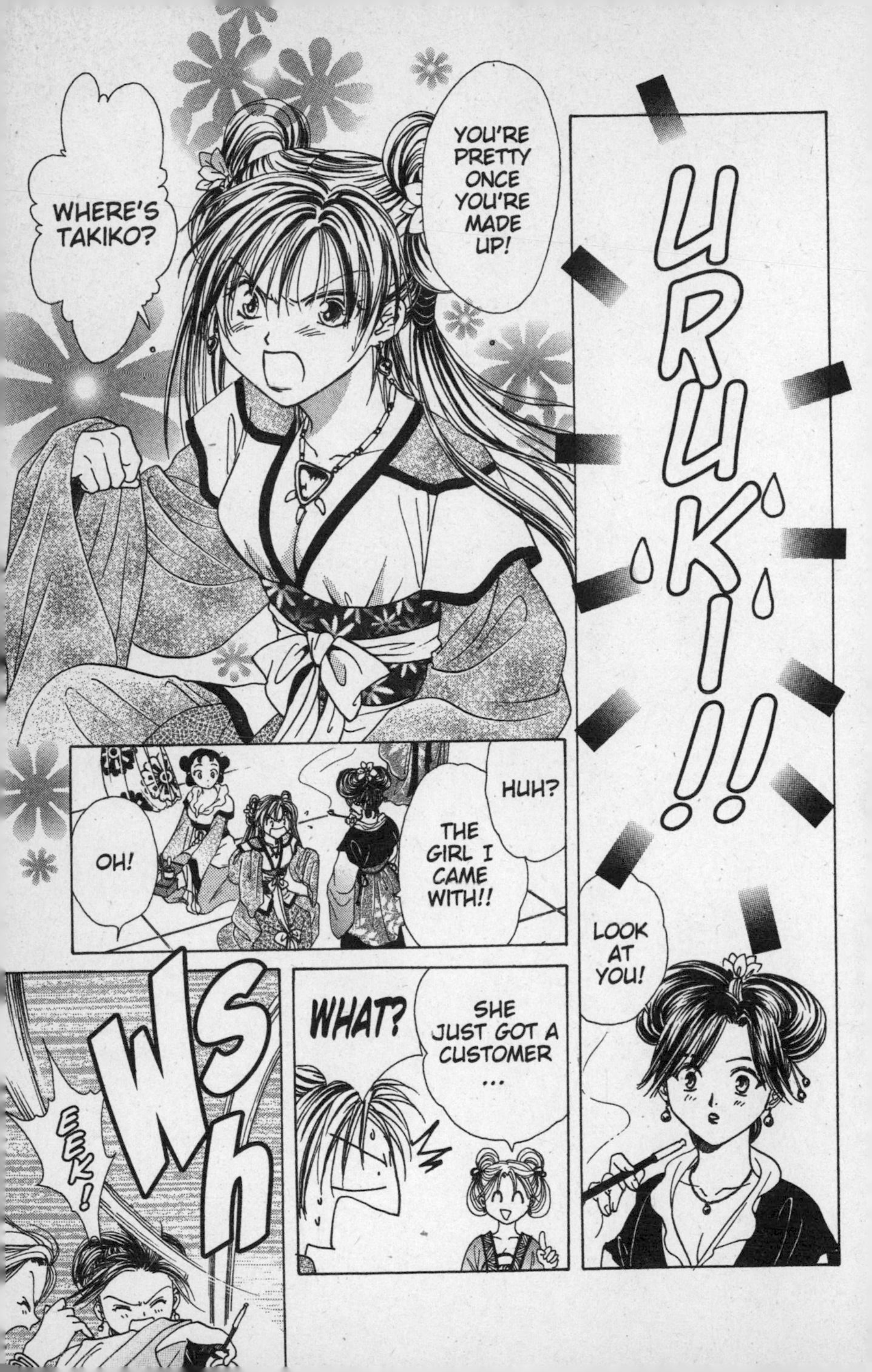
URUKI!!
LOOK AT YOU!
YOU'RE PRETTY ONCE YOU'RE MADE UP!
WHERE'S TAKIKO?
HUH?
THE GIRL I CAME WITH!!
OH!
SHE JUST GOT A CUSTOMER ...
WHAT?
WSh
EEK!

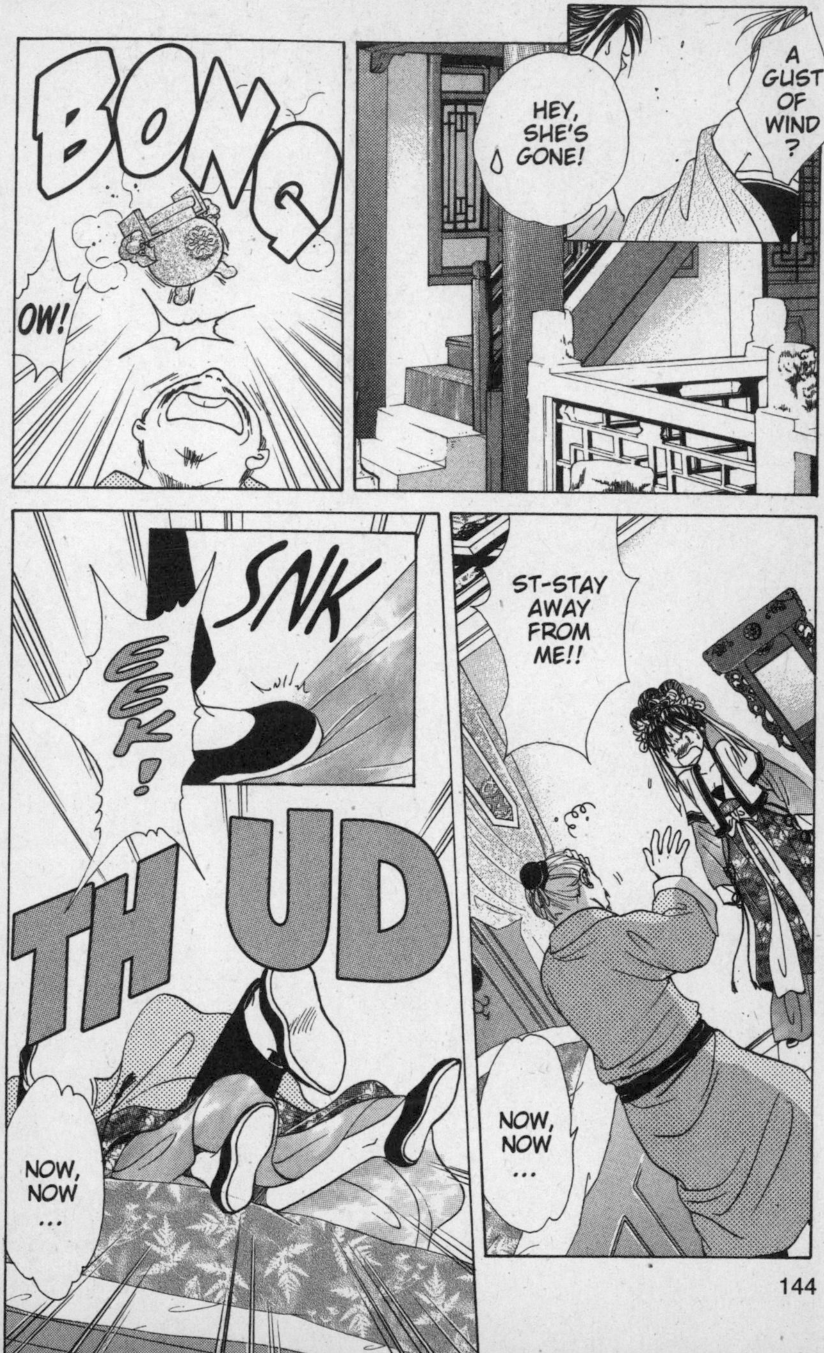
A GUST OF WIND ?
HEY, SHE'S GONE!
BONG
OW!
ST-STAY AWAY FROM ME!!
NOW, NOW ...
SNK
EEEK!
THUD
NOW, NOW ...

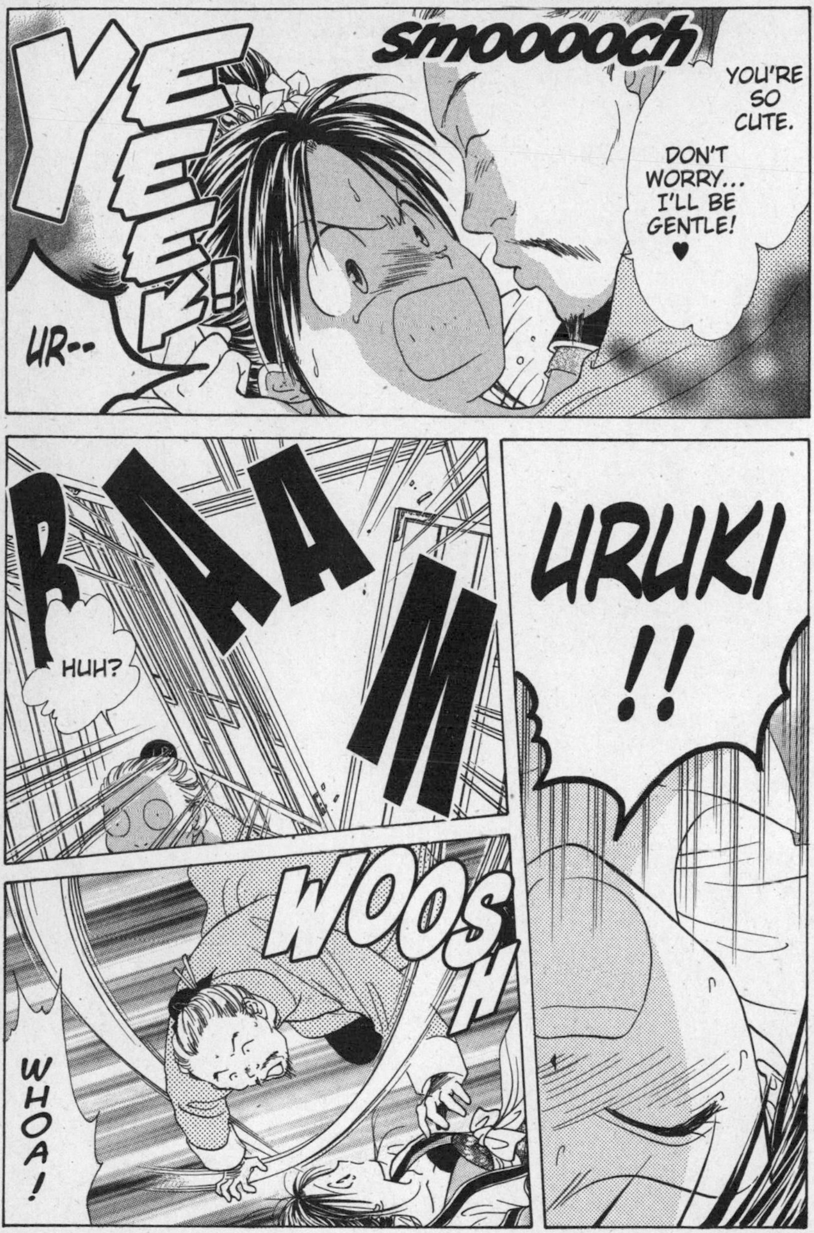
YOU'RE SO CUTE.
DON'T WORRY... I'LL BE GENTLE! ♥
smooooch
YEEEK!
UR--
URUKI !!
BAAM
HUH?
WOOSH
WHOA!

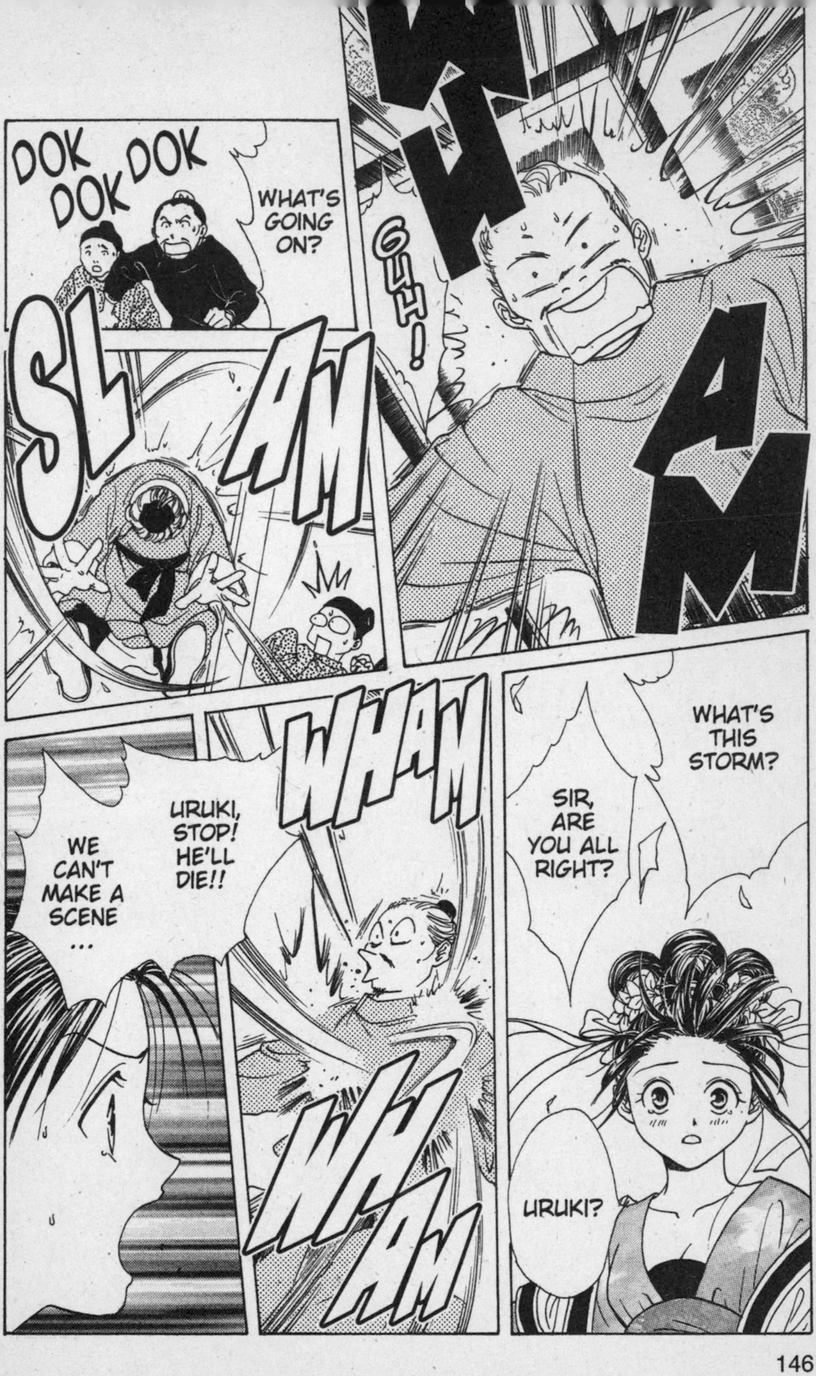
WH
GUH!
AM
DOK DOK DOK
WHAT'S GOING ON?
SLAM
WHAT'S THIS STORM?
SIR, ARE YOU ALL RIGHT?
URUKI?
WHAM
URUKI, STOP! HE'LL DIE!!
WHAM
WE CAN'T MAKE A SCENE ...

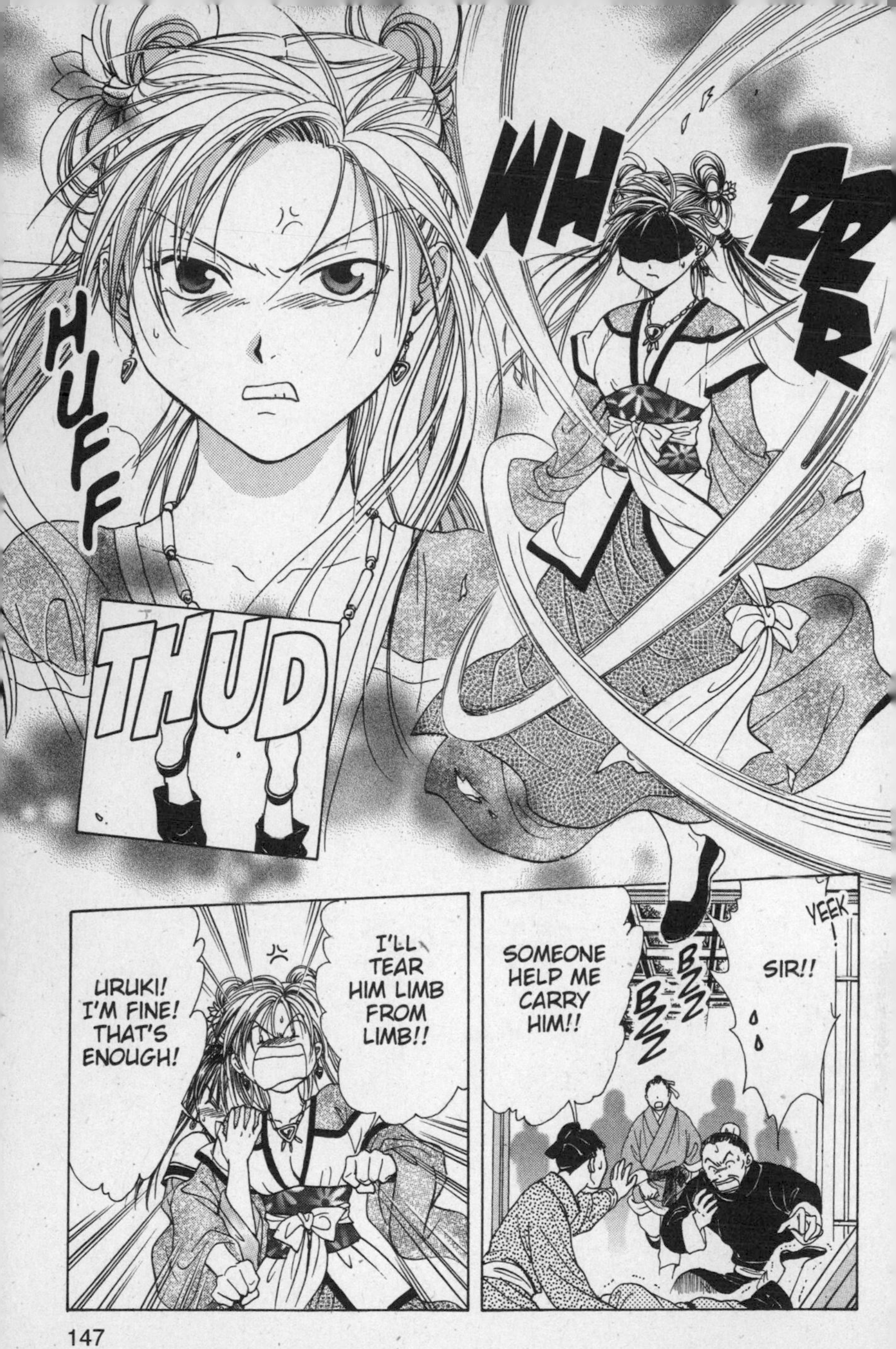
WH
RR
HUFF
THUD
YEEK!
SIR!!
SOMEONE HELP ME CARRY HIM!!
BZZ
BZZ
I'LL TEAR HIM LIMB FROM LIMB!!
URUKI! I'M FINE! THAT'S ENOUGH!

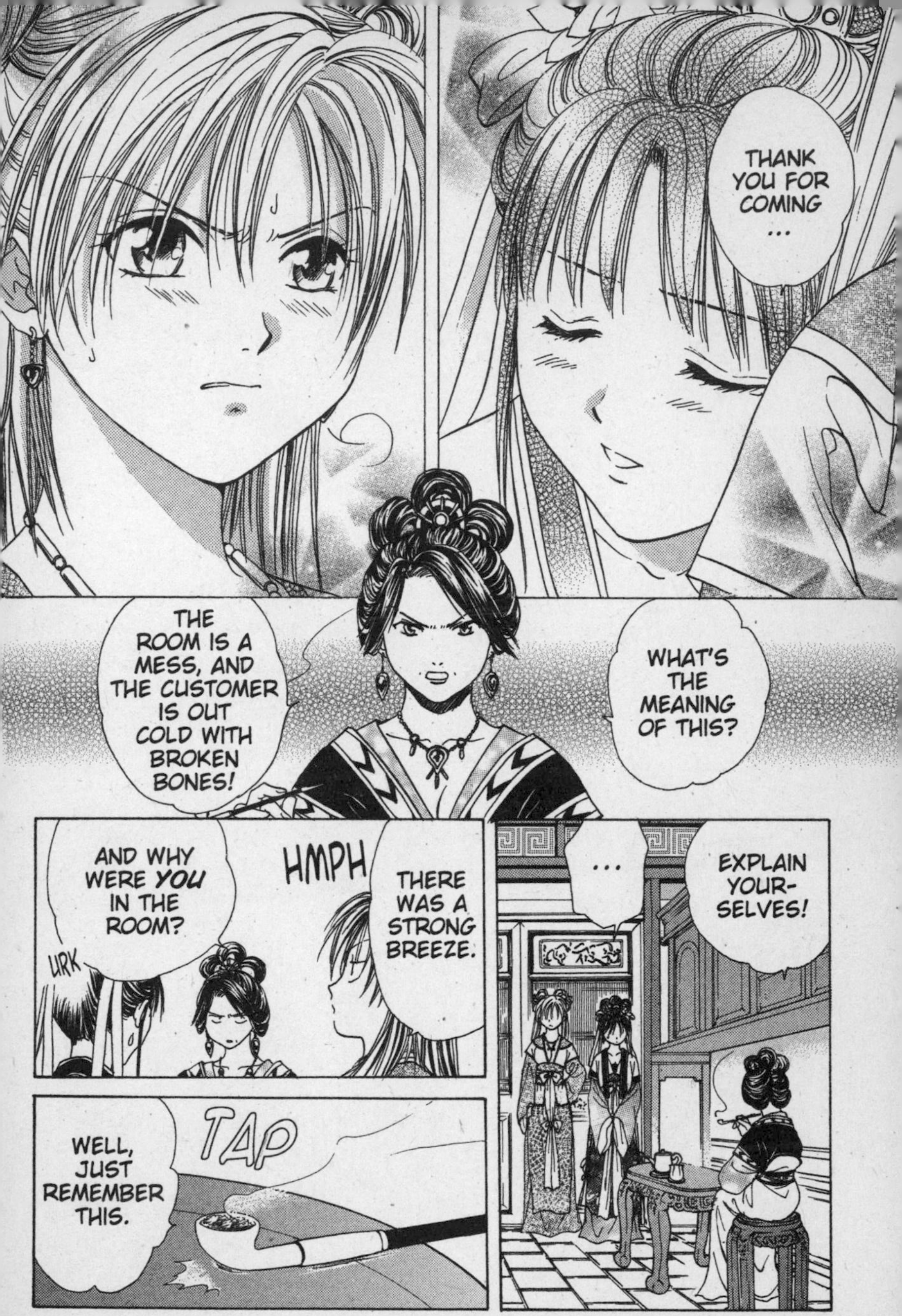
THANK YOU FOR COMING ...
WHAT'S THE MEANING OF THIS?
THE ROOM IS A MESS, AND THE CUSTOMER IS OUT COLD WITH BROKEN BONES!
EXPLAIN YOUR-SELVES!
...
THERE WAS A STRONG BREEZE.
HMPH
AND WHY WERE *YOU* IN THE ROOM?
URK
TAP
WELL, JUST REMEMBER THIS.

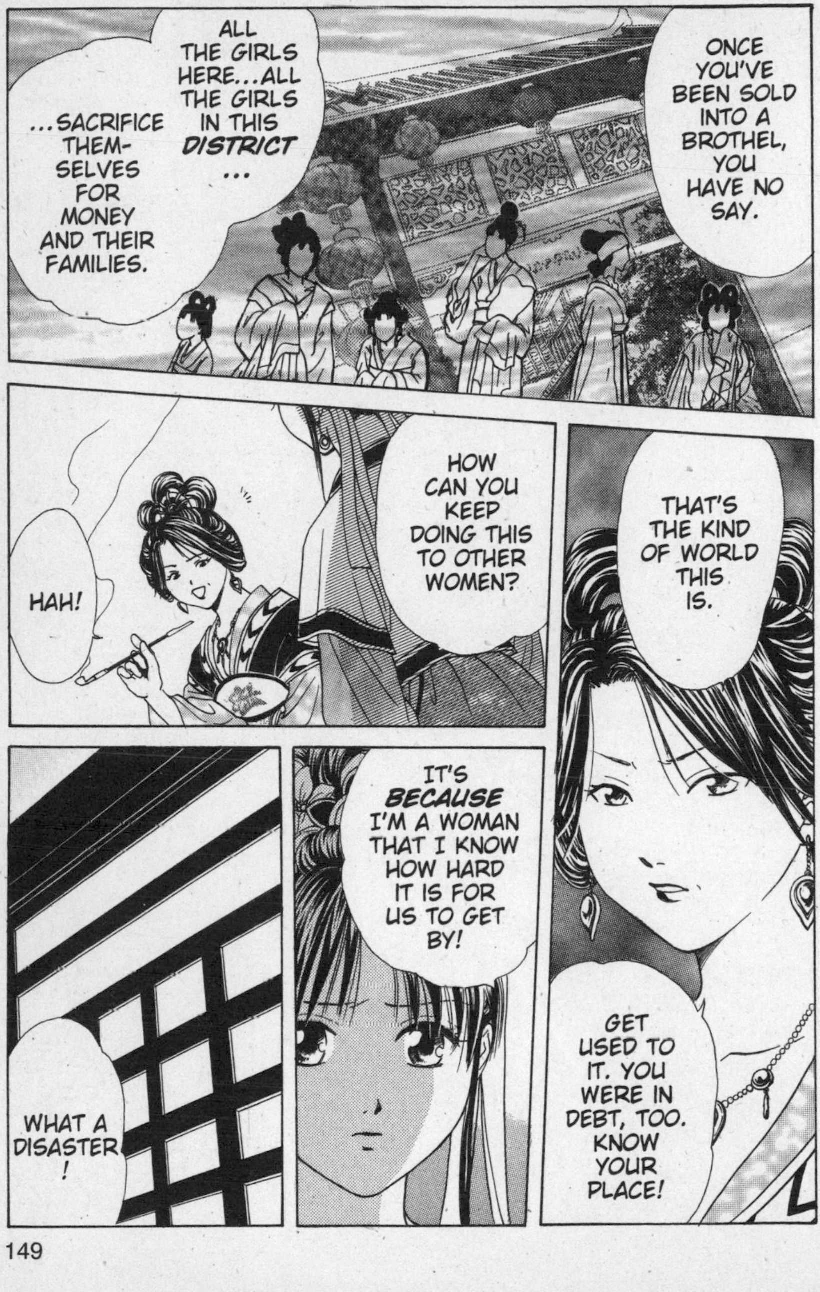
ONCE YOU'VE BEEN SOLD INTO A BROTHEL, YOU HAVE NO SAY.
ALL THE GIRLS HERE...ALL THE GIRLS IN THIS *DISTRICT*...
...SACRIFICE THEM-SELVES FOR MONEY AND THEIR FAMILIES.
THAT'S THE KIND OF WORLD THIS IS.
GET USED TO IT. YOU WERE IN DEBT, TOO. KNOW YOUR PLACE!
HOW CAN YOU KEEP DOING THIS TO OTHER WOMEN?
HAH!
IT'S *BECAUSE* I'M A WOMAN THAT I KNOW HOW HARD IT IS FOR US TO GET BY!
WHAT A DISASTER!

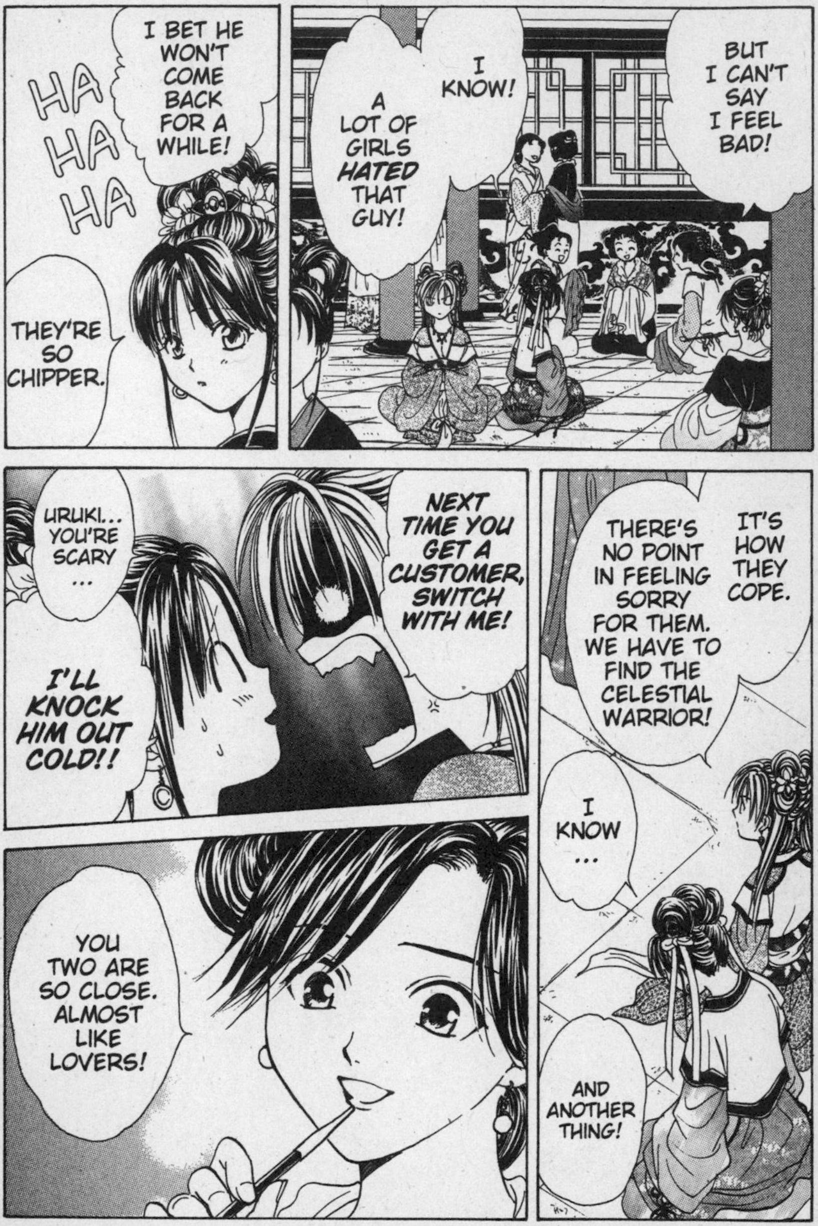
BUT I CAN'T SAY I FEEL BAD!
I KNOW!
A LOT OF GIRLS HATED THAT GUY!
I BET HE WON'T COME BACK FOR A WHILE!
HA HA HA
THEY'RE SO CHIPPER.
IT'S HOW THEY COPE.
THERE'S NO POINT IN FEELING SORRY FOR THEM. WE HAVE TO FIND THE CELESTIAL WARRIOR!
I KNOW...
AND ANOTHER THING!
NEXT TIME YOU GET A CUSTOMER, SWITCH WITH ME!
URUKI... YOU'RE SCARY...
I'LL KNOCK HIM OUT COLD!!
YOU TWO ARE SO CLOSE. ALMOST LIKE LOVERS!

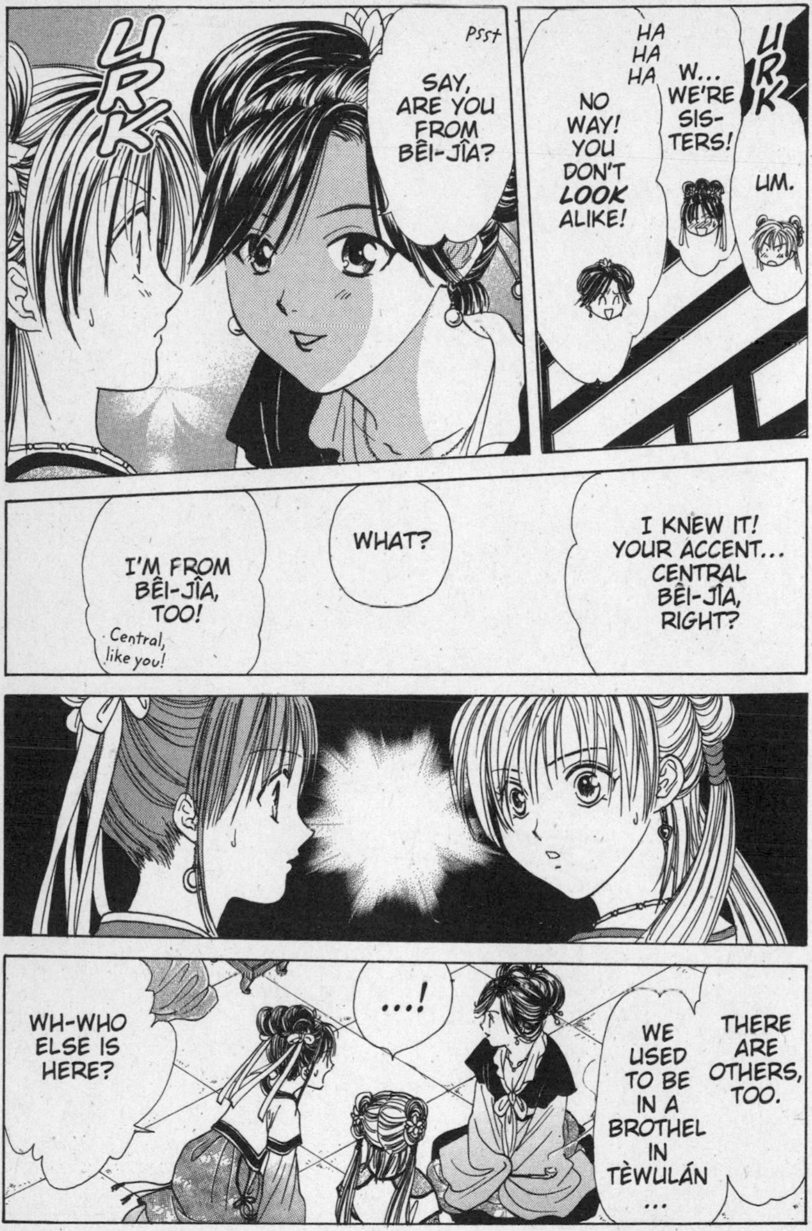
URK
W... WE'RE SISTERS!
UM.
HA HA HA
NO WAY! YOU DON'T LOOK ALIKE!
PSST
SAY, ARE YOU FROM BÊI-JÎA?
URK
I KNEW IT! YOUR ACCENT... CENTRAL BÊI-JÎA, RIGHT?
WHAT?
I'M FROM BÊI-JÎA, TOO!
Central, like you!
THERE ARE OTHERS, TOO.
WE USED TO BE IN A BROTHEL IN TÈWULÁN...
...!
WH-WHO ELSE IS HERE?

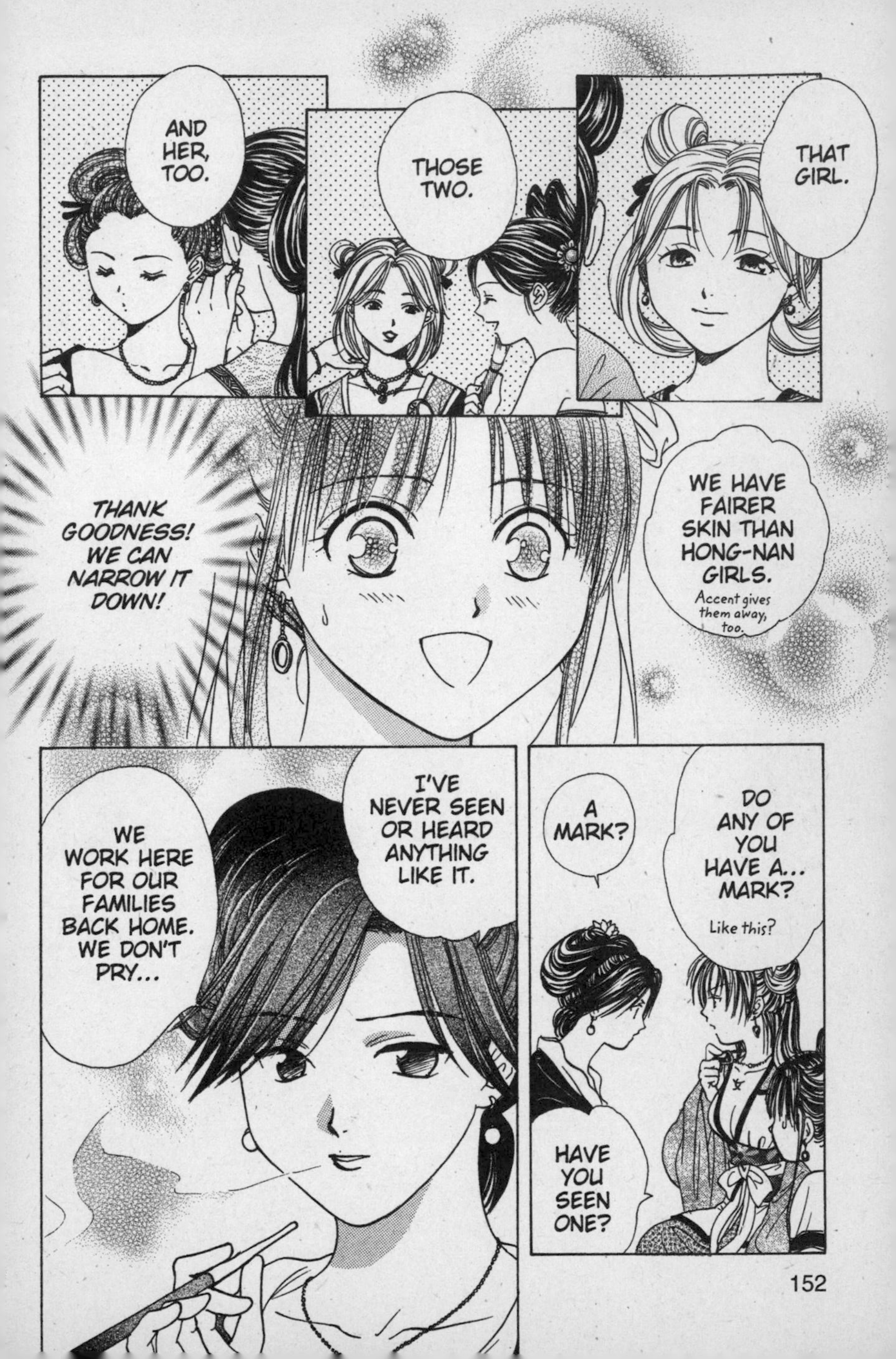
THAT GIRL.
THOSE TWO.
AND HER, TOO.
WE HAVE FAIRER SKIN THAN HONG-NAN GIRLS.
Accent gives them away, too.
THANK GOODNESS! WE CAN NARROW IT DOWN!
DO ANY OF YOU HAVE A... MARK?
Like this?
A MARK?
HAVE YOU SEEN ONE?
I'VE NEVER SEEN OR HEARD ANYTHING LIKE IT.
WE WORK HERE FOR OUR FAMILIES BACK HOME. WE DON'T PRY...

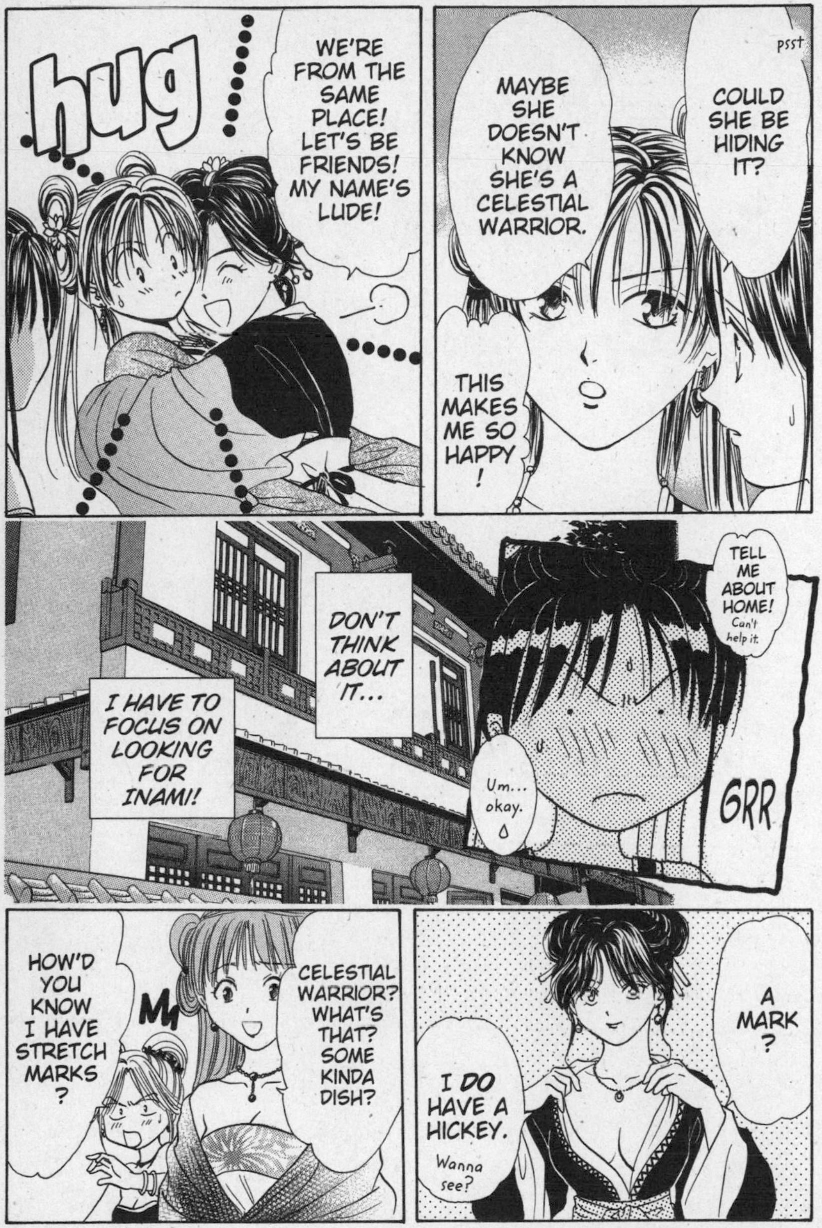
psst
COULD SHE BE HIDING IT?
MAYBE SHE DOESN'T KNOW SHE'S A CELESTIAL WARRIOR.
THIS MAKES ME SO HAPPY!
hug
WE'RE FROM THE SAME PLACE! LET'S BE FRIENDS! MY NAME'S LUDE!
TELL ME ABOUT HOME!
Can't help it.
GRR
Um... okay.
DON'T THINK ABOUT IT...
I HAVE TO FOCUS ON LOOKING FOR INAMI!
A MARK?
I *DO* HAVE A HICKEY.
Wanna see?
CELESTIAL WARRIOR? WHAT'S THAT? SOME KINDA DISH?
Mu
HOW'D YOU KNOW I HAVE STRETCH MARKS?

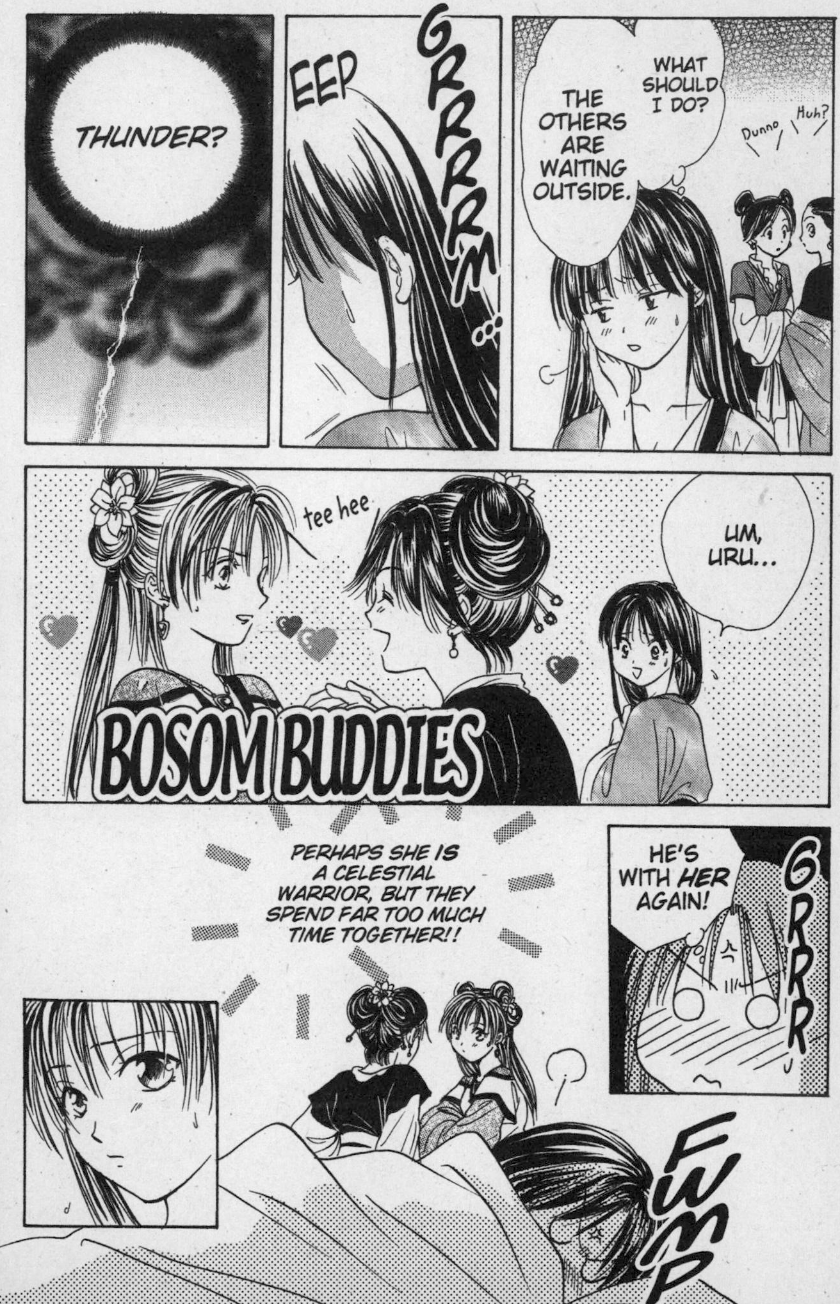
WHAT SHOULD I DO?
THE OTHERS ARE WAITING OUTSIDE.
Huh?
Dunno
GRRRRM..
EEP
THUNDER?
UM, URU...
tee hee
BOSOM BUDDIES
GRRR
HE'S WITH HER AGAIN!
PERHAPS SHE IS A CELESTIAL WARRIOR, BUT THEY SPEND FAR TOO MUCH TIME TOGETHER!!
FUMP

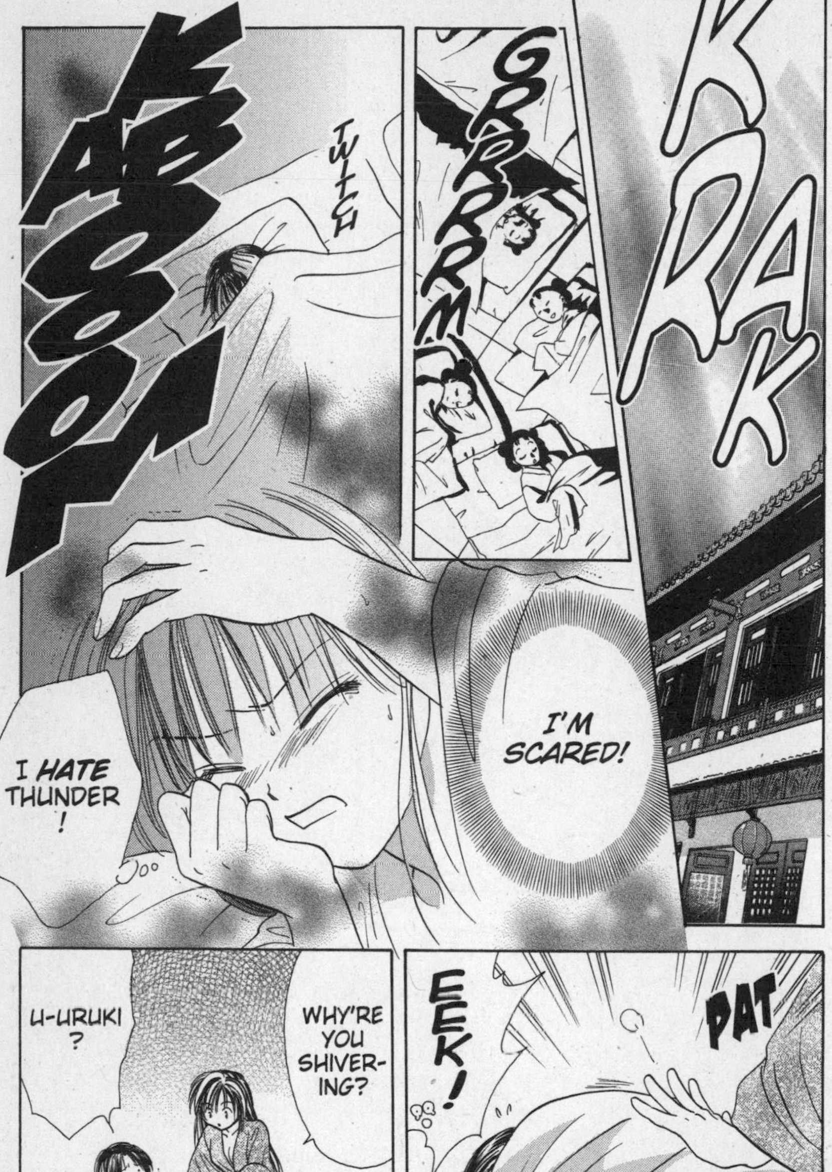
KRAKAK
GRRRM
TWITCH
I'M SCARED!
I HATE THUNDER!
PAT
EEK!
WHY'RE YOU SHIVER-ING?
U-URUKI?

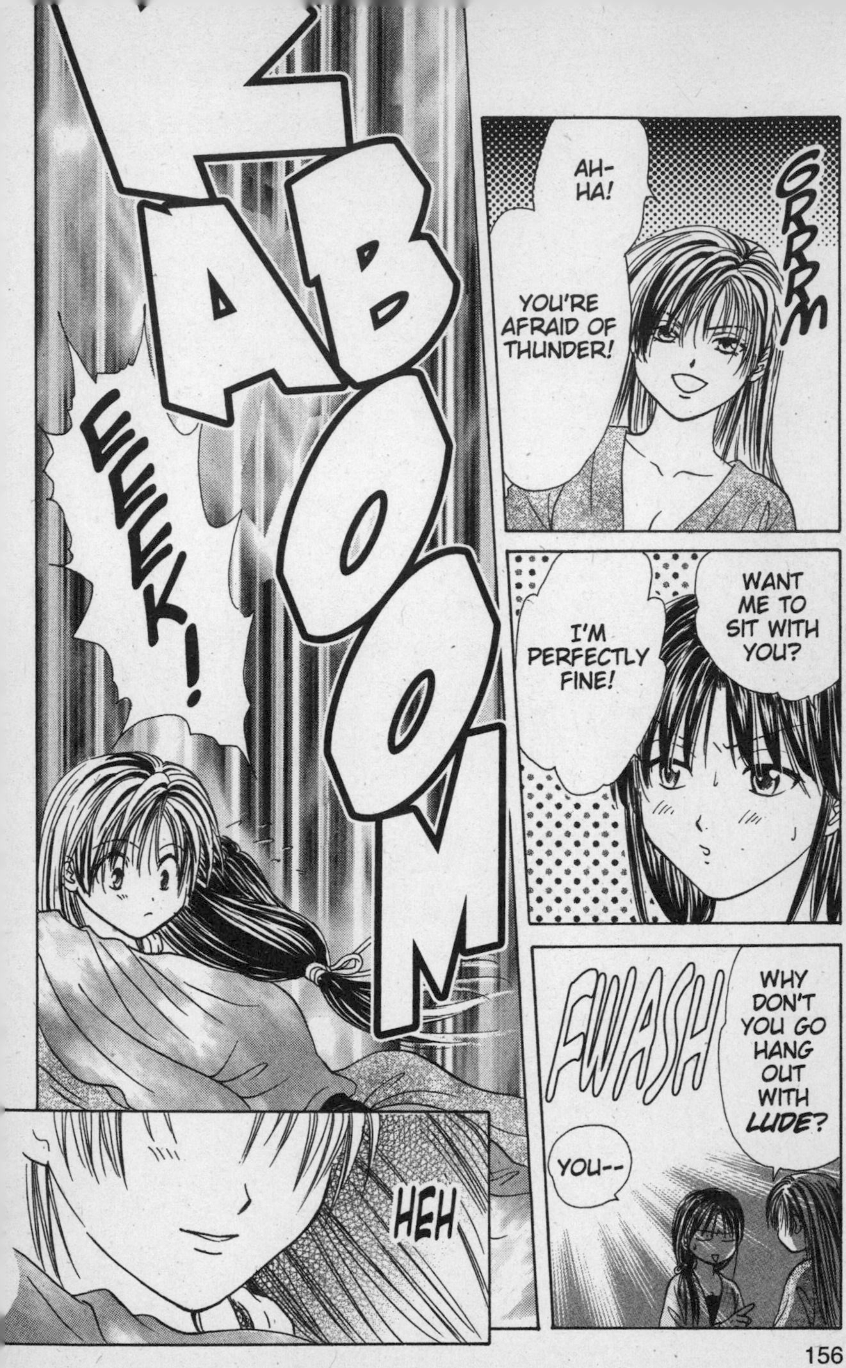
GRRRM
AH-HA!
YOU'RE AFRAID OF THUNDER!
WANT ME TO SIT WITH YOU?
I'M PERFECTLY FINE!
FWASH
WHY DON'T YOU GO HANG OUT WITH *LUDE*?
YOU--
ABOOM
EEEK!
HEH

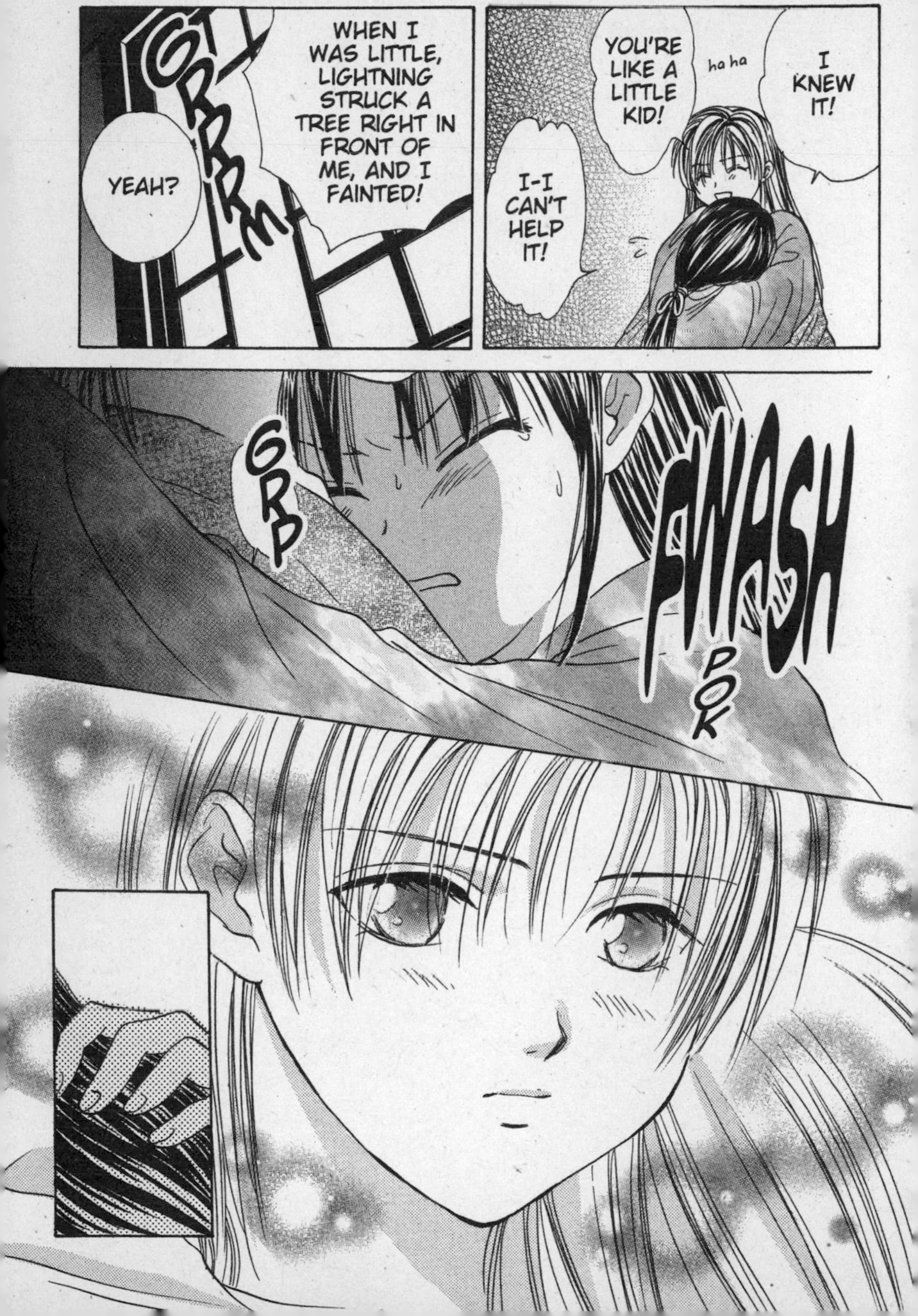
I KNEW IT!
ha ha
YOU'RE LIKE A LITTLE KID!
I-I CAN'T HELP IT!
WHEN I WAS LITTLE, LIGHTNING STRUCK A TREE RIGHT IN FRONT OF ME, AND I FAINTED!
GRRRRm
YEAH?
FWASH
POK
GRP

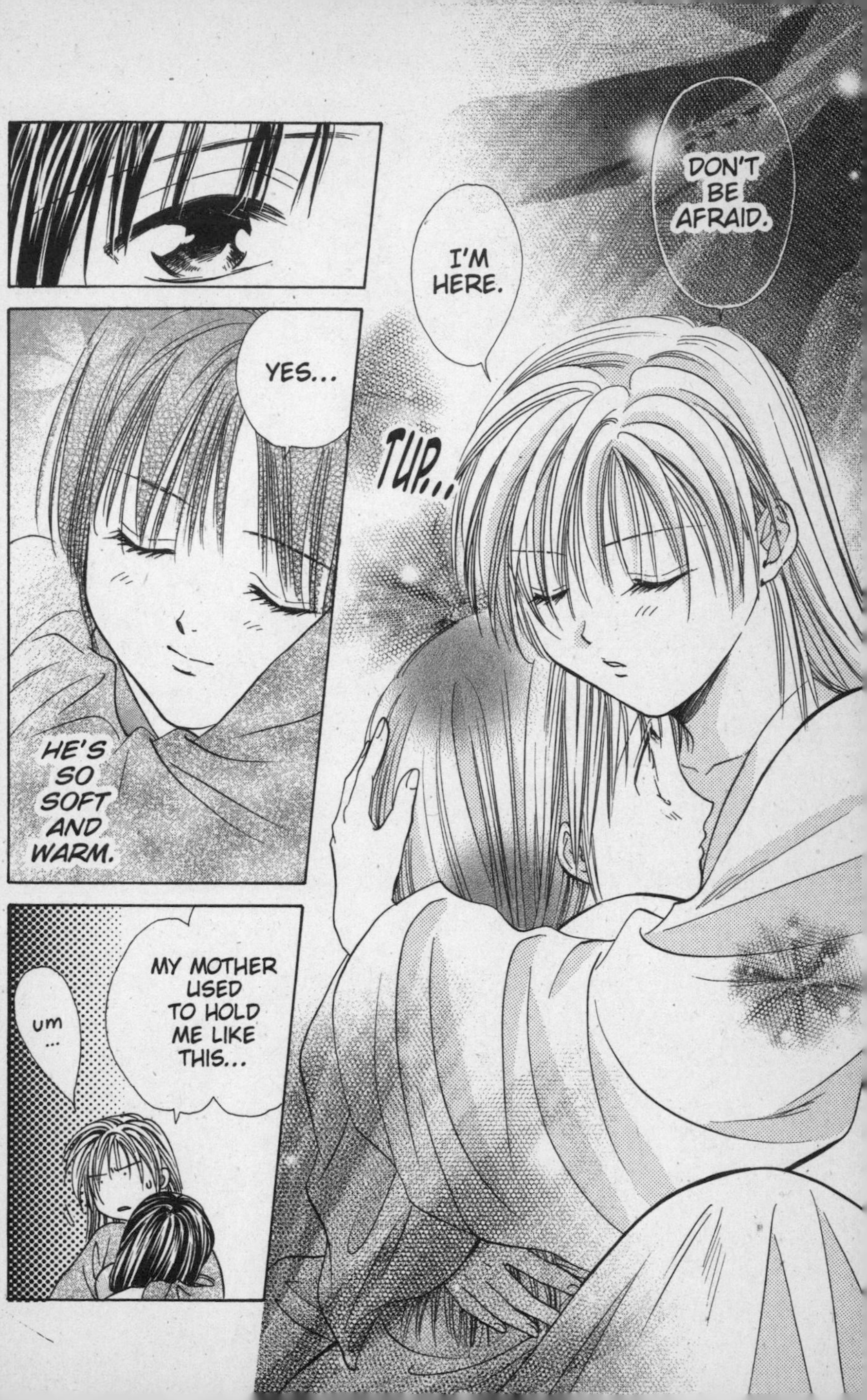
DON'T BE AFRAID.
I'M HERE.
TUP...
YES...
HE'S SO SOFT AND WARM.
MY MOTHER USED TO HOLD ME LIKE THIS...
um ...

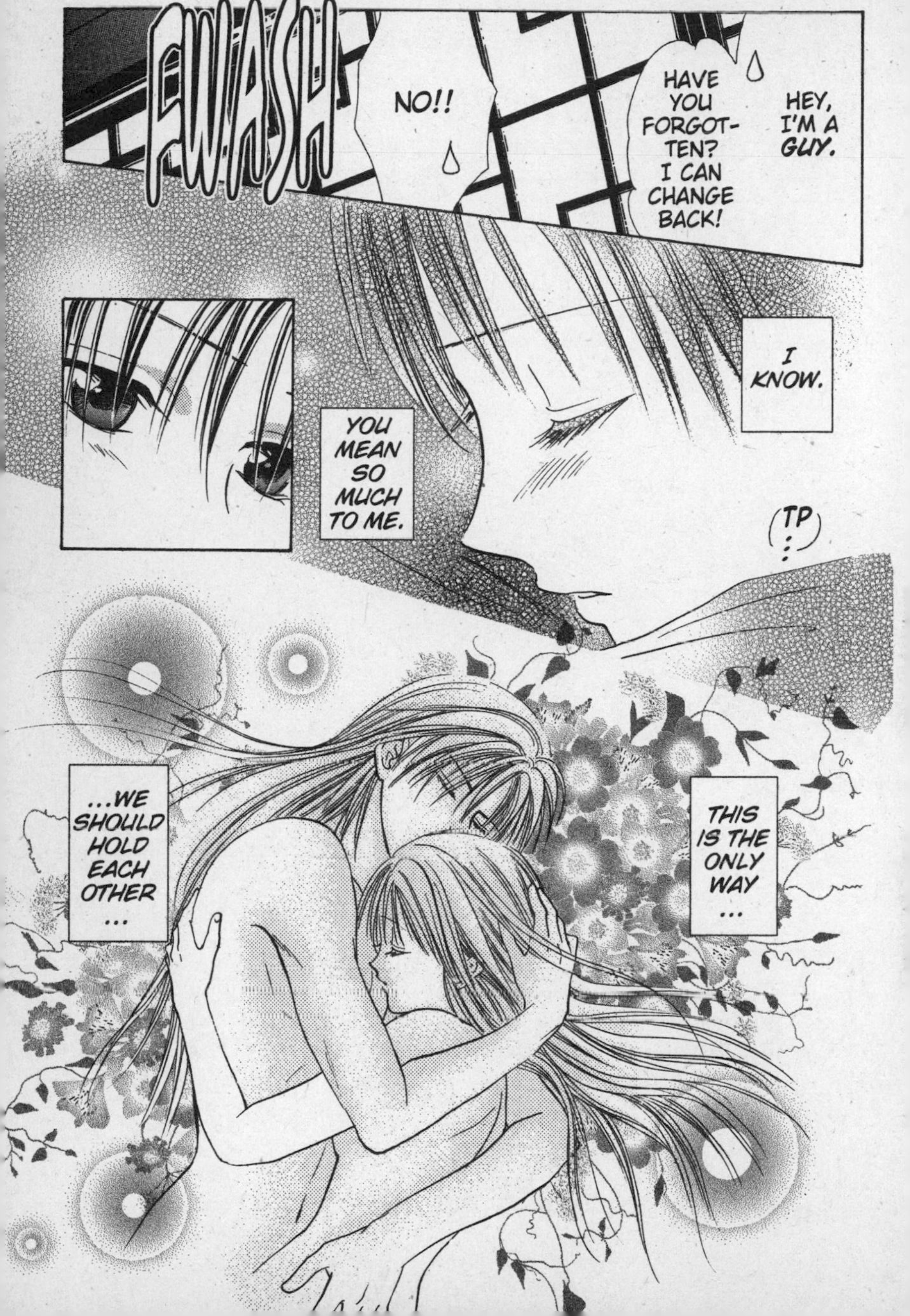
HEY, I'M A GUY.
HAVE YOU FORGOT-TEN? I CAN CHANGE BACK!
NO!!
FWASH
I KNOW.
YOU MEAN SO MUCH TO ME.
TP
THIS IS THE ONLY WAY ...
...WE SHOULD HOLD EACH OTHER ...

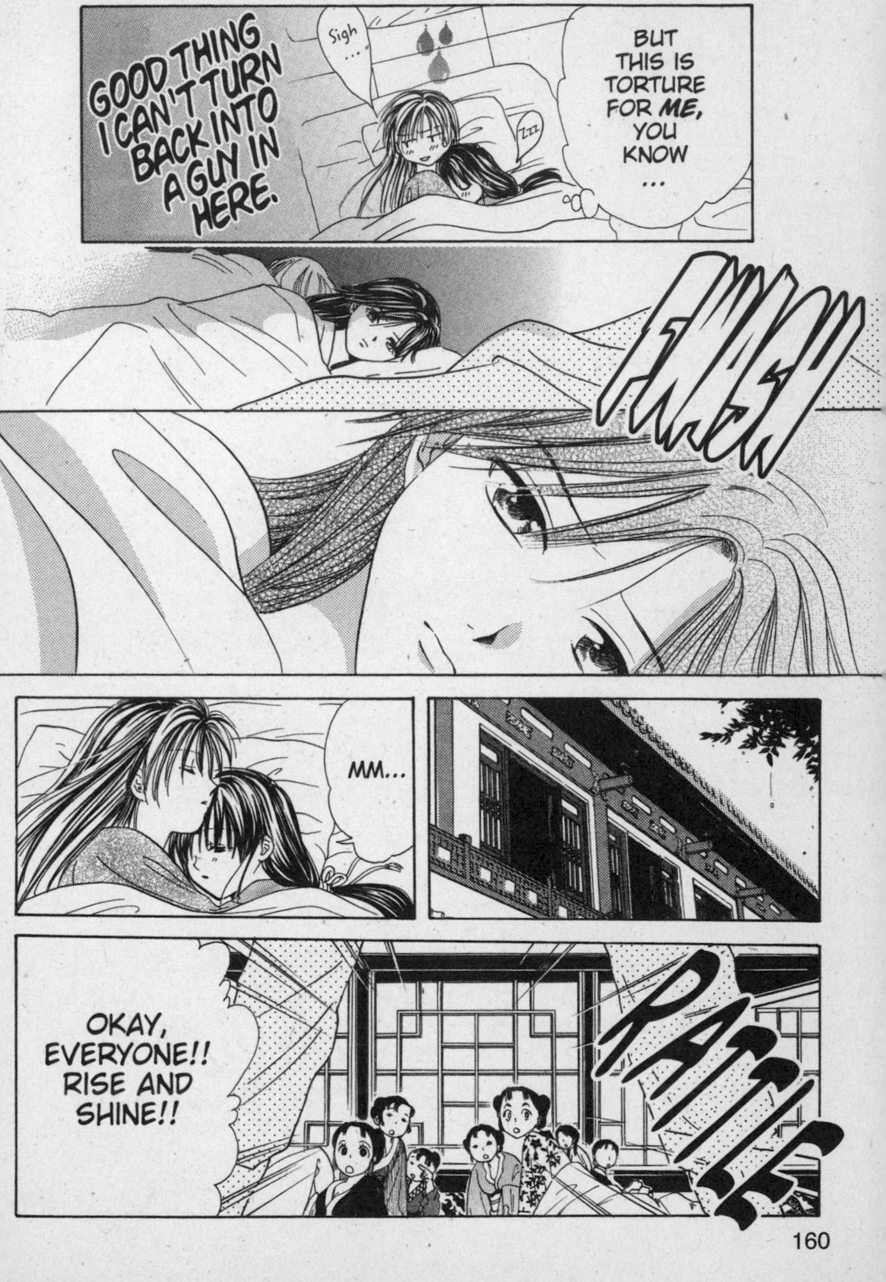
BUT THIS IS TORTURE FOR *ME*, YOU KNOW ...
Sigh ...
Zzz
GOOD THING I CAN'T TURN BACK INTO A GUY IN HERE.
FWASH
MM...
RATTLE
OKAY, EVERYONE!! RISE AND SHINE!!

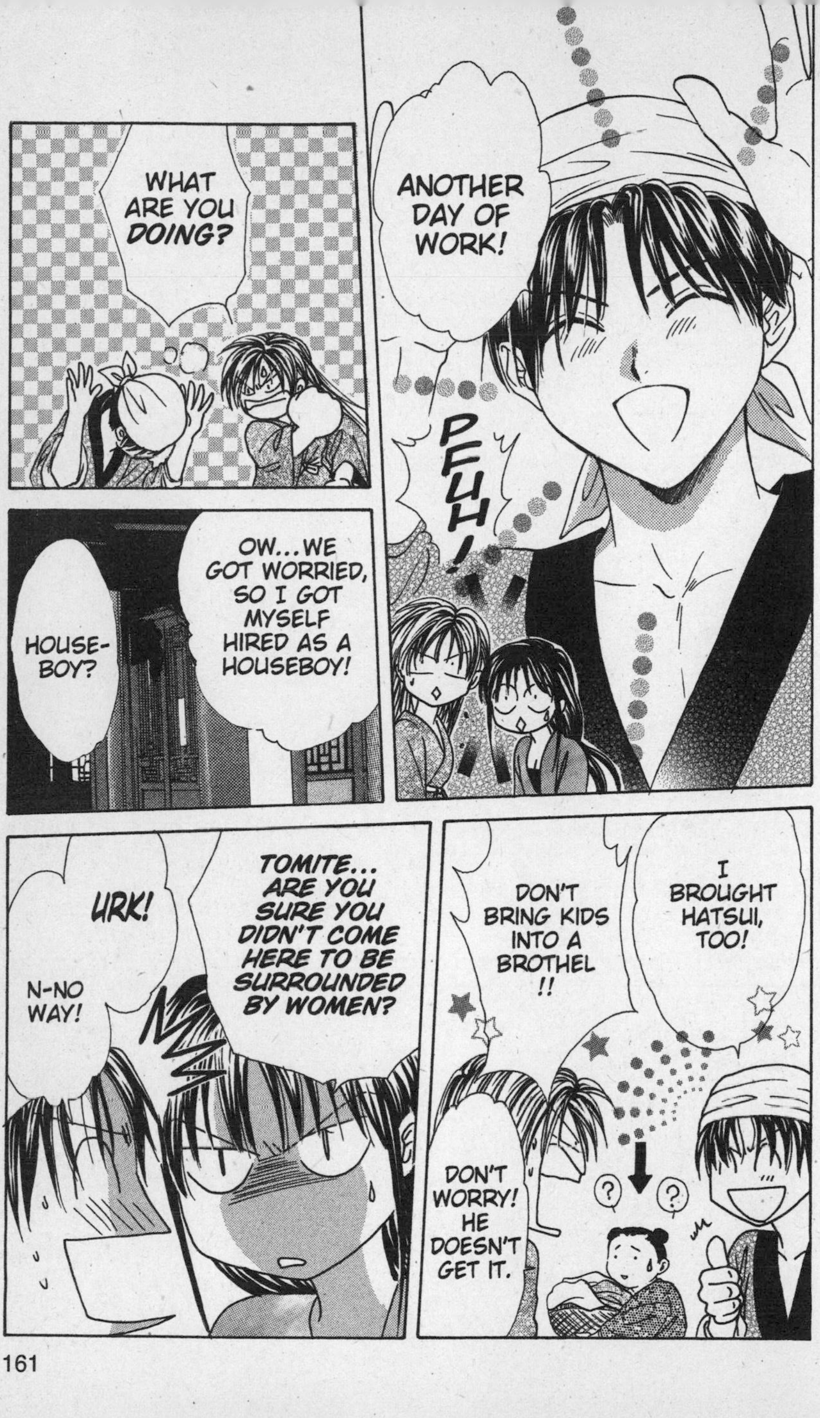
ANOTHER DAY OF WORK!
PFUH!
WHAT ARE YOU *DOING?*
OW...WE GOT WORRIED, SO I GOT MYSELF HIRED AS A HOUSEBOY!
HOUSE-BOY?
I BROUGHT HATSUI, TOO!
DON'T BRING KIDS INTO A BROTHEL !!
DON'T WORRY! HE DOESN'T GET IT.
TOMITE... ARE YOU SURE YOU DIDN'T COME HERE TO BE SURROUNDED BY WOMEN?
URK!
N-NO WAY!

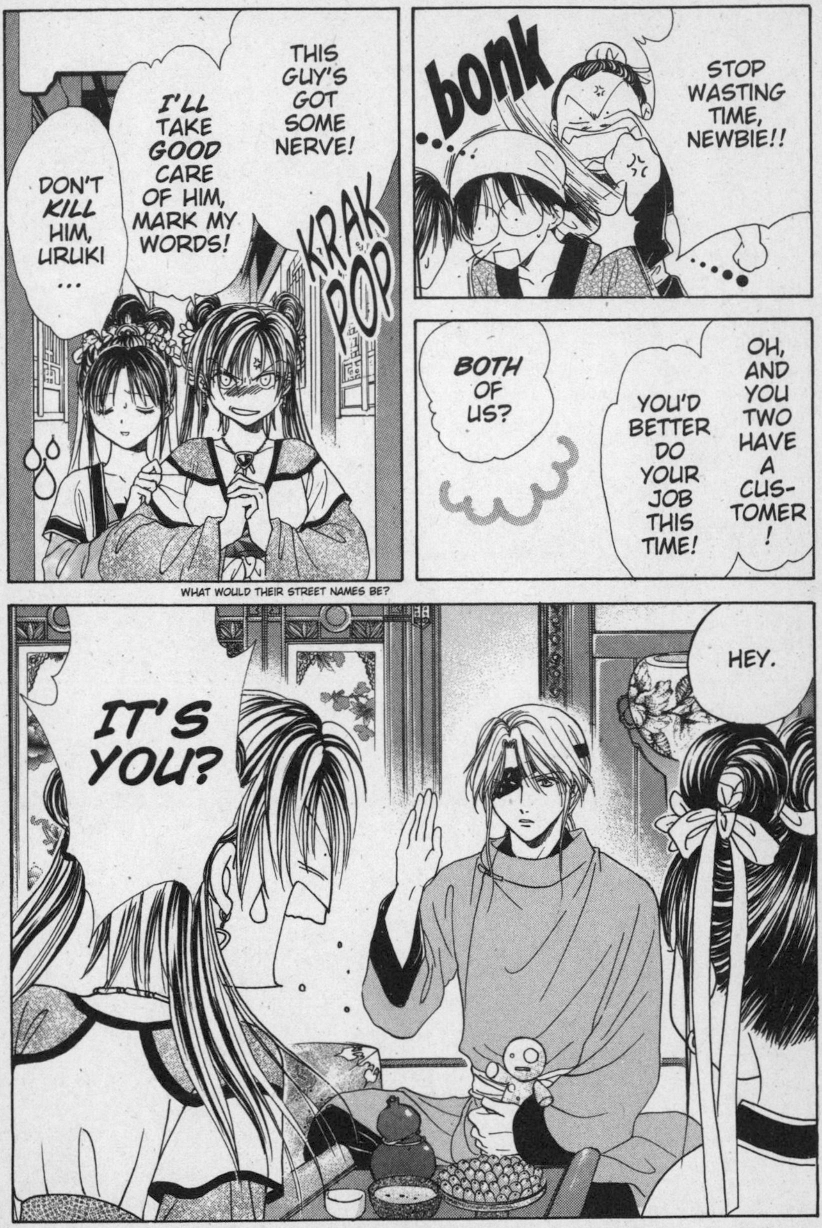
STOP WASTING TIME, NEWBIE!!
...bonk
OH, AND YOU TWO HAVE A CUS-TOMER!
YOU'D BETTER DO YOUR JOB THIS TIME!
BOTH OF US?
THIS GUY'S GOT SOME NERVE!
I'LL TAKE GOOD CARE OF HIM, MARK MY WORDS!
DON'T KILL HIM, URUKI...
KRAK
POP
WHAT WOULD THEIR STREET NAMES BE?
HEY.
IT'S YOU?

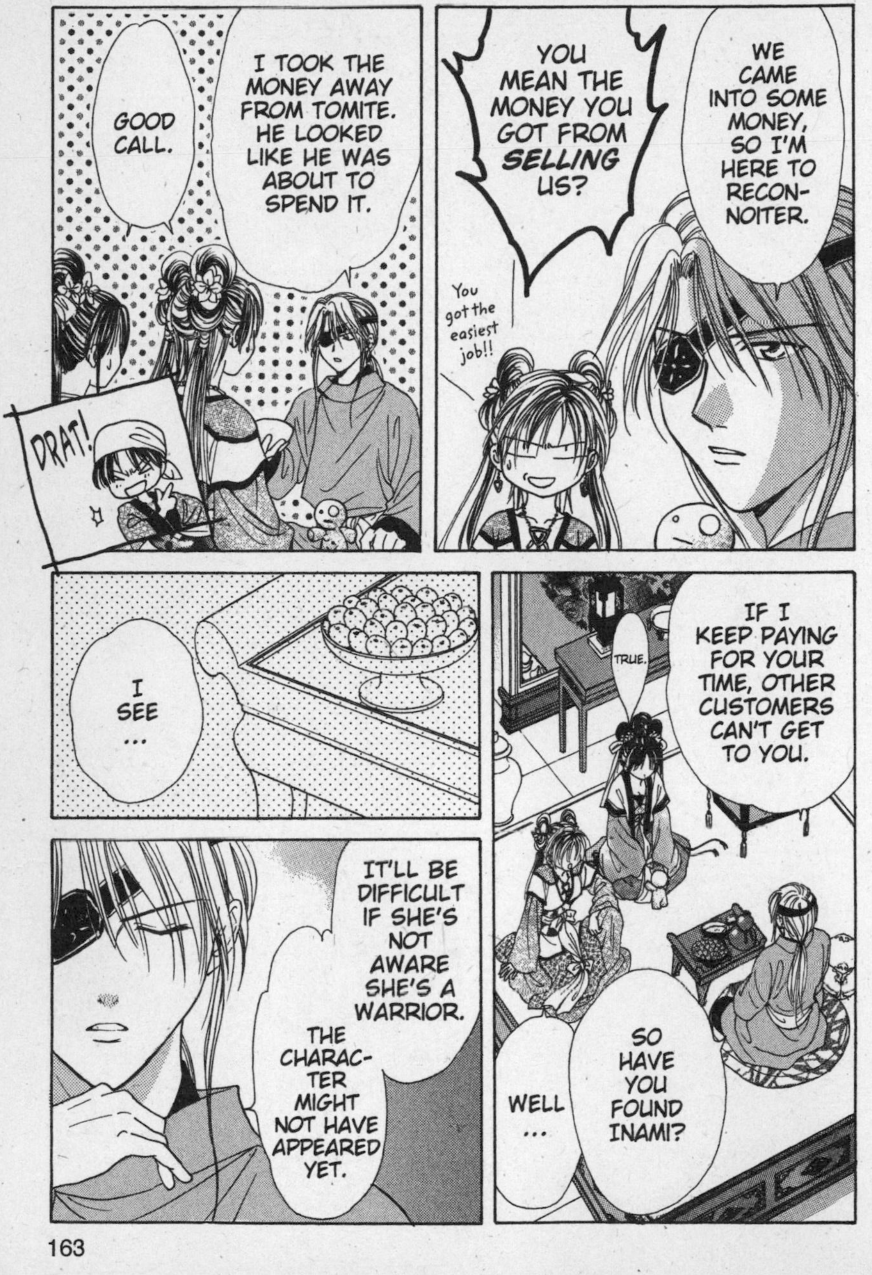
WE CAME INTO SOME MONEY, SO I'M HERE TO RECON-NOITER.
YOU MEAN THE MONEY YOU GOT FROM SELLING US?
You got the easiest job!!
I TOOK THE MONEY AWAY FROM TOMITE. HE LOOKED LIKE HE WAS ABOUT TO SPEND IT.
GOOD CALL.
DRAT!
IF I KEEP PAYING FOR YOUR TIME, OTHER CUSTOMERS CAN'T GET TO YOU.
TRUE.
SO HAVE YOU FOUND INAMI?
WELL ...
I SEE ...
IT'LL BE DIFFICULT IF SHE'S NOT AWARE SHE'S A WARRIOR.
THE CHARAC-TER MIGHT NOT HAVE APPEARED YET.

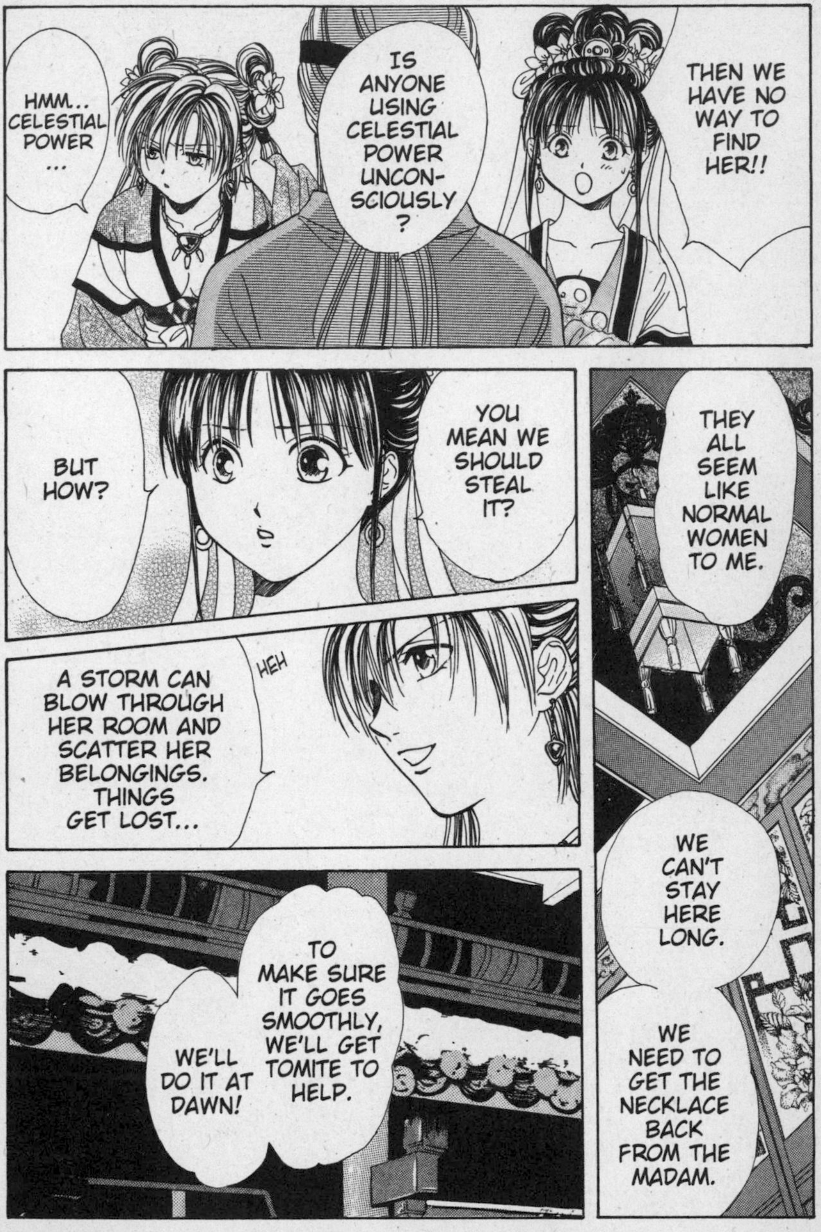
THEN WE HAVE NO WAY TO FIND HER!!
IS ANYONE USING CELESTIAL POWER UNCONSCIOUSLY?
HMM... CELESTIAL POWER...
THEY ALL SEEM LIKE NORMAL WOMEN TO ME.
WE CAN'T STAY HERE LONG.
WE NEED TO GET THE NECKLACE BACK FROM THE MADAM.
YOU MEAN WE SHOULD STEAL IT?
BUT HOW?
HEH
A STORM CAN BLOW THROUGH HER ROOM AND SCATTER HER BELONGINGS. THINGS GET LOST...
TO MAKE SURE IT GOES SMOOTHLY, WE'LL GET TOMITE TO HELP.
WE'LL DO IT AT DAWN!

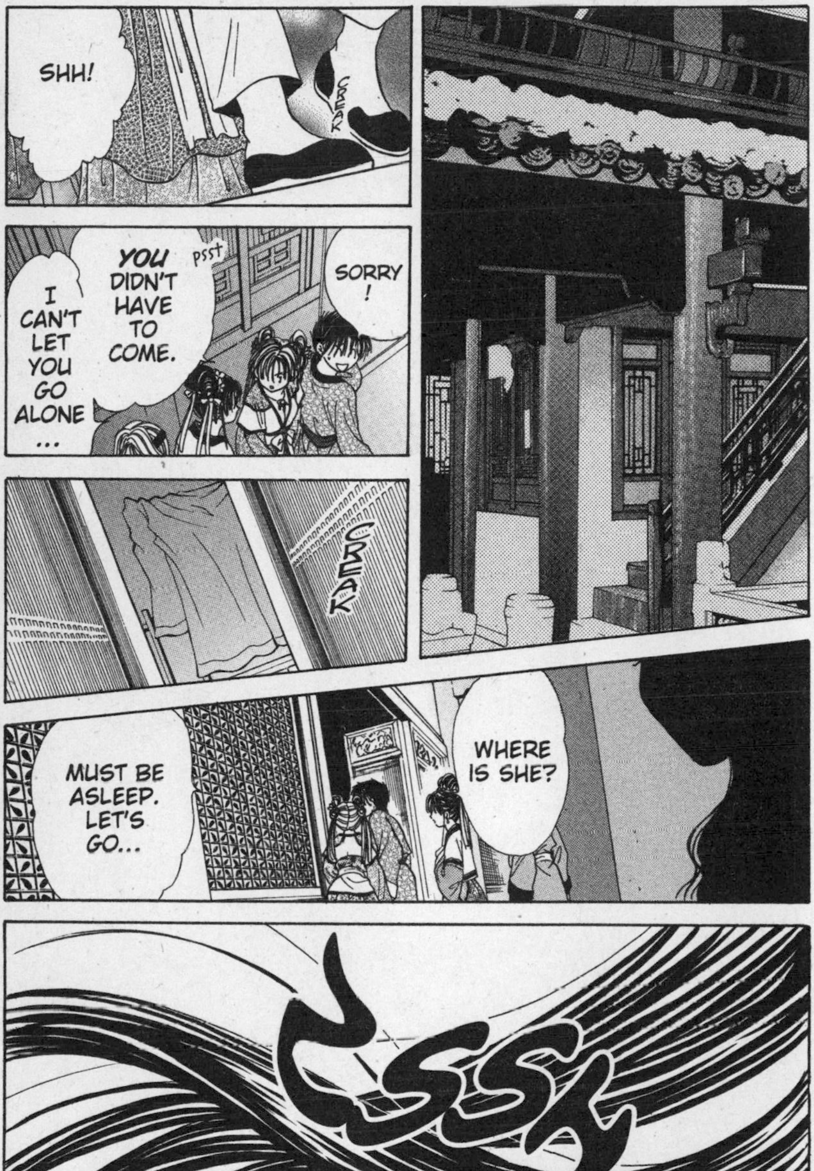
SHH!
CREAK
SORRY!
psst
YOU DIDN'T HAVE TO COME.
I CAN'T LET YOU GO ALONE...
CREAK
WHERE IS SHE?
MUST BE ASLEEP. LET'S GO...
SSSH

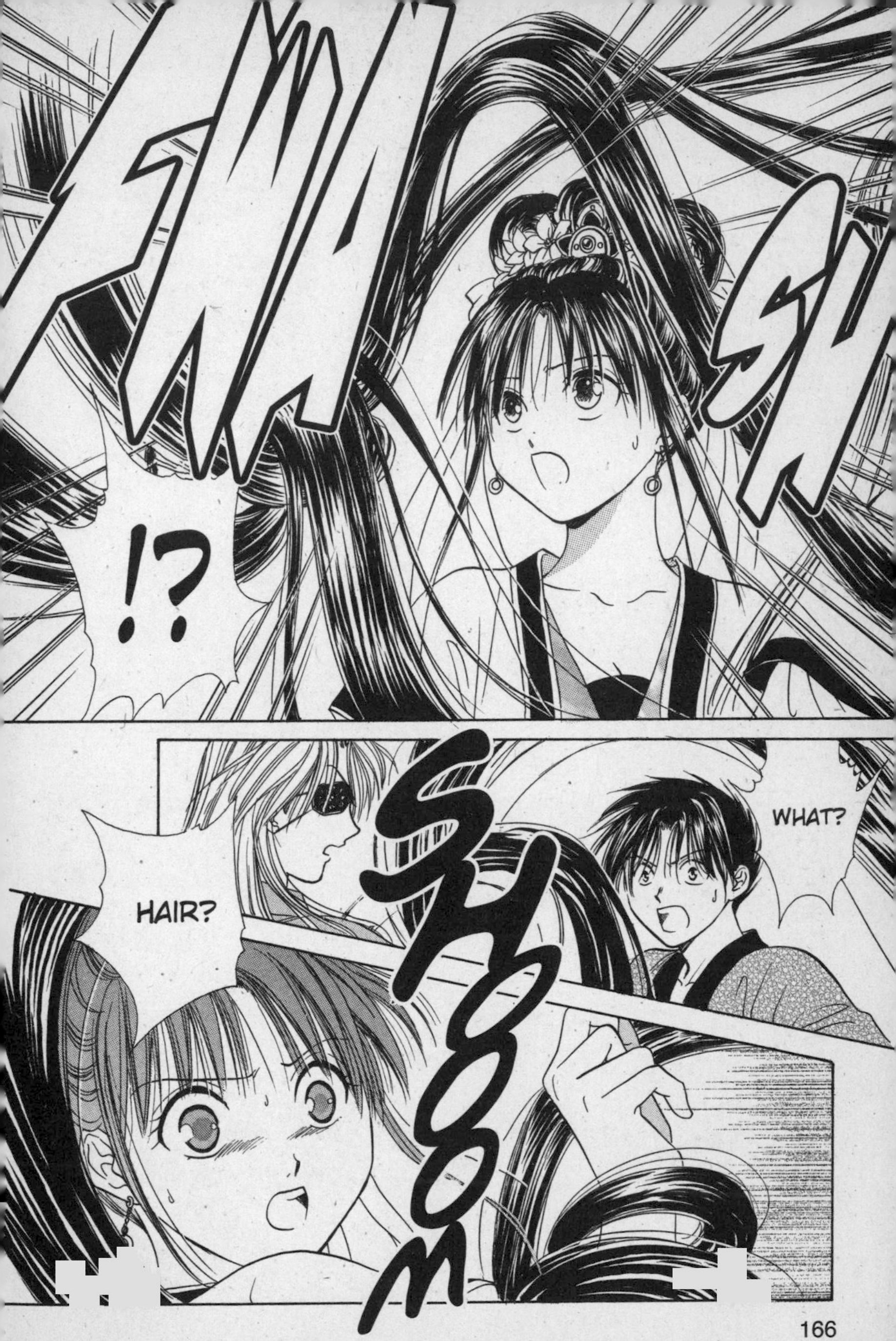
SWASH
!?
SHOOOM
WHAT?
HAIR?

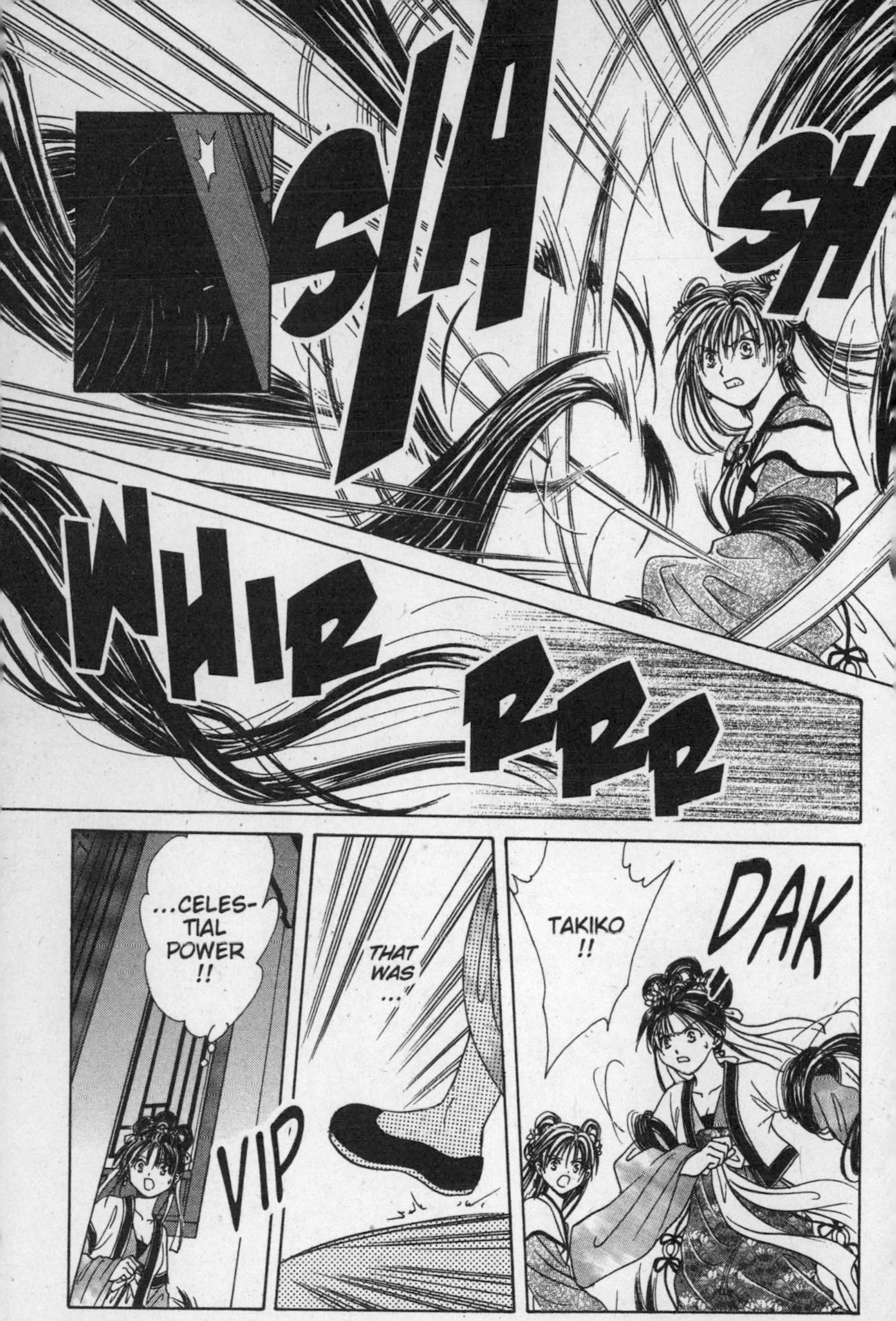
SLASH
WHIRRRR
DAK
TAKIKO !!
THAT WAS ...
VIP
...CELESTIAL POWER !!

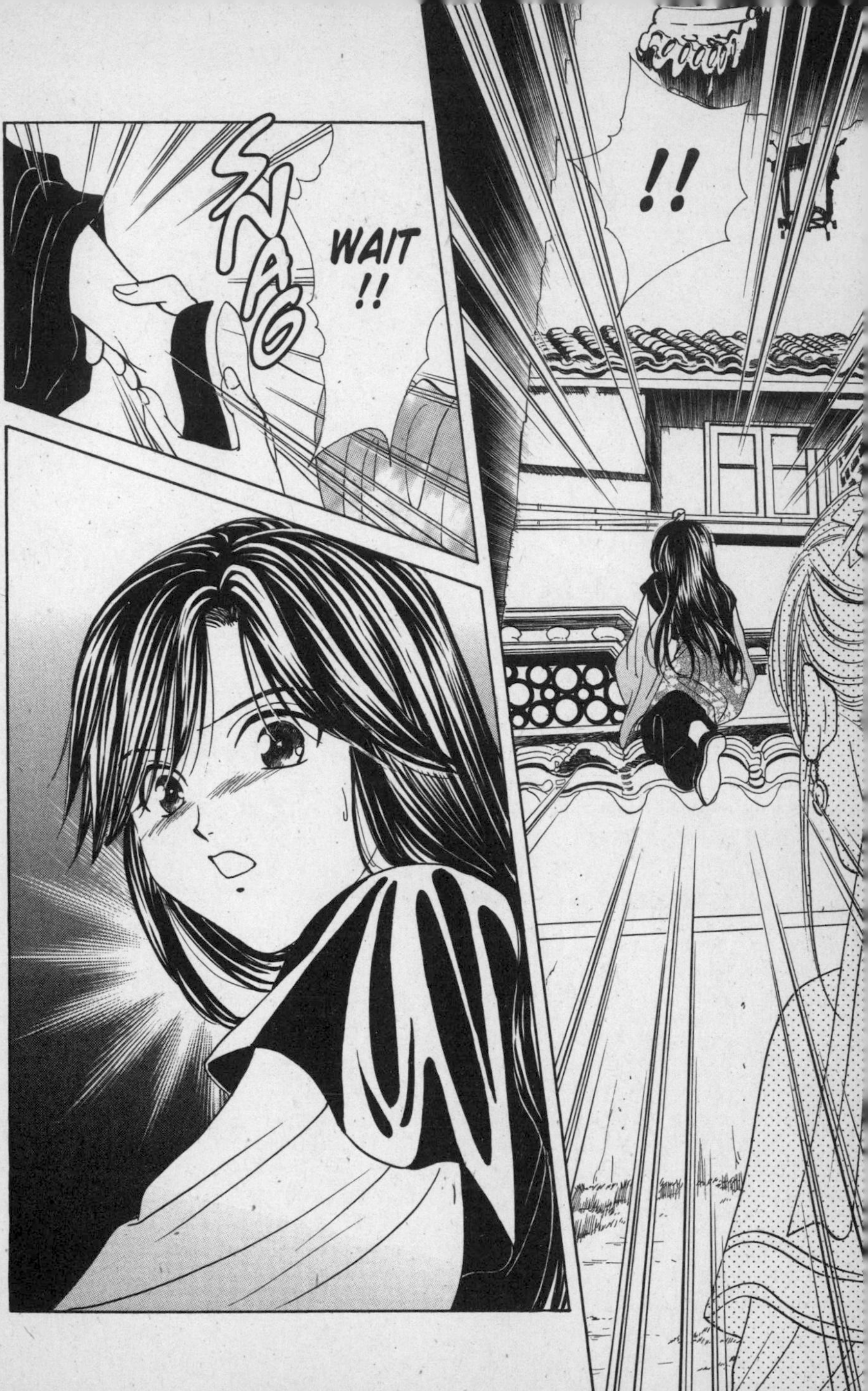
!!
WAIT !!
SNAG

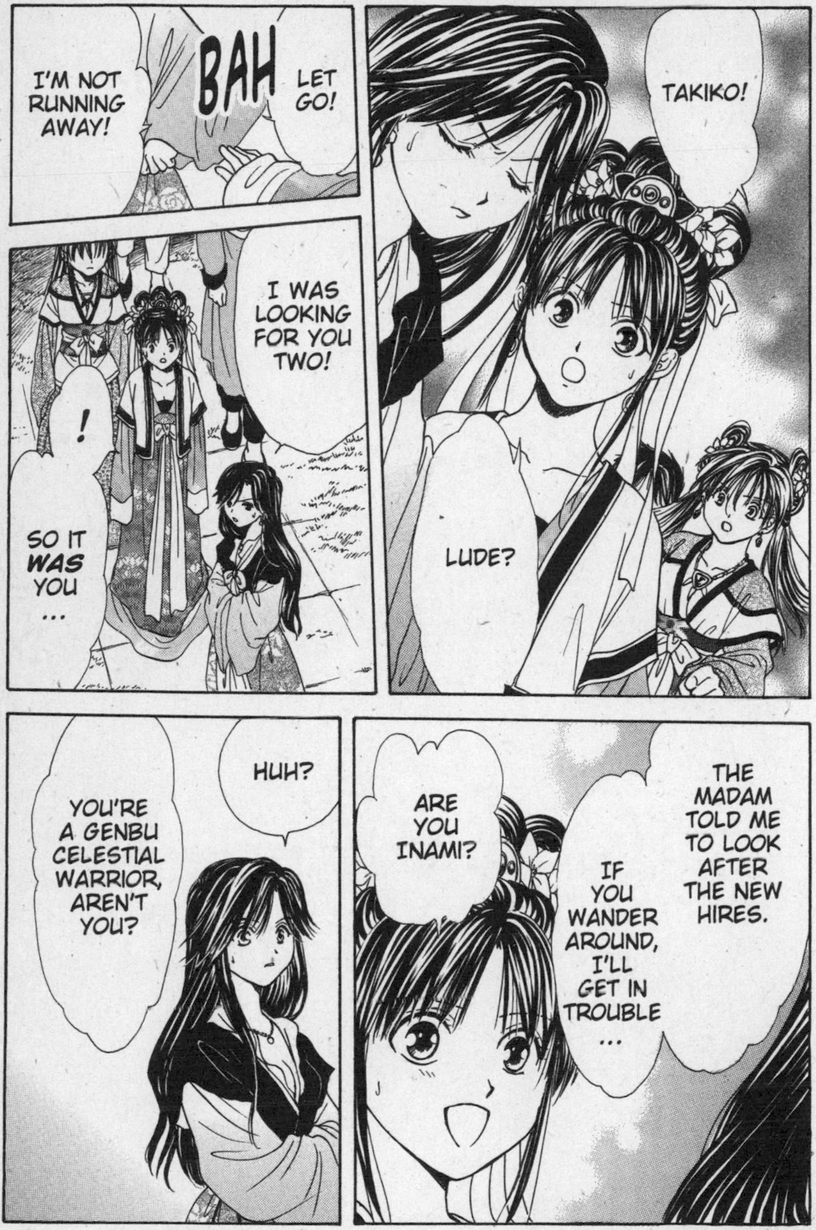
TAKIKO!
LUDE?
LET GO!
BAH
I'M NOT RUNNING AWAY!
I WAS LOOKING FOR YOU TWO!
!
SO IT *WAS* YOU ...
THE MADAM TOLD ME TO LOOK AFTER THE NEW HIRES.
IF YOU WANDER AROUND, I'LL GET IN TROUBLE ...
ARE YOU INAMI?
HUH?
YOU'RE A GENBU CELESTIAL WARRIOR, AREN'T YOU?

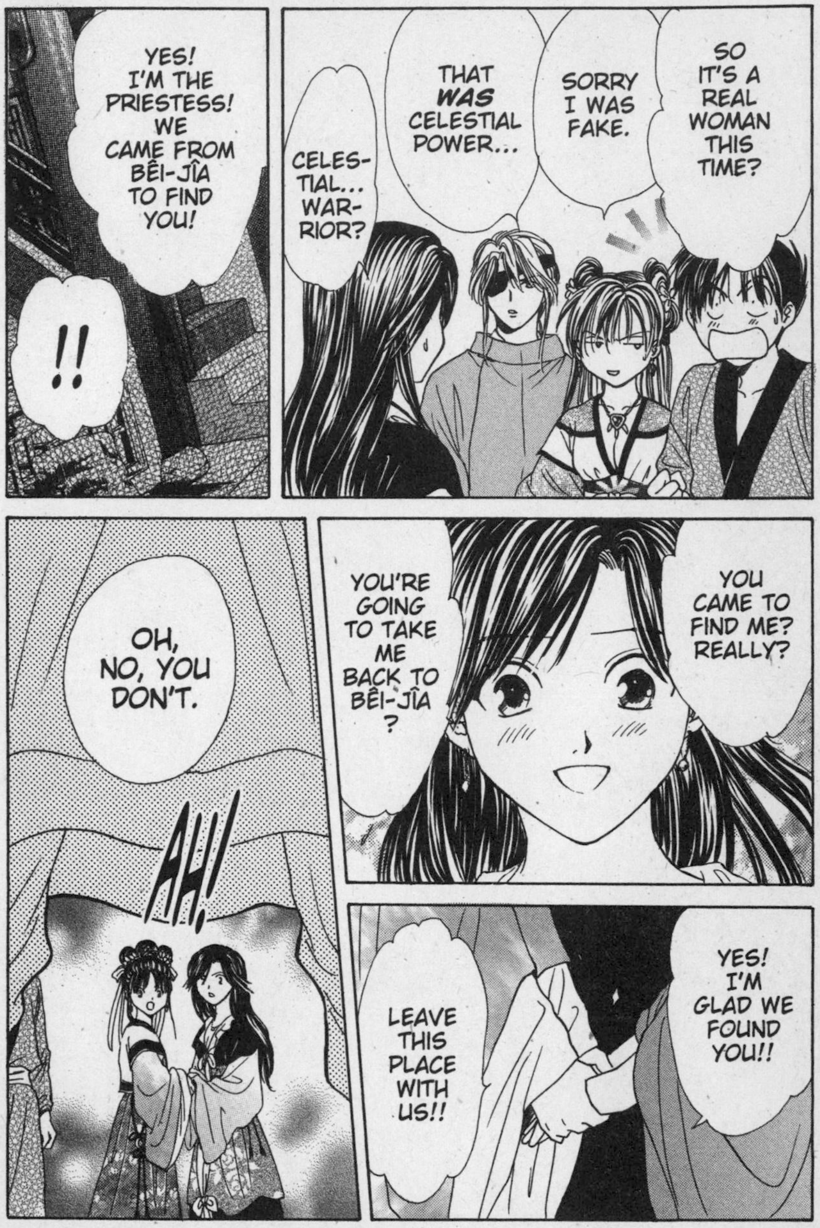
SO IT'S A REAL WOMAN THIS TIME?
SORRY I WAS FAKE.
THAT *WAS* CELESTIAL POWER...
CELES-TIAL... WAR-RIOR?
YES! I'M THE PRIESTESS! WE CAME FROM BÊI-JÎA TO FIND YOU!
!!
YOU CAME TO FIND ME? REALLY?
YOU'RE GOING TO TAKE ME BACK TO BÊI-JÎA?
YES! I'M GLAD WE FOUND YOU!!
LEAVE THIS PLACE WITH US!!
OH, NO, YOU DON'T.
AH!

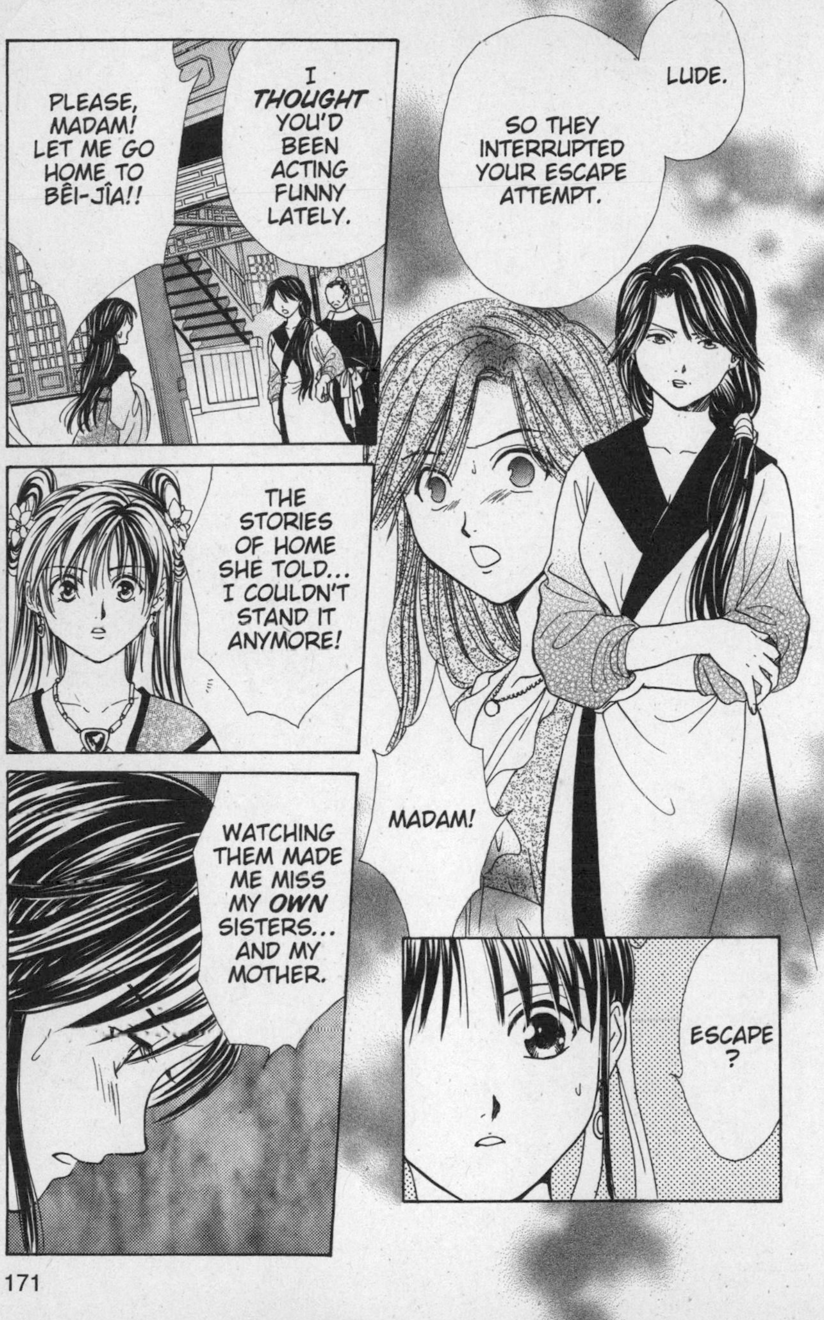
LUDE.
SO THEY INTERRUPTED YOUR ESCAPE ATTEMPT.
MADAM!
I *THOUGHT* YOU'D BEEN ACTING FUNNY LATELY.
PLEASE, MADAM! LET ME GO HOME TO BÊI-JÎA!!
THE STORIES OF HOME SHE TOLD... I COULDN'T STAND IT ANYMORE!
WATCHING THEM MADE ME MISS MY *OWN* SISTERS... AND MY MOTHER.
ESCAPE?

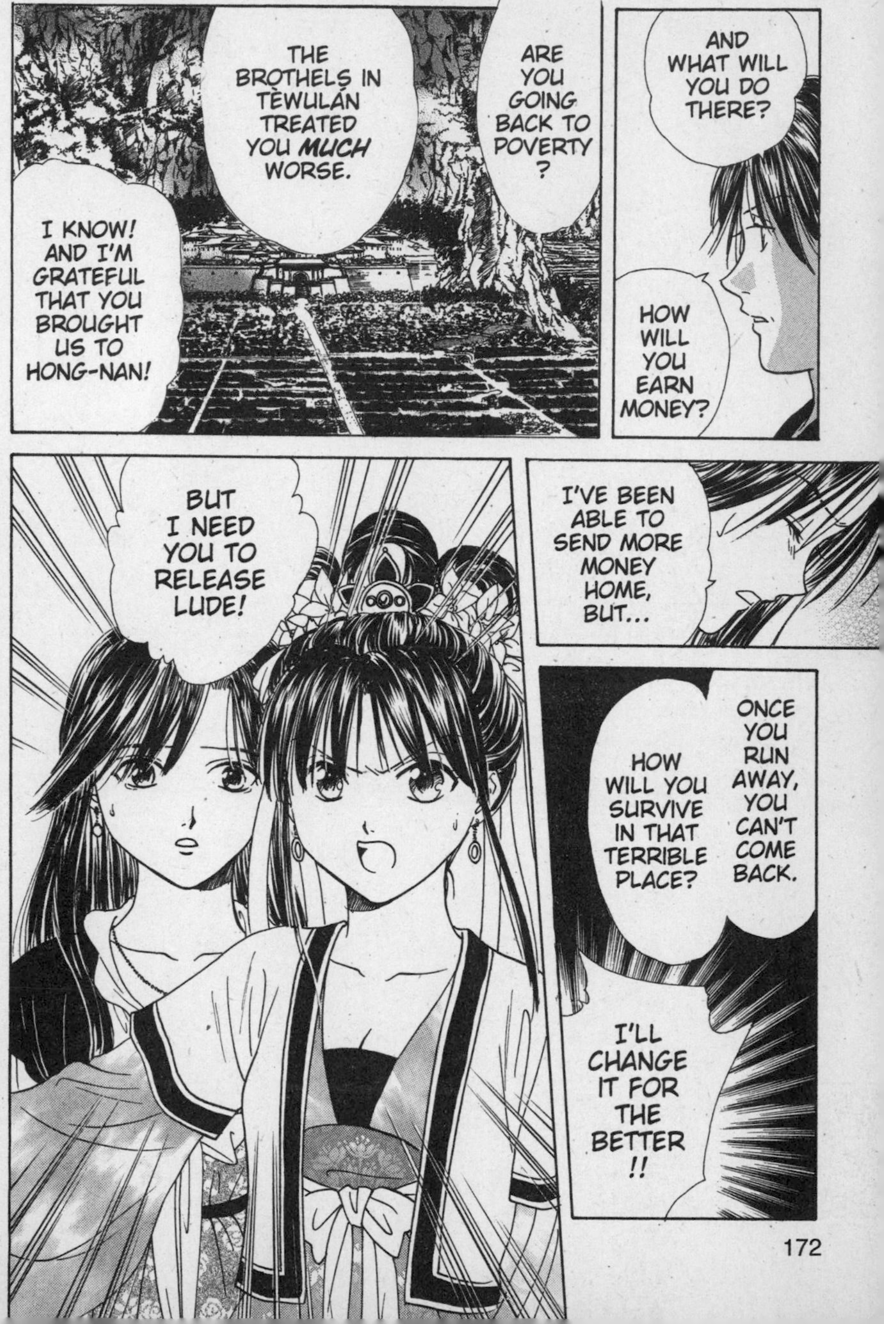
AND WHAT WILL YOU DO THERE?
HOW WILL YOU EARN MONEY?
ARE YOU GOING BACK TO POVERTY?
THE BROTHELS IN TÈWULÁN TREATED YOU *MUCH* WORSE.
I KNOW! AND I'M GRATEFUL THAT YOU BROUGHT US TO HONG-NAN!
I'VE BEEN ABLE TO SEND MORE MONEY HOME, BUT...
ONCE YOU RUN AWAY, YOU CAN'T COME BACK.
HOW WILL YOU SURVIVE IN THAT TERRIBLE PLACE?
I'LL CHANGE IT FOR THE BETTER!!
BUT I NEED YOU TO RELEASE LUDE!

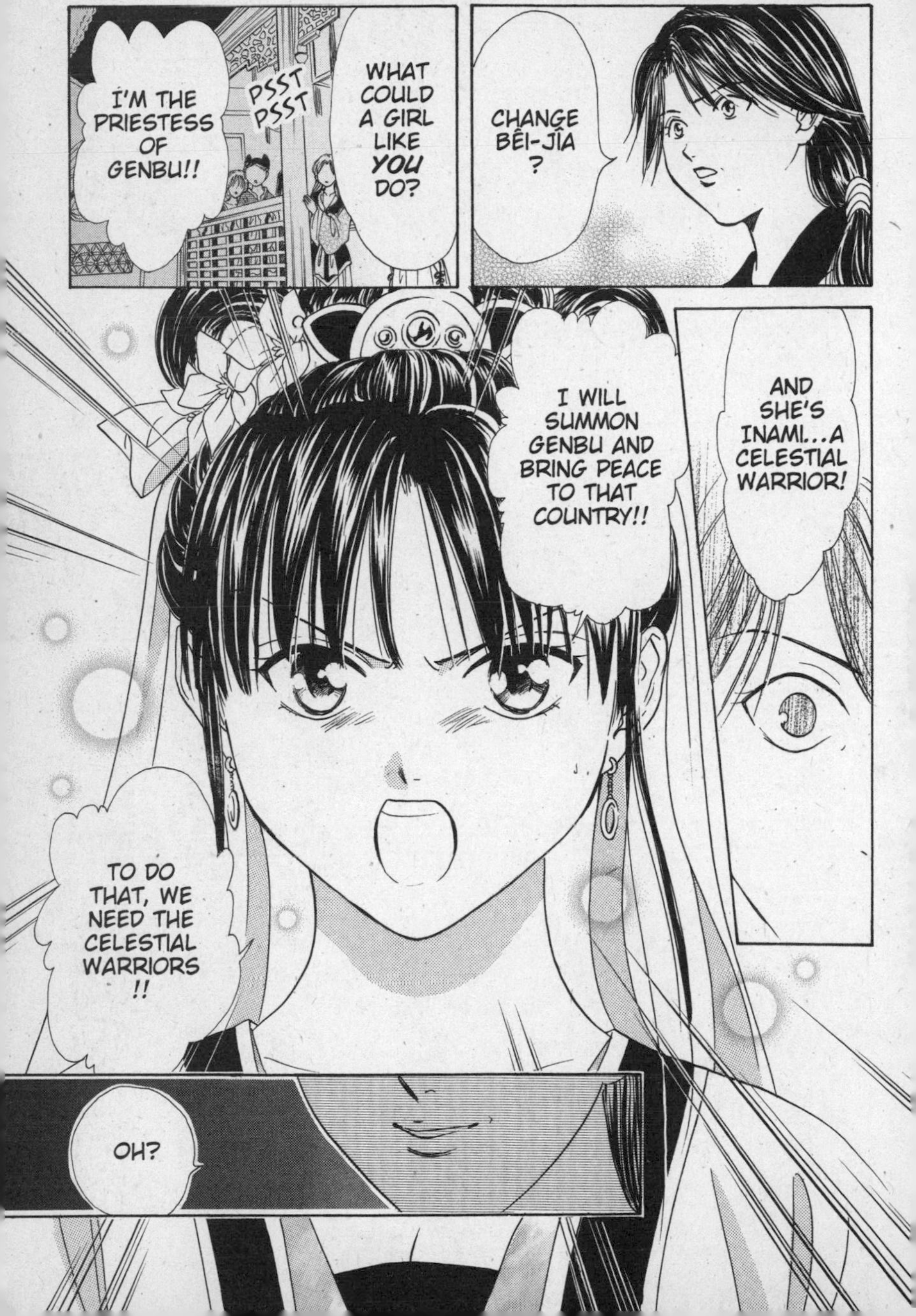
CHANGE BÊI-JÎA ?
WHAT COULD A GIRL LIKE *YOU* DO?
PSST PSST
I'M THE PRIESTESS OF GENBU!!
I WILL SUMMON GENBU AND BRING PEACE TO THAT COUNTRY!!
TO DO THAT, WE NEED THE CELESTIAL WARRIORS!!
AND SHE'S INAMI...A CELESTIAL WARRIOR!
OH?

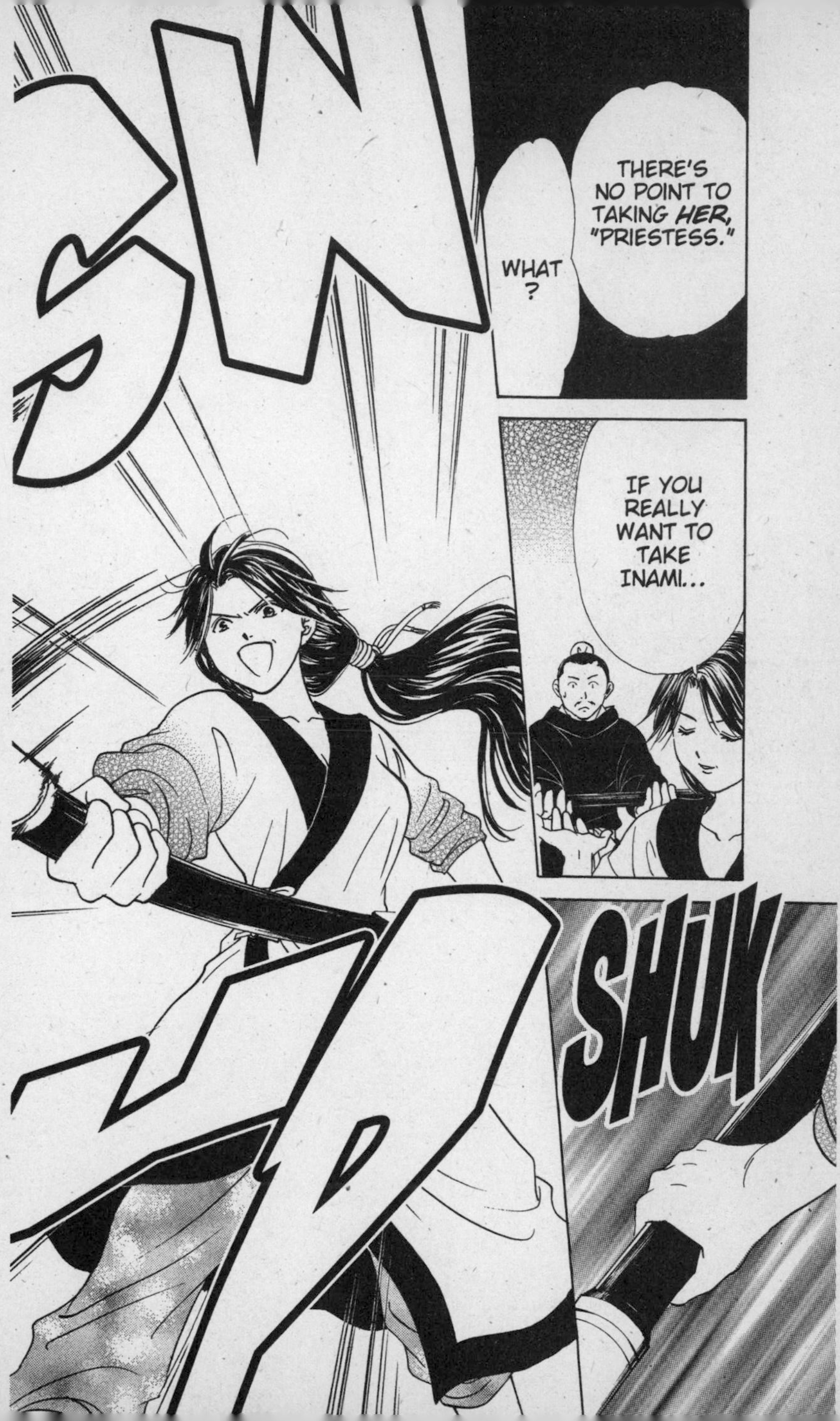
THERE'S NO POINT TO TAKING *HER*, "PRIESTESS."
WHAT ?
IF YOU REALLY WANT TO TAKE INAMI...
SHUK

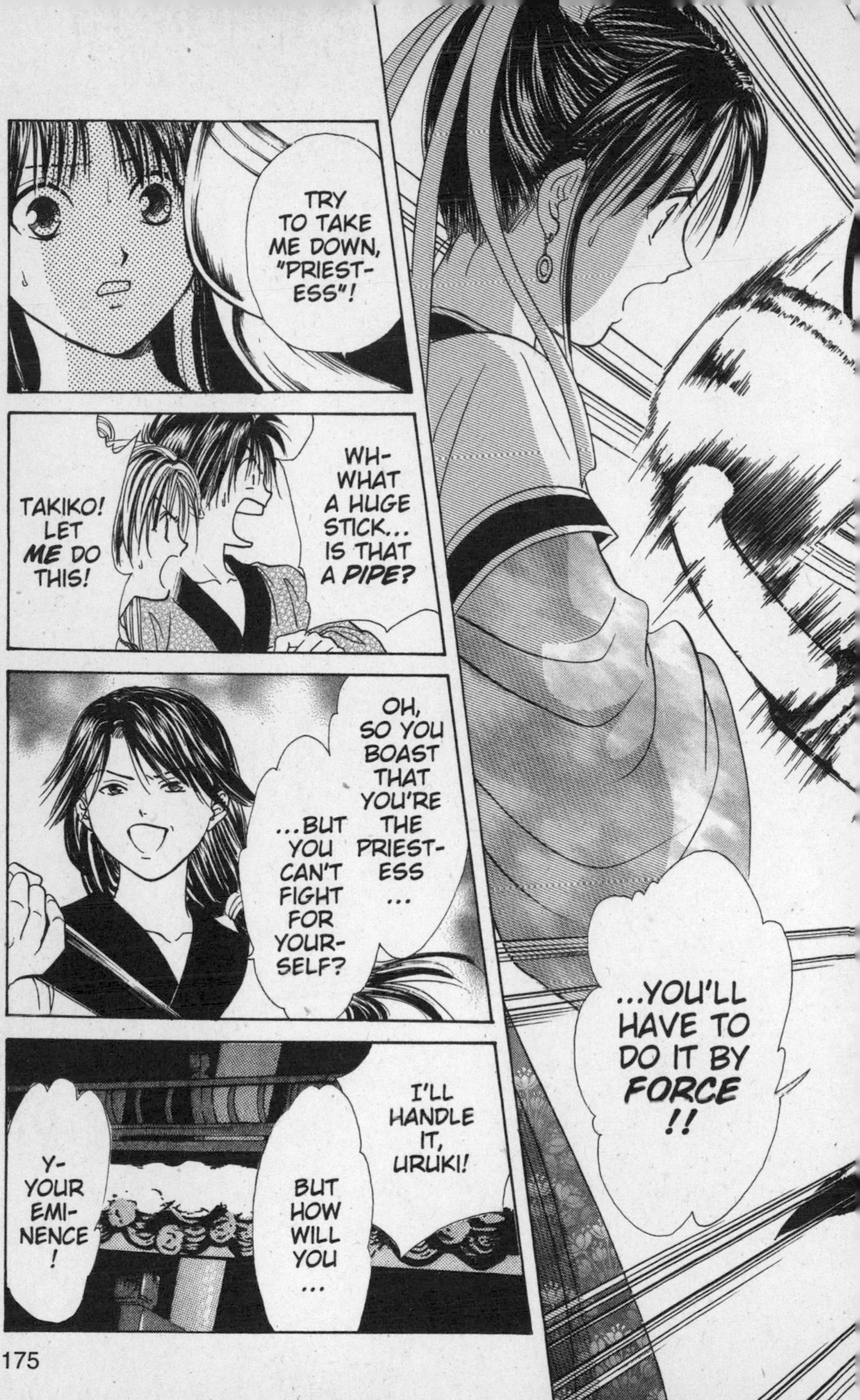
...YOU'LL HAVE TO DO IT BY **FORCE** !!
TRY TO TAKE ME DOWN, "PRIEST-ESS"!
WH-WHAT A HUGE STICK... IS THAT A ***PIPE?***
TAKIKO! LET ***ME*** DO THIS!
OH, SO YOU BOAST THAT YOU'RE THE PRIEST-ESS...
...BUT YOU CAN'T FIGHT FOR YOUR-SELF?
I'LL HANDLE IT, URUKI!
BUT HOW WILL YOU...
Y-YOUR EMI-NENCE!

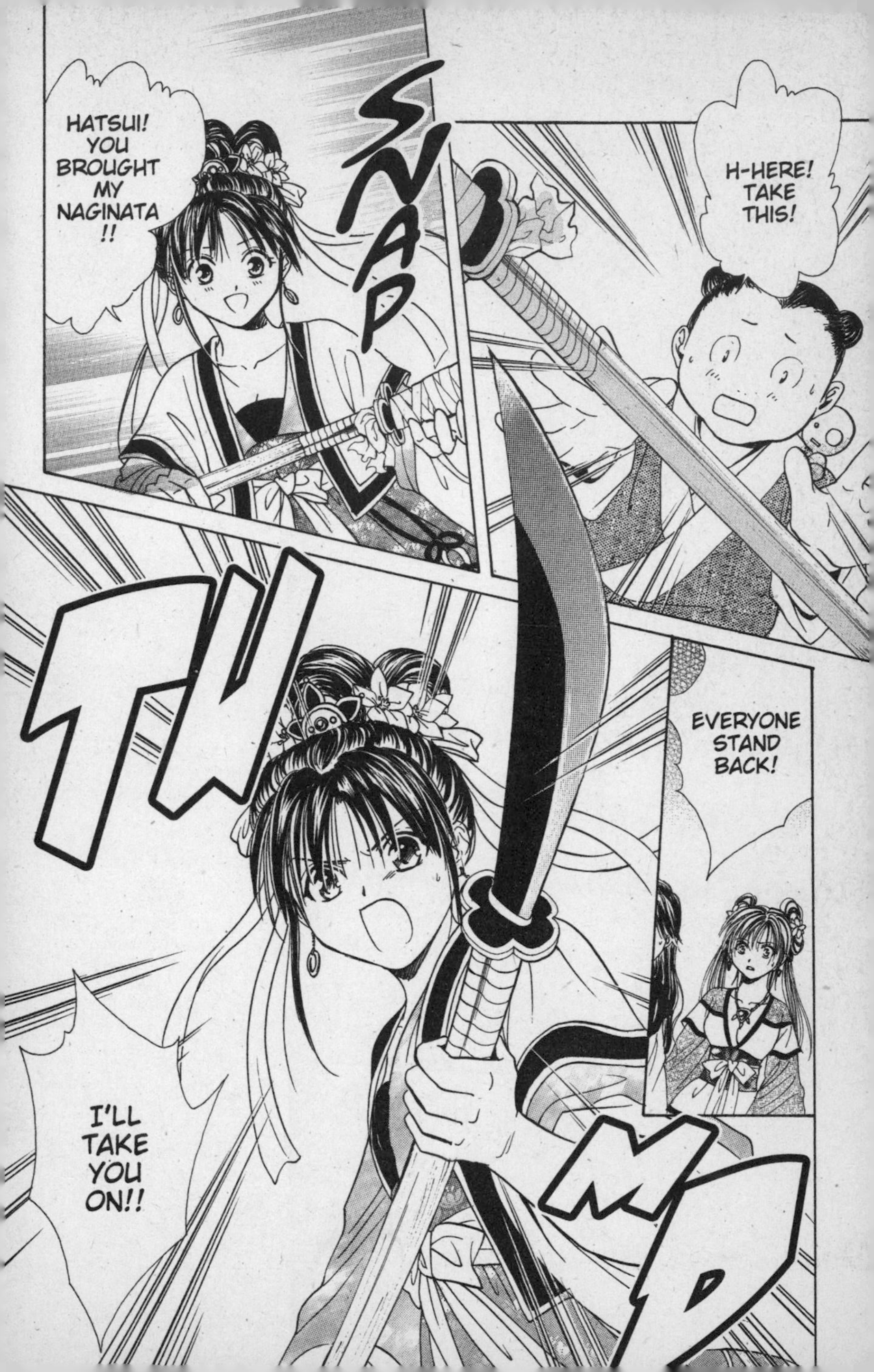
H-HERE! TAKE THIS!
SNAP
HATSUI! YOU BROUGHT MY NAGINATA!!
EVERYONE STAND BACK!
I'LL TAKE YOU ON!!

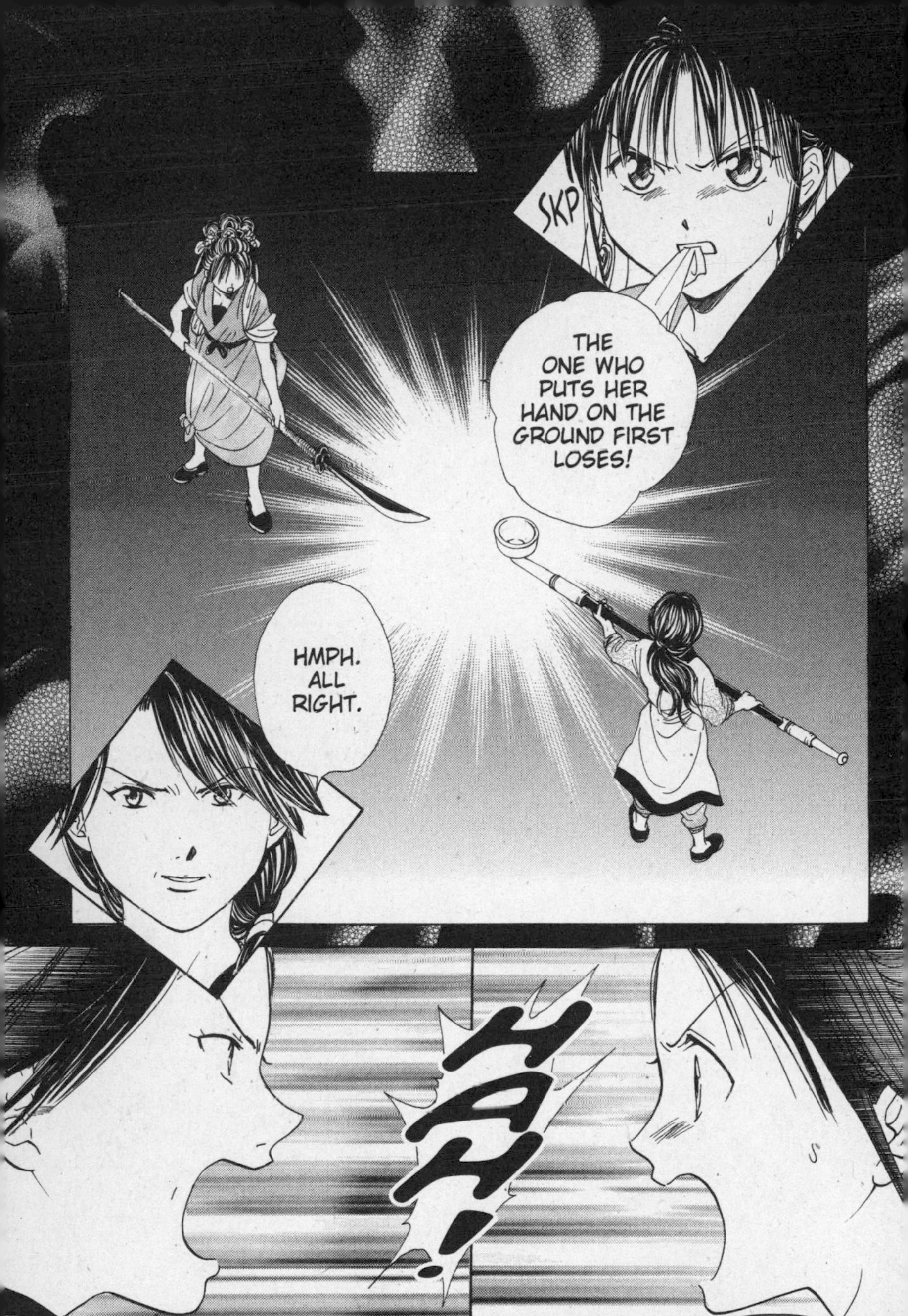
SKP
THE ONE WHO PUTS HER HAND ON THE GROUND FIRST LOSES!
HMPH. ALL RIGHT.
HAH!

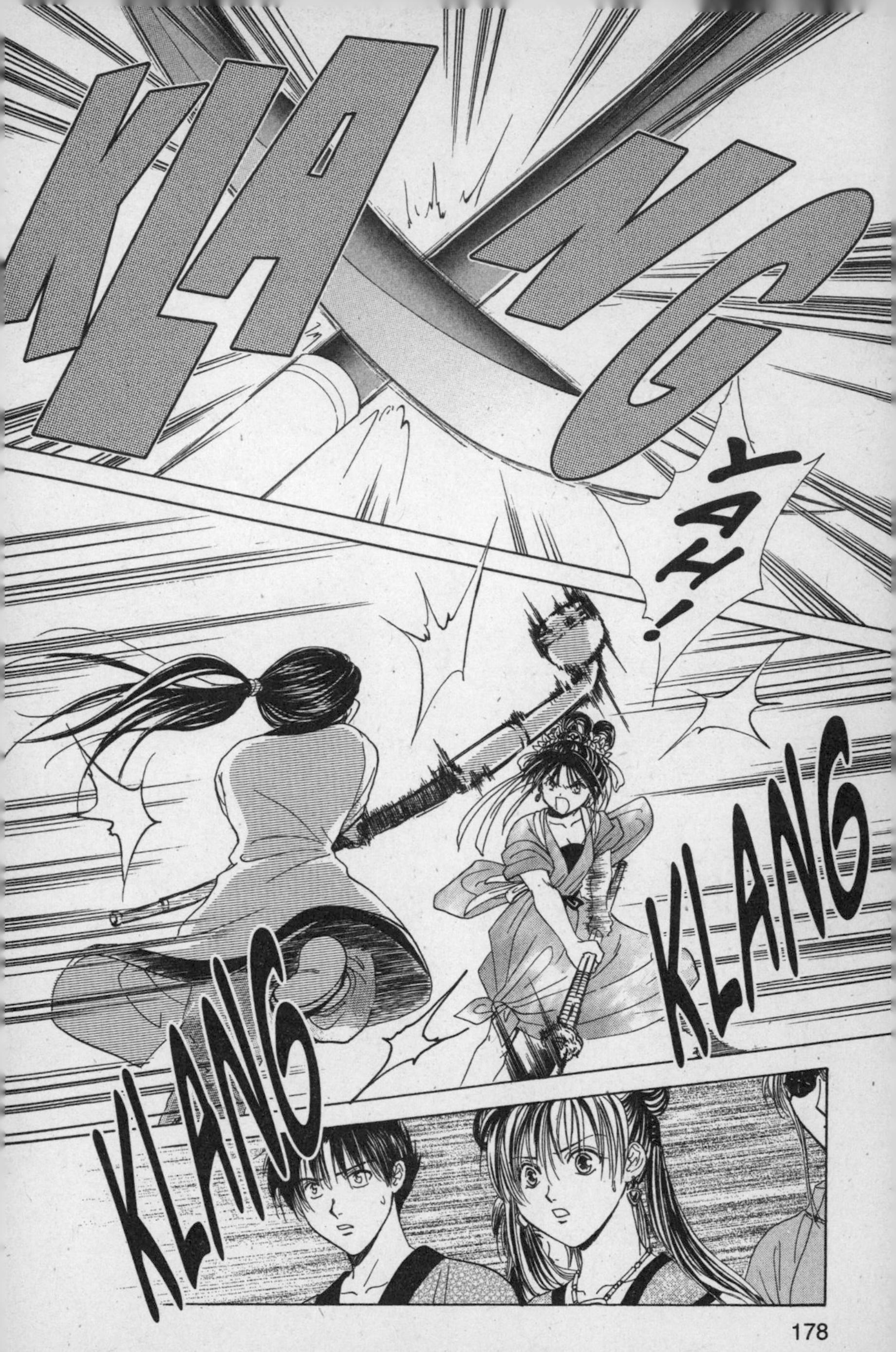
KLANG
YAH!
KLANG
KLANG

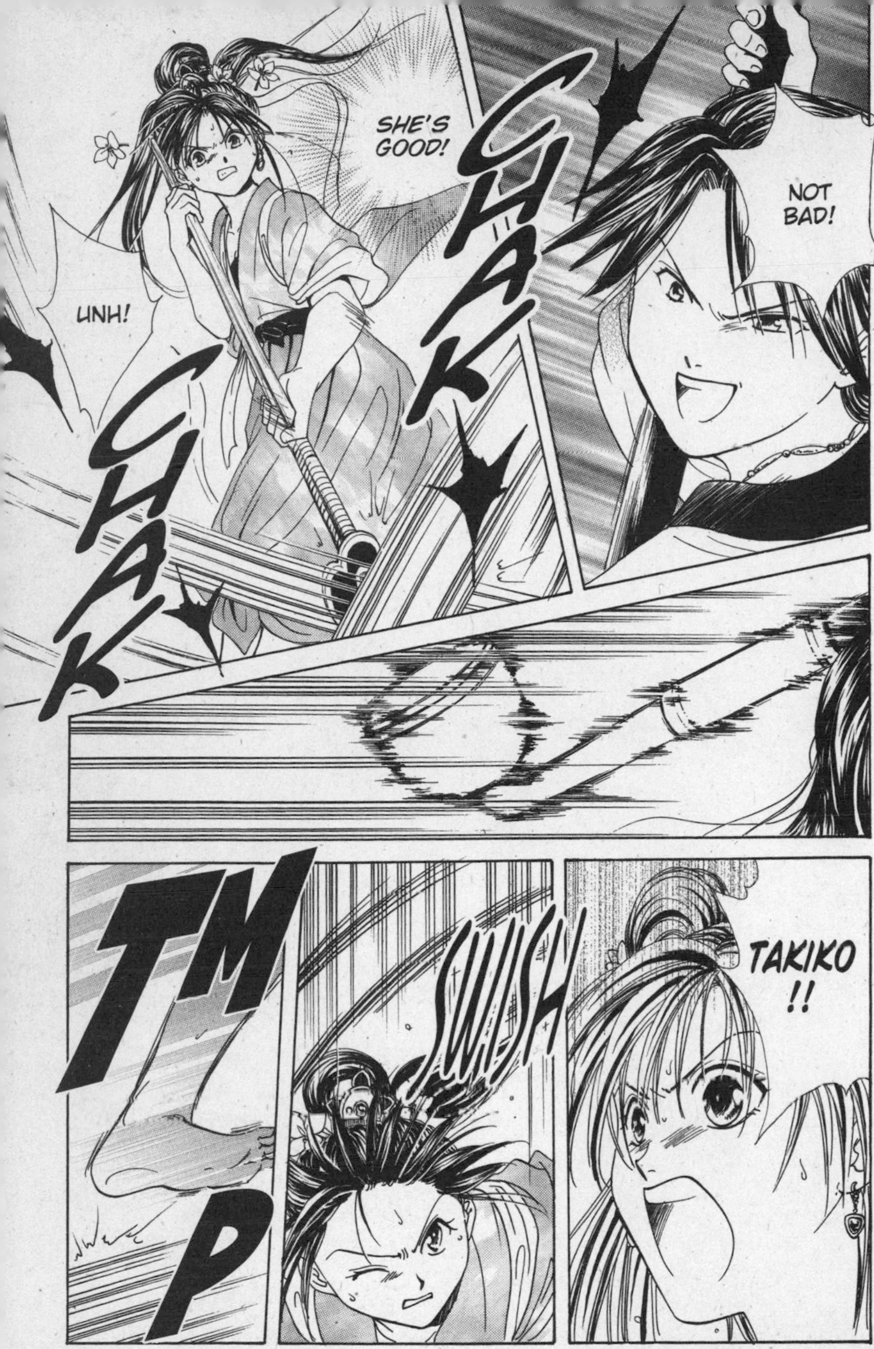
NOT BAD!
CHAK
SHE'S GOOD!
UNH!
CHAK
TAKIKO !!
SWISH
TMP

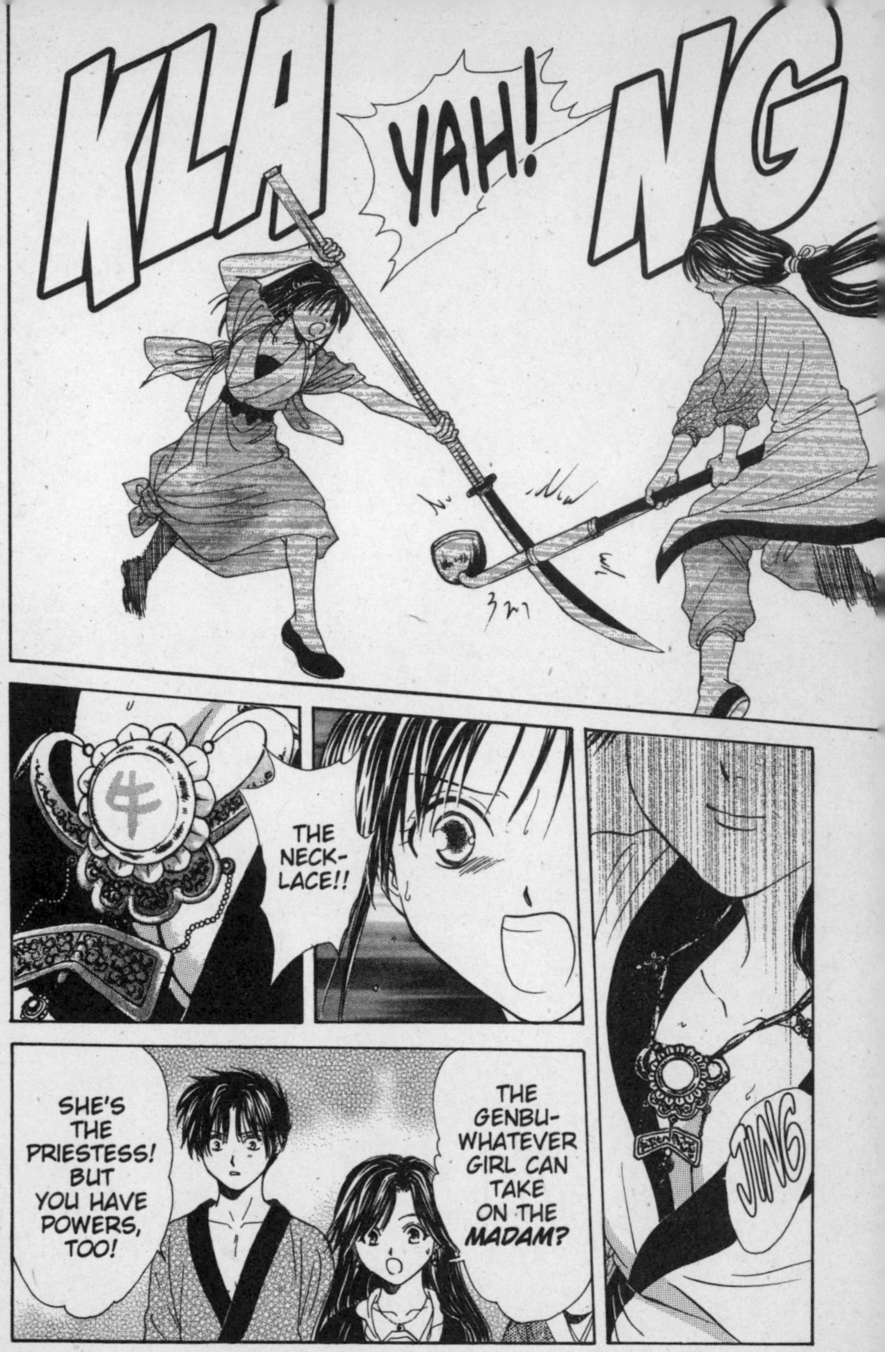

KLANG
YAH!
JING
THE NECK-LACE!!
THE GENBU-WHATEVER GIRL CAN TAKE ON THE *MADAM*?
SHE'S THE PRIESTESS! BUT YOU HAVE POWERS, TOO!

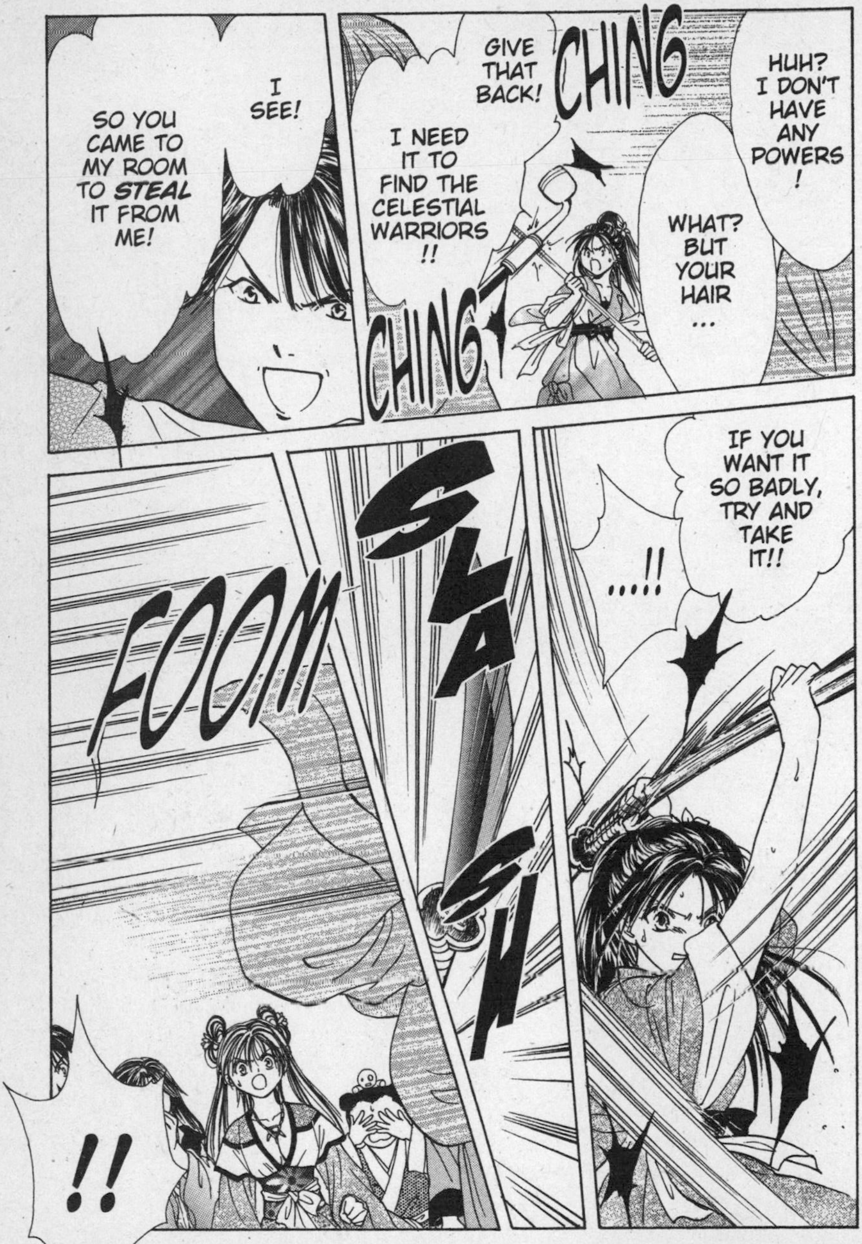
HUH? I DON'T HAVE ANY POWERS!
WHAT? BUT YOUR HAIR...
GIVE THAT BACK!
CHING
I NEED IT TO FIND THE CELESTIAL WARRIORS!!
CHING
I SEE!
SO YOU CAME TO MY ROOM TO **STEAL** IT FROM ME!
IF YOU WANT IT SO BADLY, TRY AND TAKE IT!!
...!!
SLASH
FOOM
!!

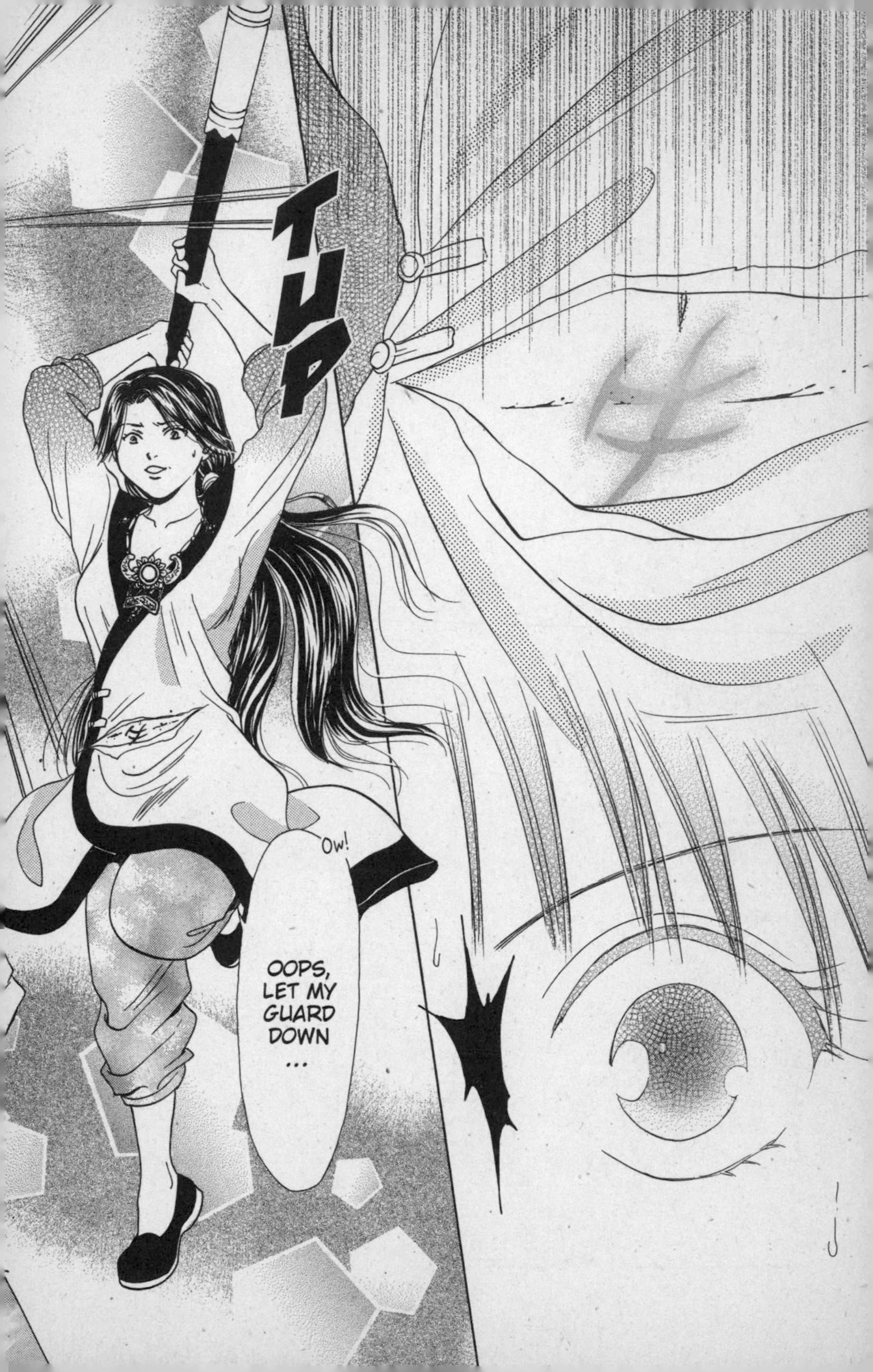
THUP
OW!
OOPS, LET MY GUARD DOWN ...

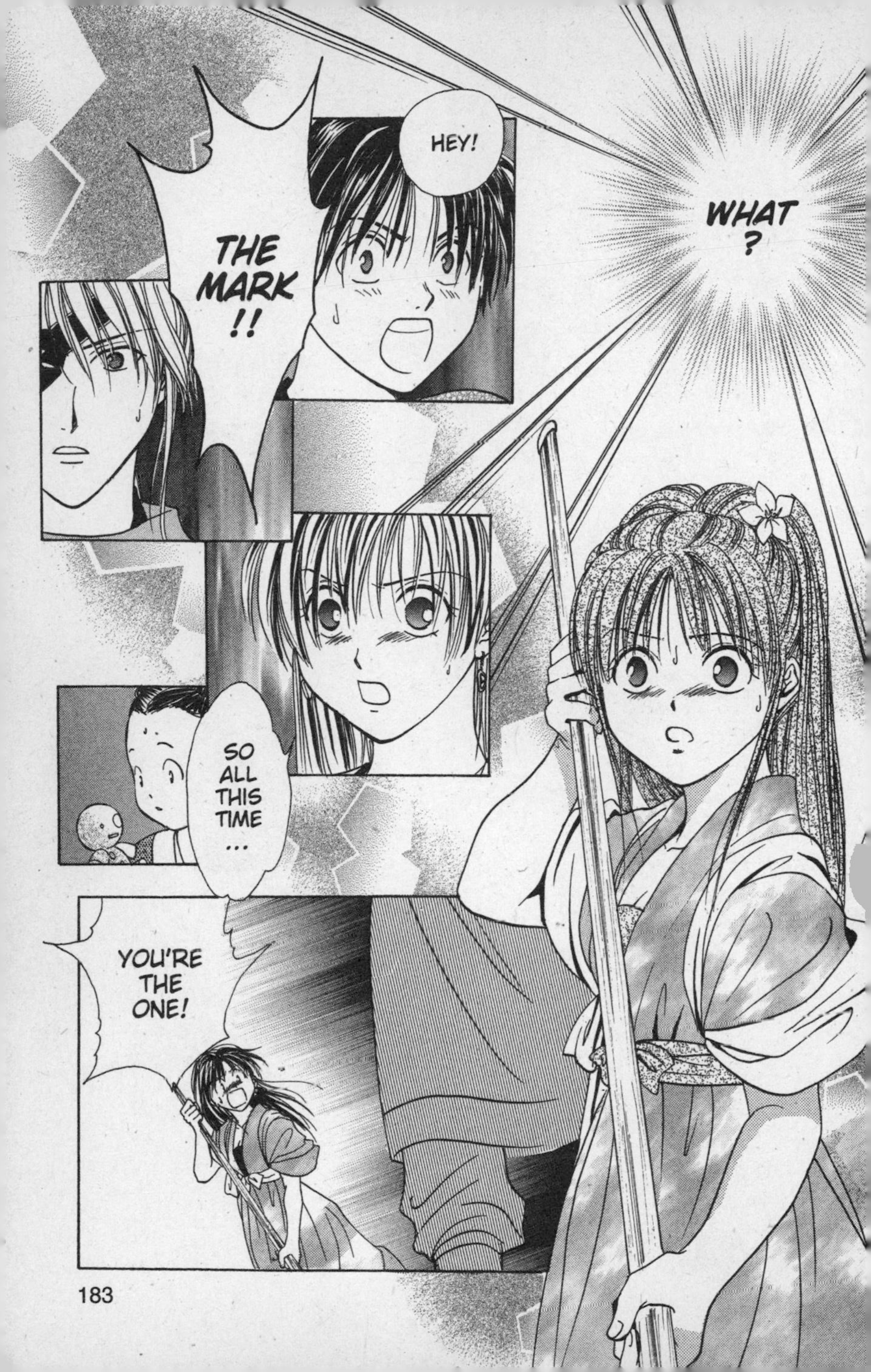
WHAT ?
HEY!
THE MARK !!
SO ALL THIS TIME ...
YOU'RE THE ONE!

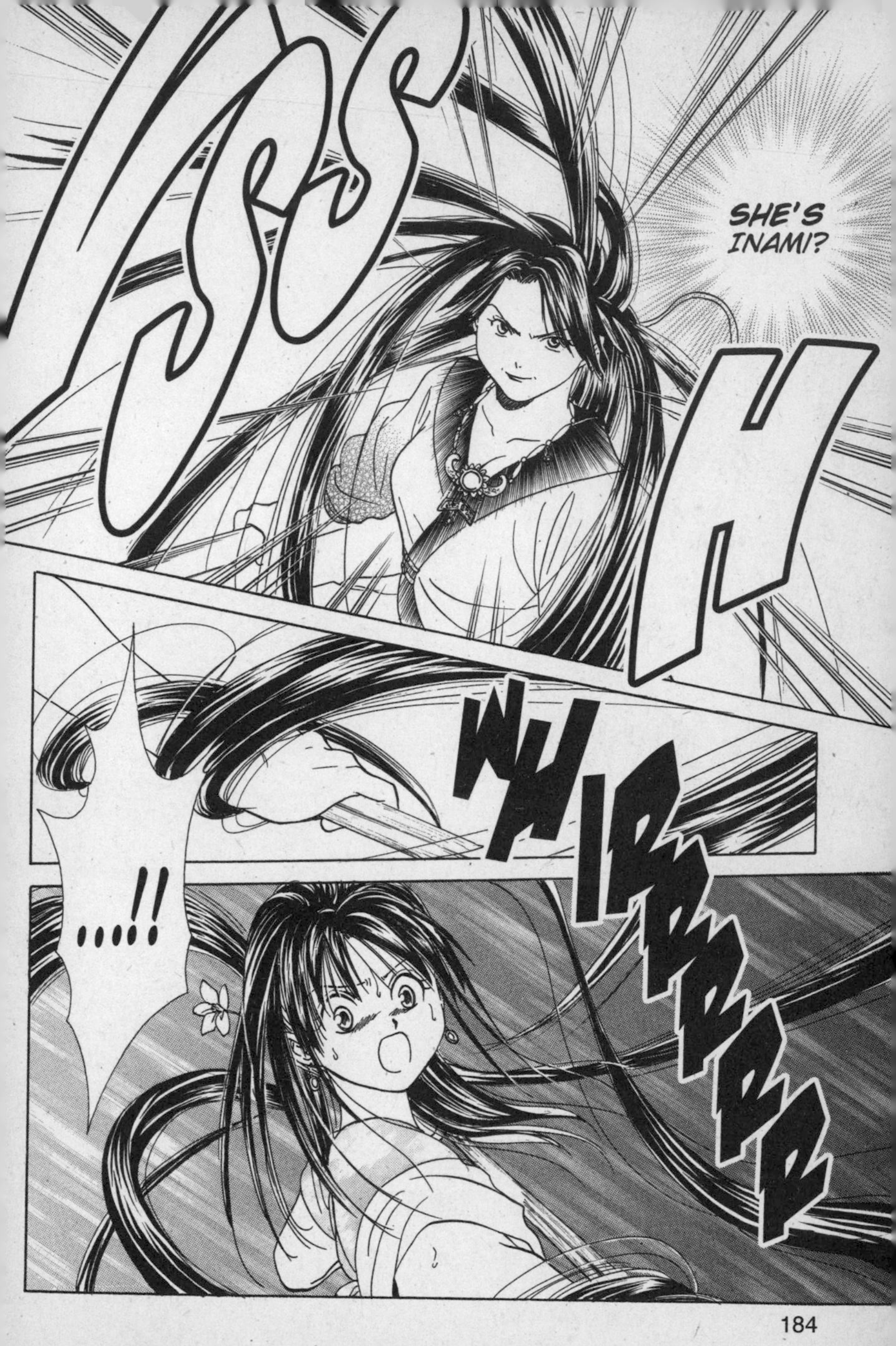
SHE'S INAMI?
....!!

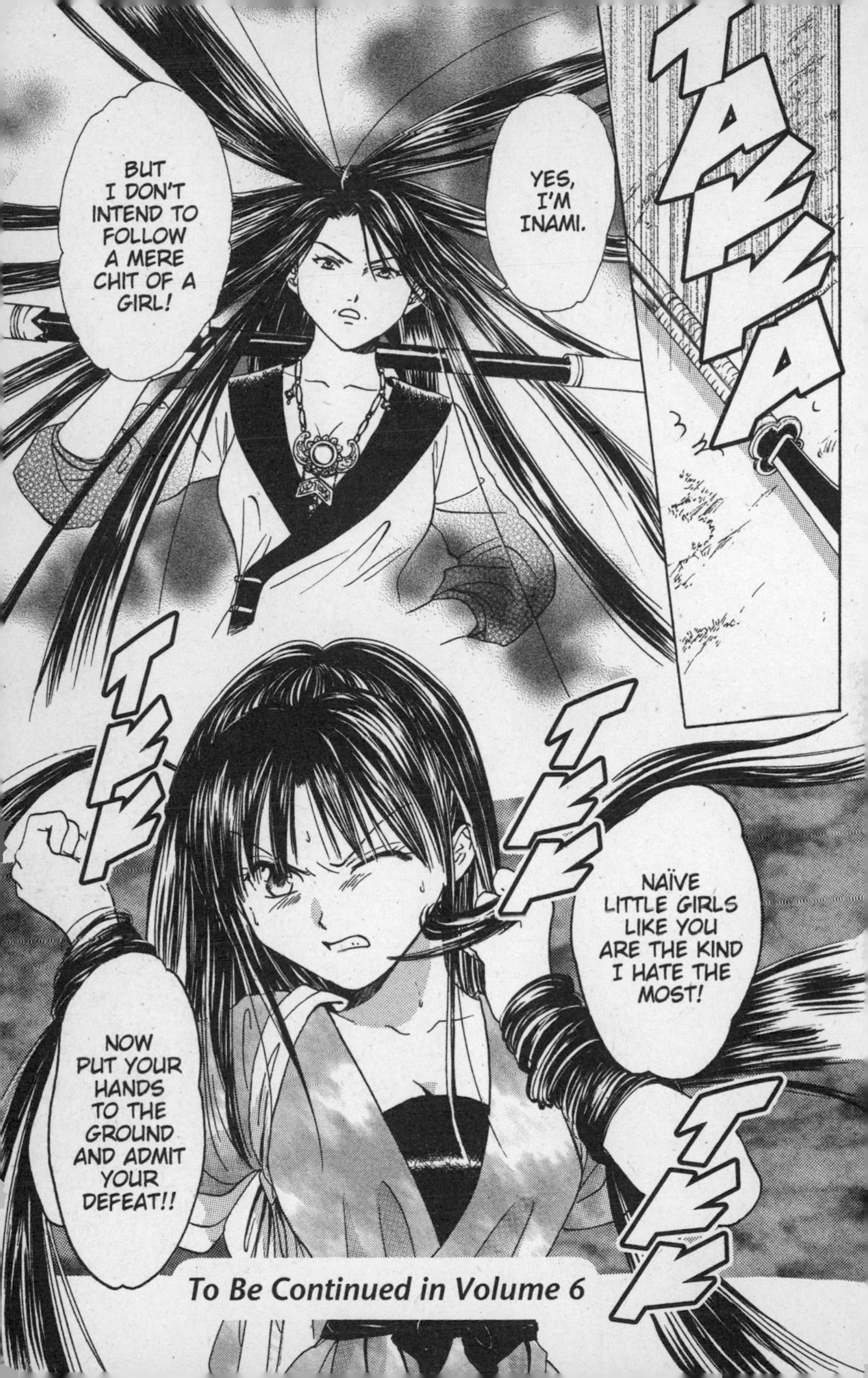
YES, I'M INAMI.
BUT I DON'T INTEND TO FOLLOW A MERE CHIT OF A GIRL!
NAÏVE LITTLE GIRLS LIKE YOU ARE THE KIND I HATE THE MOST!
NOW PUT YOUR HANDS TO THE GROUND AND ADMIT YOUR DEFEAT!!
To Be Continued in Volume 6

Yuu Watase was born on March 5 in a town near Osaka, Japan. She was raised there before moving to Tokyo to follow her dream of creating manga. In the decade since her debut short story, *Pajama De Ojama* (An Intrusion in Pajamas), she has produced more than 50 volumes of short stories and continuing series. Her latest work, *Absolute Boyfriend*, appeared in Japan in the anthology magazine *Shôjo Comic* and is currently serialized in English in *Shojo Beat* magazine. Watase's other beloved series, *Alice 19th*, *Imadoki!*, and *Ceres: Celestial Legend*, are available in North America in English editions published by VIZ Media.

Fushigi Yûgi: Genbu Kaiden Vol. 5

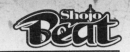

The Shojo Beat Manga Edition

STORY AND ART BY
YUU WATASE

Translation/Lillian Olsen
Touch-up Art & Lettering/Rina Mapa
Design/Amy Martin
Editor/Shaenon K. Garrity

Managing Editor/Megan Bates
Editorial Director/Elizabeth Kawasaki
Vice President & Editor in Chief/Yumi Hoashi
Sr. Director of Acquisitions/Rika Inouye
Sr. VP of Marketing/Liza Coppola
Exec. VP of Sales & Marketing/John Easum
Publisher/Hyoe Narita

Printed in Canada

Published by VIZ Media, LLC
P.O. Box 77010
San Francisco, CA 94107

Shojo Beat Manga Edition
10 9 8 7 6 5 4 3 2 1
First printing, November 2006

RATED T+ FOR OLDER TEEN

PARENTAL ADVISORY
FUSHIGI YÛGI: GENBU KAIDEN is rated T+ for Older Teen and is recommended for ages 16 and up. Contains nudity, strong language, sexual themes, and realistic and fantasy violence.

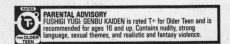

store.viz.com

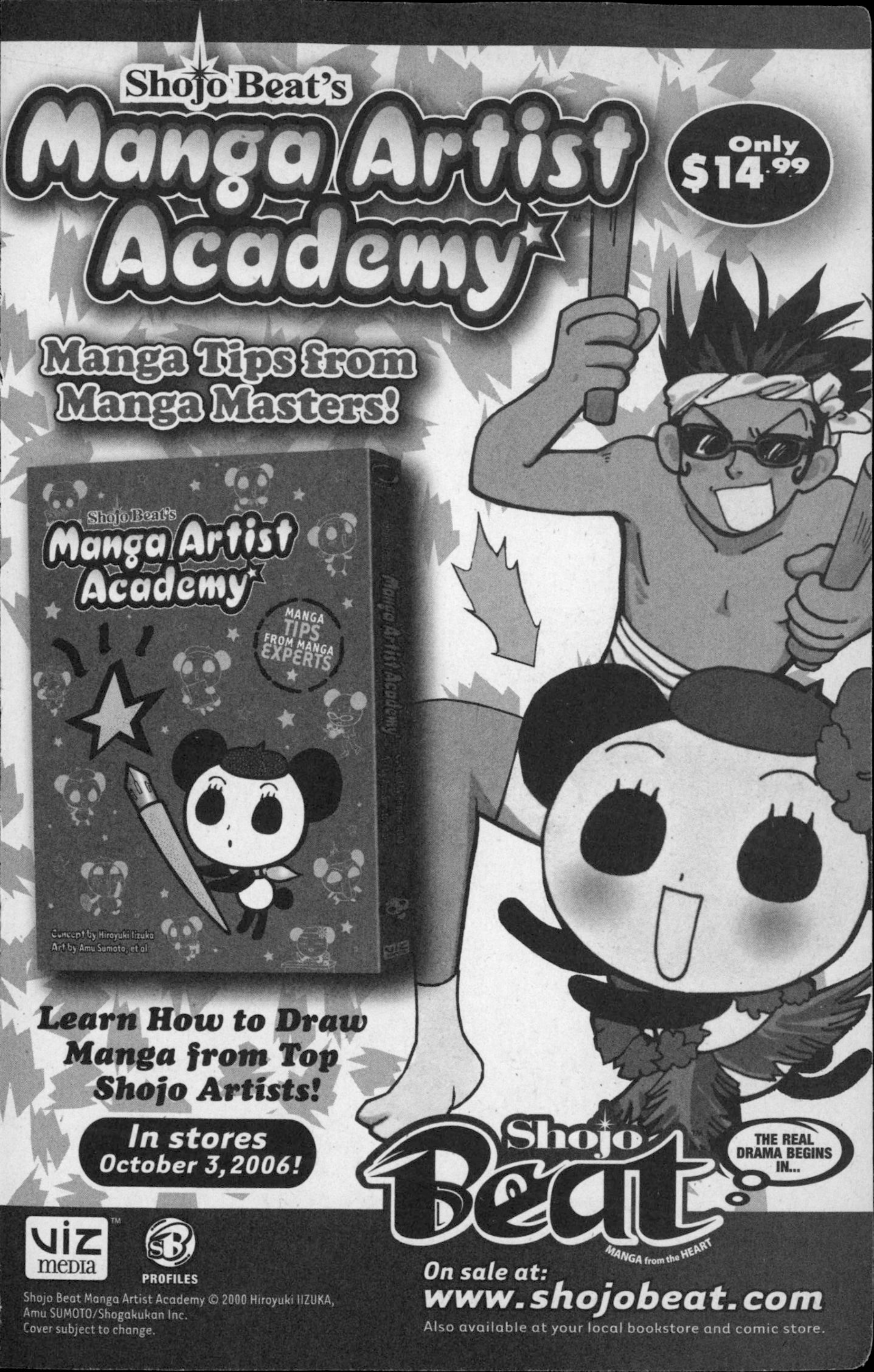
Shojo Beat's
Manga Artist Academy™
Only $14.99
Manga Tips from Manga Masters!
Shojo Beat's
Manga Artist Academy
MANGA TIPS FROM MANGA EXPERTS
Manga Artist Academy
Concept by Hiroyuki Iizuka
Art by Amu Sumoto, et al.
Learn How to Draw Manga from Top Shojo Artists!
In stores October 3, 2006!
Shojo Beat
THE REAL DRAMA BEGINS IN...
MANGA from the HEART
viz media
PROFILES
On sale at:
www.shojobeat.com
Also available at your local bookstore and comic store.
Shojo Beat Manga Artist Academy © 2000 Hiroyuki IIZUKA, Amu SUMOTO/Shogakukan Inc.
Cover subject to change.

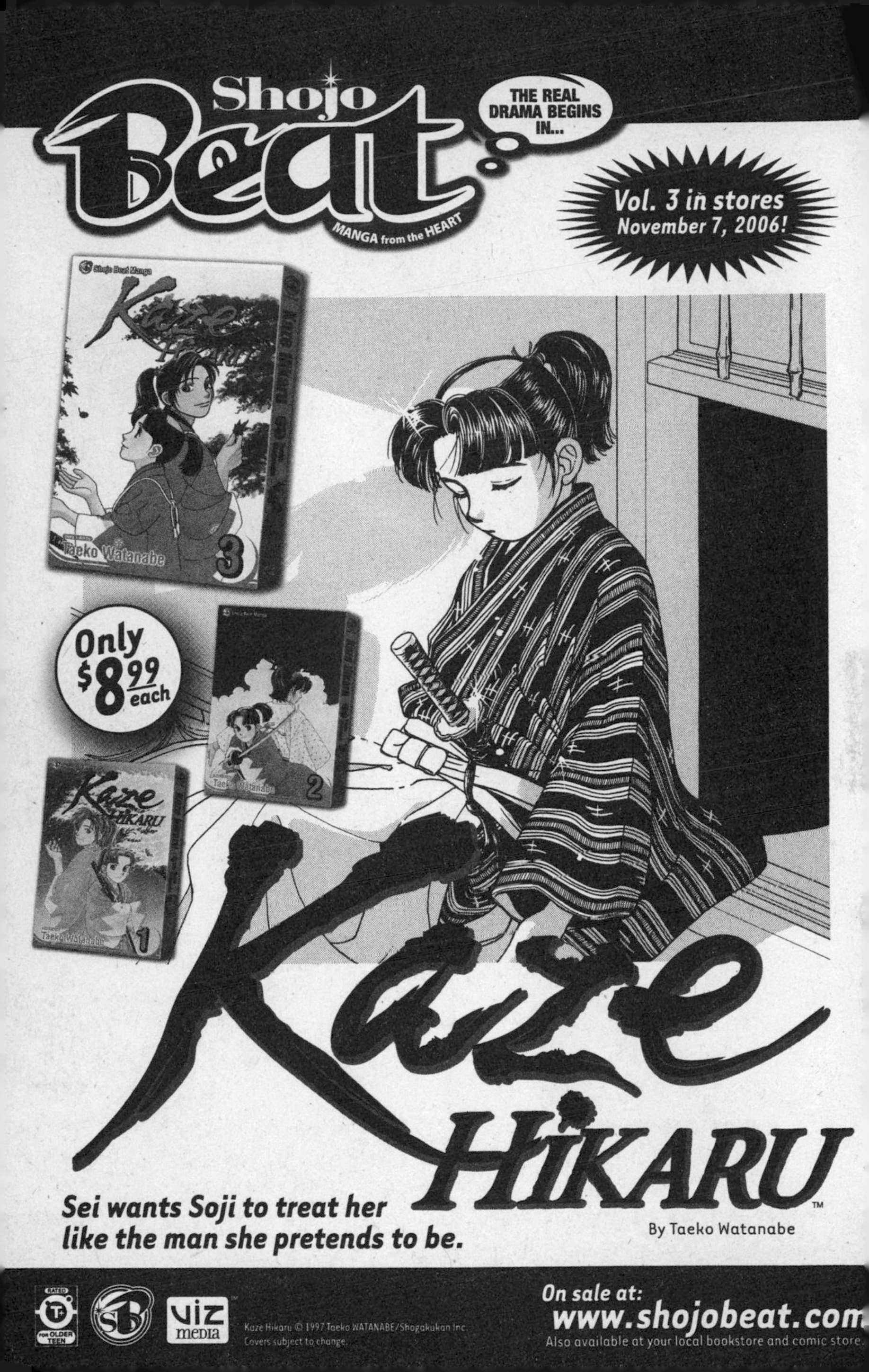
Shojo Beat
MANGA from the HEART
THE REAL DRAMA BEGINS IN...
Vol. 3 in stores November 7, 2006!
Shojo Beat Manga
Kaze Hikaru
Taeko Watanabe
3
Only $8.99 each
2
1
Kaze Hikaru™
Sei wants Soji to treat her like the man she pretends to be.
By Taeko Watanabe
RATED T+ FOR OLDER TEEN
SB
viz media
Kaze Hikaru © 1997 Taeko WATANABE/Shogakukan Inc.
Covers subject to change.
On sale at:
www.shojobeat.com
Also available at your local bookstore and comic store.

Tell us what you think about Shojo Beat Manga!

Our survey is now available online. Go to:

shojobeat.com/mangasurvey

Help us make our product offerings better!

VIZ media

Shojo Beat

THE REAL DRAMA BEGINS IN...

MANGA from the HEART

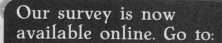

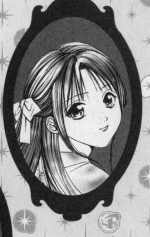

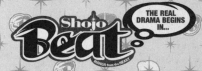

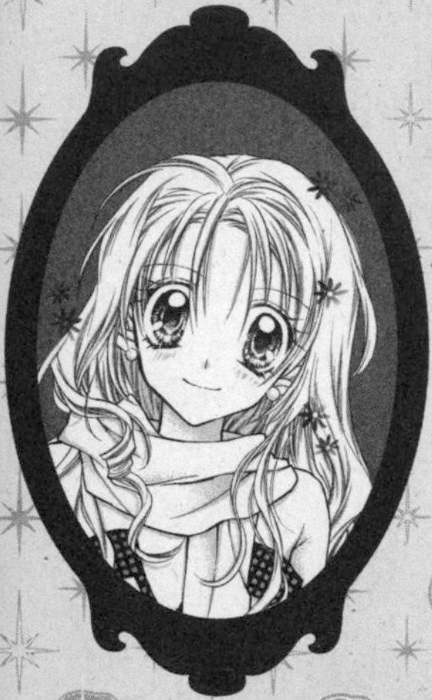

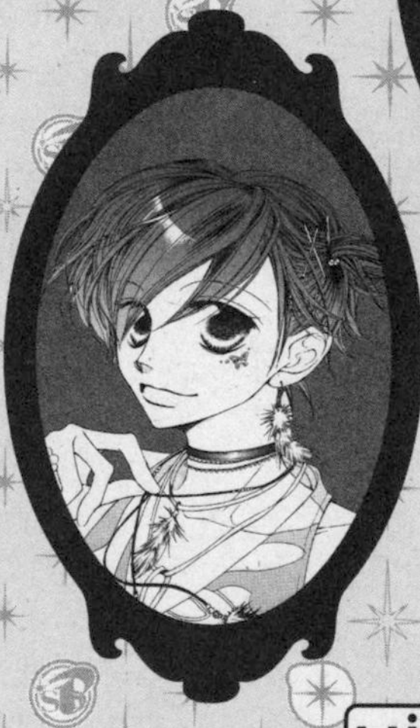